You're looking at Mekong muck...and the answer to it—

an Air Cushion Vehicle. It speeds across swamps, rice paddies, sand bars and shore lines on a cushion of air. Our GI's call it "Charlie Victor." VC's call it "quai vat"—the monster! ACV's get along without harbors, docks or landing sites. All they require is what happens to exist where they happen to be. Three "monsters" have proved this point in the Delta and in the lowlands west of Saigon. They have no equal for a variety of search and destroy, resupply and rescue missions. Bad news for the VC's will be coming off Bell production lines this fall.

Textron COMPANY Buffalo, New York

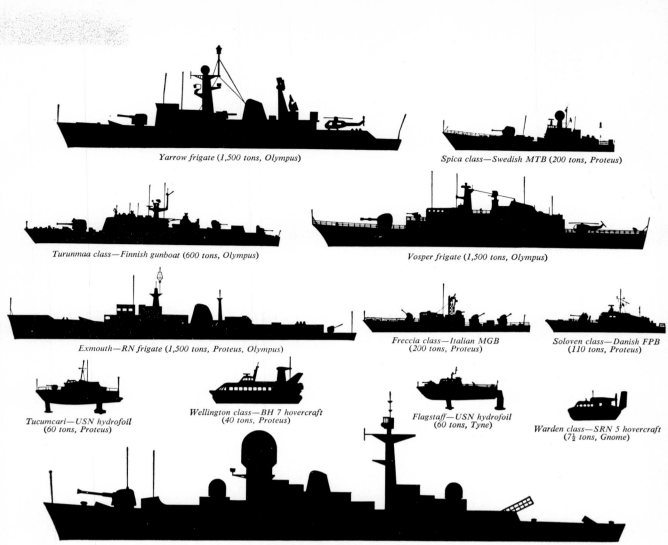

Yarrow frigate (1,500 tons, Olympus)

Spica class—Swedish MTB (200 tons, Proteus)

Turunmaa class—Finnish gunboat (600 tons, Olympus)

Vosper frigate (1,500 tons, Olympus)

Exmouth—RN frigate (1,500 tons, Proteus, Olympus)

Freccia class—Italian MGB
(200 tons, Proteus)

Soloven class—Danish FPB
(110 tons, Proteus)

Tucumcari—USN hydrofoil
(60 tons, Proteus)

Wellington class—BH 7 hovercraft
(40 tons, Proteus)

Flagstaff—USN hydrofoil
(60 tons, Tyne)

Warden class—SRN 5 hovercraft
(7½ tons, Gnome)

Type 82—RN destroyer (6,500 tons, Olympus)

Power for all— with Rolls-Royce gas turbines

RATINGS 1,050-27,200 b.h.p.   **SEA TIME** 100,000 hours

GNOME, PROTEUS, TYNE AND OLYMPUS–these are the engines which carry the RR name-plate. They have amassed their vast operating experience the hard way–in high-speed warships of navies throughout the world; in military and commercial hydrofoils and hovercraft. Ships of 12 navies, from hovercraft to the 6,500-ton Type 82 destroyer, are powered by Rolls-Royce main propulsion engines.

Rolls-Royce marine gas turbines have lower maintenance requirements than steam or diesel machinery, are easily installed, and allow refit by replacement–which means reduced engine-room complement and higher ship availability. Standardisation on a few prime movers for all ship types ensures low-cost logistic support.

If you would like to know more about these engines and their long operational experience, please write to: General Sales Manager, Industrial and Marine Gas Turbine Division, Rolls-Royce Ltd., P.O. Box 72, Coventry, England.

JANE'S SURFACE SKIMMER SYSTEMS

Edited by Roy McLeavy

Order of Contents

World Sales Distribution

North, Central and South America

McGraw-Hill Book Company,
330 West 42nd Street,
New York, N.Y.10036 U.S.A.

and

McGraw-Hill Company of Canada Ltd.
330 Progress Avenue,
Scarborough,
Ontario, Canada.

Europe, Asia, Africa and Australasia

Sampson Low, Marston & Co. Ltd.
(A part of B.P.C. Publishing Ltd.)
P.O. Box No. 2L.G.,
St Giles House,
49/50 Poland St., London,
W.I., England

EDITORIAL *communications should be addressed to:*

The Editor, Jane's Surface Skimmer Systems,

B.P.C. Publishing Limited, P.O. Box No. 2L.G., St. Giles House, 49/50 Poland Street, London, W.I., England
Telephone: 0I-437-0686

ADVERTISEMENT *communications should be addressed to:*

Jane's Yearbooks Advertising,

B.P.C. Publishing Limited, P.O. Box No. 2L.G., St. Giles House, 49/50 Poland Street, London, W.I., England
Telephone: 0I-437-0686

Built in the Rodriquez Shipyard at Messina.

The Gearbox is of paramount importance

where marine vessels are concerned. The light, high-speed diesel engines of hydro-foil-boats require equally efficient marine reversing gears. The ZF Gearbox fully satisfies this demand. It is light, easy to operate and extremely reliable. Our production range includes power transmissions from 10 to 3,000 H.P. Please ask for leaflets and installation proposals.

Sole Agent for the U.K.:
Harold Ludicke Engineers Ltd.
79, Alexandra Road
London, N.W. 8
Phone: MAlda Vale 27 29

ZAHNRADFABRIK FRIEDRICHSHAFEN AG

has helped all
hovercraft
to rise above their
lubrication problems

For details of BP Marine Services
contact :
BP Marine PO Box 148
Strand London WC2
Telephone : 01-438 2214

6 adv.

CLASSIFIED LIST OF ADVERTISERS
1968-69 EDITION

A1. ACCESSORIES

Dassault, Electronique Marcel

A2. ACV AND HYDROFOIL POWERPLANTS

Avco Lycoming Division
Maybach Mercedes-Benz Motorenbau GmbH
Rolls Royce Ltd.
Société C.R.M.

A3. ACV MANUFACTURERS

Bell Aerosystems Company
British Hovercraft Corp. Ltd.
Vosper Ltd.

A4. AERO AUXILIARY EQUIPMENT

Dassault, Electronique Marcel

A5. AIRCRAFT EQUIPMENT

Bell Aerosystems Company
Garrett International S.A.

A6. AIRCRAFT FLOATS

Garrett International SA

A7. AIRCRAFT V/STOL

Bell Aerosystems Company

A8. AIRPORT MAINTENANCE EQUIPMENT

Dassault, Electronique Marcel

A9. AIR DATA COMPUTER SYSTEMS

Dassault, Electronique Marcel

A10. AIR TRAFFIC CONTROL EQUIPMENT

Bell Aerosystems Company

A11. ASTRO-INERTIAL NAVIGATION SYSTEM

Bell Aerosystems Company

A12. AUTOMATIC CHECKOUT SYSTEMS

Dassault, Electronique Marcel

A13. AUTOMATIC VOLTAGE AND CURRENT REGULATORS

Dassault, Electronique Marcel

A14. AVIATION GASOLINE

BP Trading Ltd. (United Kingdom)
BP Marketing Companies (Overseas)
Shell-Mex & B.P. Ltd. (BP Marine Division, United Kingdom)

A15. AVIATION LUBRICATING OIL AND SPECIAL PRODUCTS

BP Trading Ltd. (United Kingdom)
BP Marketing Companies (Overseas)
Shell-Mex & B.P. Ltd. (BP Marine Division, United Kingdom)

A16. AVIATION TURBO FUELS

BP Trading Ltd. (United Kingdom)
BP Marketing Companies (Overseas)
Shell-Mex & B.P. Ltd. (BP Marine Division, United Kingdom)

B1. BATTERY CHARGERS

Dassault, Electronique Marcel

B2. BLIND FLYING INSTRUMENTS

Dassault, Electronique Marcel

B3. BOOKS

Sir Isaac Pitman & Son Ltd.

8 adv.

CLASSIFIED LIST OF ADVERTISERS—*continued*

C1. COMPUTERS
Dassault, Électronique Marcel

**C2. COMPUTERS, AERODYNAMIC,
AND DIGITAL**
Dassault, Électronique Marcel

**C3. CONTROL EQUIPMENT FOR AIR-
CRAFT**
Dassault, Électronique Marcel

C4. CONTROL SYSTEMS
Garrett International S.A.
Mitchell Hydraulics Limited

**C5. CONTROL SYSTEMS-CONSULT-
ANTS**
Mitchell Hydraulics Limited

D1. DATA PROCESSING EQUIPMENT
Dassault, Électronique Marcel

**D2. DATA RECORDER JETTISON
AND RECOVERY SYSTEMS**
Dassault, Électronique Marcel

**D3. DATA TRANSMISSION
EQUIPMENT**
Dassault, Électronique Marcel
Garrett International S.A.

D4. DE-ICING EQUIPMENT
Garrett International S.A.

D5. DIESEL ENGINES
Maybach Mercedes-Benz Motorenbau
GmbH
Rolls Royce Ltd.
Société C.R.M.

E1. ELECTRIC AUXILIARIES
Dassault, Électronique Marcel

E2. ELECTRICAL EQUIPMENT
Dassault, Électronique Marcel

E3. ELECTRONIC EQUIPMENT
British Hovercraft Corporation Ltd.
Dassault, Électronique Marcel

E4. ELECTRONICS AND GUIDANCE
Dassault, Électronique Marcel

E5. EQUIPMENT FOR AIRCRAFT
Dassault, Électronique Marcel

**F1. FINANCE—SHIPS & HOVER-
CRAFT**
Ship Mortgage Finance Company Ltd.

F2. FINISHED MACHINE PARTS
Mitchell Hydraulics Ltd.

F3. FUELS
BP Trading Ltd. (United Kingdom)
BP Marketing Companies (Overseas)
Shell-Mex & B.P. Ltd. (BP Marine
Division, United Kingdom)

**G1. GUIDED MISSILE GROUND
HANDLING EQUIPMENT**
Dassault, Électronique Marcel

G2. GUIDED MISSILES
Dassault, Électronique Marcel

H1. HELICOPTER GAS TURBINES
Avco Lycoming Division

H2. HOVERCRAFT KITS
Hoverknights

H3. HOVERCRAFT MANUFACTURER
British Hovercraft Corporation Ltd.
Sedam
Société Bertin & Cie
Vospers Ltd.

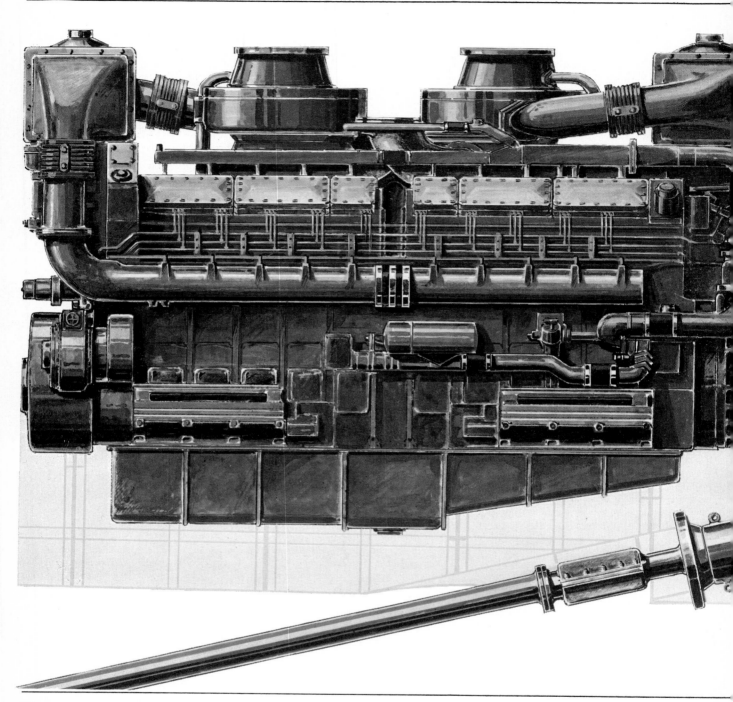

Power for 41 knots

When hydrofoil vessels start to move, they resemble traditional vessels to a very great extent until they begin to accelerate faster and faster. Then, with approximately half cruising speed the hull rises from the water and "floats" on it's steel foils above the water. Now only the resistance of the foils remains to be overcome.

If one graphically illustrates the power requirement curve of a hydrofoil vessel, one notices that it rises initially much more sharply than the cubic propeller curve of a normal displacement vessel. During the lift the maximum torque is

required. However with approximately the same power the speed will be remarkably increased – corresponding to the flatter resistance curve of the foils.

The propulsion engines for hydrofoil vessels are not only required to have an extremely low power to weight ratio and small dimensions; very special demands are also made on the operational torque. Further requirements are lower maintenance costs and longer dependable engine service life.

Maybach Mercedes-Benz diesel engines meet these requirements. By putting the hydrofoil vessels economically into service, Maybach Mercedes-Benz have made the possibilities extraordinarily favourable. So it is, that more and more of these modern vessels have been built. At the present time there are about 100 hydrofoil vessels from 30 to 60

tonnes, 90 of them running with Maybach Mercedes-Benz diesel engines. The first vessels have been in service for the past 12 years. They are still running.

This verification of competence is the deciding reason why the latest and largest hydrofoil vessel PT 150 DC will be equipped with Maybach Mercedes-Benz diesel engines; two 20 cylinder engines drive the propellers through Maybach Mercedes-Benz torque converters and ZF gearing. That means 8000 h. p. are available for the lift.

The vessel is to be put into scheduled ferry boat service for almost throughout the year in the Kattegat. On each journey 250 passengers can be transported, or 150 passengers and 8 automobiles – with 41 knots maximum speed (that's 76 km/h). In this way new standards for economic sea ferry traffic have been set.

Maybach Mercedes-Benz
Diesel Engines for Hydrofoil Vessels

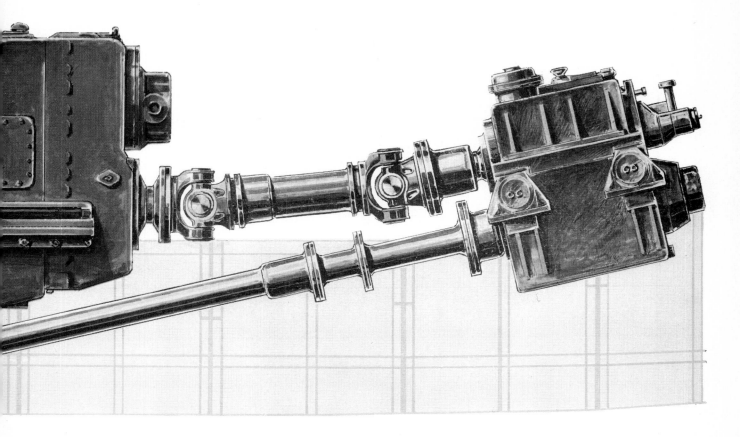

All hydrofoil vessels of type PT 20 and PT 50 which have been built up to summer 1967 were equipped with quick running Maybach Mercedes-Benz diesel engines. They were built under licence from Supramar AG, Lucerne/Switzerland, by the following shipyards:

Rodriquez, Messina/Italy
Westermoen, Mandal/Norway
Gusto, Schiedam/Holland
Hitachi, Osaka/Japan
(the new PT 150 DC is being built by Westermoen)
The PT 20 and PT 50 vessels have been put into service all over the world in passenger and mail service, such as on the following lines:

Manila - Corregidor
Buenos Aires - Montevideo
Piraeus - Passalimani - Hydra
Auckland - Waiheke Island
Naples - Capri
Hong Kong - Macao
Straits of Messina

Guernsey - Jersey - St. Malo
Copenhagen - Malmö
Malta - Gozo
Enoshima - Atami - Ito
Maracaibo - Cabimas
Livorno - Elba
Oslo-Fjord
Cannes - Nice - Monte Carlo
Kure - Imabari
Stavanger - Haugesund - Bergen
Lake Garda
Sydney - Manly
Osaka - Kobe - Awajishima - Takamatsu
Tyrrhenian Sea
Gulf of Rijeka
Lake Geneva
Lake Maggiore
Lake Como

Maybach Mercedes-Benz Motorenbau GmbH · Friedrichshafen/Germany

H4. HOVERPALLET MANUFACTUR-ERS

British Hovercraft Corporation Ltd.
Société Bertin & Cie

H5. HYDRAULIC CONTROL EQUIPMENT

Mitchell Hydraulics Limited

H6. HYDROFOIL BOATS AND SHIPS

Cantiere Navale Leopoldo Rodriquez
Supramar AG

H7. HYDROFOIL RESEARCH AND DESIGN

Supramar AG

I 1. INSTRUMENTS, ELECTRONIC

Dassault, Electronique Marcel

I 2. INSTRUMENTS, NAVIGATION

Dassault, Electronique Marcel

I 3. INSTRUMENTS, PRECISION

Bell Aerosystems Company
British Hovercraft Corporation Ltd.

I 4. INSTRUMENTS, TEST EQUIPMENT

Dassault, Electronique Marcel

L1. LORAN, AIRBORNE

Dassault, Electronique Marcel

L2. LUBRICANTS

BP Trading Ltd. (United Kingdom)
BP Marketing Companies (Overseas)
Shell-Mex & B.P. Ltd. (BP Marine
Division, United Kingdom)

M1. MICRO-WAVE TEST EQUIPMENT

Dassault, Electronique Marcel

M2. MISSILES, GUIDED

Dassault, Electronique Marcel
Bell Aerosystems Company

M3. MOTORBOAT BUILDERS

Cantiere Navale Leopoldo Rodriquez
Vosper Limited

M4. MOTOR GUN BOATS AND TORPEDO BOATS

Cantiere Navale Leopoldo Rodriquez
Vosper Limited

O1. OILS

BP Trading Ltd. (United Kingdom)
BP Marketing Companies (Overseas)
Shell-Mex & B.P. Ltd. (BP Marine
Division, United Kingdom)

P1. PATROL BOATS

Cantiere Navale Leopoldo Rodriquez
Vosper Limited

P2. PETROLEUM PRODUCTS

BP Trading Ltd. (United Kingdom)
BP Marketing Companies (Overseas)
Shell-Mex & B.P. Ltd. (BP Marine
Division, United Kingdom)

P3. PUBLISHERS

Hovercraft World
Sir Isaac Pitman & Son Ltd.

R1. RADAR FOR NAVIGATION, WARNING INTERCEPTION, FIRE CONTROL AND AIRFIELD SUPER-VISION

Dassault, Electronique Marcel

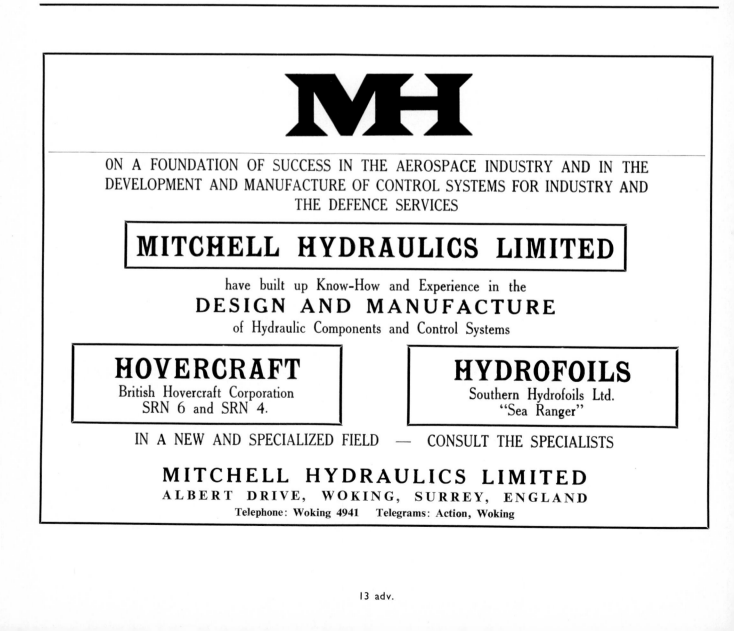

CLASSIFIED LIST OF ADVERTISERS—*continued*

R2. RADAR REFLECTORS
Dassault, Electronique Marcel

R3. RADIO NAVIGATION EQUIPMENT
Dassault, Electronique Marcel

R4. REPLACEMENT PARTS FOR DIESEL ENGINES
Société C.R.M.

R5. REVERSE—REDUCTION GEARS
Société C.R.M.

S1. SKIRT MATERIALS
Hoverknights

S2. SIMULATORS
Dassault, Electronique Marcel

S3. SPACE SYSTEMS
Dassault, Electronique Marcel

S4. SPEED CONTROL, DEVICES
Dassault, Electronique Marcel

S5. SURVEILLANCE SYSTEMS
Dassault, Electronique Marcel

T1. TEST EQUIPMENT
Dassault, Electronique Marcel

T2. TEST EQUIPMENT, AIRFIELD RADIO
Dassault, Electronique Marcel

T3. TRANSFORMER/RECTIFIER UNITS
Dassault, Electronique Marcel

V1. VALVES—DIRECTIONAL, ELECTROHYDRAULIC AND SOLENOID OPERATED SERVO
Mitchell Hydraulics Ltd.

V2. VOLTAGE AND CURRENT REGULATORS
Dassault, Electronique Marcel

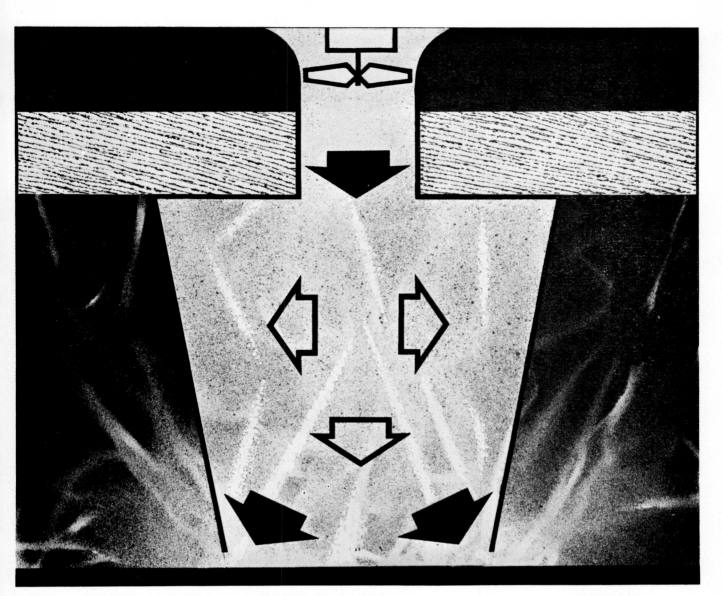

BERTIN & Cie

The Bertin independently fed multiple plenum chambers system is the ACV Technique most suited for the adaptation of light weight flexible skirts.
Through this technique,

stability
manœuvrability
low cost of production
low cost of maintenance
comfort.

are unequalled

Research goes on at Bertin & Cie, meanwhile :

"Terraplane" and **"Naviplane"** vehicles are developed by
SEDAM 42, avenue Raymond-Poincaré - Paris XVIe

Suburban and intercity **"Aerotrain"** are developed by
Société de l'Aerotrain. 80, Avenue de la Grande-Armée - Paris XVIe

special **handling** problems are also tackled through Air Cushion Systems by Bertin & Cie .

techno-paris
promotion

 BERTIN & Cie ☐ BP N° 3 ☐ 78 Plaisir ☐ tel.: 462.25.00

Société d' Etudes et de Développement des Aéroglisseurs Marins, Terrestres et Amphibies

80, Avenue de la Grande Armée - PARIS 17eme - Tel: 380.17.69

NAVIPLANE ''N 300''

TERRAPLANE'' B C 7''

☐ CIVILIAN USE
☐ MILITARY USE
☐ TRANSPORT
☐ SERVICE

INDUSTRIE FRANÇAISE DES VEHICULES SUR COUSSIN D'AIR

The **BERTIN technique** *insures the basic qualities*

of

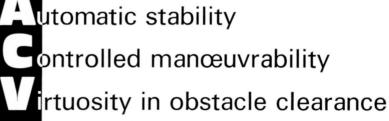

Automatic stability

Controlled manœuvrability

Virtuosity in obstacle clearance

Simplicity in construction and maintenance

BERTIN technique *has led to the development of the*

''AÉROTRAIN'' by the   SOCIÉTÉ AÉROTRAIN - 42, Av. R. Poincaré - PARIS 16ᵉ

JANE'S
SURFACE SKIMMER
SYSTEMS

SECOND EDITION

COMPILED AND EDITED BY
ROY McLEAVY

1968-69

NEW YORK:
McGRAW-HILL BOOK COMPANY

Printed in Great Britain

WARDEN (SR.N5) CLASS

WINCHESTER (SR.N6) CLASS

WELLINGTON (BH.7) CLASS

MOUNTBATTEN (SR.N4) CLASS

experience is the key

There is a world of difference between thinking and knowing. That difference is experience—in the case of BHC, world-wide hovercraft operating experience.

Over 60,000 hours of operation in 43 countries.

More than 2,000,000 sea miles logged.

Close on 2,000,000 fare-paying passengers carried.

Proven performance in full tropical heat and humidity.

Hundreds of high-speed sorties along fast-flowing rivers and over treacherous rapids.

Extended operations over ice and snow under Arctic conditions.

Comprehensive desert trials.

First to set up hovercraft production lines, BHC to-day has the 'Warden' (SR.N5), 'Winchester' (SR.N6), 'Wellington' (BH.7) and 'Mountbatten' (SR.N4) Classes in full production. Non-marine air-cushion applications include heavy-load road and cross-country transporters and 'FLOTALOAD' hoverpallets for industrial use.

BRITISH HOVERCRAFT—WORLD LEADERS IN THE HOVER TRANSPORT REVOLUTION

 **british hovercraft corporation**
EAST COWES · ISLE OF WIGHT · ENGLAND

 BRITISH HOVERCRAFT CORPORATION LIMITED IS A SUBSIDIARY OF WESTLAND AIRCRAFT LIMITED

FOREWORD

Air cushion vehicles and hydrofoils are still in their infancy but slowly and surely they are taking their place in the pattern of waterborne transport. Overwater speeds of 35-50 knots are now a normal occurrence and passenger travel aboard the world's skimmers has become an accepted practice in thirty countries.

The total number of passengers carried to date by hydrofoils is estimated to be 35 million; in 1968 alone hovercraft carried in excess of 700,000 passengers.

The purpose of the second edition of Jane's Surface Skimmer Systems, like the first, is to describe and illustrate every new commercial and military air cushion vehicle, every hydrofoil and every air-lubricated pallet and conveyor system. In one volume we aim, year by year, to provide descriptions of all forms of craft and load carriers which skim across land or sea at interface level.

In this edition we have greatly extended our coverage of the field, and have also covered each craft in greater detail. Two further innovations are the inclusion of the first-ever attempt to provide a skimmer glossary, and the presentation of features from two 'guest' contributors — Baron Hanns von Schertel, the pioneer hydrofoil designer and head of Supramar Ltd, and E. K. Liberatore, the air cushion vehicle designer and President of Aeromar Corporation. Baron von Schertel assesses the safety, reliability and maintainability of Supramar hydrofoils, more than 100 of which are now in service, and Mr Liberatore provides a survey of the advanced ACV programmes now being pursued in the United States.

It can be said that the development of skimmers—ACVs, tracked ACVs and hydrofoils—will be of benefit to countries at all stages of industrial growth: those at the apex of their growth, with overcrowded air space, but undersized waterways; those with dense populations requiring constant evolution in their transport systems, and those which are still underdeveloped and requiring flexible craft as mobile bases from which to attack clearance and development work over vast areas. In short, skimmers do not simply represent a further refinement of transport systems. They will work to the benefit of the world at large.

ROY McLEAVY.

ACKNOWLEDGEMENTS

Because of its increased size and new three-column layout, this second edition has involved a greater amount of supporting activity than the first edition.

Editorial and other help has been kindly given by many people this year. We should, in particular, like to express gratitude to the following: Baron Hanns von Schertel, Supramar; William M. Ellsworth, US Navy Hydrofoil Special Trials Unit; Bremerton, Washington; Dr. F. H. Todd, Dept. of the Navy, Office of Naval Research; E. K. Liberatore, Aeromar Corporation; Cdr. R. L. von Gerichten, JSESPO; A. G. Simmons, British Hovercraft Corporation; The Leopoldo Rodriquez Shipyard; Donald Nigg; W. J. Eggington, Aerojet-General Corporation; William A. Burbaum, Bell Aerosystems; H. M. Dubois, Aeroglide Systems, Inc; John S. Stratford, Hovercraft Division, Vosper Thornycroft; Sheenagh Wallace, National Physical Laboratory; S. J. Wornom, General Dynamics, Electric Boat Division; Selwyn Sharp, Rolls-Royce Ltd; Eric Falk, General Electric Company; Roger Eastwood, Hovermarine; Herbert Snowball, Airavia Ltd; Dr. William R. Bertelsen, Bertelsen Manufacturing Company; John K. Roper, Atlantic Hydrofoils, L. R. Burrows, Cushioncraft Ltd; S. Hirai, Mitsubishi Heavy Industries; Y. Kaneko, Smaller Craft Section, Mitsubishi, Shimonoseki Shipyard; Gerald O. Rennarts, International Hydrolines Inc; K. Ito, Mitsui Shipbuilding and Engineering Co; J. J. MacRostie, FMC Corporation; G. W. J. Cook, Anglian Development Ltd; L. Flammand, Bertin & Cie; Blohm & Voss AG; J. F. Lstiburek, Water Spyder Marine Ltd; F. de Jersey, De Havilland Aircraft of Canada Ltd; M. W. Beardsley, Skimmers Inc; A. F. Gillingham, Denny Hovercraft Ltd; J. M. Berthelot, Société de l'Aerotrain; J. Bruce Deam, US Army Aviation Material Laboratories; Robert Lee, General Electric Transportation Systems Division; Jan A. Eglen, Eglen-Cull; J. B. Frenzinger, Cushionflight Corporation; T. V. Sloss, Southern Hydrofoils; Franklin A. Dobson, Dobson Products Co; Andrea Marzotto, Seaflight; Tom Gunderson, Gunderson Hovercraft Co; Prof. L. Kobylinski, Gdansk Ship Research Institute; Herbert L. Bartlett, Bartlett Flying Saucer; Arthur Read, British Rail Hovercraft Ltd; James Eder and Barry Palmer, Air Kinetics Inc; Hover-Air Ltd; John Vass, Daily Express; Cedric Wren, Barwren Hover Ltd; G. G. Harding; Capt. W. W. Barrow, US Coast Guard; A. R. Hawker, Airbearings Ltd; Nigel Seale, Coelacanth Gemco; N. Kirpitznikoff, Israel American Motor Corporation; P. Watson, Urba; M. Monbeig-Andrieu, SEDAM; Geoffrey L. Green, Hovergem (A'Asia) Ltd; James R. Wynne and John D. Gill, Wynne-Gill Associates Inc; Hoverlloyd; Ted Mitchell, Hovergem Ltd; John A. Cox, Pratt & Whitney Aircraft; Ronald G. Moyer, American Aerocar Company; William I. Niedermair, Northwest Hydrofoil Lines Inc; W. J. Brockman, Hovertravel Ltd; and Mrs. I. Smith, Novosti Press Agency.

Grateful acknowledgement is also made for the use of extracts from the following papers and publications:

William H. Ellsworth, *The US Navy Hydrofoil Development Program—A Status Report*; AIAA/SNAME Advanced Marine Vehicles Meeting, May 1967.

Dr. P. Magini and Dr. J. Burroughs, *Control of the Hydrofoil Ship*, Institute of Navigation, July 1967.

Dr. Alfred Skolnick and Z. G. Wachnik (JSESPO), *Jets, Props and Air Cushions*, ASME, Gas Turbine & Products Show, Washington, March 1968.

Glossary of Terms Relating to Air Cushion Vehicles, British Standards Institution.

Hydrofoils, by Christopher Hook and A. C. Kermode, Pitman, (Widout Formulae Series).

Dictionary of Marine Engineering and Nautical Terms, by G. O. Watson, Newnes.

Finally we should like to thank Rowland D. Hunt and Christopher Hook for their valued assistance with the Glossary, Peter Jarvis for editorial assistance, and Derek Wood of Airavia and International Defense Review for the loan of the Strela-type patrol craft photo.

When you tell most people that Avco Lycoming turbines have gone to sea this sort of picture comes to mind

Probably our own fault. After all, when you get the reputation as the world's number one producer of gas turbine engines for helicopters, you can't expect the world to go hook, line and sinker for your "just as great" marine turbines overnight.

Not that the sea is anything new to Lycoming. We've been powering ships since the 1920s. In 1958, soon after the T53 was born, several of them went to sea — in the Army's "Flying Duck" and the Navy's "Halobates" hydrofoils.

Since then a lot of water has gone under the bridge. And a lot of Lycoming-powered aircraft have gone over it. Through this experience, we've learned to make compact gas turbines that cover the waterfront, from 800 to 3,500 SHP.

We've got propulsion systems for amphibious craft, hydrofoils and air-cushion vehicles. We've got powerplants for conventional boats, auxiliary power systems for larger ships, and even have a rig that melds the economy of diesel power with the performance of a gas turbine. And puts them just a flick of the switch apart.

Actually, our marine powerplants have little in common with our aircraft engines.

Little, except Lycoming's 8 million plus hours of operational know how.

And that's no fish story.

AVCO LYCOMING DIVISION
STRATFORD, CONN.

19 adv.

CONTENTS

Dolphin Hydrofoil demonstrates high performance and economy

- **50 knots in 8 to 10-foot waves**
- **116 passengers**
- **less than 3 cents per seat-mile total owning and operating cost**

The Grumman Dolphin Hydrofoil has exceeded its original design specifications for both top speed and ability to operate in heavy seas. This outstanding performance was proved by #1 Dolphin which recently completed a season of commercial passenger operation in the Canary Islands.

To handle the anticipated production schedule, Grumman is obtaining manufacturing facilities in Florida, in addition to the Dolphin production currently underway at the Blohm & Voss yards in Hamburg. This year, #1 and #2 Dolphins will enter commercial operation in the United States.

The Garrett Corporation has joined with Grumman to handle world-wide Dolphin sales, marketing, and distribution responsibility.

For more information on Dolphin performance, economics and application, please contact Mr. John W. Calvert, Director Hydrofoil Sales, The Garrett Corporation, 9851 Sepulveda Boulevard, Los Angeles, California 90009. Telephone (213) 776-1010. Cable Garrettair, Los Angeles.

The Garrett Corporation

Garrett is one of The Signal Companies

AIR CUSHION VEHICLE PROGRESS REPORT

AIR CUSHION VEHICLE PROGRESS REPORT

Despite a welter of minor technical setbacks, and despite the criticisms, the world's ACV constructors and operators can on the whole count 1968 as their most successful year so far. More people travelled in air cushion vehicles in more parts of the world than ever before, and more commercial operators and government bodies, including armed services, confirmed their faith in ACVs by placing orders for them.

BHC's Winchesters and the Mountbatten prototype carried between them nearly 700,000 fare-paying passengers on routes in Italy, Denmark, Japan and the United Kingdom alone. One out of every 3 passengers and one out of every 5 cars carried across the English Channel by surface transport in 1969 on the Kent to French coast corridor will go by hovercraft. Since only four BHC Mountbattens will be involved, these figures, based on the predictions of British Rail and Hoverlloyd, indicate clearly the dramatic impact that hoverferries are likely to have in future on short sea routes of high traffic volume. It is expected that British Rail and Hoverlloyd will share at least 20% of the complete market in four to five years time.

As the development of the passenger/car hoverferry progresses, more and more conventional ferryboat operators will inevitably shift over to the new mode of water transport, and although many have still to be convinced of the reliability, safety and economics of the air cushion vehicle, there seems no reason to doubt that the commercial outlook for the big passenger/car hoverferry, at any rate, is bright indeed.

No companies have worked harder to prove the viability of these craft than BHC and British Rail Hovercraft Ltd. Their joint efforts led to the introduction in August of the ten-week service operated between Dover and Boulogne which was the most important ACV event of 1968. Before the service closed to enable BHC to fit the Mountbatten with a new skirt and introduce various minor modifications, the craft made 482 crossings, carrying 27,000 passengers and 3,000 cars. Passenger reaction to travel across the channel in waves up to 5 ft has been extremely good.

British Rail will re-open this service in April 1969, and subject to negotiations will take delivery of a second craft for the same route late in the summer of 1969. Hoverlloyd Ltd. has also ordered two BHC Mountbattens at a total cost of £3½ million, and these will enter service in 1969 on the Ramsgate/Calais route. The crossings will take 40 minutes and there will be fourteen return trips a day in summer, and three a day during the winter. The company's hoverport covers 12½ acres below the cliffs at Pegwell Bay. In the summer of 1969, Hoverlloyd estimates it will fill nearly 800,000 seats and 100,000 car spaces.

A completely new type of skirted hoverferry, due to make its debut in early April 1969, is the 76 ton Vosper Thornycroft VT 1, which has been designed from the outset to be commercially competitive with conventional ships. This is a semi-amphibious, 40-knot craft, using controllable-pitch water propellers, driven by two Lycoming marine gas turbines. The propellers are carried beneath the hull on deep skegs, which are arranged in such a way as to allow the craft to nose up a beach ramp, with only about 5 ft of water aft, and settle in a slightly nose-down attitude to load and unload. In this condition the VT 1 can accept a 3 ft rise or fall of tide before it has to be moved, which allows ample time for normal turn-round. The design also takes account of the effects of onshore swell. Water rudders are used for directional control and a skirt-shift system provides a means of countering roll forces generated in turns. The skirt is designed to give passengers a "soft" ride and this has been effectively demonstrated on the VT 1M, a 40% scale model used by the company for research. The first VT 1 has been ordered by Hovertravel and there is an option on the second.

In the design stage at present are three other craft of 75-80 tons; the Hovermarine HM.3, British Hovercraft Corporation's BH.8, and a new Mitsubishi project. Mitsubishi are also planning to build a 170 ton passenger car-ferry, but this class will not be laid down until the company has had further time to assess the Japanese and Pacific markets.

Mitsui, who began trials with their MV-PP5 Hakusho in September, are also planning much bigger ferry craft.

A newcomer to the passenger ferry scene is SEDAM's 90-seat N 300 Naviplane, two of which will be introduced on a regular passenger service along the Cote d'Azur by Société Naviplane Cote d'Azur in June 1969. The design is based on the Bertin principle of separately fed multiple skirts and the two craft were taken to Nice in September 1968 for a series of experimental services and also to undergo trials conducted by the French armed services. N 300 variants will include a mixed passenger/car ferry (up to 8 cars) and an all-freight version with a cargo capacity of 13 tons.

SEDAM is now completing the design of the N 500, an open-sea, mixed-traffic hoverferry, which will transport 400-500 passengers and 30-40 vehicles. French Railways are reported to be interested in operating the craft across the English Channel in the early 1970s.

Without a doubt, the air cushion principle provides a means of making a long overdue advance in the speeds associated with waterborne transport, and nowhere was this more quickly appreciated than in the United States. In 1966 the President sent a message to the Senate concerning transportation in which he said that he was directing the Secretary of Commerce, with the Secretary of Defence, and the President's Scientific Adviser, to conduct a study of advanced vessel concepts. The work of the team, he said, would include research in an ocean-going surface effect vessel capable of skimming over the water at speeds of more than 100 knots. A charter was issued establishing the Joint Navy-Commerce Surface Effect Ships Program, and the Joint Surface Effect Ships Program Office (JSESPO) has been charged with establishing the feasibility of designing and operating multi-thousand ton ships.

Dr. Alfred Skolnick, Director of Technology at JSESPO, forecasts that large or ship-size air cushion vehicles will almost certainly stimulate new markets and new trade opportunities. He estimates that the journey from New York to Southampton could be accomplished in about 30 hours. Passenger and mixed-traffic ferry services, and the transporting of large volumes of perishables are among the commercial applications foreseen.

At the same time the multi-mission capability of surface effect ships will have a tremendous impact on military operations Dr Skolnick states: "Unquestionably, naval tacticians will develop effective uses for a large volume platform able to move from point to point at very high speeds and capable of carrying a substantial payload. In particular, immediate applications come to mind for use in antisubmarine warfare (hover-listed: dash-attack), and in aircraft carrier design, where relative landing speeds are so substantially reduced as to transform naval aircraft into veritable short take-off and landing (STOL) vehicles, with perhaps significant and advantageous effect upon naval structural design characteristics".

In its commercial form the surface effect ship could provide tourists with a means of high speed intercontinental transportation which would carry them and their cars at low price. The SES could ultimately prove to be a far greater sociological mixing force than air travel.

The JSESPO programme follows a parallel technology and system engineering approach. The technology portion will investigate and solve crucial problems in such areas as aerohydrodynamics, propulsion, and related technologies, thus forming a sound and fundamental basis in depth for advancing the programme. The system engineering portion will serve to combine the necessary technologies into an overall system. The systems effort will also provide the actual verification of studies, analysis, and technological developments by use of major experimental test craft (90-ton and multi-hundred ton) including operations, test, reporting, and the preparation of design manuals for future surface effect ships.

Since the inception of this programme, JSESPO has constructed or modified and tested, both 1½-ton and 15-ton test craft, and has undertaken work in aerohydrodynamics propulsion structure, and related technologies. In addition, they have conducted design studies for a 90-ton test craft and initiated key subsystem developments including supercavitating propellers and lift fans. The Office is currently negotiating the design construction and test of a 100-ton test craft which is expected to be completed during fiscal year 1971.

There is a growing demand for smaller and middleweight cushion vehicles. Production now in hand of an initial batch of four of BHC's 45-ton Wellingtons, orders for which have been placed by both the Imperial Iranian Navy and the Royal Navy. Currently BHC is producing 60 Warden (SR.N5) and Winchester (SR.N6) craft and has made provision for the extension of the line to 80 units. In 1968 the ubiquitous Winchester took part in cold weather trials in Canada and Finland; operated the first Mediterranean hoverferry service; saw service in Singapore with the world's first fully operational military hovercraft unit, and undertook an extended tour of South America—the most ambitious hovercraft demonstration attempted to date. The first stage involved operations in areas remote from servicing and technical support facilities in the headwaters of the Amazon above Iquitos in Peru. The second stage took the form of a scientific expedition from Manaus in Brazil up the Negro and Orinoco rivers to the Caribbean Sea and Trinidad, and the third and final stage involved demonstrations in Port-of-Spain, Caracas, Georgetown, Rio de Janeiro and Buenos Aires. The craft successfully demonstrated that it could negotiate rapids and operate in waters which no other powered craft can navigate.

In developed form, the Winchester's sister craft, the Warden, has become Bell's first production machine. In February 1968 three SK-5 Model 7255s left the company's assembly line to be used for assault operations and transport duties by the US Army. The craft were airlifted to Vietnam in May 1968 and are now operating in the Mekong Delta. Three US Navy SK-5s (Model 7232s) are also operating in Vietnam on a second combat tour which was due to be completed at the end of 1968.

Air cushion vehicles are now being built for a growing range of specialist applications where their speed and other features make them superior to existing equipment.

In the field of hydrographic survey the new Hovermarine survey craft, developed in association with Decca, will offer the hydrographer the advantage of high speed in rivers and estuaries where restricted draught conditions present a hazard to conventional vessels. Hovermarine has also designed a high speed fire tender for tackling port and harbour fire outbreaks and casualty evacuation.

British Hovercraft Corporation had developed a medical centre and airfield crash rescue versions of the Winchester, and in Australia, Hovergem (A'Asia) Pty Ltd. is building a 1½ ton amphibious utility vehicle to transport equipment, freight and cattle station personnel across flooded areas in the Northern Territory and Queensland during the wet season. The craft can be quickly converted from platform truck configuration into a 14 seat personnel carrier.

Of significance to the world's farmers, is the introduction in Twin Valley, Minnesota, USA, of the simple, sturdily constructed Gunderson Flying Saucer Crop Sprayer, which is the first ACV in the world to be specifically designed for agricultural use. Spray booms mounted beneath and on both sides of the hull enable the vehicle to spray a 32 ft swath. The craft which has been employed extensively during the past two years, normally operates over land at 15 mph and at this speed will cover 8 acres with 20 gallons of chemicals.

Just as the fast skirted or sidewall hovercraft will have an increasing impact on overwater travel, so tracked hovercraft are destined to have an increasing impact on travel over land. The greatest advances to date having been made in France by Société de l'Aerotrain and Compagnie d'Enegetique Lineaire (URBA). The Aerotrain 01 half-scale prototype, after nearly three years of test runs at speeds up to 215 mph (346 km/h) has accumulated all the necessary data for the design and costing of full-scale vehicles, which will operate at these speeds, and now the new 02 half-scale prototype is producing data for vehicles designed to operate at speeds above 215 mph.

Long range, intercity Aerotrains will operate at speeds above 200 mph (322 km/h) and those designed for medium range intercity services will have a speed of 160-200 mph (257-322 km/h). The first leg of the future Orleans to Paris line—a track 11·5 miles (18·5 km) long—is under construction. Designed for a service speed of up to 250 mph (402 km/h), the track which is made from 67 ft (20 m) long prefabricated concrete beams which are mounted on 16 ft (4·90 m) pylons along the entire 70 mile (113 km) route to allow the track to be built across roads and cultivated land. The standard vehicle used on the line will carry 80 passengers in an air-conditioned and soundproof cabin, and have a speed of 155-185 mph ((230-300 km/h).

A 44-passenger suburban vehicle is now being built by the company. On multistop suburban lines average speeds as high as 95 mph (153 km/h) will be possible with this vehicle where the distances between stations are from 2-5 miles (3·2-8 km). The prototype is equipped with a linear induction motor, but later an alternative propulsion system will be fitted using an automotive engine driving tyred wheels, which will exert just sufficient pressure on the track to provide the propulsive power required.

The latest tracked ACV system for mass public transportation to be developed in France is a form of suspended monorail, designed by Maurice Barthalon. The vehicle is suspended from its track by an air lift system in which the pressure is sub-atmospheric. The prototype, the URBA 4, was demonstrated at Lyon in March 1968. The company's future programme includes the construction of an 820 ft track with curves, an incline and points, and the demonstration of a 100 passenger prototype along a 1 km track at speeds up to 65 mph in August 1969. The first commercial installation is due to be opened in January 1971. In the United Kingdom a 16-passenger test vehicle which will be tested on a 20 mile track near Cambridge, is in the design stage.

In the USA, the Transportation Systems Division of the General Electric Company has been awarded a contract by the Department of Transportation to make a design study of a 300 mph (483 km/h) vehicle suitable for intercity services. LTV Aerospace Corporation will undertake design studies for selected parts of the vehicle.

No survey of ACV activity would be complete without reference to the companies specialising in lightweight craft. Many of their products have proved extremely practical little machines and though designed at the outset for sports and pleasure several have proved suitable for light utility applications. The range available includes the Hover Air Hover Hawk, the Barwren Crested Wren, the Cushionflight Airscat and the Dobson Air Car. A newcomer is the Bertelsen Aeromobile 13 which introduces advanced new ideas on lift/propulsion and control, and is bound to set the manufacturers of large craft thinking. The ACV world is becoming full of craft of all kinds and all sizes for a variety of applications.

Whether big or small, their successes in 1968 have created a new mood for the world ACV industry which can now see dazzling possibilities ahead as the hover market begins to take a definite shape.

AIR CUSHION VEHICLE MANUFACTURERS

AUSTRALIA

overgem
VERGEM (A'ASIA) PTY LTD
AD OFFICE:
8 Franklin Street, Adelaide
LEPHONE:
4-6861
ORKS:
hird Street, Brompton, South Australia
LEPHONE:
5-2201
RECTORS:
ervyn S. Paddon, Managing Director
eoffrey L. Green, Technical Designer/
Director
len Cully, Engineering
orris Hoy, Engineering
raham H. Treloar, Secretary
hief Test Driver, Morris Hoy
n the completion of an encouraging
lve-month test programme by the proto-
e Gemcraft (JSSS, 1967-8 edition), the
ectors of Ross Aviation Facilities and
offrey L. Green formed Hovergem (A'Asia)
Ltd on December 22nd 1967. Since
n two new experimental craft, the GX-2c
-2d have been completed, and the
npany has started work on the Hovergem
, a 1½ ton passenger/utility vehicle for
tle station owners. The prototype is
ected to be ready for tests in early 1969.
the design stage is the G-5 Spencer, twice
size of the G-4, and designed for a payload
36 passengers and up to 6 tons of freight.

VERGEM GX-2d
n experimental four-seater powered by a
gle 145 hp GM-H automotive engine, the
-2d is similar to the earlier Gemcraft but
twin lift ducts and twin airscrews.

During public demonstrations across the beach and sea at Port Gawler, South Australia in August 1968, with two passengers and a driver aboard it reached ground speeds of 60-70 mph (97-113 km/h).

GX-2d has been developed via the 2c, a twin-duct design built on the original 7 ft 6 in (2·28 m) wide Gemcraft hull. On the 2d the hull has been widened by 4 ft 4 in (1·32 m) increasing the cushion area by more than 80%, with a negligible increase in weight and a considerable improvement in lateral stability.

LIFT AND PROPULSION: Power is supplied by a single 145 hp GM-H 186X2 six-cylinder automobile engine which drives through an automobile clutch assembly and Uni-Royal toothed belts two parallel, horizontal shafts. A 20 in (508 mm) diameter, 7-bladed axial-flow fan, mounted at the forward end of each shaft, directs air via a 90° elbow to an underfloor duct, which feeds cushion air beneath the craft through front and rear apertures. Each shaft extends through the rear of the duct elbow to a reversible-pitch McCauley constant speed, two-bladed airscrew of 54 in (1·37 m) diameter. These are similar to those fitted to the Cessna 185, and have been modified for independent pitch control, using an engine driven hydraulic system. A 15 in (381 mm) deep skirt of natural rubber sheet surrounds and retains the air cushion.

CONTROLS: The air cushion is divided into three compartments with vanes controlling the flow to each part. The vanes to the two forward sections are inter-connected with the aerodynamic rudders behind the propulsion

airscrews giving directional control. Hovering yaw control is provided by differential pitch of the propellers. Fore and aft trim is provided by the vane controlling flow to the rear compartment.

ACCOMMODATION: An operator and up to three passengers are carried in an enclosed cabin with a sliding, aircraft type canopy.

DIMENSIONS:
Length overall (approx) 23 ft 5 in (7·13 m)
Beam overall (approx) 11 ft 10 in (3·6 m)
Height overall 8 ft 2 in (2·48 m)
Skirt depth 14 in (356 mm)

PERFORMANCE:
Max speed Has attained ground speeds of 60-70 mph (97-113 km/h)

HOVERGEM G-4
Enquiries from cattle station owners and other potential users in the Northern Territory and Queensland showed the need for an amphibious craft, slightly bigger than the GX-2, able to transport agricultural equipment, freight and personnel across flooded areas during the wet season. This led to the development of the G-4, a 1½ ton utility vehicle which can be quickly converted from platform truck configuration into a 14-seat personnel carrier. A hinged loading ramp is fitted.

LIFT AND PROPULSION: Two variants will be available—the G-4A, a single-engine model, intended for use over reasonably smooth terrain and calm water, and the G-4B, a more powerful model with twin engines, probably 175 hp Rolls-Royce Continental GO-300s, with increased ground clearance for operation over rougher terrain.

During demonstrations across the beach and sea at Port Gawler, South Australia, GX-2d (one 145 hp GM-H 186X2) has reached 70 mph

AIR CUSHION VEHICLE MANUFACTURERS
HOVERGEM: Australia

Each engine will drive a 36 in (915 mm) diameter axial flow lift fan and a 62 in (1,575 mm) diameter reversible pitch propeller directly, eliminating the need for intershaft transmission. The lift/propulsion system will be similar in most respects to that employed on the GX-2 and Gemcraft prototype.

The prototype, a G-4B, is scheduled for completion early in 1969.

CONTROL: Two aerodynamic rudders, operated by foot pedals, provide directional control. Other controls in the operator's cabin include airscrew pitch control levers, lateral and fore and aft trim controls and the engine throttle(s). Speed and yaw can be controlled by the airscrew pitch settings.

HULL: Construction is mainly of marine quality aluminium alloy, with some glass fibre components. Buoyancy is provided by watertight cells with polyurethene foam. To reduce abrasion, the light alloy airscrews and fan blades will be given a heavy nickel/chrome finish. All exposed steel fittings are cadmium plated.

ACCOMMODATION: Both models, G-4A and B, will be available in freight or passenger forms. The lightweight cabin structure for the 14-16 seat passenger configuration will fit directly onto the freight platform on the removal of the side fences and the loading ramp. The conversion can be carried out quickly, the seat fixings picking up the freight tie-down points. It is expected that most operators will purchase the freight model and the passenger cabin for maximum utilisation.

DIMENSIONS:
Length overall	29 ft 8 in (9·06 m)
Beam overall	15 ft 0 in (4·57 m)
Height overall (skirt inflated)	10 ft 6 in (3·20 m)
Height overall on landing pads	8 ft 6 in (2·59 m)
Work platform	12 ft 10 in (3·91 m) × 8 ft 0 in (2·43 m)
Skirt depth	2 ft 0 in (0·60 m)
Passenger cabin seating space	10 ft 2 in (3·09 m) × 8 ft 0 in (2·43 m)

PERFORMANCE:
Max speed, calm air conditions (est)
65 mph (105 km/h)
Cruising speed (est) 35-40 mph (56-64 km/h)
Endurance at cruising speed (est 4 hours)
Price, G-4A app $A25,000

HOVERGEM G-5 SPENCER CLASS

The G-5, at present in the project stage, is roughly twice the size of the G-4 and will carry up to 36 passengers and 6 tons of freight. It is intended primarily for services in the Spencer Gulf area of Southern Australia.

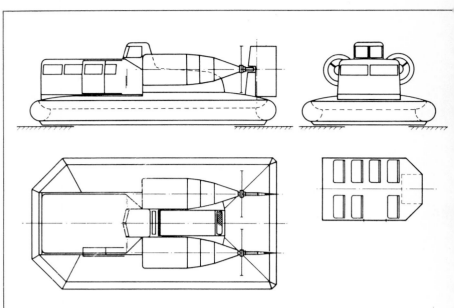
Hovergem G-4 equipped with a lightweight cabin structure and seats for 14-16 passengers

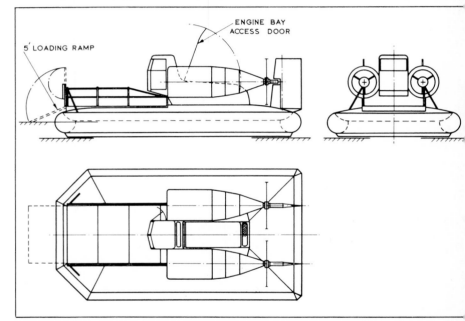
Hovergem G-4 as a utility truck, with 12 ft 10 in (3·91 m) × 8 ft 0 in (2·43 m) freight platfor

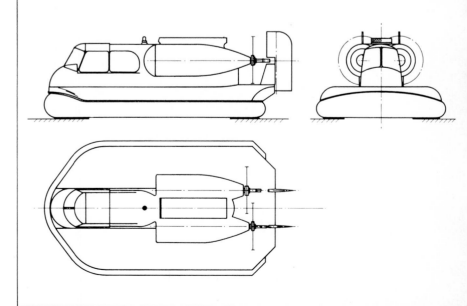
Hovergem GX-2d experimental four-seater powered by a 145 hp GM-H automotive engine

Hovergem Limited (handwritten)

overgem
OVERGEM LIMITED

HEAD OFFICE AND WORKS:
PO Box 83, R.R.5, Ottawa
TELEPHONE:
(613) 822-1472
DIRECTORS:
Ronald M. Stern
Theodore J. Mitchell
Geoff Voyce
EXECUTIVES:
Geoff Voyce, General Manager
Theodore J. Mitchell, Technical Director

OVERGEM

A two-seat, amphibious sports ACV manufactured in Canada for the Canadian and United States markets, the Hovergem is powered by three 17½ hp JLO air-cooled engines, one for lift and two for propulsion, and has a maximum speed over water of knots.

Trials of the prototype were completed on May 30th, 1968. Two pre-production models are being built before series production starts.

LIFT AND PROPULSION: The craft is powered by three JLO 297 two-stroke, air-cooled engines. Two, mounted in ducts at the rear of the craft, drive 36 in (915 mm) two-bladed Banks-Maxwell propellers for thrust, and the left engine, mounted ahead of the cabin, powers two aluminium, centrifugal fans.

An 8 gallon fuel tank is installed aft of the cabin. Recommended fuel is 80/88 octane with 20 : 1 fuel/oil mixture.
CONTROLS: Directional control is provided by twin rudders and differential throttling of the propellers. The rudders are operated by a 'butterfly' steering wheel. Dashboard controls include three car-type ignition switches (with key operated master switch), three engine tachometers and starting buttons.
HULL: The craft designed for series production. The base of the machine is made from extruded aluminium sections, and foam is attached to this for buoyancy. The cabin, a fibreglass structure, is attached to this, followed by the engine/fan assembly. A one-piece fibreglass hull is then fitted, and this is followed by the installation of the propulsion engines, ducts, rudders windscreen and a vinyl-covered nylon bag skirt. When the batteries and fuel are added the craft is ready to fly. The hull is designed to carry 400 lb (181 kg) at an all-up weight of 1,100 lb (498 kg). Reserve buoyancy is 100%.
ACCOMMODATION: Driver and passenger sit in tandem beneath a full-vision canopy.
SYSTEMS:
ELECTRICAL: 12 volt electrical system with 56 Ah battery, and three charging rectifiers. Supplies instrumentation, engine starters and internal and external lights.

DIMENSOINS:

Length overall	16 ft 1 in (4·9 m)
Beam overall	7 ft 6 in (2·28 m)
Height overall	4 ft 6 in (1·37 m)

WEIGHTS:

All-up weight	1,100 lb (499 kg)
Gross weight	700 lb (317·5 kg)
Normal payload	400 lb (181·4 kg)
Maximum payload	600 lb (272·1 kg)

PERFORMANCE:

Max speed over land	45 mph (72·4 km/h)
Max speed over water	30 knots (54·7 km/h)
Endurance at cruising speed	4 hours
Vertical obstacle clearance	1 ft (305 mm)

PRICE: Approximately $3,500 Canadian

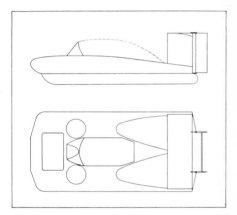

Hovergem two-seat amphibious sports ACV

A glassfibre hull, enclosed two-seat cabin and two 17½ hp JLO thrust engines with ducted propellers are features of the Hovergem, which has been designed for series production

FRANCE

Bertin
SOCIETE BERTIN & CIE
OFFICE AND WORKS:

BP No 3, Plaisir (les Yvelines)

DIRECTORS:

Jean Bertin, President Director General

Benjamin Salmon, Director General

Societe Bertin & Cie has been engaged in the design and development of ACVs incorp-orating the Bertin principle of separately fed multiple plenum chambers surrounded by flexible skirts since 1957. A research and design organisation, the company has a staff of over 500, mainly scientists and design engineers.

Société de l'Aerotrain is responsible for the construction and development of Bertin tracked air cushion vehicles, and *Société d'Études et de Développment des Aéroglisseurs Marins* (SEDAM) is responsible for devel-ing and marketing the Naviplane a Terraplane series. ACV designs by Bertin described in this section in the entries these two companies.

The Bertin principle of separately fed mu iple plenum chambers is being applied materials handling. The company's produ in this field are described in the section Applicators, Conveyors and Pallets.

Beaudequin
JACQUES BEAUDEQUIN
HEAD OFFICE:

85 Rue Republique, 92 Suresnes, Paris, France.

M. Jacques Beaudequin, President of the Club Aeroglisseur Francais, is the designer of Moise III, an experimental single-seat amphibious ACV based on an inflatable cata-maran hull. Larger models, including two and six-seat sports-craft, are being developed with quantity production in view.

MOISE III
Moise 111 is a lightweight, amphibious single seater with an inflatable, catamaran hull. It is in use as both a development and a demonstration craft.

LIFT AND PROPULSION: The craft is of plenum design. A 25½ in (600 mm) diameter Varipal lift fan is mounted at the forward end of the central intake/nacelle and is driven by a 250 cc Velocette Viceroy opposed twin through a toothed belt. The driver sits astride the nacelle saddle-fashion. Thrust is provided by a rear-mounted 3 ft (0·91 m) diameter Regy propeller, powered by a 125 cc JLO engine. Tests are also being made with water screw propulsion.

HULL: The two hulls and their lateral struts are made of rubber and are inflatable. Total buoyancy is 882 lb (400 kg). Decking is of marine ply covered with polythyrene. Neoprene loop skirts are fitted across the bow and stern.

DIMENSIONS: (hull inflated)

Length	11 ft 8 in (3·55 m)
Width	5 ft 11 in (1·80 m)
Height	3 ft 2 in (0·96 m)
Skirt depth	2 in (51 mm)

WEIGHTS

Normal gross weight	481 lb (218 kg)
Normal payload	209 lb (95 kg)
Maximum payload	264 lb (120 kg)

PERFORMANCE

Max speed over calm water (designed)

27 knots (50 km/h)

Beaudequin Moise III, an experimental single s ACV with an inflatable catamaran hull.

Turning circle at 12 knots	66 ft (20
Vertical obstacle clearance	6 in (153 m
Price	F 10,000 appr

Sedam
SOCIETE D'ETUDES ET DE DEVELOPPE-MENT DES AEROGLISSEURS MARINS
HEAD OFFICE:

80 Avenue de la Grande-Armée Paris 17 ème

OFFICERS:

Abel Thomas, Chairman General

Charles Marchetti, Managing Director

SEDAM was incorporated on July 9, 1965, to study, develop and test over-water ACV's based on principles conceived by Bertin & Cie. It has built a single-seat test vehicle, the Naviplane N 101, and the first two 27-ton 90-passenger Naviplane N 300s, which will be operated along the Côte d'Azur by Society Naviplane Côte d'Azur from June 1969 onwards. The company is also com-pleting the design of a light multi-purpose ACV, the Naviplane N 102, and studies of a 200-220 ton open-seas passenger/car hover ferry, the N 500. Trials of a lightweight sportscraft designed by the company began in September 1968. The company is also responsible for the development, manufac-ture and sales of the Bertin Terraplane series.

NAVIPLANE BC 8
This ACV consists basically of a light alloy buoyancy hull, able to float on water. The high-set driver's cab, machinery and control surfaces are concentrated at the rear end, leaving most of the flat deck clear for pay-load.

LIFT AND PROPULSION: A single 400 shp Turboméca Artouste shaft-turbine drives two aircraft tractor propellers through external gearboxes. Airflow for the lift system is provided by a Turboméca Marboré turbojet (880 lb = 400 kg st) and is ducted to the individual skirts through special channels which cool the hot gases and entrain addition-al air to augment the efflux. The front skirt has a diameter of 8 ft 6½ in (2·60 m) and height of 2 ft 5½ in (0·75 m); the other six skirts each have a diameter of 6 ft 10¾ in (2·10 m).

As a result of the use of seven separate flexible air cushion skirts and the method of propulsion by aircraft propellers, the BC 8 is able to travel with equal facility over prepar-ed or rough terrain marshland or water. large deck and high payload make it suitab for a wide range of applications; and it off particular versatility as an airfield cra rescue vehicle. In the case of airfields ne water, a BC 8 would be able to take the pla of both the land and water vehicles normal needed for emergency services and wou offer higher speed than either form of existi vehicle. In its fully-equipped crash resc mode it will carry foam firefighting equi ment, a rescue derrick, a winch and oth emergency gear.

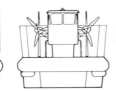

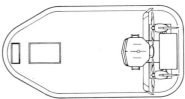

General arrangement of the BERTIN NAVIPLANE BC 8

DIMENSIONS:

Length overall	32 ft 9½ in (10·00 m)
Width overall	16 ft 4¾ in (5·00 m)
Height	14 ft 1¼ in (4·30 m)

WEIGHTS:

Weight empty	5,180 lb (2,350 kg)
Payload	4,410 lb (2,000 kg)

PERFORMANCE:

Max speed over runway or water	62 mph (100 kmh)
Over rough ground	31 mph (50 kmh)

NAVIPLANE N 101

This experimental over-water ACV is a one-fifth scale research "model" of the Naviplane N 300, which is being developed with French government support. It utilises the familiar Bertin multiple-skirt principle.

LIFT AND PROPULSION: Two axial fans, turning at 3,100 rpm, feed the eight individual skirts, which have a total cushion area of 100 sq ft (9·34 m²). Propulsion is provided by two twin-blade metal variable-pitch propellers and fans driven by a 44 hp Nelson H-63B four-cylinder two-stroke engine with integral cooling fan.

CONTROLS: Two stick controls, on each side of the driver, enable him to vary the propeller pitch mechanically to provide forward and rearward travel and rotation. The engine is controlled by a foot-operated accelerator.

DIMENSIONS:

Length overall	17 ft 11 in (5·45 m)
Width overall	9 ft 5 in (2·86 m)
Cushion area	100 sq ft (9·34 m²)
Height at rest	5 ft 11 in (1·80 m)
Height overall, skirts inflated	6 ft 10 in (2·09 m)

WEIGHTS:

Basic weight	390 kg
Normal all-up weight	472 kg

PERFORMANCE:

Max forward speed	37 mph (60 kmh)
Obstacle clearance	12 in (0·40 m)

NAVIPLANE SPORTS ACV

Trials of this lightweight amphibious ACV began on September 6th 1968. Developed from the N 101, it is designed as a sports and pleasure craft for the private owner.

LIFT AND PROPULSION: A single 7CV J LO L197 driving a fan immediately aft of the driver provides air for the multiple skirt system. Two 4·3 CV JLO L 101s drive two shrouded airscrews for propulsion.

WEIGHTS:

Normal gross weight	441-551 lb (200-250 kg)
Empty weight	298 lb (135 kg)

PERFORMANCE:

Max speed, calm water	34 mph (55 km/h)
Max wave height	2 ft (0·60 m)

NAVIPLANE N 102

A light, single-engine ACV using the Bertin multiple skirt principle, the Naviplane N 102 is designed for a wide range of civil and applications including customs and river police patrol, water-taxi, light cargo and ambulance work, conservancy board survey, military reconnaissance and dual control training for drivers of larger Naviplanes.

LIFT AND PROPULSION: A Turboméca Astazou gas turbine, rated 450 hp, powers the integrated cushion lift/propulsion system. Mounted at the rear of the central load carrying cabin, the Astazou drives a 1·70 m diameter axial lift fan and two, three-blade variable-pitch propellers carried on outriggers for propulsion.

HULL: Construction is mainly in marine corrosion resistant aluminium alloy.

ACCOMMODATION: The central cabin superstructure can be quickly removed to provide a freight deck. The two gull-wing entrance doors permit full utilisation of the cabin space. As an ambulance the craft will accommodate three stretcher cases with two attendants.

The normal cabin seating arrangement is for a pilot and eight to ten passengers.

The craft has been designed for ease of stowage aboard aircraft and ships.

DIMENSIONS:

Length	32 ft 6 in (9·9 m)
Beam	15 ft 6 in (4·7 m)
Height, hovering	10 ft 6 in (3·2 m)
Height, on landing pads	8 ft 0 in (2·4 m)
Cushion area	300 sq ft (27·8 m²)

WEIGHTS:

Empty weight (basic craft)	4,000 lb (1,816 kg)
Disposable load:	
Full for three hours' endurance	1,100 lb (498 kg)
Pilot and passengers	1,980 lb (899 kg)
Additional fittings	220 lb (100 kg)
Total disposable load	3,300 lb (1,498 kg)
Total weight	7,300 lb (3,307 kg)

PERFORMANCE:

Max speed over calm water	75 mph (120 km/h)
Endurance at cruising speed	3·5 hours
Maximum wave capability	3-5 ft (0·9-1·5 m)

Naviplane single seat amphibious sports ACV developed from the N 101. Maximum speed over calm water is 34 mph (55 km/h)

Impression of the NAVIPLANE N 102. A Turboméca Artouste IIC drives a 1·70 m diameter axial fan for lift, and two three-blade variable-pitch propellers for thrust

AIR CUSHION VEHICLE MANUFACTURERS
SEDAM: France

NAVIPLANE N 300

A 27-ton multi-purpose transport for amphibious operation, the N 300 is the first full-scale vehicle in the Naviplane series designed for commercial use.

The first two N 300s were built at Biarritz at the Breguet factory and started tethered hovering and preliminary handling trials in December 1967. Afterwards they were transported by sea to the SEDAM test centre at l'Etang de Berre. In September 1968 N 300-01 and -02 went to Nice for a series of experimental services and tests to be conducted by the French armed services. In June 1969 the craft will be introduced on regular passenger services along the Côte d'Azur by Societe Naviplane Côte d'Azur.

N 300 variants will include a mixed passenger and car ferry (up to 8 cars) capacity of 13 tons. These will have open freight decks to permit cars and freight lorries to be driven straight on and off. The first two craft have been completed as 90-seat passenger ferries and have a lightweight cabin structure above the open deck.

LIFT AND PROPULSION: Motive power is provided by two Turbomeca Turmo 111-D3 gas turbines located in separate engine rooms, port and starboard and drawing filtered air from plenum compartments behind the forward fan ducts. Each engine is coupled via a main gearbox located directly beneath each propeller pylon to a 3-bladed Ratier-Figeac 11 ft 10 in (3·60 m) diameter, variable and reversible pitch propeller and via a secondary gearbox to two 11-blade 6 ft 3 in (1·90 m) diameter axial lift fans. The main gearboxes are cross-connected by a shaft so that in the event of one engine failing or malfunctioning the four fans and two propellers can all be driven by the remaining engine. The fans deliver air to eight individual Bertin skirts, each 6 ft 7 in (2 m) deep and with a hemline diameter of 10 ft 2 in (3·09 m). These are in turn surrounded by a single wrap-round skirt.

Sedam Naviplane N.300

The 90 seat Naviplane N 300-02 will operate a service along the Cote d'Azur starting in June 1969

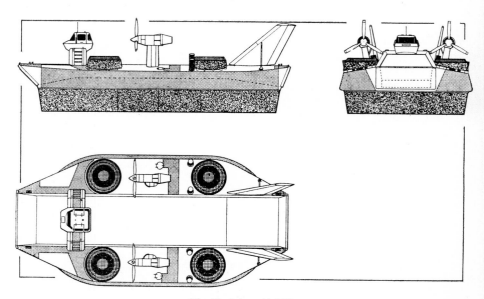

The Naviplane N. 300

NTROLS: The wheelhouse which seats a
ptain and navigator is located above a
idge spanning the foredeck to provide a
0° view. The main driving controls and
e instrumentation are positioned in front
the port seat.

The wheel of a control column varies the
tch of the two propellers differentially and
re and aft movement of the column alters
tch collectively.

ULL: The hull is a raft-like structure built
marine corrosion resistant aluminium
oys. Main buoyancy compartments are
neath the freight deck. Fans and machinery
e installed in separate structures on either
e of the freight/passenger deck, port and
rboard.

CCOMMODATION: Aircraft-type seats are
ovided for 90 passengers. Baggage areas
e provided in the centre of the passenger
loon, port and starboard, and at the rear
the saloon where there is also a dinghy
wage area. Access to the passenger
mpartment is by steps built into the bow
d stern ramp/doors.

MENSIONS:

Length overall	78 ft 9 in (24 m)
Beam	34 ft 5 in (10·5 m)
Height overall	24 ft 7 in (7·5 m)
Skirt depth	6 ft 7 in (2·0 m)
Cabin floor area	861 sq ft (80 m²)
Cushion area	1,722 sq ft (160 m²)

EIGHTS:

Basic weight	14 tonnes
Passengers	90/100
Freight	13 tonnes
Normal all-up weight	27 tonnes

ERFORMANCE:

Max speed	57/62 knots
Cruising speed	44/50 knots
Endurance	3 hours

AVIPLANE N 500

An open seas, mixed traffic hover ferry for
e 1970s, the N 500 will transport 400-500
ssengers and 30-40 vehicles. Gross weight
ll be 200-220 tons and the maximum speed
the region of 75 knots.

wer for Sedam's N 300 is supplied by two
00 shp Turbomeca Turmo III D/3 shaft tur-
es driving two 11 ft 6 in (3·5 m) diameter
opellers for thrust and four 6 ft 3 in (1·9 m)
meter lift fans. The fans feed eight Bertin
xible skirts, each 6 ft 7 in deep, which in turn
e surrounded by a lightweight, wrap-round
rt

Interior of the Naviplane N 300, 90-seat passenger ferry

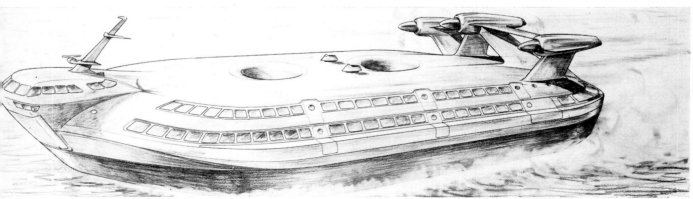

Artist's impression of the Naviplane N 500, 4/500 passenger, 30/40 vehicle, mixed traffic hover ferry

AIR CUSHION VEHICLE MANUFACTURERS
SEDAM: France

NAVIPLANE N 520

In the planning stage is a 250 ton ASW system based on the Naviplane N 500 design, and with a maximum speed of 150/160 km/h. Maximum endurance would be about 10 hours.

TERRAPLANE BC 14

The Terraplane is designed as a rugged, reliable means of transport suitable for developing countries where it is necessary to rely on natural or only very cursorily levelled tracks for communications between population centres. It can be operated by any person capable of driving a car and is capable of relatively high speeds of between 31-43 mph (50-70 km/h) over rudimentary rocky or muddy tracks, cleared by a bulldozer in places where this is absolutely necessary.

It can cross water or marshes and requires neither bridges nor any other structure, except simple access ramps for entering and leaving.

The company believes that Terraplanes would enable emergent countries to get their economy moving by providing the necessary means of transport by land without the pre-requisite of a road system, the construction of which is beyond their means either for the time being or permanently.

The Terraplane BC 14 is a project for a four-seat 44-50 mph (70-80 km/h) "shuttle" vehicle for underdeveloped territories.

The company envisages a possible Terraplane network operated by BC 7s and 14s, leading off from the main natural highways formed by rivers and used by large Naviplanes.

Also, where airfields exist, simple Terraplane tracks could be laid out from them to the main traffic roads to ensure permanent service and satisfy both charter and regular air requirements. To enable individuals to travel more easily a small vehicle like the BC 14 would be provided, which, like the BC 7, is a combined ground effect and wheeled vehicle.

LIFT AND PROPULSION: Propulsion will be provided by a propeller mounted inside a shroud at the rear. A single automotive engine mounted in front of the cabin will drive the wheels, the lift fan and the propeller. Airflow from the lift system will be ducted to large lift cells in the front and rear, and six smaller lift cells beneath the cabin.

CHARACTERISTICS:

Length and width of the BC 14 will be
17 ft 6 in (5·35 m) and (6 ft 5 in) 1·95 m

Terraplane BC 7 demonstrating its amphibious capability. Special paddle vanes can be attach to the wheels to propel the vehicle across water at about 10 km/h (6 mph)

The Terraplane BC 7, a combined ground effect machine and wheeled vehicle, is designed for use developing countries where it is necessary to rely on only cursorily levelled tracks for commu cations. Available with either a truck or coach body. it can be operated by any person capable driving a car and has a maximum speed of 50 mph (80 km/h). It can cross water with or witho air cushion support

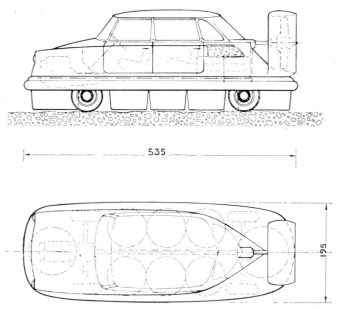

BC 14, a 50 mph four seater designed for underdeveloped territories

TERRAPLANE BC 7

The Terraplane BC 7 is a combined ground effect machine and wheeled vehicle, driven like a car or truck, but with the essential difference that it can be run at speeds up to 50 km/h over uneven ground, water and even liquid mud.

Since 1967, the BC 7 has been tested extensively in both Europe and Canada. The BC 7 02 was taken to Montreal to undergo tests across agricultural terrain and in forestry areas.

LIFT: Cushion lift is provided by a 150-180 hp Chevrolet V8 driving three centrifugal fans through a notched belt and pulley system. The airflow is ducted to ten individual neoprene-coated tergal skirts, each 1·5 m in diameter and 0·55 m high.

PROPULSION: The wheels, which provide steering and propulsion, are fitted with agricultural type tyres with a pressure from 1 to 1·8 atmospheres, and are driven by two separate 45 hp Renault petrol engines, one mounted at the front and one at the rear. A normal steering wheel, operating the front wheels, controls the direction of travel. Disc brakes are fitted with direct hydraulic control. Additional mechanical braking is provided for the rear wheels.

A three-stage hydraulics system allows selection of weight transference to the road wheels ranging from 5—20% of the total load. Special paddle vanes which can be attached to the wheels allow travel over water at about 10 km/h.

An automatic lifting system is used to raise the wheels above obstacles. Pressure is applied against the ground by two hydraulic cylinders, the amount of pressure being set by the driver who can also adjust the front/rear weight distribution. According to the pressure exerted against the cylinders by the obstacles, so either one or several wheels are lifted automatically without the driver having to intervene.

CONSTRUCTION: The BC 7 is built in light alloy, with the driver's cabin in plastic. Standard vehicle electrical equipment is carried, plus air conditioning equipment for the cab. Buoyancy for over water operation is provided within the body of the vehicle by inflatable rubber tanks. It can cross water with or without air cushion support.

ACCOMMODATION: It is available in three versions: a platform truck with a payload of 2,500 to 3,000 kg; an open back truck with a payload of 2,000 to 2,500 kg; or as a coach or bus with seats for twenty passengers and a driver.

DIMENSIONS:

Length	31 ft 6 in (9·6 m)
Width	10 ft 2 in (3·1 m)
Height	9 ft 10 in (3·0 m)

WEIGHTS:

Weight empty	5,510 lb (2·5 tonnes)
Payload	5,510 lb (2·5 tonnes)
Weight loaded	11,020 lb (5 tonnes)

PERFORMANCE:

Max speed:	
On levelled ground	50 mph (80 km/h)
Uneven ground	31 mph (50 km/h)
Over water	6 mph (10 km/h)
Endurance	3-5 hour

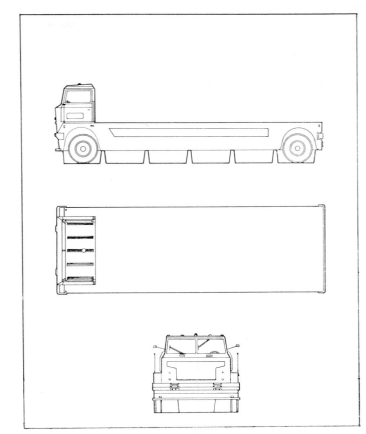

The Bertin TERRAPLANE BC 7

An automatic lifting system is used to raise the BC 7's wheels above obstacles. Pressure is applied against the ground by two hydraulic cylinders. According to the pressure exerted by the obstacles so either one or several wheels are lifted automatically.

Obstacle clearance
  4 in at 50 mph (10 cm at 80 km/h)
  12 in at 31 mph (30 cm at 50 km/h)
  16-20 in (40-50 cm at lower speeds)

WHEEL POSITIONS:
Height retracted   14 in (350 mm)

Height lowered   8 in (200 mm)

Operating positions
            driving, parking and water
Adherence setting
            5-30% of max loaded weight

AIR CUSHION VEHICLE MANUFACTURERS
ISRAEL AMERICAN MOTOR CORPORATION: Israel

ISRAEL

Israel American Motor Corporation
ISRAEL AMERICAN MOTOR CORPORA-TION LTD
HEAD OFFICE:
28 Haneviim Street, Tel-Aviv, Israel
TELEPHONE:
224230-229775
DIRECTORS:
Nathan Kirpitznikoff
Ora Kirpitznikoff

Israel American Motor Corporation was formed in 1964 to develop and produce air cushion vehicles, primarily for export. The company has since built and tested several plenum-chambered development craft, including the NX-1 Orale and the NX-2 Lady Bird. The latter craft provided axial fan data for the N-2 Lady Bird, described below.

N-2 LADY BIRD
The prototype N-2 Lady Bird was due to start sea trials in mid-October, 1968. This strikingly elegant craft is built in fibreglass, reinforced plastics with welded tubular steel members to support the lift and propulsion engines and transmission. For hard surface landings and to assist stowage four landing wheels protrude from beneath the plenum chamber.

LIFT AND PROPULSION: A 230 shp automotive engine drives two contra-rotating 1·42 m axial fans flanking the cabin for lift and a 230 hp flat-six aero-engine drives a reversible-pitch airscrew for propulsion.

The craft, which is of the simple plenum type with a 23 in (582 mm) skirt, is balanced prior to moving off by an electro-mechanical weight shifting arrangement. Twin rudders operating in the airscrew slipstream and mounted behind the propulsion shroud provide directional control.

ACCOMMODATION: Upward opening doors provide access to the six-seat cabin.

DIMENSIONS:

Length	39 ft 6 in (12·02 m)
Beam	20 ft 1 in (6·10 m)
Height	11 ft 10 in (3·6 m)
Skirt depth	1 ft 11 in (0·58 m)

WEIGHTS:

Max loaded weight	7,607 lb (3,450 kg)
Empty weight	5,622 lb (2,550 kg)

PERFORMANCE:

Max speed	75 mph (120 km/h)
Cruising speed	60 mph (96 km/h)
Ground clearance	21½ in (0·550 m)
Daylight clearance (fully loaded)	8 cm
Max range with max load	186 miles (300 km)

Full-scale model of the Lady Bird 2 under construction prior to the moulding of the fibreglass reinforced plastic hull. Welded tubular steel members will support the lift and propulsion engine and transmission

The outstandingly clean lines of the N-2 Lady Bird are displayed by this scale model. A six-seat craft capable of more than 60 knots over calm water, it has been designed with an eye to the North American Export market

JAPAN

Hitachi

HITACHI SHIPBUILDING & ENGINEERING CO

HEAD OFFICE:
47, Edabori 1-chome, Nishi-ku, Osaka, Japan

It was announced in August 1967 that

Hitachi is developing a range of air cushion vehicles. No details had been received at the time of going to press.

Mitsubishi

MITSUBISHI HEAVY INDUSTRIES LTD

HEAD OFFICE:
10, 2-chome Marunouchi, Chiyoda-ku, Tokyo, Japan

TELEPHONE:
(212)-3111

WORKS:
1130 Hikoshima Shimonoseki, Yamaguchi-Pref

TELEPHONE:
(66) 2111

CABLES:
Dock Shimonoseki

DIRECTORS:
F. Kono
K. Kita

SENIOR EXECUTIVES:
S. Katsumata, General Manager
T. Kaneko, Sales Manager
Y. Kaneko, Chief Designer

R.N5-M

The SR.N5-M is similar in most respects to the standard BHC Warden class craft, apart from the installation of a 900 shp Ishikawa-jima Marima IM100-IH gas turbine (licence built GE LM-100) in place of the original Marine Gnome, to power the integrated lift/propulsion system. Cruising speed in

The Mitsubishi SR.N5-M, powered by a 900 shp Ishikawajima Harima IM100-IH gas turbine. The craft seats 20 passengers and cruises at 45-55 knots

waves up to 1 in high is 45-55 knots.

In its standard passenger form, the craft accommodates a driver and up to twenty passengers. The company will also supply military variants to order. Structural details can be found under the entry for the BHC Warden in the UK section.

DIMENSIONS, EXTERNAL:

Length	38 ft 9 in (11·8 m)
Beam	23 ft 0 in (7·01 m)
Height overall on landing pads	12 ft 11 in (3·94 m)
Skirt depth	4 ft 0 in (1·22 m)
Cushion area	490 sq ft (45·7 m²)

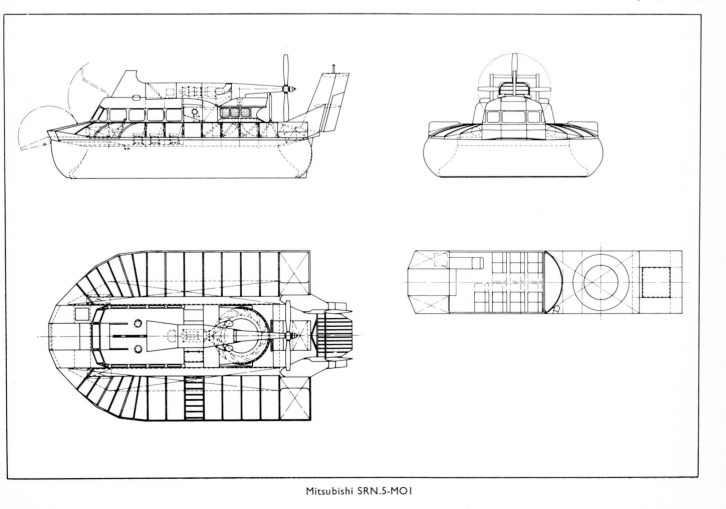

Mitsubishi SRN.5-M01

AIR CUSHION VEHICLE MANUFACTURERS
Mitsubishi: Japan

DIMENSIONS, INTERNAL:

Cabin length	11 ft 10 in (3·6 m)
Max width	7 ft 8 in (2·34 m)
Size and position of doors in the front of the craft	5 ft 9½ in (1·76 m) high by 3 ft 3 in (0·99 m) wide
Baggage holds	each 36 cu ft (1 m³) (two at sides of rear deck)
Baggage holds	each 36 cu ft (1 m³) (two at sides of rear deck)

WEIGHTS:

Normal all-up weight	14,987 lb (6,800 kg)
Normal payload	4,408 lb (2,000 kg)

PERFORMANCE (Normal all-up weight):

Max speed over calm water	64 knots (119 km/h)
Cruising speed (IAS) in 3 ft 4 in (1 m) waves	45-55 knots (82-101 km/h)
Endurance at max continuous power	3-5 hours
Max gradient	1 : 6
Vertical obstacle clearance	3 ft 7 in (1 m)

The Mitsubishi SR.N6-M (re-engined SR.N6 with a 900 hp LM100-IH gas turbine) was operated by Kyushu Shosen Company on the first Japanese hovercraft passenger service between September 1967 and May 1968

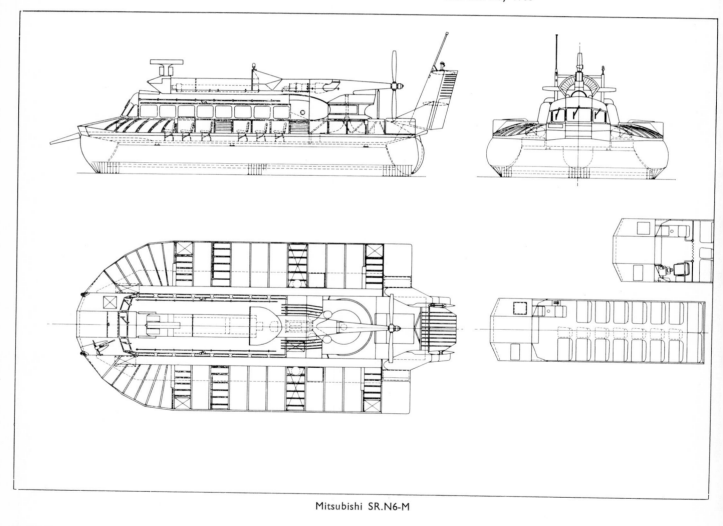

Mitsubishi SR.N6-M

SR.N6-M

The first craft of this type was imported by Mitsubishi Heavy Industries from British Hovercraft Corporation. A 900 shp Ishikawajima Harima IM100-IH gas turbine (licence-built GE LM100) replaces the original Marine Gnome to power the integrated lift/propulsion system, but apart from this the craft differs only in minor items from the standard BHC Winchester. The cabin is air-conditioned and seats 38 passengers. Cruising speed is 40-45 knots in waves up to 1 m in height. The craft is now in commercial operation with Kuyushu-Shosen Co Ltd in the Kuyushu district. Mitsubishi will supply military variants to order. Structural details can be found under the entry for the BHC Winchester in the UK section.

DIMENSIONS, EXTERNAL:

Length	48 ft 5 in (14·76 m)
Beam	23 ft 3 in (7·01 m)
Height overall on landing pads	14 ft 11 in (4·54 m)
Skirt depth	4 ft 0 in (1·22 m)
Cushion area	80 sq ft (66·7 m²)

DIMENSIONS, INTERNAL:
Cabin length   21 ft 8 in (6·6 m)
Max width   7 ft 8 in (2·34 m)
Floor area   166 sq ft (15·4 m²)
Size and position of doors in the front of
the craft:
  Height   (1·76 m)
  Width   (0·95 m)
Baggage holds, two at sides of rear cabin:
                              each 36 cu ft (1 m³)

WEIGHTS:
Normal all-up weight   20,394 lb (9,253 kg)
Normal payload   6,777 lb (3,075 kg)
PERFORMANCE (Normal all-up weight):
Max speed (max power over calm water)
                              59 knots (109 km/h)
Max speed (max continuous power)
                              55 knots (101 km/h)
Cruising speed (IAS) in 3 ft 4 in (1 m) waves
                           40-45 knots (74-84 km/h)
Endurance (max continuous power)
                                      3·5 hours
Max gradient   1 : 10
Vertical obstacle clearance   3 ft 7 in (1 m)

Mitsubishi SR.N6-M

Mitsubishi's 3-ton GEM, an experimental craft with a peripheral jet.   A 260 shp Continental 10-470
F drives an axial-flow fan for lift, and thrust is provided by a 145 hp Continental 0-300-A driving a
fixed pitch propeller.   The craft seats three and has a maximum speed of 35 knots.

AIR CUSHION VEHICLE MANUFACTURERS

MITSUI: Japan

Mitsui

Mitsui Shipbuilding & Engineering Co. Ltd.

HEAD OFFICE:

6-4 Tsukiji 5-Chome, Chuo-Ku, Tokyo, Japan

TELEPHONE:

543-3111

TELEX:

TK 2821, 2924

CABLE:

Mituizosen Tokyo

DIRECTORS:

Mr S. Tanaka, President (Representative Director)

Mr T. Asano, Executive Vice-President (Representative Director)

Mr I. Yamashita, Executive Vice-President (Representative Director)

Mr S. Sakamoto, Managing Director (Representative Director)

M. Fukuyama, Managing Director

S. Kudo, Managing Director

K. Karashima, Managing Director

J. Komatsu, Managing Director

H. Noda, Director

Y. Ishihara, Director

K. Kato, Director

S. Massaki, Director

S. Takeuchi, Director

K. Hamano, Director

R. Kawazura, Director

K. Nagai, Director

T. Teramura, Diroector

K. Maeda, Director

S. Takato, Audotir

T. Mizuno, Auditor

Mitsui's Hovercraft Department was formed on May 1st 1964, following the signing of a licencing agreement in 1963 with Hovercraft Development Ltd and Vickers Ltd, whose ACV interests were later merged with those of British Hovercraft Corporation. In addition the company was licenced by Westland S.A. in 1967, following the formation of BHC.

The company has built two eleven-seat MV-PP1s, one of which has been supplied to the Thai Customs Department, and it completed the prototype of the 50-seat MV-PP5 in August 1968. Work has now started on the design of new passenger craft with twice the seating capacity of the MV-PP5.

MV PP5

The MV-PP1 is a small peripheral jet ACV built for river and coastal services and fitted with a flexible skirt. It seats a pilot and ten passengers and cruises at 40 knots.

Two craft of this type have been built to date—the prototype, which was completed in July 1964 and has been designated RH-4, and the first production model, the PP1-01.

The latter was sold to the Thai Customs Department, for service in the estuary of the Menam Chao Phya and adjacent waters, and has been named Customs Hovercraft 1. It has been in service with the Thai Customs Department since September 1967.

HULL: The basic structural member is a light alloy buoyancy hull of mainly riveted construction with a pointed bow. On either side are further tanks for reserve buoyancy. Honeycomb boards with aluminium cores are employed as strengthening

Mitsui MV-PP5 prototype during sea trials

RH4, the prototype of the Mitsui MV-PP1. The Thai Customs Department now operates the fi production model in the Menam Chao Phya estuary

members in the main structure, which contains the passenger space and the fan gearbox spaces.

The main deck is above the buoyancy hull, the space between them forming fore and aft plenum chambers and containing the deck support structure.

LIFT AND PROPULSION: Above each plenum chamber is a 5 ft (1·5 m) diameter aluminium alloy centrifugal fan, driven by a 250 hp Continental 10-470 aero-engine mounted centrally at the front of the cabin. A second 250 hp Continental 10-470 driving either a 2-bladed McCauley or Sumitomo fixed or reversible-pitch airscrew propels the craft. Air is ejected from the plenum chamber in the form of a simple, peripheral curtain through a segmented skirt of single-ply neoprene-nylon fabric. An athwartship stability trunk is fitted and this also is in

neoprene-nylon sheet. The skirt outrigge and skirt are easily removable for transpo ation.

ACCOMMODATION: The cabin seats eitł 9 or 10 passengers and 1-2 crew membe Cabin access is through two gull-wing e trance doors, one port and one starboa Emergency window exits are provided at t sides and in the rear of the cabin. A f range of safety equipment is carried includi 11 life jackets, a fire alarm system, o manually activated fire extinguisher for t engine casing and one portable extinguish

CONTROLS: Directional control is pro ded by two aerodynamic rudders hinged the rear of the two fins and operating in t airscrew slipstream. A pair of hydraulical operated water rods, controlled by fo pedals, provide auxiliary steering and bra ing.

SYSTEMS: Electrical: One 24V × 1 kW
C/DC generator. One 24V × 70Ah battery
s electric power source. Hydraulics:
) kg/cm² hydraulic system for actuating
ater rods.

OMMUNICATIONS: SSB or VHF radio
»ptional).

IMENSIONS, EXTERNAL:

Length overall	34 ft 4 in (10·4 m)
Beam overall	15 ft 3 in (4·7 m)
Height overall on landing pad	
	10 ft 0 in (3·0 m)
Skirt depth	11 ft 6 in (0·5 m)
Draft afloat	9 in (0·2 m)
Cushion area	35·5 m²

IMENSIONS, INTERNAL:

Cabin: Length	2 ft 4 in (3·5 m)
Max width	8 ft (2·4 m)
Max height	5 ft (1·5 m)
Floor area	20 ft (6·0 m)
Size of doors	
Two 2 ft 1 in (0·65 m) × 4 ft (1·2 m)	
Position of doors	One each side of cabin
Baggage hold volume	10 cu ft (0·2 m³)

VEIGHTS:

Normal all-up weight	3·8 tons
Normal gross weight	2·8 tons
Normal payload	1·0 tons

ERFORMANCE:

Max speed over calm water	45 knots
Cruising speed, calm water	40 knots
Turning circle diameter at 30 knots	
abt 300 m without water-rod less than	
150 m with water-rod.	
Still air range and endurance at cruising	
speed	120 nautical miles; 3 hrs
Max gradient, static condition	12 : 1
Vertical obstacle clearance	10 ft (0·25 m)

V-PP5

Mitsui's first large hovercraft is the 50-seat
V-PP5, a gas-turbine powered craft
ntended primarily for fast ferry services on
apanese coastal and inland waters. The
rototype began its sea trials in August 1968.

IFT AND PROPULSION: All machinery
located aft to reduce to a minimum the
oise level in the passenger cabin. A single
HI IM-100 gas-turbine (license-built General
lectric LM100) with a maximum continuous
ating of 1,050 hp at 19,500 rpm drives the
ntegrated lift/propulsion system. Its output
naft passes first to the main gearbox from
hich shafts extend sideways and upwards
o two 3-bladed Hamilton/Sumitomo vari-
ble-pitch propulsion propellers of 8 ft 6 in
·59 m) diameter. A further shaft runs
rward to the fan gearbox from which a
rive shaft runs vertically downwards to a
ft 7 in (2·27 m) 13-blade lift fan mounted
eneath the air intake immediately aft of
ne passenger saloon roof. The fan is
onstructed in aluminium alloy and the disc
late is a 1½ in (40 mm) thick honeycomb
ructure.

To prevent erosion from water spray the
ropeller blades are nickel plated.

Fuel is carried in two metal tanks, with a
otal capacity of 416 gallons (1,900 litres),
ocated immediately ahead of the lift fan
ssembly. JP-5 and similar fuels are
ecommended.

ONTROLS: Twin aerodynamic rudders in
ne propeller slipstream and differential

Mitsui MV-PP5-01 Hakucho (Swan) ascending the slipway at its base during trials in September 1968

thrust from the propellers provide directional
control. The rudders are cable-controlled
from the commander's position. In addition
two retractable water rods, located slightly
aft or amidships on each side of the main
buoyancy tank, can be extended downwards
to prevent drift when turning and these also
assist braking at high speeds. The water
rods are operated hydraulically by foot-
pedals. When used in conjunction with the
rudders, the turning radius is reduced to
about a third of that taken when only air
rudders are used.

A thrust-port air bleed system provides
lateral control at slow speeds. The thrust
ports are actuated by air extracted from the
engine compressor and are located beneath
the passenger door entrances, port and starboard.

HULL: Construction is primarily of high
strength AA502 aluminium alloy suitably
protected against the corrosive effects of sea
water. The basic structure is the main buoyancy chamber which is divided into eight
water-tight sub-divisions for safety, and includes fore and aft trimming tanks. Two further
side body tanks, each divided into three
watertight compartments, are attached to
the sides of the main buoyancy chamber.
To facilitate shipment the side body tanks
can be removed, reducing the width to 12 ft
4 in (3·75 mm).

The outer shell of the main buoyancy
chamber, the machinery deck space, the
forward deck and the passage decks around
the cabin exterior are all constructed in
honeycomb panels with aluminium cores.

The lift fan air intake, radar cover, part of
the air conditioning duct, and inside window
frames are in glass-fibre reinforced plastic.

Design loads are as required by the Provisional British ACV Safety Regulations.

SKIRT: The flexible skirt was designed by
Mitsui in the light of research conducted
with aid of the RH-4 (MV-PP1 prototype)
It is made of $\frac{1}{32}$ in (0·8 mm) thick chloro-
prene-coated nylon sheet. A fringe of finger
type nozzles is attached to the skirt base at
the bow and on both sides. At the stern a

D-section bag skirt is used to avoid scooping
up water.

A transverse stability bag and keel are
fitted.

ACCOMMODATION: The passenger cabin
is sited above the forward end of the main
buoyancy chamber. Seats for the two crew
members are on a raised platform at the front
of the cabin. All controls, navigation and
radio equipment are concentrated around the
seats. The windows ahead are of reinforced
tempered glass and have electric wipers.

The two cabin entrance doors are divded
horizontally, the lower part opening sideways, the top part upwards. The standard
seating arrangement is for 42 passengers but
eight additional seats can be placed in
the centre aisle.

In accordance with Japanese Ministry of
Transport regulations a full range of safety
equipment is carried, including two inflatable
life rafts, 52 life jackets, one automatic,
manually activated fire extinguisher for the
engine casing and two portable fire extinguishers in the cabin. Other standard equipment includes ship's navigation lights, marine
horn, searchlight and mooring equipment,
including an anchor. The twelve side windows can be used as emergency exits and are
made of acrylic resin.

SYSTEMS:

ELECTRICAL SYSTEM: Two 2 kW, 24
volt ac/dc generators driven by belts form
the main gearbox. 1 24 volt, 68 Ah battery
for engine starting.

HYDRAULIC AND PNEUMATIC SYS-
TEM: a 995·6 lbf/in² (70 kg/cm²) hydraulic
system pressure for water rods and (56·8-
99·5 lbf/in² (4·7 kg/cm²) operating pneumatic
system for thrust port operation.

COMMUNICATION AND NAVIGATION:
Standard equipment includes a single SSB
radio and radar. A gyro-compass can be
fitted as an optional extra.

PERFORMANCE:

Max speed, calm water 55 knots (102 km/h)
Cruising speed, calm water

45 knots (83 km/h)

AIR CUSHION VEHICLE MANUFACTURERS
MITSUI / COELACANTH: Japan / Trinidad

Still air range and endurance at cruising speed of about 160 nautical miles, 4 hours

Vertical obstacle clearance 2 ft (0·6 m) app

DIMENSIONS, EXTERNAL:

Length overall	52 ft 6 in (16·0 m)
Beam overall	28 ft 2 in (8·6 m)
Height overall on landing pad	
	14 ft 5 in (4·4 m)
Skirt depth	3 ft 11 in (1·2 m)
Draft afloat	11 in (0·2 m)
Cushion area	741 sq ft (88· m²)

DIMENSIONS, INTERNAL:

Cabin:

Length	23 ft 4 in (7·1 m)
Max width	12 ft 6 in (3·8 m)
Max height	6 ft 3 in (1·9 m)
Floor area	280 sq ft (26 m²)

Doors:

Two (0·65 m) × (1·4 m), one each side of cabin

Baggage-hold volume	24 cu ft (0·6 m³)

WEIGHTS:

Normal all-up weight	12·0 tons
Normal payload	5·5 tons

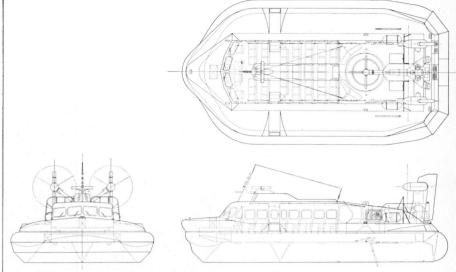

Mitsui MV-PP5 50-seat hovercraft, designed for fast ferry services on Japanese coastal and inlan[d] waters

POLAND

Institute of Agricultural Mechanisation and Electrification

INSTITUTE OF AGRICULTURAL MECHANISATION AND ELECTRIFICATION

HEAD OFFICE:

Rakowieka 8, Warsaw, Poland

The Institute of Agricultural Mechanisation and Electrification is developing a range of small air cushion vehicles intended principally for agricultural applications, including crop-spraying. Latest of these is reported to be the TP-2R Domino. a modular type load-carrying platform built of welded steel tubing and measuring app 8 ft 3 in (2·5 m) long, 5 ft 7 in (1·7 m) wide and 1 ft (0·3 m) high. As many as 8-12 of these platforms can be bolted together to form a variety of ACVs of different load carrying capacities. Each platform has a single 22 hp air-cooled motorcycle engine driving a centrally moun[t]ed fan for lift. Hover height of the bas[ic] module is 3 in (0·11 mm).

Small capacity ACVs built up from th[e] basic platforms would be pushed by a man [or] towed by a tractor or a horse. Larg[e] multiple units will be fitted with propulsiv[e] airscrews and will have a control cabi[n] based on that of the Latka SM-4 helicopt[er] at the front.

TRINIDAD

Coelacanth Gemco Ltd.

COELACANTH GEMCO LTD

HEAD OFFICE:

1 Richardson Street, Point Fortin, Trinidad, W.I.

TELEPHONE:

Point Fortin 2439

CABLES:

Coelacanth, Trinidad

DIRECTORS:

Hugh Ammon

V. R. F. Richardson

Nigel Seale

Coelacanth Gemco Ltd, the first company to specialise in the design and construction of air cushion vehicles in the West Indies, has recently purchased land on Guapo Beach, Trinidad, where an ACV factory and a hover-port will be built. Guapo Bay and the neighbouring Antilles Bay will be used by the company for sea tests and a disused runway adjacent to the site will be used for overland tests.

The company also plans to build a two-mile long, 100 ft wide ACV roadway between Guapo Beach and the Point Fortin Industrial Estate. A freight operation is planned with ACVs taking aboard finished goods from the Industrial Estate, and delivering them to Port-of-Spain, 40 minutes away at a speed of 60 knots.

Craft at present under development by the company are the Pluto, Jupiter, Venus and Arcturus.

PLUTO

The Pluto is a two-seat test vehicle, bui[lt] in marine ply, and designed to provide dat[a] for a four-seat craft which will be markete[d] under the same name.

LIFT AND PROPULSION: A 7 hp Brigg[s] & Stratton motor mower engine, drives a[n] axial, 42 in diameter tractor fan for lift an[d] a second engine of the same type drives [a] ducted, 42 in diameter air conditionin[g] cooling tower fan for propulsion. Direction[al] control is provided by a rudder operating i[n] the slipstream.

Lift and propulsion engines are due to b[e] replaced by 20 hp engines. Two Rotafo[il] fans, now on order, will replace the singl[e] heavy duty tractor fan and a propeller wi[ll] replace the propulsion fan.

DIMENSIONS, EXTERNAL:
Length   14 ft 0 in
Width   7 ft 10 in
Height   5 ft 4 in

WEIGHTS:
Empty weight   725 lb

PERFORMANCE:
Speed over water   6 mph
Speed over land (with one person)   9 mph
Est. speed with new 20 hp engines for lift
  and propulsion   40 mph
Vertical obstacle clearance   4 in
Est. clearance with 20 hp lift engine 12 in

VENUS

This craft has been designed principally for carrying oil company executives to and from wells in the Gulf of Paria, in Soldado and other areas in the West Indies. Ten and fifteen seat versions will be built, and like the Jupiter, the craft will be available in either amphibious form with a continuous skirt or as a rigid sidewall type with bow and stern skirts.

A manned scale model of the craft was due for completion in December 1968.

JUPITER

A projected four-seat ACV runabout, Jupiter is designed around the basic hull of the company's Super Bee cabin cruiser, and will be available either as an amphibious craft, with a continuous peripheral skirt, or as a rigid sidewall type with bow and stern skirts.

Lift will be provided by a 75 hp modified outboard driving two Rotafoil fans, and propulsive thrust by a 90 hp modified outboard driving a reversible-pitch, ducted propeller.

DIMENSIONS:
Length   18 ft 0 in
Beam   10 ft 0 in
Height   7 ft 0 in

WEIGHT:
Weight, incl fuel   2,810 lbs

PERFORMANCE:
Max speed (est)   50 knots

ARCTURUS

The Arcturus is a 35-seat amphibious ACV designed by Nigel Seale. Motive power for the lift and propulsion system will be supplied by high speed diesel generators driving Lear Siegler Electric Motors.

Work has started on a manned scale model.

The first of Coelocanth Gemco's Pluto series is this manned test model of a 4-seat cabin version. Test runs are made in the nearby bay at Point Fortin

UNITED KINGDOM

Airbearings
AIRBEARINGS LTD

HEAD OFFICE:
126 Bishopsgate, London E.C.2
TELEPHONE:
London Wall 4925/6/7
WORKS:
Barnham Broom Hall, Norfolk
TELEPHONE:
Barnham Broom 640
DIRECTORS:
A. R. Hawker, Chairman
J. E. Cook, Secretary
C. R. W. Hughes
SENIOR EXECUTIVES:
N. Seymour, General/Works Manager
A. R. Hawker ⎫ Chief Designers
J. E. Cook ⎭
C. R. W. Hughes, Sales Director

Airbearings Ltd. was founded in March
1965 to manufacture light ACVs employing
the company's own integrated lift/propulsion
system and skirt design. The first production model designed by the company is the
HC.10 Falcon.

H.C.10 FALCON

The Falcon is a 3-seat lightweight sports
ACV intended for large-scale production.
The design is based on the company's
experience with H.C.9, a smaller but similar
craft, and earlier prototypes.

The designers have paid careful attention
to safety aspects. Thrust is provided by fan
air rather than by an air propeller and the
neoprene/nylon skirt has integral buoyancy
to avoid any possibility of a collapse in poor
overwater operating conditions.

LIFT AND PROPULSION: Motive power
for the integrated lift/propulsion system is
provided by a 100 bhp Johnson V.100 outboard motor driving a single 34 in diameter
wood laminate fan. Thrust is provided by
ejecting fan air horizontally from the rear of
the hull.
CONTROLS: Deflector foils operating in the
air stream provide directional control.
Braking is by reverse thrust.
HULL: The hull is built in glass reinforced
plastics throughout except for the engine
mounting. It is stressed for 6 g. A continuous 1 ft 1½ in (342 mm) deep peripheral
skirt is fitted.
ACCOMMODATION: Access to the three-
seat cabin is via a door on the port side. An
emergency exit is fitted on the starboard side.
Cabin heating can be installed as an optional
extra.
SYSTEMS:
ELECTRICAL: A 12 volt 18 Ah battery is
installed for engine starting, operating the
ballast pump, lights and the windscreen
wiper.
COMMUNICATIONS AND NAVIGATION:
A compass is fitted as standard. Radio and
other equipment is optional.
DIMENSIONS, EXTERNAL:
Length overall   15 ft 3 in (4·64 m)
Beam overall, skirt inflated
                           9 ft 6 in (2·89 m)
Beam, power off   7 ft 6 in (2·28 m)
Height overall on landing pads
                           3 ft 9 in (1·14 m)
Skirt depth   1 ft 1½ in (0·32 m)
Draft afloat   1 ft 6 in (0·45 m)
Cushion area   87 sq ft (8 m²)

DIMENSIONS, INTERNAL:
Cabin:
Length   5 ft 0 in (1·5
Width   4 ft 9 in (1·4
Height   3 ft 3 in (0·9
Floor area   22·5 sq ft (2·45 m
WEIGHTS:
Normal all-up weight   1,500 lb (680 k
Empty weight   1,000 lb (454 k
Normal payload   500 lb (227 k
PERFORMANCE (at normal operati
weight):
Max speed over calm water
                           43 mph (69 km
Cruising speed, calm water
                           38 mph (61 km
Turning circle diameter at 30 knots
                           600 ft (182
Still air range and endurance at cruisi
speed   114 miles (183 km), 3 hou
Max gradient, static conditions   1 ir
Vertical obstacle clearance 14 in (365 m

Airbearings H.C. 10 Falcon 3-seat sports A

ir Vehicle Developments
R VEHICLE DEVELOPMENTS

EAD OFFICE AND WORKS:
Sun Hill, Cowes, Isle of Wight

ELEPHONE:
Cowes 3194/2118

PARTNERS:
P. H. Winter, MSc
C. D. J. Bland

Air Vehicle Developments was formed in February 1968. Its activities include the development of long distance conveyor systems and off-the-road transport vehicles, and the construction and testing of hovercraft propulsion and lift systems. The firm also undertakes project studies and technical evaluations, and acts as a purchasing agent for small air cushion vehicles and associated equipment.

arwren
ARWREN HOVER LTD

EAD OFFICE AND WORKS:
Diamond Road, Whitstable, Kent

ELEPHONE:
Whitstable 2236

IRECTORS:
L. G. Barton, Chairman
R. L. Barton, Secretary
C. H. Wren

Barwren Hover Ltd was formed in November 1967 to produce the Crested Wren, a uccessful lightweight amphibious two-seater esigned by Cedric Wren, and winner of the)67 amateur hovercraft rally at Apethorpe, orthamptonshire. Main structure of the aft is of marine plywood and both lift and ropulsion engines are Inca 400 cc air-cooled -strokes. The craft has a normal all-up eight of 1,000 lb (454 kg) and is marketed £1,250 ex-works.

RESTED WREN

IFT AND PROPULSION: Lift is provided y a 24 in (610 mm) diameter 13-blade ulti-wing fan driven by an Inca Power 00 cc air-cooled vertical twin 2-stroke. The hrust engine, of the same type, is mounted n four chromium-plated tubular members ft of the cabin, and drives a fixed pitch, -bladed wooden propeller. The propeller s stainless steel tipped and as a safety neasure is guarded by a heavy wire mesh age. The single rudder is hinged to the rear f the cage structure.

A 5-gallon fuel tank is located at the rear f the hull beneath the lift engine. Fuel is upplied to the engine by an S.U. 12 v lectric pump.

ONTROLS: Directional control is provided y the single rudder located in the slip-tream, and operated by a joystick and 10 wt cables passing over a pulley system to teel stays on the control surface.

IULL: The main hull structure is of marine ly. The cabin is a multi-ply box, fitted vith a forward sliding fibreglass canopy with Perspex side windows, and laminated glass vindscreen to prevent scratching. A glass-ibre "knock-out" panel in the roof provides n emergency exit. Transverse stiffening of he floor is provided by ½ in thick ply, and a ly bulkhead separates the cabin from the ift engine bay. Aft of the cabin is a one-iece fibre-glass intake duct fitted above the ift engine and fan. The main well is below he engine bay, and surrounding the bay is watertight stressed-skin torsion box, ttached to which is a 12 in bag skirt in pvc. Four landing skids are attached to the under urface to prevent skirt damage.

The Crested Wren two-seater amphibious ACV, powered by two Inca 400 c.c. twin 2-stroke engines

ACCOMMODATION: A bench seat, covered with Vynide Flexnit, provides seating for two. Emergency safety equipment includes a hand-operated fire extinguisher.

SYSTEMS:

ELECTRICAL: Both engines are equipped with Siba-Dynastart generator units to charge a 12v battery for the operation of running lights, engine starting etc.

DIMENSIONS:

Length overall	12 ft 6 in (3·81 m)
Beam overall	6 ft 0 in (1·82 m)
Height overall on landing pads	5 ft 10 in (1·77 m)
Skirt depth	9 in (299 mm)
Draft afloat	2 in (51 mm)
Cushion area	35 sq ft (3·25 m²)

WEIGHTS:

Normal all-up	1,000 lb (453 kg)
Normal payload	440 lb (199 kg)

PERFORMANCE:

Max speed over calm water
45 mph (72 km/h)
Cruising speed   30 mph (48 km/h)
Water speed in 15 knot headwind
25 mph (40 km/h)
Max wave capability 9-12 in (229-305 mm)
Still air range and endurance at cruising speed 50 miles (80 km) at 30 mph (48 km/h
Max gradient static conditions   1 : 10
Vertical obstacle clearance   9 in (229 mm)

PRICE AND TERMS:

Approximate cost of craft f.o.b. £1,250, plus £85 despatch and packing. Terms of payment: Cash on delivery to docks.

BHC
BRITISH HOVERCRAFT CORPORATION
HEAD OFFICE:
East Cowes, Isle of Wight
DIRECTORS:
D. C. Collins, Chairman
R. Stanton-Jones, Managing Director
W. Oppenheimer, Assistant Managing Director, Finance
L. Boddington CBE, Assistant Managing Director, Technical
E. F. Gilberthorpe, Works Director
R. F. Dunlop, Commercial Director
T. Bretherton, Finance Director and Secretary
NON-EXECUTIVE DIRECTORS:
J. C. Duckworth
D. Hennessey
J. S. Booton

The British Hovercraft Corporation is the world's largest hovercraft manufacturer. It was formed in 1966 to concentrate the British hovercraft industry's major technical and other resources under a single management.

The Corporation deals with a wide variety of applications of the air cushion principle, the emphasis being on the development and production of amphibious hovercraft. Other activities include the development and production of overland load transporters and floatload hoverpallets.

The capital of the Corporation is £5 million, 65% held by Westland Aircraft Ltd., 25% by Vickers Ltd, and 10% by National Research and Development Corporation.

BHC established the world's first full-scale hovercraft production line in 1964. Currently it is producing 60 Warden (SR.N5) and Winchester (SR.N6) Class craft at its plant at Itchen, Southampton and an initial batch of four 168-ton Mountbatten (SR.N4) Class craft at East Cowes. Provision has been made for the extension of the Warden/Winchester line to 80 units and the initial production batch of Mountbattens to six.

The first Mountbatten entered service with British Rail Hovercraft Ltd on the Dover/Boulogne route in August 1968 and the second and third craft are scheduled to enter service with Hoverlloyd Ltd on the Ramsgate/Calais route early in 1969.

BHC craft have seen service in all parts of the world with commercial and military operators. Warden hovercraft are now in service with the British Armed Services, the US Army and the US Navy.

The world's first fully operational military hovercraft unit—200 squadron, Royal Corps of Transport, currently in Singapore—is equipped with military variants of the Winchester. A further Winchester is in service with the Royal Navy as a fast amphibious communications and support craft for Royal Marine Units in the Falkland Islands.

Winchesters have been employed during 1967-68 in trials and sales demonstrations in Canada, Denmark, Finland, South America and the Far East.

Cold weather trials, organised by Hoverwork (Canada) in conjunction with the Canadian Department of Defence, were conducted in Canada at Fort Churchill, Manitoba on Hudson Bay.

Cold weather trials in Finland were designed to evaluate the Winchester as a coastguard and rescue craft, and were conducted in conjunction with the Finnish Navy and Coastguard. On the return to the UK the craft operated on a short-term passenger-carrying service in Esjberg, Denmark.

The South American tour was the most ambitious ever attempted by BHC and involved operations in areas remote from sophisticated servicing and technical support facilities. The first stage involved operations in the headwaters of the Amazon above Iquitos in Peru, and the second stage took the form of a scientific expedition from Manaus in Brazil up the Negro and Orinoco Rivers to the Caribbean Sea and Trinidad. This expedition was organised by the Geographic Magazine and Hoverwork Limited.

The third and final phase took the craft to demonstrations in Port-of-Spain, Trinidad, Caracas, Venezuela, Georgetown, Guyana, Rio de Janeiro, Brazil and Buenos Aires, Argentina.

Production is also in hand of an initial batch of four 45-ton Wellington Class hovercraft. Orders for this class have been placed by both the Imperial Iranian Navy and the Royal Navy.

The Corporation is also developing the BH.8 80-ton overwater hovercraft and is conducting design studies on craft up to 300/400 tons and ocean-going hoverships of up to 4,000 tons.

MOUNTBATTEN (SR.N4)
The world's largest hovercraft, the Mountbatten is a 173-ton passenger car/ferry designed for stage lengths of up to 100 n. miles (184 km) or coastal water routes. It has an average service speed of 40-50 kn in waves up to 10 ft (3·04 m) in height and able to operate in 12 ft (3·7 m) seas at a spe of about 20 knots.

The first craft entered commercial serv with British Rail Hovercraft Lts. in Aug 1968 on the Dover/Boulogne route for initial ten-week period in service. BHR v re-open this service in April 1969 and subj to negotiations will take delivery of a seco craft for service on the same route late in t summer of 1969.

Two further craft will also enter serv with Hoverlloyd Limited in 1969 on Ramsgate/Calais route.

The first BRH Mountbatten is one of initial batch of four craft but provision already been made to extend production cater for anticipated deDand.

LIFT AND PROPULSION: Power is sup ed by four 3,400 shp Marine Proteus fr turbine, turboshaft engines located in pa at the rear of the craft on either side of t vehicle deck. Each engine is connected one of four identical propeller/fan units, t forward and two aft. The propuls propellers, made by Hawker Siddeley, are the 4-bladed, variable and reversible pit type. 19 ft (5·79 m) in diameter. The fans, made by BHC, are of the 12-blad centrifugal type, 11 ft 6 in (3·5 m) in diamet

Since the gear ratios between the engi fan and propeller are fixed, the pow distribution can be altered by varying t propeller pitch, and hence changing the spe of the system, which accordingly alters t power absorbed by the fixed pitch fan. T power absorbed by the fan can be vari from almost zero shp (i.e. boating w

British Rail's SR.N4 Mountbatten is capable of carrying 254 passengers and 30 cars at speeds up 50 knots. The craft crosses the English Channel between Dover and Boulogne in about 35 minute reducing the time taken by conventional sea ferries by almost an hour.

nimum power) to 2,100 shp, within the opeller and engine speed limitations. A pical division on maximum cruise power uld be 2,000 shp to the propeller and 1,150 p to the fan; the remaining 250 shp can be counted for by engine power fall-off due to e turbine rpm drop, transmission losses and ixiliary drives.

The drive shafts from the engines consist flanged light-alloy tubes approximately ft 6 in (2·28 m) long supported by steady earings and connected by self-aligning coup- gs. Shafting to the rear propeller/fan units comparatively short, but to the forward iits is approximately 60 ft (18·27 m).

The main gearbox of each unit comprises a piral bevel reduction gear, with outputs at e top and bottom of the box to the vertical ropeller and fan drive shafts respectively. he design of the vertical shafts and couplings similar to the main transmission shafts, xcept that the shafts above the main gearbox e of steel instead of light alloy to transmit e much greater torque loads to the pro- ler. This gearbox is equipped with a ower take-off for an auxiliary gearbox with rives for pressure and scavenge lubricating l pumps, and also a hydraulic pump for e pylon and fin steering control.

The upper gearbox, mounted on top of the ylon, turns the propeller drive through 90° nd has a gear ratio of 1·16 : 1. This earbox has its own self-contained lubricating ystem.

Engines and auxiliaries are readily access- le for maintenance from inside the craft, hile engine, propellers, pylons and all earboxes can be removed for overhaul rithout disturbing the main structure.

The fan rotates on a pintle which is attach- d to the main structure. The assembly may e detached and removed inboard onto the ar deck without disturbing the major tructure.

CONTROLS: The craft control system is ssentially a double SR.N3 system in which he thrust lines and pitch angles of the ropeller can be varied either collectively or lifferentially. The pylons, fins and rudders nove through ±35°, ±30° and ±40° espectively.

Demand signals for pylon and fin angles are ransmitted from the commander's controls lectrically. These are compared with the ylon or fin feed-back signals and the lifferences are then amplified to actuate the ydraulic jacks mounted at the base of the ylon or fin structure. Similar electro- hydraulic signalling and feed-back systems re used to control propeller pitches.

The commander's controls include a rudder oar which steers the craft by pivoting the propeller pylons differentially.

For example, if the right foot is moved forward, the forward pylons move clockwise, viewed from above, and the aft pylons and fins move anti-clockwise, thus producing a turning moment to starboard. Rudder bar movement also varies the propeller blade angles differentially so as to increase the craft's turning moment produced by the pylon and fin movement. The foregoing applies with positive thrust on the propellers, but if negative thrust is applied, as in the case of using the propellers for braking, the pylons and fins are automatically turned to apposing

The first Mountbatten hovercraft entered scheduled service with British Rail Hovercraft Ltd. on August 1st, 1968. The craft is seen leaving Dover harbour en route to the first continental hover-port at Le Portel, Boulogne.

Control cabin of the SR.N4. Basic manning requirements is for a commander, a first officer and a radar operator/navigator. A seat is provided for a fourth crew member or a crew member in training. The moving map display of the Decca Flight Log is located above the commander's windscreen at the left

angles, thus maintaining the turn. A wheel mounted on a control column enables the commander to move the pylons and fins in unison to produce a drift to either port or starboard as required. Collective variation of the propeller pitch angles, and hence control of the distribution of power between propellers and fans, is by fore-and-aft movement of the control wheel, used in conjunction with the engine throttle levers. HULL: Construction is primarily of high strength, aluminium-clad, aluminium alloy, suitably protected against the corrosive effects of sea water. To simplify e.g. arrangements the Mountbatten is designed around a central load-carrying cabin.

The basic structure is the buoyancy chamber, built around a grid of longitudinal and transversal frames, which form twenty-

four water-tight sub-divisions for safety. The design ensures that even a rip from end-to-end would not cause the craft to sink or overturn. The reserve buoyancy is 250%, the total available buoyancy amounting to more than 550 tons.

Top and bottom surfaces of the buoyancy chamber are formed by sandwich construction panels bolted onto the frames, the top surface being the vehicle deck. Panels covering the central 16 ft (4·9 m) section of the deck are reinforced to carry unladen coaches, or commercial vehicles up to 9 tons gross weight (max axle load 13,000 lb (5,900 kg), while the remainder is designed solely to carry cars and light vehicles (max axle load 4,500 lb (2,040 kg). An articulated loading ramp, 18 ft (5·5 m) wide, which can be lowered to ground level, is built into the bows, whilst doors

AIR CUSHION VEHICLE MANUFACTURERS
BHC: United Kingdom

extending the full width of the centre deck are provided at the aft end.

Similar grid construction is used on the elevated passenger-carrying decks and the roof, where the panels are supported by deep transverse and longitudinal frames. The buoyancy chamber is joined to the roof by longitudinal walls to form a stiff fore-and-aft structure. Lateral bending is taken mainly by the buoyancy tanks. All horizontal surfaces are of pre-fabricated sandwich panels with the exception of the roof, which is of skin-and-stringer panels.

Double curvature has been avoided other than in the region of the air intakes and bow. Each fan air intake is bifurcated and has an athwartships bulkhead at both front and rear, supporting a beam carrying the transmission main gearbox and the propeller pylon. The all-moving fins and rudders behind the aft pylons pivot on pintles just ahead of the re bulkhead.

A system of peripheral trunks with athwa ship stability trunk, similar to that on pre ous BHC hovercraft, has been used Mountbatten. A modification has, howeve been introduced in the method by which t air is directed into the cushion. The perip eral slot used on previous hovercraft has be substituted by a system in which the air

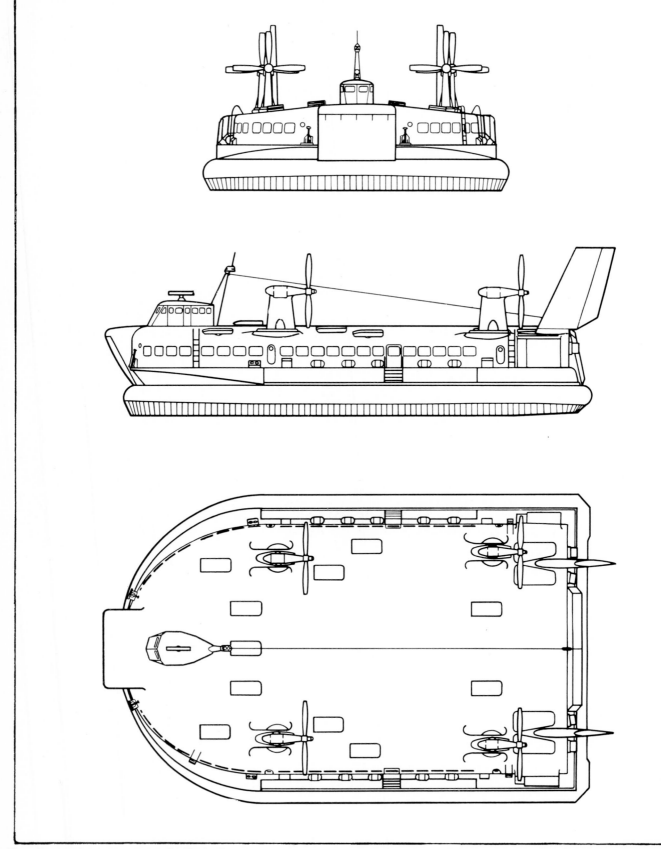

Typical internal arrangements on the SR.N4 Mountbatten include an all-passenger layout seating 609, and passenger car ferries for either 174 passenge and 34 cars or 254 passengers and 30 cars.   Average service waterspeed is 40-50 knots (74-93 km/h)

e side and bow trunks is directed into the
shion through a series of fingers which form
e lower part of the trunks. The aft and
ability trunks are similar in construction,
t differ from the side trunks in that the air
directed into the cushion through inverted
nes.

The material used for the trunks is neoprene-
ated nylon fabric, and although that of
e fingers and cones is the same material, it
of a much lighter weight. The greater
xibility of the lower portion of the trunks
ntributes to improved control, stability
d comfort.

CCOMMODATION: The basic manning
quirement is for a commander, an engineer/
dio operator and a radar operator/navi-
tor. A seat is provided for a fourth crew
ember or a crew member in training. The
mainder of the crew, i.e. those concerned
th passenger service or car handling, are
ated in the main cabins. The arrangement
y be modified to suit individual operator's
quirements.

The control cabin is entered by either of
o ways. The normal method, when the
rs are arranged in four lanes, is by a hatch
the cabin floor, reached by a ladder from
e car deck. When heavy vehicles are carri-
on the centre land, or if for some other
ison the ladder has to be retracted, a door
the port side of the passenger cabin gives
cess to a ladder leading onto the main
bin roof. From the roof an entrance door
es access into the control cabin.

The craft currently in production will carry
4 passengers and 30 cars but the basic
sign permits variations from an all-passeng-
craft (609 seats) to one carrying 174
ssengers and 34 cars.

The car deck occupies the large central area
the craft, with large stern doors and a bow
mp providing a drive-on/drive-off facility.
Separate side doors give access to the
ssenger cabins which flank the car deck.
e outer cabins have large windows which
tend over the full length of the craft. The
ntrol cabin is sited centrally and forward
top of the superstructure to give maximum
ew.

DIMENSIONS, EXTERNAL:

Overall length   130 ft 2 in (39·68 m)
Overall beam   78 ft 0 in (23·77 m)
Overall height on landing pads
                      37 ft 8 in (11·48 m)
Skirt depth   8 ft 0 in (2·44 m)

DIMENSIONS, INTERNAL:

Passenger/vehicle floor area
                      5,800 sq ft (539 m²)
Vehicle deck headroom-centre line
                      11 ft 3 in (3·43 m)
Bow ramp door aperture size (height ×
width) 11 ft 6 in × 18 ft (3·51 m × 5·48 m)
Stern door aperture size (height × width)
      11 ft × 31 ft (3·51 m × 9·45 m)

WEIGHTS:

Normal gross weight   168 tons
Fuel capacity
      4,500 Imp gallons (20·456 litres)

PERFORMANCE (at normal gross weight at
5°C):

Max waterspeed over calm water, zero wind
(cont power rating) 65 knots (120 km/hr)
Average service waterspeed
      40-50 knots (74-93 km/hr)

Top: Cars being loaded aboard the SR.N4 via the 18 ft (5·49 m) wide articulated bow door/ramp
Centre: Stern door aperture is 31 ft wide × 11 ft 6 in high (9·45 m × 3·51 m). The two doors
extend the full width of the vehicle deck

Bottom: Panels covering the central 16 ft (4·9 m) of the vehicle decks are reinforced to carry unladen
coaches or commercial vehicles up to 9 tons gross weight while the remainder is designed solely
to carry cars and light vehicles

AIR CUSHION VEHICLE MANUFACTURERS
BHC: United Kingdom

Normal stopping distance from 50 knots	700 yards (640 m)
Endurance at max cont power on 2,800 Imp gallons	2·5 hours
Negotiable gradient from standing start	1 : 14

WARDEN (SR.N5)

The Warden was the first hovercraft to be put into quantity production. It has been evaluated in all parts of the world and currently craft of this type are operating in the United States, Canada, South East Asia and the United Kingdom.

It can be equipped for a variety of uses including firefighting, crash rescue, coast-guard work and off-shore patrol. As a commercial transport it can seat up to 18 people or carry 2 tons of freight. In military form, it can carry 15 fully-equipped troops; a davit hoist and stretcher mountings for search and rescue operations, or a variety of other specialised equipment.

LIFT AND PROPULSION: Power for the integral lift/propulsion system is provided by a single 900 shp Rolls Royce Marine Gnome shaft turbine mounted on top of the craft, to the rear of the cabin. A 12-bladed, 7 ft (2·13 m) diameter light alloy lift fan is driven through a primary reduction gearbox and a secondary bevel gearbox. From the top of the bevel gearbox, an extension shaft runs to a 9 ft (2·74 m) diameter Dowty-Rotol four-blade reversible-pitch propeller.

CONTROL: Steering is by means of two rudders hinged to the rear of the tail fins, each with an integral bucket-rudder operating in air-flow ducted from the plenum chamber to increase control effectiveness at low speeds. Directional control is further assisted by a hydraulically-operated skirt-lift system and forward and aft thrust ports. Two electrically actuated elevator control surfaces are mounted between the tail fins and give pitch trim at cruising speed.

HULL: The hull and superstructure of the Warden are built of conventional aircraft light alloys. The basic structure comprises a buoyancy tank at the rear and cabin floor forward. This layout reduces the height and frontal area of the vehicle by sinking the cabin to the bottom of the rigid structure.

The lift fan bay forms part of the plenum chamber, the top skin of which is of Warren girder construction to allow the air to be distributed to the forward and side skirts. The side buoyancy tanks which support the peripheral skirts are readily detachable to facilitate transportation by aircraft, ship or road.

The skirts are made of neoprene-coated nylon cloth and are 4 ft (1·22 m) deep, enabling the Warden to clear 3 ft 6 in (1·07 m) walls or 5 ft (1·50 m) earth banks in cross country operations. Fuel is contained in a 265 Imp gallon (1,205 litres) tank mounted above the buoyancy chamber immediately aft of the cabin.

Right: An SR.N5 Warden supplied to the Canadian Department of Transport for coastguard and rescue duties. The craft is based at Sea Island Airport, Vancouver

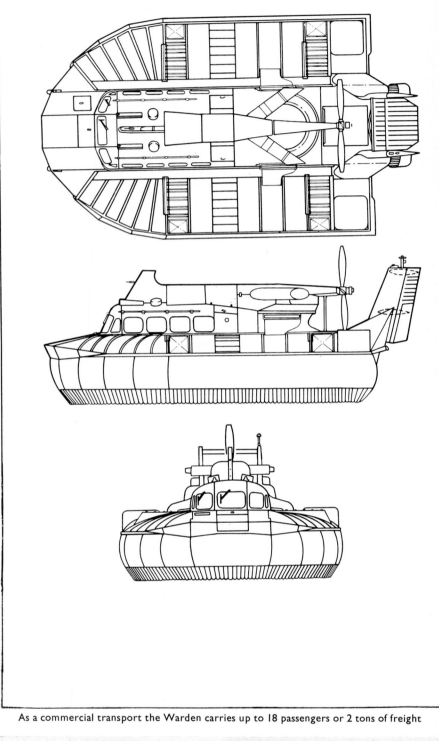

As a commercial transport the Warden carries up to 18 passengers or 2 tons of freight

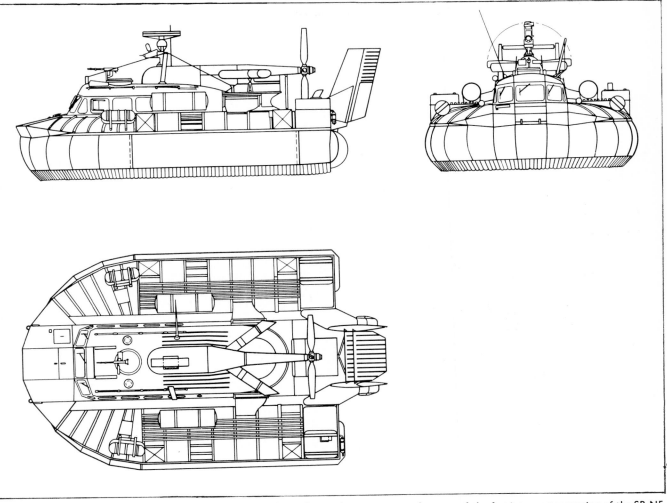

roof hatch gun ring, armour plating for the engine and an auxiliary electrical generator are features of the fast interceptor version of the SR.N5 Warden, designed for patrol in sheltered waters

ACCOMMODATION: All accommodation and machinery is contained within a central road carrying section only 8 ft 3 in (2·51 m) wide. This allows the draft to be air-lifted or transported by road with a minimum of dismantling. The cabin is 12 ft (3·66 m) long and 7 ft 8 in (2·33 m) wide and is entered via an upward-hinged bow loading door and ramp.

DIMENSIONS:

Overall length	38 ft 9 in (11·87 m)
Overall beam	23 ft 0 in (7·01 m)
Overall on pads	12 ft 11 in (3·96 m)

WEIGHT:

Normal gross weight	6·7 tons

PERFORMANCE (at normal gross weight at 15°C):

Max waterspeed over calm water zero wind, max cont power   60 knots (111 km/hr)
Average service waterspeed
          33-40 knots (61-74 km/hr)
Endurance at max cont power rating on 265 Imp gall fuel   3·6 hours

WINCHESTER (SR.N6) COMMERCIAL

The Winchester is similar in design and construction to the SR.N5 Warden and incorporates many of the components and systems of its predecessor. Designed primarily as a fast ferry for operation in sheltered waters, it can accommodate either 38 passengers or 3 tons of freight.

LIFT AND PROPULSION: Power for the integrated lift/propulsion system is provided

An SR.N5 Warden of 200 Squadron Royal Corps of Transport during trials.

by a Rolls-Royce Marine Gnome gas turbine with a maximum continuous rating at 15°C of 900 shp. This drives a BHC 12-blade centrifugal 7 ft (2·13 m) diameter lift fan, and a Dowty Rotol 4 blade variable pitch 9 ft (2·14 m) diameter propeller for propulsion.

Fully amphibious it can operate from relatively unsophisticated bases above the

high water mark, irrespective of tidal state.

Directional control is achieved by twin rudders and a thrust port system. Two electrically actuated elevators provide pitch trim at cruising speed. Winchesters have been in regular commercial service since 1964 and current operators include: Aeronave SPA, British Rail Hovercraft Ltd., Hoverlloyd Ltd., Hovertravel Ltd and Townsend

AIR CUSHION VEHICLE MANUFACTURERS
BHC: United Kingdom

Car Ferries Ltd. A Winchester is also used by Shell (Brunei) Ltd. for off-shore oil rig support.

Military models are in service with 200 Squadron Royal Corps of Transport, the world's first fully-operational military hovercraft unit, and the Royal Navy. A contract has also been received for Winchesters from the Imperial Iranian Navy.

DIMENSIONS, EXTERNAL:

Overall length	48 ft 5 in (14·76 m)
Overall beam	23 ft (7·01 m)
Overall height on landing pads	15 ft (4·57 m)
Skirt depth	4 ft (1·22 m)

DIMENSIONS, INTERNAL:

Cabin size (length × width)
21 ft 9 in × 7 ft 8 in (6·62 m × 2·34 m)

Cabin headroom-centre line   6 ft (1·83 m)

Door aperture size (height × width)
5 ft 9 in × 3 ft 3 in (1·75 m × 0·99 m)

One of two SR.N6 Winchesters operated by Hovertravel Ltd. between Ryde, Southsea and Gosport

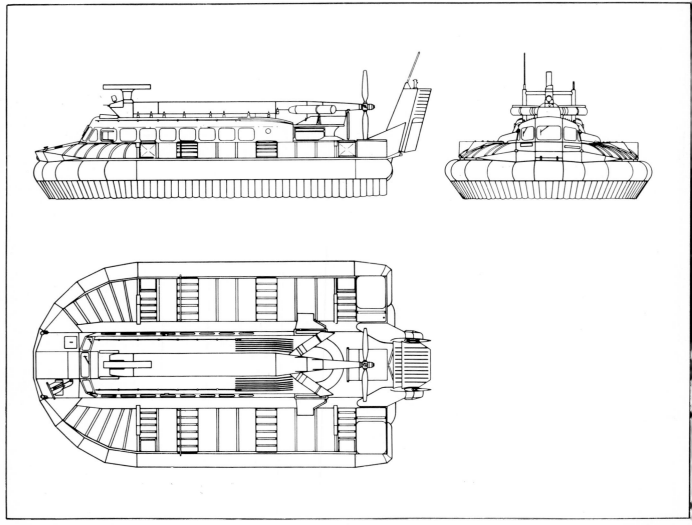

A fast, amphibious passenger ferry for services in sheltered coastal waters, the Winchester carries up to 38 passengers or 3 tons of freight at speeds up to 52 knots

EIGHT:

Normal gross weight   10 tons

ERFORMANCE (at normal gross weight at 15°C):

Max water speed over calm water zero wind (cont power rating)   52 knots (96 km/hr)

Average service waterspeed in sheltered coastal waters   30-35 knots (55-65 km/hr)

Endurance at max cont power rating on 265 Imp gall of fuel   3·6 hours

INCHESTER (SR.N6) UTILITY

This variant differs mainly from the standard commercial craft in having a wider bow or and a topside hatch amidships to facilise the loading of freight either by crane rough the roof or through the bow.

Palletised loads can be 'floated' in and out the cabin by hoverpallets supplied with from the main engine compressor.

Loads of up to ½-ton which are too long for e cabin may be secured on strengthened le decks.

Tie-down points are provided in the cabin or and rear bulkhead.

DIMENSIONS, EXTERNAL:

Overall length   48 ft 5 in (14·76 m)

Overall beam   23 ft (7·01 m)

Overall height on landing pads

   15 ft (4·57 m)

Skirt depth   4 ft (1·22 m)

DIMENSIONS, INTERNAL:

Cabin size (length × width)

   21 ft 9 in (6·62 m) × 7 ft 8 in (2·34 m)

Cabin headroom—centre line   6 ft (1·83 m)

Door aperture size (height × width)

   5 ft 9 in (1·75 m) × 4 ft 3 in (1·29 m)

Roof hatch size (length × width)

   7 ft (2·13 m) × 7 ft 6 in (2·29 m)

WEIGHT:

Normal gross weight   10·7 tons

PERFORMANCE (at normal gross weight at 15°C):

Maximum waterspeed over calm water, zero wind (cont power rating)

   50 knots (92 km/hr)

Average service waterspeed in sheltered coastal waters   28-33 knots (51-62 km/hr)

Endurance at cont power rating   3·6 hours

WINCHESTER (SR.N6) MOBILE DISPENSARY/MEDICAL CENTRE

This is based on the standard commercial craft, with the cabin converted to provide a comprehensive medical centre.

A waiting room tent is stowed in the starboard pannier to provide additional covered accommodation for patients when the craft is stationary and operating as a clinic. Within the cabin, which is fully air-conditioned, are an examination room and an operating theatre. The examination room is also fully equipped as a dispensary, with storage space and stretcher stowage. Through this room there is easy access for stretchers to the operating theatre. The theatre has an operating table and a dental treatment chair, each with separate equipment stores but sharing refrigeration and sterilisation facilities. Oxygen and gases required for surgery are stored in bottles adjacent to the operating table.

A tank for fresh water is externally mounted to serve the dispensary. Additional power for lighting and surgery equipment is provided by a small auxiliary electrical generator unit while the main engine is stopped. In the medical role the SR.N6 carries a team of four but, with the heavy equipment removed, the craft could be used in the evacuation role and carry up to fifty people.

Dimensions, weights, performance, given for the Winchester Utility apply equally to this variant.

WINCHESTER CRASH RESCUE CRAFT

This version of the Winchester is designed for crash rescue service at airports situated on shore lines where an aircraft, through overshooting or undershooting, may land on mudflats, marshes, shallow water or coral reefs.

Modifications include a revised bow, wide external walkways with handrails and side rescue platforms which, together with a low rail line when resting on the ground or water, facilitate rescue operations. Access to the cabin is by a large midships hatch. The fire fighting monitor is above the cabin where its operator can direct rescue operations and provide a protecting foam curtain. Sufficient water is carried for foam generation during a rescue, but provision is made for picking up additional water when prolonged fire fighting is required.

In addition to carrying 50 survivors in the cabin, inflatable liferafts enable a further 52 to be rescued in one sortie.

The five-man crew is accommodated in the forward compartment. For normal operations the crew comprises: a commander, a navigator/pump operator and three firemen.

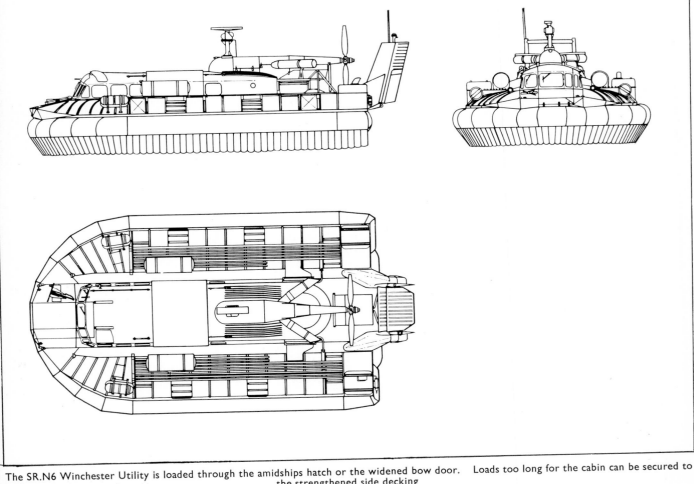

The SR.N6 Winchester Utility is loaded through the amidships hatch or the widened bow door. Loads too long for the cabin can be secured to the strengthened side decking

AIR CUSHION VEHICLE MANUFACTURERS

BHC: United Kingdom

A sustained cruising speed of 45 knots can be maintained over calm water or flat land surface in ISA + 15°C conditions. Areas containing isolated vertical obstacles up to 3 ft (1 m) in height, may be crossed at a speed of 15 knots, and the craft is capable of operating in 6 ft (2 m) of surf. As a displacement craft, in semi-boating condition, it can maintain 5 knots in a calm sea.

Dimensions, weights and performance details given for the Winchester Utility also apply to the Crash Rescue variant.

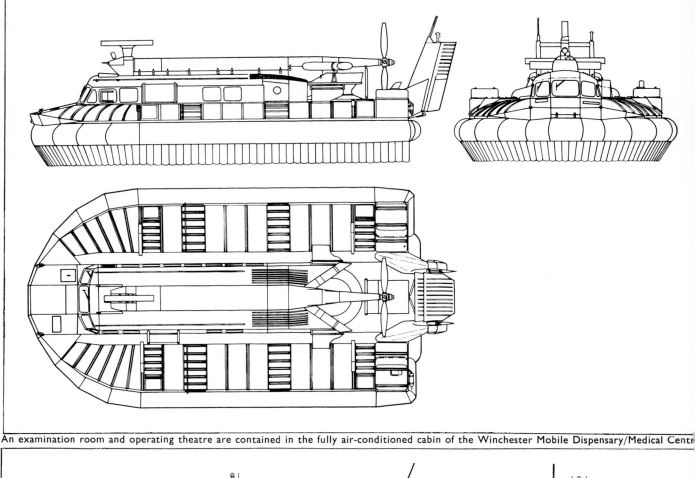

An examination room and operating theatre are contained in the fully air-conditioned cabin of the Winchester Mobile Dispensary/Medical Centre

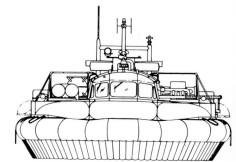
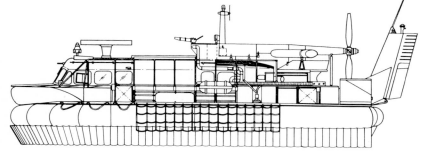
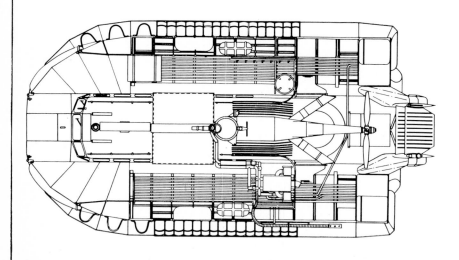

Airport crash rescue variant of the Winchester, conceived after trials by the Royal Air Force, using a Warden class craft in a similar role

NCHESTER (SR.N6) MILITARY
he wider bow door, topside hatch and engthened side decks of the Utility version

are also present in the military model to facilitate the loading of stores, weapons and equipment.

A roof gun hatch position can be located on the port side of the cabin. Provision can also be made for armour plating to protect

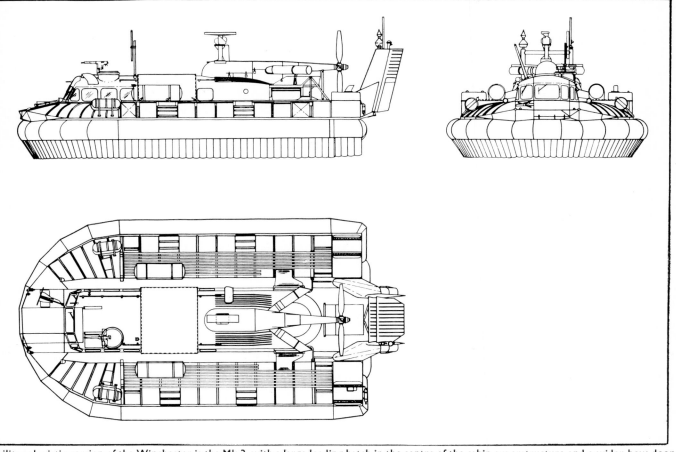

e military logistic version of the Winchester is the Mk.3, with a large loading hatch in the centre of the cabin superstructure and a wider bow door

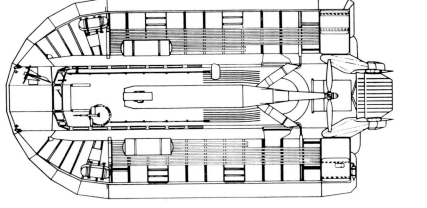
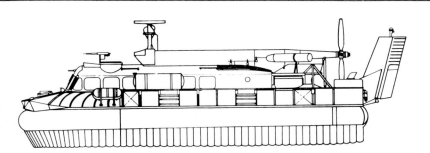
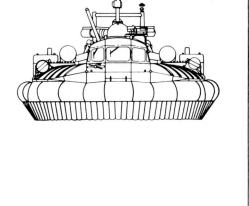

0 1 2 3 4 5 6 7 8 9 10
SCALE—FEET

atures of the Winchester Mk. 4 Fast Attack include a roof gun ring, armour plating for the engine and occupants and an air conditioning system housed in the dorsal fairing

AIR CUSHION VEHICLE MANUFACTURERS
BHC: United Kingdom

the engine, and vital electrical equipment and there are fittings to accept extra armour to give protection against 7·62 mm ammunition for 20 troops sitting on the floor.

A small auxiliary generator unit is fitted for use when electrical power is needed for prolonged periods while the main engine is stopped. Communication equipment is concentrated behind the rear cabin bulkhead with doors for easy access.

TYPICAL USES: Logistic support; troop and weapon carrying; coastal patrolling; casualty evacuation.

TYPICAL MILITARY LOADS: 30 armed troops or 105 mm howitzer and crew or 120 mm anti-tank gun and crew or 3 NATO pallets.

Other military variants designed specifically for patrolling and interception duties are also in production.

DIMENSIONS, weights and performance, details given for the Winchester, Utility, also apply to the above model, with the following exceptions:

Cabin size (length × width)
19 ft × 7 ft 8 in (5·78 m × 2·33 m)
Endurance at cont power rating:
On basic fuel   3·25 hours
With additional fuel   5·7 hours

WELLINGTON (BH.7) COMMERCIAL

The latest addition to the BHC range of commercial craft is the 48-ton Wellington, a fast ferry with competitive economics and designed for short haul operations in coastal waters. Contracts for military variants have been placed by the Imperial Iranian Navy and the Royal Navy.

LIFT AND PROPULSION: Power for the integrated lift/propulsion system is provided by a Rolls-Royce Marine Proteus with a maximum continuous rating at 15°C of 3,400

A Winchester Mk. 4 fast attack craft (in the lead) accompanied by a Mk. 3 logistic support variar Both craft are in service with the Imperial Iranian Navy.

shp (3,447 c.v.). This drives a BHC 12-blade, centrifugal, 11 ft 6 in (3·5 m) diameter lift fan and an HSD, 4-blade, variable-pitch 19 ft (5·79 m) diameter propeller for propulsion.

CONTROLS: Directional control is achieved by the swivelling propeller pylon and a thrust port system similar to that used on the Winchester.

HULL: Construction is mainly of corrosion resistant light alloy. Extensive use is made of components and techniques employed on the Mountbatten. The engine, transmission, gearboxes and propellers are identical to those used on the larger craft.

ACCOMMODATION: The interior can be fitted out to meet the particular traffic demands of different routes. As a mixed traffic craft, 72 passengers and six to eight cars can be carried, the latter being housed in the main central cabin. On all variants a large bow door is used for loading and unloading.

SYSTEMS: Auxiliary power unit: One Rov IS/90 gas turbine engine.
DIMENSIONS, EXTERNAL:
Overall length   77 ft 2 in (23·50 ɪ
Overall beam   45 ft 6 in (13·73 ɪ
Overall height on landing pads
33 ft 0 in (10·05 ɪ
Skirt depth   5 ft 6 in (1·67 ɪ
DIMENSIONS, INTERNAL:
Bow door size
13 ft 9 in × 7 ft 6 in (4·18 m × 2·24 ɪ
Vehicle deck headroom centre line
7 ft 6 in (2·28 ɪ
WEIGHT:
Normal gross weight   48 toɪ
PERFORMANCE (at normal gross weight 15°C):
Max waterspeed over calm water zero wiɪ (cont power) rating 65 knots (120 km/hɪ
Average service waterspeed in coast waters   35-40 knots (65-74 km/hɪ
Endurance at max cont power rating c 850 Imp gall fuel   3 houɪ

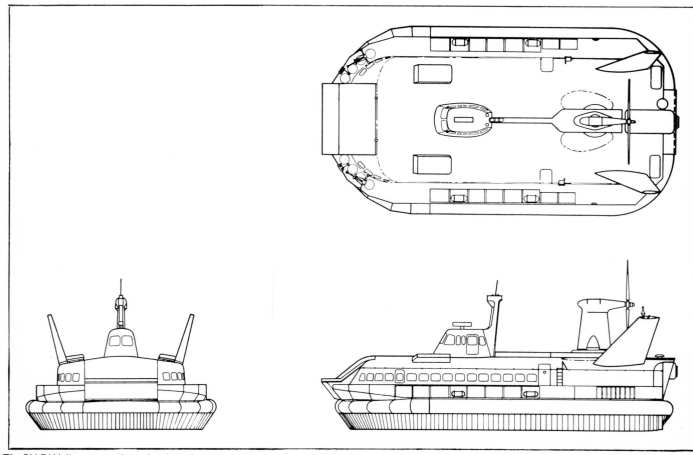

The BH.7 Wellington, a 48 ton fast ferry for short-haul operations in coastal waters.   The mixed traffic version will carry 72 passengers and up to 8 caɪ

[W]ELLINGTON (BH.7) FAST ATTACK

[A]rmament of the Fast Attack variant of [the] Wellington can include a rapid-fire [me]dium calibre gun and/or surface-to-[sur]face or surface-to-air missile installations. [T]he large cabin area permits a variety of [op]erational layouts. In a typical arrange-[me]nt, the operations room is placed directly [ben]eath the control cabin and contains [com]munication, navigation, search and strike [equ]ipment and associated displays.

[T]he craft has an endurance of 11 hours [un]der cruise conditions but this can be [ext]ended considerably as it can stay 'on [wa]tch' without using the main engine. [P]rovision can be made for the crew to live [abo]ard for several days.

[DI]MENSIONS, EXTERNAL:

[L]ength	75 ft 6 in (22·9 m)
[B]eam	41 ft 3 in (12·6 m)
[H]eight on landing pads	33 ft (10·1 m)
[S]kirt depth	5 ft 6 in (1·7 m)

[Th]e 48 ton BH.7 Wellington fast ferry for [ope]ration in coastal waters. Powered by a [Mar]ine Proteus gas turbine, it will have a service waterspeed of 35-40 knots

POWER PLANT AND SYSTEMS:

Main engine: Rolls-Royce Marine 'Proteus' at 3,400 shp maximum cont power
Auxiliary power plant: Two Rover IS/90 gas turbines
Fan: BHC, 12-bladed centrifugal 11 ft 6 in (3·5 m) dia
Propeller: Hawker Siddeley Dynamics, (HSD), 4-bladed, variable pitch 19 ft (5·8 m) dia

Fuel load at 45 tons AUW	9 tons
Max fuel capacity	12·5 tons

WEIGHTS:

Normal gross	45 tons

PERFORMANCE (at normal gross weight at 15°C):

Max waterspeed, calm water, zero wind, cont power   65 knots (120 km/hr)
Rough waterspeed in 4½ ft (1·37 m) seas (depending on heading and wave length)   35-50 knots (65-92 km/hr)
Endurance at max cont rating on 9 tons of fuel (with 10% reserve)   8 hours

WELLINGTON (BH.7) LOGISTIC AMPHIBIOUS

ACCOMMODATION: In this role, the main hold floor area of 600 sq ft (56 m²) provides an unobstructed space suitable for loading wheeled vehicles, guns and military stores.

Two side cabins, filled with paratroop-type seats, can accommodate up to 60 troops and their equipment.

Access at the bow is through a 'clamshell' door.

Machine guns can be fitted in gun rings on the roof on either side of the cabin and provision can be made for armour plating to protect personnel, the engine and vital electrical components.

SYSTEMS: Two Rover IS/90 gas turbine APUs provide electrical power independently of the main engine.

TYPICAL MILITARY LOADS: 170 fully equipped troops or 3 field cars and trailers plus 60 troops or 2 armoured scout cars or up to 20 NATO Pallets.

DIMENSIONS, EXTERNAL:

Overall length	76 ft 6 in (23·3 m)
Overall beam	41 ft 3 in (12·6 m)
Overall height on landing pads	33 ft (10·1 m)

DIMENSIONS, INTERNAL:

Main cabin floor area	600 sq ft (56 m²)
Main cabin headroom—centreline	7 ft 10 in (2·38 m)
Access door aperture (height × width)	7 ft 10 in (2·3 m) × 13 ft 9 in (4·2 m)

WEIGHTS:

Normal gross weight	45 tons
Fuel load at 45 tons AUW	9 tons
Max fuel capacity	12·5 tons

PERFORMANCE (at normal gross weight at 15°C):

Max waterspeed, calm water, zero wind, cont power rating   65 knots (120 km/hr)
Rough waterspeed in 4½ ft (1·37 m) seas depending on heading and wave length   35-50 knots (65-92 km/hr)
Endurance at max cont power rating with 9 tons of fuel (with 10% reserve)   8 hours

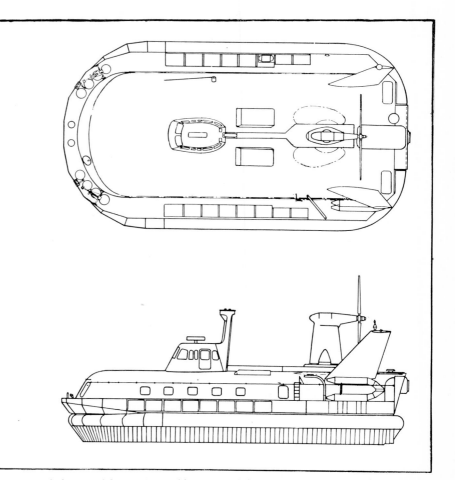

[Ar]mament of the fast attack version of the BH.7 Wellington can include a rapid fire medium calibre gun with full fire control and/or surface-to-surface or surface-to-air missiles

AIR CUSHION VEHICLE MANUFACTURERS

BHC: United Kingdom

BH.8

Designed initially for military logistic-support duties the BH.8 is a twin-engined, 80-ton, open-water hovercraft with bow and stern loading doors.

It is the largest hovercraft that can be readily transported in one piece as deck cargo, thus facilitating world-wide delivery. Capable of carrying 3-ton vehicles, the craft will be suitable for a wide range of civil, as well as military roles, including passenger ferry, mixed passenger/car ferry and freight carrier.

According to the internal arrangements, typical civil payloads at 90 tons all-up weight would be 280 passengers, 14 cars plus 110 passengers or 35 tons of freight.

Two 3,400 shp Rolls-Royce Marine Proteus gas turbines power the integrated lift/propulsion system.

DIMENSIONS:
Length   96 ft 0 in (29·26
Beam   56 ft 0 in (17·07
Height   32 ft 0 in (9·75
PERFORMANCE (at 90 tons all up weigh
Max continuous calm water speed
                    75 knots (136 km/l
Speed in 4·5 ft (1·2-1·5 m) waves
                    45-55 knots (74-91 km/l
Max endurance   8 hou

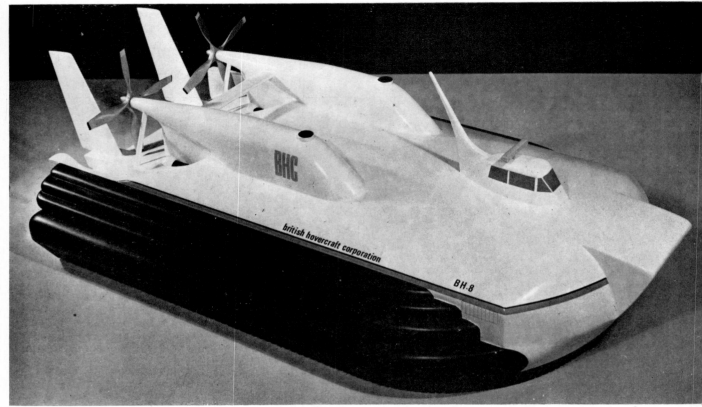

A typical payload of the BH 8 (CIVIL) at 90 tons auw would be 14 cars plus 110 passengers

oss & Jackson
OSS & JACKSON LTD
AD OFFICE:
ower Aghada, Co Cork, Ireland

ushioncraft
SHIONCRAFT LTD
AD OFFICE:
he Duver, St. Helens, Isle of Wight
LEPHONE:
Bembridge 2711
LEGRAMS:
ushair Ryde
RECTORS:
. Bretherton
. R. J. Britten
. D. Norman

ushioncraft Ltd was formed in 1967 from
e Hovercraft Division of Britten-Norman
d. The first ACV built by Britten-Norman
s the three-seat CC-1 in 1960. This was
lowed by three of the larger, ten-seat
shioncraft CC-2s. Experience with these
d to the design and construction of two
ther prototypes, the CC-4 and CC-5. The
mpany is at present fully engaged on
veloping the CC-7, which is now approach-
g production. The CC-4 and CC-7 proto-
pes have been purchased by the NPL
overcraft unit for their research and
velopment programmes.

-7
The CC-7 is a direct development of the

TELEPHONE: Middleton 61333
DIRECTORS:
F. G. Cross, BSc(eng), AFRAeS
G. L. M. A. Jackson, AMIPlantE
H. L Walter

CC-5, but incorporates a United Aircraft of
Canada ST-6B-60 free-turbine, rated at 390
shp continuous, and a refined fan-jet propulsion system. It is designed as an 8-10 seat
light amphibious communications craft, but
is suitable for many alternative roles from
freighter to dual-control trainer. Design
started in March 1967 and the prototype,
which has been purchased by the Ministry of

Cross & Jackson is building an ACV prototype which is scheduled for completion at
the end of 1968. No details of the craft has
been released for publication at the time of
going to press.

Technology for use by the NPL Hovercraft
Unit was completed in March 1968.
LIFT AND PROPULSION: Power for the
integrated lift/propulsion system is provided
by a single United Aircraft of Canada ST-
6B-60 free-turbine with a maximum continuous rating of 390 bhp at 6,000 rpm. This is
mounted behind the passenger cabin with
the output shaft towards the rear of the craft.

The Cushioncraft CC-7 8-10 seat light amphibious communications craft, freighter or dual-control
trainer

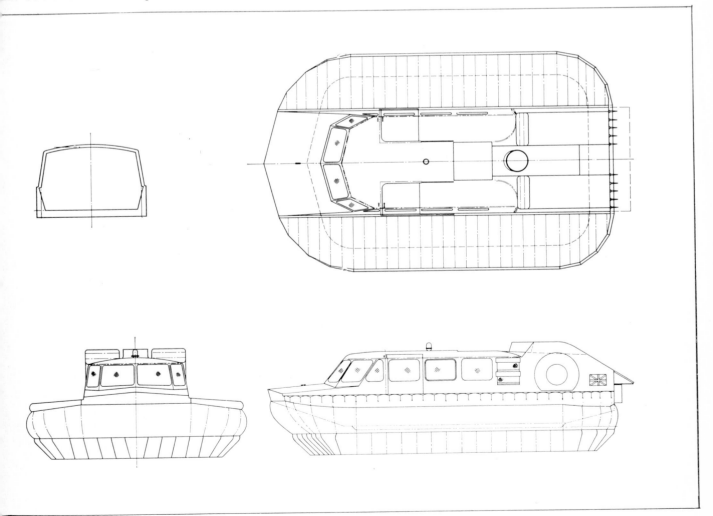

Cushioncraft CC-7 (One 390 bhp ST-6B-60 free-turbine)

AIR CUSHION VEHICLE MANUFACTURERS
CUSHIONCRAFT / DAILY EXPRESS: United Kingdom

The drive is taken to a Salisbury differential gearbox with a ratio 2·88 : 1. The two fan output shafts from the differential have Pollard flange-mounted bearings at their outer ends.

The two centrifugal fans, which are designed and made by Cushioncraft, are of light alloy construction, 1 ft 3 in (0·38 m) wide and 3 ft 6 in (1·06 m) in diameter. The volute casings are in glass fibre.

CONTROLS: Craft direction is controlled by deflection of the thrust from the low pressure fan jet system and differential use of the reverse thrust system. Thrust air is expelled aft through two sets of multiple rudders, five port and five starboard. In each of the two thrust ports, ahead of the rudders, is a reverse thrust bucket. Both are interconnected with louvres set in forward facing openings at the top of the port and starboard volute casings. Two whipstaves, one each side of the commander's seat, control the louvres and buckets to provide reverse thrust for braking or reversing. Port and starboard systems can be operated independently for low speed steering control. The rudders are operated by a rudder bar, and the engine throttle, of twist grip type, is at the top of the starboard whipstave.

HULL: Construction is primarily of corrosion resistant light alloys. The basic structure is a punt-like hull, divided into eight watertight subdivisions. A feature of the craft is the use of inflatable ⅛ in (3·17 mm) thick rubber sidebodies, each 4 ft (1·21 m) wide and attached to each side of the hull. These are of simple mattress construction and can be folded to facilitate transport on lorries or aircraft. Overall dimensions of the craft with sidebodies deflated is 7 ft 6 in (2·28 m). A bag type skirt is fitted, with a finger skirt below. Skids, which extend beneath the hull, are provided for setting down.

ACCOMMODATION: The commander sits on the left of the craft, with a passenger seat to the right. In the eight seat cabin layout, there are three double seats behind. Two additional tip-up seats adjacent to the doors, will be fitted in the ten-seat layout. The cabin is heated and ventilated and all windows are of the "push out" variety to provide emergency exits. Safety equipment includes a fire extinguisher. A fireproof bulkhead divides the cabin from the engine bay.

COMMUNICATIONS AND NAVIGATION: Optional extras to suit customers' requirements.

SYSTEMS:

ELECTRICAL: 24 volt system with engine driven generator supplying power for side body inflation compressor, starting, light and instruments.

DIMENSIONS, EXTERNAL:

Length overall	24 ft 6 in (7·46 m)
Beam overall	15 ft 2 in (4·62 m)
Skirt depth	2 ft 0 in (0·60 m)
Height overall, hovering	7 ft 9 in (2·36 m)
Cushion area	2,330 sq ft (216 m²) at

DIMENSIONS, INTERNAL:

Cabin floor area	70 sq ft (6·50 m²) at
Door size 2 doors, each 2 ft 6 in (0·76 m) wide

WEIGHTS:

Normal all-up weight	6,000 lb (2,722 kg)
Disposable load	3,000 lb (1,361 kg)
Basic weight, empty	3,000 lb (1,361 kg)

PERFORMANCE (design):

Max speed	40 knots (76 km/h)
Cruising speed	35 knots (66·5 km/h)
Max range	100 miles (161 km)
Max gradient	1
Vertical obstacle clearance	2 ft (0·60 m)

Daily Express
DAILY EXPRESS

HEAD OFFICE:
Fleet Street, London E.C.4
TELEPHONE:
Fleet Street 8000

Since September 1966 the Daily Express has been encouraging its readers to become hovercraft conscious by inviting them to become hovernauts. The new two-seat Air Rider has been designed especially for construction by schools. By late October 1968, well over 100 British schools were building the craft and orders for plans had been received from several hundred overseas educational establishments. The first inter-schools hovercraft building contest was

organised jointly by BP and The Daily Express in September 1968.

TWO-SEAT AIR RIDER

One of the most popular British light air cushion vehicle designs to date, the new Express Air Rider is an amphibious two-seater capable of land speeds up to 50 mph and water speeds of up to 32 knots. The prototype was completed in April 1968 and trials ended in June.

LIFT AND PROPULSION. A single 250 cc Velocette engine mounted immediately ahead of the cockpit drives a 22 in diameter Multiwing axial lift fan. Aft of the cockpit is a 33 bhp Greeves Scramble engine which

drives a 4 ft 6 in diameter two-bladed Rollason propeller via vee belts.

FUEL: A single 3 gallon tank is located aft of the cockpit on the port side with the refuelling neck immediately above.

CONTROLS: An aerodynamic rudder operating in the propeller slipstream provides directional control. Braking is achieved by partially cutting off air to the cushion and increasing the skirt pressure. Throttle controls are fitted to the rudder handbar.

HULL: The boat-shaped hull is built up from ⅜ in (9·5 mm) ply formers with a 0·07 in (2 mm) ply skin. Buoyancy boxes are provided in the bow, stern and along both sides. The skirt is of the peripheral bag type.

A line-up of Express two-seat Air Riders.

ACCOMMODATION: Operator and passenger share a canvas seat in the central open cockpit.

SYSTEMS:

ELECTRICAL: An engine operated generator supplies 12 volts to an aircraft type battery for engine starting.

DIMENSIONS, EXTERNAL:

Length overall	12 ft 6 in (3·81 m)
Beam overall	6 ft 6 in (1·98 m)
Height overall on landing pads	7 ft 4 in (2·23 m)
Skirt depth	1 ft 0 in (0.30 mm)
Draft afloat	3 in (77 mm)
Cushion area	70 sq ft (6·5 m²)

DIMENSIONS, INTERNAL:

Cockpit	3 ft × 3 ft (0·91 m × 0·91 m)

WEIGHTS:

Normal all-up weight	400 lb (181 kg)
Normal gross weight	700 lb (317 kg)
Normal payload	300 lb (136 kg)
Max payload	600 lb (272 kg)

PERFORMANCE (normal operating weight):

Max speed over calm water approx	32 knots (57 km/h)
Max speed over land	50 mph (80 km/h)
Cruising speed, calm water	25 knots (75·5 km/h)
Turning circle diameter at 30 knots	210 ft (64 m)
Still air endurance at cruising speed	45 minutes
Max gradient	15°
Vertical obstacle clearance	10 in (254 mm)

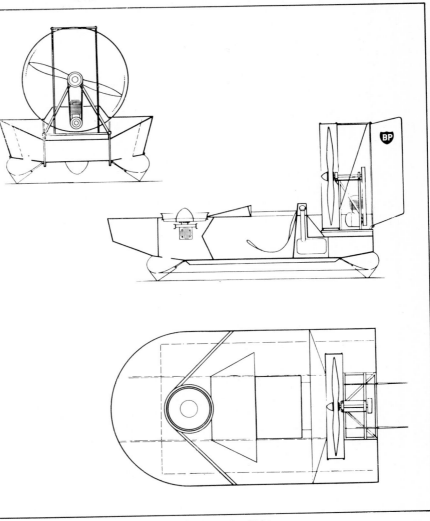

Daily Express 2 seat Air Rider

Denny
DENNY HOVERCRAFT LIMITED

HEAD OFFICE:
City Gate House, Finsbury Square, London EC2

TELEPHONE:
01-638 8595

TELEGRAMS:
Hovercraft, London

DIRECTORS:
F. Tyrer, Chairman
A. F. Gillingham
Sir John Onslow, Bt
J. Chappel
S. R. Hogg

Denny Hovercraft Ltd has three craft of the D2 series, of which one, D2-002, is in operation with Norwest Hovercraft on the route Fleetwood-Morecambe-Barrow. 003 and 004 are being modified on similar lines to the 002.

One of the craft will be operated by a subsidiary company—Jamaica Hovercraft Ltd—on a service in Kingston Harbour, Jamaica.

The company is currently completing a design study for the D2 Mk 11, a 40 knot vessel for 100 passengers, with lift and propulsion systems based on that of the D2. A much larger craft, the D3, is at present in the design stage.

D2

An 85-seat rigid sidewall craft, the D2 is designed for ferry services of short stage

The Denny D2-002 rigid sidewall passenger ferry. The craft seats 85 passengers and has a service speed of 25 knots.

lengths. The craft has a service speed of 25 knots and can negotiate waves up to 4 ft (1·21 m) without loss of speed on scheduled runs.

LIFT AND PROPULSION: Two Caterpillar D.336TA diesels, each developing 400 hp, provide propulsion power, and two Caterpillar D.330 TAs developing 180 hp each, drive the lift fans. The two propulsion engines drive two 20 in (508 mm) diameter aluminium-bronze propellers through a vee drive.

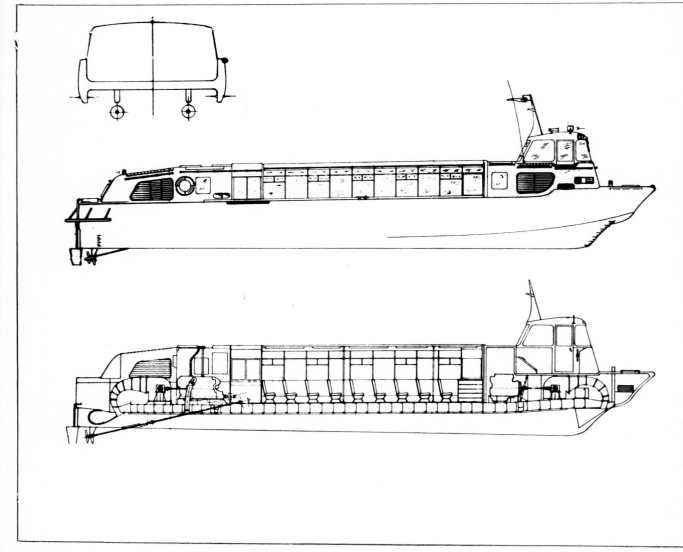

HULL. The craft has glass fibre sidewalls and frames and marine ply inner and outer bottoms. A fingered bag skirt is fitted across the bow and a loop skirt is fitted aft. Both skirts are of nylon reinforced neoprene.

ACCOMMODATION: Passengers are accommodated in a single cabin with seats for 85. Access is through four sliding doors, located forward and aft, port and starboard. Separate entry doors, port and starboard, are provided in the raised wheelhouse for the captain and crew.

COMMUNICATIONS AND NAVIGATION:
Radio: Marconi Harbafone 20 vhf radiotelephone. Radar: Decca Type 101.

DIMENSIONS:

Length overall	81 ft 6 in (24·8 m)
Beam overall	19 ft 0 in (5·79 m)
Skirt depth	3 ft 0 in (0·91 m)
Draft	5 ft 0 in (1·52 m)
Draft hovering	2 ft 0 in (0·60 m)
Cushion area	1,235 sq ft (114·7 m²)

INTERNAL:
Cabin (excluding wheelhouse):

Length	30 ft 0 in (9·15 m)
Max witdh	17 ft 0 in (5·18 m)
Max height	8 ft 0 on (2·44 m)
Floor area	510 sq ft (74·4 m²)

Baggage holds, position and volume:

One, aft of cabin	544 cu ft (14·3 m³)

WEIGHTS:

Normal all-up weight	30 tons
Normal payload	5 tons
Maximum payload	6 tons

PERFORMANCE (at normal operating weight):

Max speed, over calm water	27 knot
Cruising speed, calm water	25 knot
Turning circle diameter at 25 knotsf	300 ft (90 m
Water speed in 4 ft waves and 15 kno headwind	16 knot
Max wave capability on scheduled runs	3-4 ft (0·92-1·22 m
Max wave height (off cushion)	8-10 ft (2·44-3·05 m
Still air range and endurance at cruisin speed	150 miles (240 km
Range and endurance in 4 ft waves, 15 kno headwind	120 miles (192 km

Price and terms: Approximate cost of craft fob £70,00

Harding—Wotsit II

GEOFFREY HARDING

ADDRESS:

Passenger Transport Department, County Borough of Wallasey, Seaview Road, Wallasey, Cheshire

Geoffrey Harding, the General Manager of the Wallasey Passenger Transport Department, is also a successful amateur ACV designer and constructor. His latest design, the Wotsit 11 beach rescue craft prototype, is a novel combination of air cushion and wheeled vehicle, with a British Anzani lift

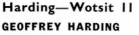

The Wotsit II light ACV, designed for beach rescue. The craft uses wheels for thrust an directional control instead of the normal combination of propeller and aerodynamic rudder

gine, and a Renault 754 automotive engine, ving two rubber tyred wheels through a nventional car gearbox for thrust. The ft is intended for use in the Mersey and nilar estuaries where an obstacle clearance ility of about 10 in (254 mm) is necessary order to negotiate boulders and rock tcrop.

t is available to the Wallasey Fire Brigade beach rescue work, when the water is nd to be too deep to reach marooned holidaymakers with a Land Rover, and too shallow for a lifeboat. When used on rescue operations the craft is equipped with a standard ambulance vhf radio-telephone.

WOTSIT 11

Wotsit 11 is basically a two-seat plenum chamber design of ply and aluminium construction. The use of wheels for thrust and directional control, instead of the more usual combination of propeller and aero-dynamic rudder, was considered essential in view of the rapid acceleration and positive control needed for beach rescue in the face of strong cross and head-winds.

The craft is capable of land speeds of the order of 50 mph (80 km/h) and water speeds up to 10 knots.

For rescue work up to 3 stretcher cases can be carried on top of the hull, in addition to which two persons can comfortably lie down on the inflated sidebodies, port and starboard,

---

over Air
OVER-AIR LIMITED
EAD OFFICE AND WORKS:
South Street, Crowland, Lincs
ELEPHONE:
Crowland 464
RECTORS:
Barbara, Lady Brassey, Managing Director
G. Levenson
NIOR EXECUTIVES:
E. G. C. Westmorland, General Manager
B. J. Jaffray, Joint Chief Designers
M. Hart
VERSEAS ASSOCIATES:
Hover-Air (South Africa) Pty Ltd
PO Box 398, Kaysna, Cape, South Africa
ANAGING DIRECTOR:
Cdr John Kerr

Hover-Air was formed in 1966 to design nd manufacture light air cushion vehicles or private and agricultural use. The ompany's latest craft are the two-seat HA-5 Iover Hawk Mk 11 and a crop-spraying ariant which was due to be marketed in the utumn of 1968.

HA-5 HOVER HAWK Mk II

Derived from the earlier Hoverbat and Iovertwin, the Hover Hawk is a two-seat, lass-fibre hulled sports ACV powered by hree Velocette Viceroy engines, one for lift nd two for propulsion. The craft is mphibious and has a maximum speed over alm water of 30 mph.

LIFT AND PROPULSION: Lift is provided by a single 16 hp Velocette Viceroy driving a 2 ft (0·61 m) diameter centrifugal fan of welded aluminium construction. Engine and fan are mounted on a frame to form a complete lift assembly unit which slides into position through an access panel. Thrust is supplied by two outrigged 16 hp Velocette Viceroys driving two Hordern-Richmond laminated wood propellers of 31 in (788 mm) diameter housed in glass fibre ducts. Leading edges of the propellers have stainless steel anti-erosion strips.
CONTROL: Craft direction is controlled by twin rudders in the propellers' slipstream and by differential throttling of the propulsion engines.
HULL: The hull is of moulded glass reinforced plastic construction. It incorporates two full-length longitudinal beams, and two transverse beams of polystyrene—one forward of the cabin and one aft. These are 12 in (306 mm) deep by 4 in (103 mm) wide and skinned with glass and resin. Around the periphery of the craft is a 4 in (103 mm) slab of polystyrene foam. The integral foam structure provides 150% buoyancy and sealed chambers within the hull increase this to 250%. The skirt is of bag type, in nylon reinforced pvc, with an inflated depth of 10 in (255 mm).
ACCOMMODATION: Access to the cabin is through two 2 ft (610 mm) wide gullwing doors, one each side. Side-by-side contoured seats are provided for two, with the driver seated to the right. An emergency push-out panel exit is provided and standard safety equipment includes a fire extinguisher.

SYSTEMS:
ELECTRICAL: 12 volts, supplied by engine driven alternators.

DIMENSIONS, EXTERNAL:
Length overall	15 ft 6 in (4·72 m)
Beam overall	8 ft 0 in (2·44 m)
Skirt depth	10 in (254 mm)
Draft afloat	4 in (102 mm)
Cushion area	86 sq ft (7·98 m²)

WEIGHTS:
Normal all-up weight	900 lb (408 kg)
Normal gross weight	1,250 lb (567 kg)
Normal payload	350 lb (159 kg)
Max payload	420 lb (190 kg)

PERFORMANCE (at normal operating weight):
Max speed over calm water, max power
30 mph (48 km/h)
Max speed over calm water, max cont power
27 mph (43 km/h)
Cruising speed, calm water
25 mph (40 km/h)
Max wave capability on scheduled runs
1 ft (0·30 m)
Max survival sea state 2 ft (0·60 m)
Still air range and endurance at cruising speed 65 miles 2½ hours
Max gradient, static conditions 1 : 8
Vertical obstacle clearance 9 in (229 mm)

PRICE AND TERMS:
Approx cost of craft f.o.b. £1,595
Terms of payment: Cash on pro-forma invoice or letter of credit for overseas customers

The Hover-Air Hover Hawk Mark II, fibreglass-hulled amphibious sports ACV

AIR CUSHION VEHICLE MANUFACTURERS
HOVERCRAFT DEVELOPMENT / N.P.L. HOVERCRAFT UNIT: United Kingdom

Hovercraft
HOVERCRAFT DEVELOPMENT LTD

HEAD OFFICE:
Kingsgate House, 66-74 Victoria Street, London SW1

DIRECTORS:
D. Hennessey, FRIPA, Chairman

M. W. Innes
Professor W. A. Mair
P. N. Randell, Secretary
J. E. Rapson, Chief Engineer

Hovercraft Development Ltd is now purely a licensing body handling the international licensing arrangements of air cushion vehicles employing the Hovercraft principle, evolved

and developed by C. S. Cockerell, CBE, ⟨ associated patents.

It was formed in January 1959 and carr⟨ out extensive research and development the hovercraft field. Its responsibilities this work were transferred to the Natio⟨ Physical Laboratories Hovercraft Unit April 1967.

N.P.L. Hovercraft Unit
NATIONAL PHYSICAL LABORATORY HOVERCRAFT UNIT

HEAD OFFICE:
Teddington, Middlesex

TELEPHONE:
Teddington Lock 3222

TRIALS UNIT:
St. John's Street, Hythe, Hants

TELEPHONE:
Hythe 3065

Since April 1967, the Hovercraft Unit of the National Physical Laboratory, Ministry of Technology has been responsible for the research and development activities previously conducted by Hovercraft Development Ltd.

Its research facilities include a test tank 280 ft (85·34 m) long and 30 ft (9·14 m) wide, with a water depth of 2 ft 6 in (0·76 m), enabling model speeds of 50 ft/sec (15·24 m/sec) to be attained, and it also operates full scale hovercraft vehicles for experimental purposes. In addition to the HD.1, the company has the experimental HD.2, designed and constructed by the HDL Technical Group, and is now operating the Cushioncraft CC-4, which after extensive modification is designated HU.4.

Amphibious hovercraft in particular are subject to such a wide range of aerodynamic and hydrodynamic forces when operating in their natural environment, that it is virtually impossible to simulate these complicated conditions in the laboratory. Although experiments with radio-controlled models in the open air or over suitable natural water

surfaces can be very realistic, it is not easy to measure motions and performance with free models. Man-carrying experimental craft are therefore employed by the Hovercraft unit to demonstrate that a new principle or technical improvement can be adopted reliably and safely as well as to make accurate 'on board' measurements of behaviour and performance under realistic conditions. Data obtained from experimental craft can be compared with the results from theoretical studies and model experiments to help in developing better methods of predicting the performance and behaviour of future craft.

HD.1
One of the earliest experimental hovercraft, HD.1 was constructed in 1963 for what was then the Technical Group of Hovercraft Development Ltd. Initially designed to evaluate the performance of a typical craft with rigid sidewalls, HD.1 was later fitted with flexible sidewall segments and thus became amphibious, playing an important part in establishing the segmented skirt, devised by HDL, as a practicable device. HD.1 is now being modified for further work, including the evaluation of new methods of measuring the speed of hovercraft over water.

The craft has a nylon-sheathed hull of conventional boat-building timber and marine ply construction, with the control cabin at the front and a test observer's cabin amidships. Lift is provided by fore and aft fans driven by two 80 hp Coventry Climax engines. Originally propelled by two 145 hp Rolls-Royce/Continental 0-300D, six-cylinder

horizontally-opposed aero-engines, driv⟨ McCauley two-blade fixed pitch propelle⟨ HD.1 was modified late in 1964. Modifica⟨ tions consisted of replacing the front prop⟨ sion unit only with a Rolls-Royce/Continen⟨ G10-470-A, six-cylinder horizontally-oppos⟨ aero-engine, driving a McCauley two-bla⟨ reversible-pitch propeller, and the fitting ⟨ new control surfaces. The original fore a⟨ aft single fin and rudder units were replac⟨ by a single, all-moving control surface a⟨ forward and twin all-moving control surfa⟨ aft.

DIMENSIONS:
Overall length	50 ft (15·24
Beam	17 ft (5·18
Overall beam across flexible sidewalls	
	23 ft (7·01
Height overall	13 ft 6 in (4·11 ⟨
Skirt depth	2 ft 6 in (0·76 ⟨

WEIGHTS:
Normal all-up weight	20,000 lb (9,070 ⟨
Overload all-up weight	22,000 lb (10,430 ⟨

PERFORMANCE:
Max speed	32 knots (61 km/⟨
Cruising speed	28 knots (53 km/⟨
Vertical obstacle clearance	
	2 ft 0 in (0·61 ⟨
Range	100 nautical miles (185 k⟨

HD.2
This experimental hovercraft was design⟨ by the HDL Technical Group in 1966 a⟨ was constructed by them at Hythe. Co⟨ struction was completed in 1967 after t⟨ HDL Technical Group became the NP⟨ Hovercraft Unit. HD.2 was designed prin⟨ arily to investigate methods of improvi⟨

The HD.1 has been used to evaluate rigid sidewalls segmented skirts and methods of measuring the speed of ACVs over water. In the foreground ⟨ the HV.4 (formerly CC-4), currently providing data on fan propulsion systems, skirts and inflated secondary structures

vercraft controllability and manoeuvrabil-
, particularly in terminal areas. It is
refore fitted with a wide range of power
isted lateral control systems. The pilot
s thirteen separate controls which may be
ected independently or used in combination.
e craft is fitted with dual control.

he craft weighs 5 tons and is 30 ft (9·14 m)
g. It is powered by three 150 hp Rover
/150 gas turbines; one of these drives the
fan and the other two, for propulsion,
ve propellers specially designed for low
speed. The designed maximum speed in
m conditions is nearly 50 knots and the
rmal hover height is 2 ft (0·61 m). HD.2
ries a crew of two and up to six observers.

periscope is fitted for observing the
tion of the skirt from within the air cushion
speed. Water speed is measured by a
ppler unit which is beamed into the
shion area where surface conditions are
atively calm.

FT AND PROPULSION: The three
wer plants are basically identical Rover
/150 gas turbines, each developing 145 bhp,
stalled in separate fire restricting bays.

All three engines draw intake air from the
num chamber through knit mesh filters
d exhaust to atmosphere through the craft
o shell.

ach engine is mounted on a tubular
b-frame to facilitate attachment to the
ucture and removal for servicing, as well
providing an integral mounting for the
duction gearboxes.

he lift engine is mounted transversely in
e rear of the craft and drives two rearward
cing axial fans of 27 in (686 mm) diameter
rough a reduction gearbox (wl.ich also
ives the hydraulic and electric ancilliaries),
horizontal shaft and two 90°, 1 : 1 bevel
xes, enclosed in the fan-hub fairings.

he propulsion engines are mounted fore
d aft on the craft centreline. Each drives a

Designed by the HDL Technical Group in 1966, the HD.2 has been built primarily to investigate methods of improving hovercraft controllability and manoeuvrability in terminal areas

reversible-pitch propeller, mounted on top of a swivelling pylon through a 90°, 1·5 : 1 reduction gearbox and a vertical torque shaft to a second 90°, 2·16 : 1 reduction gearbox enclosed in a "pod" fairing.

This final reduction box contains the propeller pitch-change hydraulic system which is signalled electrically from the engine throttle control, providing two propeller pitch positions of ± 27° approximately.

HULL: The configuration of the HD.2 is generally in accordance with the layout requirements of a larger (85-90 ton) side-loading, car-carrying hovercraft. The hull shape is consistent with the hydrodynamic requirements of the larger craft.

The structure is of light alloy using normal manufacturing techniques. Use has been made of standard stringer sections in aircraft alloys. The decision to use this type of construction was influenced mainly by the knowledge and experience of the design and

workshop staff together with the available facilities. Other factors which influenced the choice were the high power/weight ratio required and the case of modification necess-ary in an R. & D. craft.

The basic structure comprises a series of transverse frames using back-to-back channel sections with tubular bracing members. These carry the transverse bending loads and transmit the local loads to the two main longitudinal frames. These frames are spac-ed 5 ft (1·52 m) apart and have 22 swg shear webs with angle section stiffeners and extrud-ed T section booms. The landing strakes are of laminated spruce bolted to the under-side of the transverse frames.

The pylon mountings for the upper bevel gearbox and propellers are machined from steel tube and are mounted on taper roller bearings. The rotation of these pylons is at present restricted by mechanical stops ± 30°. The taper roller bearings are mounted in a

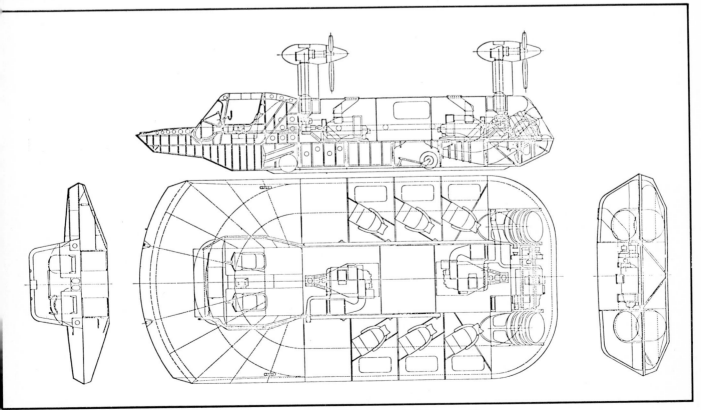

The HD2, powered by three 150 hp Rover 2s/150 gas turbines

AIR CUSHION VEHICLE MANUFACTURERS
N.P.L. HOVERCRAFT UNIT: United Kingdom

machined housing, which is built into a stressed skin box spanning the two main longitudinal frames.

The foredeck and the top of the craft are of a sandwich construction using an expanded pvc core with light alloy facings. Sandwich type material is also used for the bulkheads that divide up the central box into compartments. Two of these compartments are engine bays whilst the central one, which is located at the centre of gravity, houses the craft instrumentation and the Marconi Doppler speed meter. The fuel tanks are of nitrile rubber and are mounted in a box below the plenum top between the two longitudinal frames.

The buoyancy, which also forms the bottom of the craft, is constructed as a series of individual cells, which bolt into place between the lattice structure of the underside of the craft.

The bottom part of each buoyancy unit has to withstand water impact loads and is made of a sandwich structure with glass reinforced plastic facings on expanded pvc core.

The upper part of the box is a thin shell of GRP filled with an expanded polystyrene foam of low density.

SYSTEMS:

CONTROL: The control systems include swivelling propellers, cushion thrust ports in the skirt, and a method of shifting the skirt laterally. Two propellers are mounted in tandem on pylons which at present rotate $\pm$ 30°, with a future capability of $\pm$ 90°; low velocity air jets can be controlled through 'puff ports' in the side skirts to give some control of side force and yawing movement. The centre of the air cushion can be moved transversely, relative to the centre of gravity, so inducing a rolling moment, by moving the side segments of the skirt laterally relative to the hard structure of the craft.

HD.2 is the first hovercraft to be fitted with a wrap-around loop-segment skirt derived from earlier tests, and has segments the full depth of the cushion. The skirt surrounds the air cushion which is a single-cell plenum chamber without the usual compartmentation normally considered necessary to give stability in roll and pitch. On HD.2 'peripheral' stability is obtained from changes in the cushion area due to deformation of the angled segments of the skirt, as the craft rotates relative to the surface over which it is travelling.

The main advantage of this type of skirt is that all the flexible material is accessible from outside the craft even when the craft is off-cushion. A new skirt can be fitted easily within two hours, and individual segments can be unbuttoned and replaced in minutes. The skirt material weighs about 1 lb per square yard and is a synthetic weave coated with artificial rubber. Segments of different material are fitted at convenient points on the periphery to access their resistance to abrasion, delamination, and tearing when operating in a true marine environment.

HD.2 has now completed more than 150 hours operation on-cushion and has carried out static tests over land and water using a number of different lift fans.

Control and manoeuvre experiments have established the relative importance of the various control systems and have shown that

HU.4 will be used to evaluate a modified fan propulsion system, inflated secondary structures a skirts

relatively low values of pitch and roll stiffness can be safely used with a high thrust line and propellers which swivel up to $\pm$ 30°. The roll control was originally envisaged as a means of preventing the craft from heeling in a side wind, but has proved to have other valuable uses. At higher forward speeds the application of roll control induces a sympathetic yawing movement on the craft; this is due to asymetric drag from the side segments in the rolled condition and turns can be made with this single control.

HYDRAULICS: Hydraulic power is supplied by a Lockheed Mk 9 radial piston pump in conjunction with a cutout valve set to control system pressure between 2,500 and 3,000 psi. An 80 cu in (1,310 cc) air charged accumulator provides an emergency reserve for pylon controls in the event of a supply or pipe failure. Controls and services supplied by the hydraulic system are: pylon vectoring, lateral skirt shift, rear skirt shift and puff ports.

INSTRUMENTATION: This includes a Marconi Doppler to indicate water speeds; Brooks & Gatehouse equipment to give relative air speeds and wind directions; Magnesyn compass, a Marconi VHF transmitter/receiver, and a 25 channel ultra violet galvo recorder to make permanent records of various parameters to evaluate flight trials.

DIMENSIONS:

Length overall	30 ft 9 in (9·37 m)
Width overall	19 ft 0 in (5·79 m)
Height overall	17 ft 6 in (5·33 m)
Cushion area	342 sq ft (31·7 m²)
Plan area	429 sq ft (39·8 m²)

WEIGHTS:

Design all-up weight	9,000 lb (4,081 kg)
Overload weight	12,000 lb (5,441 kg)
Max fuel load	800 lb (363 kg)

PERFORMANCE:

Max speed, calm water, still air	
	Over 45 knots (83 km/h)
Endurance	2 hours

HU.4

This was originally the Cushioncraft CC—4 but it is now, after extensive modification, designated HU.4, and will shortly be used

to evaluate a modified fan propuls system following theoretical studies wh indicate that the efficiency of this system c considerably be improved. Other purpo for which HU.4 will be used are the practi evaluation of inflated secondary structu and the effectiveness in improving r characteristics over waves of a deep cush of greater than normal height-length rat

The HU.4 is a six-seater with an integra lift/propulsion system. Low pressure jets are used for propulsion in place aircraft-type propellers.

LIFT AND PROPULSION: Power is su plied by a single 240 hp Rolls-Royce L 8 V8 liquid-cooled 8-cylinder engine, mount with its output shaft towards the front the vehicle. The drive is taken through Borg and Beck motor-car clutch to a standa Salisbury rear-axle differential gearb Two output shafts from the differential ea carry at their outer end a pair of spec pulleys from which the lift and propuls fans are driven by nylon-faced tooth belts. There are four 12-blade light al fans of 42 in (1·077 mm) diameter mount vertically in tandem pairs in volutes (ducts) on each side at the rear of the vehic Approximately one-third of the airflow fr the fans is ducted into the plenum chamb The remaining two-thirds is ejected throu the open ends of the volutes for forwa propulsion. To avoid reduction in hov ing height that would follow eng in hovering height that would follow eng throttling, forward thrust is controlled two sliding gates which vary the size of t jet apertures at the rear of the volut Directional control is by means of two pa of rudders, on each side of the apertur Reverse-thrust louvres in the sides of t volutes are used for braking, moving ba wards and manoeuvring.

HULL: Basic structure of the HU.4 is flat box-type hull made of 1¼ in (32 m square spruce with ⅛ in (3·2 mm) thick bi plywood webs. Two main side fram extend the full length of this hull structu The original vee bow has been modified one with a curved surface giving bet characteristics during plough-in from

awed condition. The box-type structure
ormed by the longitudinal and transverse
rames is largely filled with polystyrene foam
o give positive buoyancy. A feature of
he craft is the use of flexible, inflated side
tructures.

.CCOMMODATION: The cabin superstruc-
ure, mounted on the front of the hull, is
nade of thin-gauge light alloy, with Triplex
vindscreens and Perspex side windows. The
river is seated centrally in front, with two
ndividual seats for observers behind him
nd a bench seat for three more observers
.t the rear of the cabin.   There is a rearward-
inged car type door on each side of the cabin
.t the rear.

Immediately aft of the cabin on the
ortside is a 35 Imp gallon fuel tank, followed
y the power plant.

Safety equipment carried includes manual
nd remote fire extinguishers, and a life raft.

OMMUNICATIONS AND NAVIGATION:
quipment includes Pye VHF and a gyro
ompass.

SYSTEMS:
LECTRICAL: 24 v battery, generator
riven from a fan shaft.

DIMENSIONS:
Length overall, over cushion
        25 ft 1½ in (7·65 m)
Beam overall, over cushion
        17 ft 6 in (5·33 m)
Height overall on landing pads
        8 ft 1¼ in (2·47 m)
Skirt depth   2 ft 0 in (0·60 m)
Cushion area   240 sq ft (22·3 m²)

WEIGHTS AND PERFORMANCE:
Not known. Trials in progress at time of
   going to press.

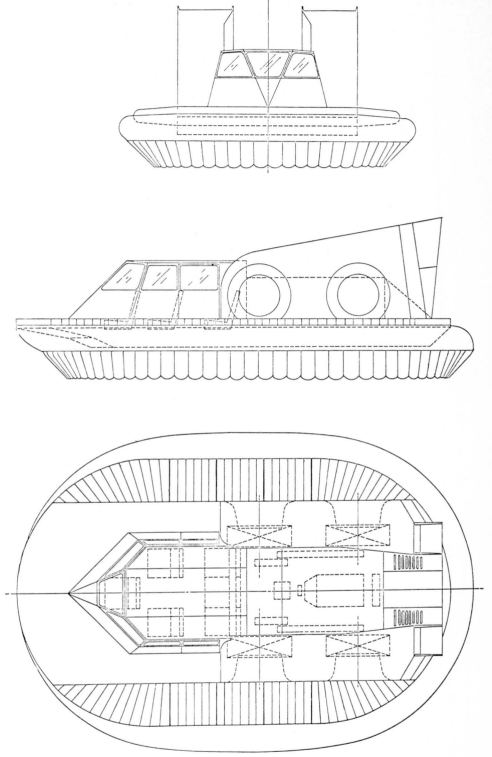

The NPL Hovercraft Unit HU4

Hoverknights
HOVERKNIGHTS
HEAD OFFICE:
  95 Rickmansworth Road, Pinner, Middlesex
TELEPHONE:
  01-868-0556

PROPRIETOR:
  Colin D. Knight
Hoverknights was formed in April 1968 to
provide technical advice and basic materials
and parts to schools, colleges, youth organis-

ations and clubs intending to build air
cushion vehicles. The company is now
planning to market a lightweight single-seat
sports craft designed by Colin Knight and
known as the Hoverscout.

AIR CUSHION VEHICLE MANUFACTURERS
HOVERMARINE: United Kingdom

Hovermarine
HOVERMARINE LIMITED

HEAD OFFICE:
Clifford House, New Road, Southampton
TELEPHONE:
Southampton 28038/9
DIRECTORS:
N. D. Piper, Managing Director
G. C. Hodgson
E. G. Tattersall BSc(Eng)
H. M. Watson
J. D. C. Stone, FCA, Secretary
A. de Boer
D. Collinson
Hovermarine has three overseas subsidiaries:

Hovermarine (Mediterranea) S.r.
ADDRESS:
Piazza Cavour 25, Rome, Italy
DIRECTORS:
Cav Lav Ing Raoul Chiodelli
Dott Claudio Chiodelli
Ing Ronald R. Rolo
N. D. Piper
G. C. Hodgson
C. A. Bekhor

Hovermarine (Canada) Ltd
ADDRESS:
Suite 311, 85 Sparks Street, Ottawa 4, Canada
DIRECTORS:
N. D. Piper
G. C. Hodgson
E. G. Tattersall
G. Perley-Robertson
K. L. Dyer (Chief Executive)

Hovermarine Incorporated
ADDRESS:
200 Park Avenue, New York, NY 10017 USA
N. D. Piper
G. C. Hodgson
E. G. Tattersall
J. E. Hughes

Hovermarine was formed in 1965 to undertake the development and construction of low-cost, rigid sidewall ACVs for overwater use. The company is licensed by HDL and there are currently four craft under production, development or design, the HM.2, HM.3, HM.4 and Hovercat. The HM.2 is in production and HM.3 and HM.4 are in the design stage. The latter are scheduled to be in production in 1970 and 1971 respectively.

The Manx Hovercat has been acquired from Manx Hovercat Limited and is now being redesigned and marketed as the Hovermarine Hovercat, Mk. 1 and 2.

William Cory and Son Limited have acquired a considerable interest in the company and C. Czarnikow Ltd and Baring Brothers and Co. Ltd. are also shareholders.

At the present time glass reinforced plastic hulls and superstructures for the production HM.2s are built by Halmatic Ltd. of Havant and the craft are fitted out by Camper and Nicholson Ltd and Port Hamble Ltd. Hovermarine is building its own factory on the River Itchen at Woolston, Southampton, where it will construct larger hulls.

HM.2
A sidewall craft designed for ferry services on light density routes of short stage lengths, the HM.2 can be integrated with an existing ferry boat system, and can be crewed by personnel experienced in the operation of conventional passenger ferries.

The basic craft carries 60-65 passengers or 5 tons of freight, but variants are offered for hydrographic survey, patrol, customs, fire-fighting and military applications.

Detail design started in December 1966, construction of the first craft moulds and tools started in March 1967 and the first hull was moulded in October. The prototype was completed in January 1968.

On completion of trials in March 1968, the HM.2 was given a certificate of construction and performance by the Air Registration Board and a Permit to Fly by the Board of Trade Air Safety Division.

By the end of June 1968, orders had been placed for ten HM.2 passenger craft and hydrographic survey variants.

LIFT AND PROPULSION: Two turbocharged VT8-370M eight-cylinder V marine diesels, each developing 320 bhp at 2,800 rpm provide propulsive power, and a single Cummins V6-215M diesel rated at 185 bhp at 2,800 rpm, drives the lift fans. The lift engine drives two pairs of forward fans through toothed belts and one aft fan through a hydraulic system. Air for the forward fans is drawn through inlets at each forward cabin quarter and in the base of the wheelhouse structure. Air for the aft fan is drawn through an inlet in the rear companionway. The lift fans are of glass-fibre construction.

The two propulsion engines drive two 15 in (381 mm) diameter AB Alcometaller nickel aluminium bronze propellers through a fluid drive system, a reversing gearbox and 1 : 1 ratio Vee box. Short skegs projecting from the base of the sidewalls protect the propellers from driftwood and grounding. A waterjet propulsion system for the HM.2 is under development.

Fuel is carried in reinforced rubber tanks, two beneath the aft companionway holding 150 gal. (680 litres) and one under the main lift fan holding 40 gal. (181 litres).

Two refuelling points are provided on the transom and one on the starboard side of the main air intakes.

CONTROLS: Craft direction is controlled by twin balanced rudders angled out to provide inward banking on turns. The rudders are operated from the wheelhouse by a car-type

Three Hovermarine HM.2 rigid sidewall ACVs at speed in the Solent. They are, left to right, one of two HM.2s operated by Seaspeed between Portsmouth and Ryde; the first craft built for Humber Hovercraft Services for services between Grimsby and Hull and the Surveymarine prototype

ering wheel. Additional control is provid-
by differential use of propulsion engine
ver.

LL: The craft is built in glass reinforced
stic and g.r.p. sandwich panels. The hull
ne homogeneous laminate into which are
ded g.r.p. bonded panel frames and
kheads. A one-piece deck laminate is
ded to the hull and transverse frames and
erstructure mouldings are bonded to the
k and bulkheads. A separate cabin
erstructure is bolted to the hull and isolat-
from the main primary structure by
ible seals.
luminium alloy members carry heavy
ns of machinery and also form the mount-
facility for small machinery items.

IRT: Front and rear skirts are of loop

segment form and designed for a cushion
height of three feet.

ACCOMMODATION: Controls are all sited
in an elevated wheelhouse with a 360° view,
located at the front end of the passenger
compartment. The commander is seated on
the right, with the principal instrumentation
and the radar operator and auxiliary instrumentation is located to the left. The craft
is operated by the commander, plus an
optional crew made up by a first officer and
two deck hands or stewardesses.

Accommodation is normally for 60 seated
passengers but the number can be increased
to 65. Seats are normally three abreast in
3 banks of seats. Toilets are fitted aft.
Access is through two forward gull wing
doors, one each side of the wheelhouse, and

one double door aft, down a companion
way.

Two "knock-out" emergency windows are
provided in the passenger saloon. Safety
equipment includes Beaufort life rafts, and
Beaufort aircraft-type life jackets under the
seats, Graviner fire detectors and fire-resistant
cladding. Hand fire extinguishers are carried,
plus an Essex Featherspray fire extinguisher
controlled from the wheelhouse.

Heating for the passenger saloon and
wheelhouse is from the freshwater circuit of
the engine cooling systems, via two heat-
exchanger blowers through ducts at floor
level. Air conditioning can be fitted if
required.

SYSTEMS:

ELECTRICAL: 24 volt DC from engine-
driven alternators (2 × 60 amp) with 165 Ah

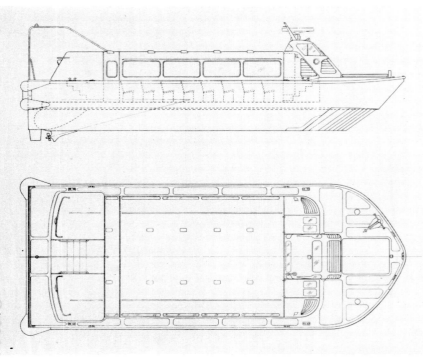

Hovermarine HM.2 004, the second craft supplied to British Rail for its Seaspeed service between
Portsmouth and Ryde, Isle of Wight. Length of the route is 4 nautical miles (8 km) and the journey
duration is 10 minutes. Block speed is 24 knots

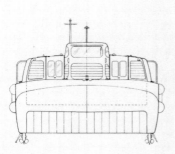

HM.2 60-65 passenger rigid sidewall ACV

AIR CUSHION VEHICLE MANUFACTURERS
HOVERMARINE: United Kingdom

Dagenite batteries. Supplies instruments, radio and radar and external and interior lights.

HYDRAULICS: System to operate steering and rear fan, 800 psi max and 2,400 psi max respectively.

APU: For air conditioning, where requested, by Petter.

COMMUNICATIONS AND NAVIGATION: Radar and Radio: To customer's requirements, currently using Kelvin C. Hughes KH 17, Decca 202 or 101 radar, and Redifon, Phillips and Kelvin C. Hughes radio.

Other Navigation Equipment: Magnesium compass or Sperry CL2 or marine direct-reading compass.

DIMENSIONS, EXTERNAL
Length overall	51 ft 0 in (15·54 m)
Beam overall	20 ft 0 in (6·10 m)
Height above hovering waterline	12 ft 0 in (3·66 m)
Draft floating with water screws	4 ft 10 in (1·47 m)
Draft floating with waterjets	3 ft 6 in (1·06 m)
Draft hovering with water screws	2 ft 3 in (0·69 m)
Draft hovering with waterjets	1 ft 0 in (0·3 m)
Cushion area	627 sq ft (584 m²)

DIMENSIONS, INTERNAL:
Cabin (excluding wheelhouse, galley and toilets):
Length	22 ft 0 in (6·7 m)
Max width	16 ft 0 in (4·8 m)
Max height	6 ft 6 in (1·9 m)
Floor area	352 sq ft (32·7 m²)

DOOR SIZES:
Rear door
4 ft 0 in (1·2 m) wide × 6 ft 3 in (1·9 m) high; two forward doors 2 ft 6 in (0·7 m) wide × 6 ft 0 in (1·8 m) high

BAGGAGE HOLDS:
Basic craft 60 cu ft (1·69 m³) aft of cabin and 24 cu ft (0·67 m³) forward of cabin

FREIGHT HOLDS:
None on standard passenger version. Freight carried in main cabin in freight version.

WEIGHTS:
Normal all-up weight	16 tons
Normal gross weight	16·4 tons
Normal payload	60 passengers or 5 tons of frieght
Max payload	65 passengers

PERFORMANCE (at normal operating weight):
Max service speed	35 knots (65 km/h)
Water speed in 4 ft waves and 15 knot headwind	20 knots (37 km)
Max wave capability on scheduled runs	4 ft 0 in (1·2 m)
Still air range and endurance at cruising speed	140 n. miles (224 km) 4 hours

PRICE:
Approximate cost, about £80,000.

HM.2 SURVEYMARINE

The Decca Navigator Company and Hovermarine have worked together to produce a complete hydrographic survey system—Decca providing the instrumentation and Hovermarine the craft. The system is titled Surveymarine. The craft will operate at 30 knots with waterjet propulsion and at faster speeds with water screws. At these speeds, echo sounding and position fixing is recorded automatically. The data is processed by a small computer so that the time cycle from the recording of the sounding to the production of the survey chart is significantly reduced.

Similar in basic design, construction and power plant to the HM.2, the survey craft is offered with waterjets to reduce the hovering draught to 1 ft and permit operation in shallow water. Spacious cabin and deck spaces are provided on a near rectangular platform. More cabin and deck space is available than on a displacement vessel similar length.

The craft offers the hydrographer advantage of high speed in rivers, lagoo and estuaries where restricted draught co ditions present a hazard to conventio vessels.

The superstructure layout is adaptable t variety of other uses from work boat and ri patrol craft, to personnel carrier.

One Surveymarine HM.2 will be delive to the East Pakistan Inland Water Transp Authority in December 1968.

DIMENSIONS:
Length overall	51 ft (15·5
Beam overall	20 ft (6·09
Height above hovering waterline to top wheelhouse	13 ft (3·95
Draft hovering	1 ft (0·31
Draft afloat	3 ft 6 in (1·07

WEIGHTS:
Craft all-up weight, fully loaded	16 tons (15,720
Normal disposal load	5 tons (4,920

PERFORMANCE:
Cruising speed, fully loaded, calm water	30 knots (50 km/
Normal operating range	200 n. miles (320 k

HM.3

Design of the HM.3 started in 1968. sidewall ACV intended for fast passenger- ferry or freight operation, the craft will propelled by either water propellers waterjets. The standard passenger fe version will carry 250, but the cabin can fitted out in a variety of ways to meet t demands of traffic on different types routes. Long-range variants will have b and lounges with a subsequent reduction seating capacity. The craft is scheduled be in production in 1970.

LIFT AND PROPULSION: High spe diesels or gas turbines will provide moti

Impression of the Surveymarine HM 2 hydrographic survey craft. Decca has provided the instrumentation, and data is processed by a small comput to reduce the time between the recording of the soundings and the production of the survey chart

wer for the lift and propulsion systems.
rotected waterjets or water propellers built
to the sidewalls will be used for propulsion.
eversal of the waterjets will be achieved
rough the use of baffles to reverse the
aterflow.

ULL: The main structure will be built in
ass reinforced plastics, with certain alumin-
im alloy components including the machin-
ry mountings and the car deck floor.
egmented skirts will be fitted at the bow
nd stern.

CCOMMODATION: Controls will be sited
a an elevated wheelhouse at the fore end of
le payload deck. The crew will normally
omprise a commander, first officer and two
r three deck hands or stewardesses. The
andard passenger version will seat 250
assengers, and a typical passenger and car
ayout will be for 100 passengers and 10 cars.
he car bay will have doors at the bow and
ern to permit through loading.

Details of systems and communications
nd navigation equipment were not available
t the time of going to press.

DIMENSIONS, EXTERNAL:

Length overall	100 ft 0 in (30·4 m)
Beam overall	37 ft 0 in (11·27 m)
Height, top of wheelhouse	
	20 ft 0 in (6·09 m)
Draft hovering	2·5 ft (0·76 m)
Draft floating	6·5 ft (1·98 m)

DIMENSIONS, INTERNAL:

Cabin, dependant upon configuration:
Vehicle bay length, width and height (two
lane loading)
90 ft (27·3 m) × 18 ft (5·4 m) × 10 ft
(3 m)

Max axle load	3 tons

WEIGHTS:

Normal all-up weight	75 tons
Payload	27 tons

PERFORMANCE (at normal operating
weight):

Service speed in calm conditions	
	40-42 knots
Speed in 4 ft (1·22 m) waves	30-32 knots
Max wave capability on scheduled runs	
	6 ft 0 in (1·8 m)
Range	160 n. miles (258 km)

HOVERMARINE-MERRYWEATHER FIRE TENDER

Using the same design construction and
powerplant arrangement as the survey craft,
the Hovermarine-Merryweather sidewall fire
tender is equipped for tackling port and
harbour fire outbreaks and casualty evacuation.

The craft layout includes a casualty station
with dispensary and stretcher bays, crew
mess and galley, fire-fighting deck and hose
store and the engine/pump room. At the
scene of the outbreak two Merryweather
MM2-8 pumps would be connected to the
Cummins propulsion engines through a clutch
and would deliver over 2,000 gallons (9·1
m. litres) per minute each at 100 lb/in²
(7 kg/cm²). Higher pressures are available
for foam generation. Through the use of
fluid drives the engines may be used simultaneously to drive the waterjets to keep the
craft in position against the thrust of the
monitors.

The sidewalls and floor are compartmented
to provide additional strength and buoyancy
should the craft be badly holed. All internal

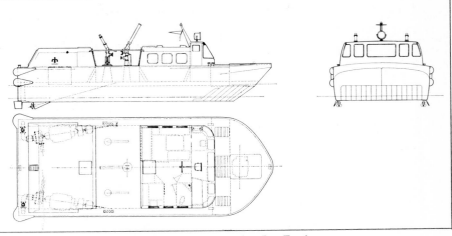

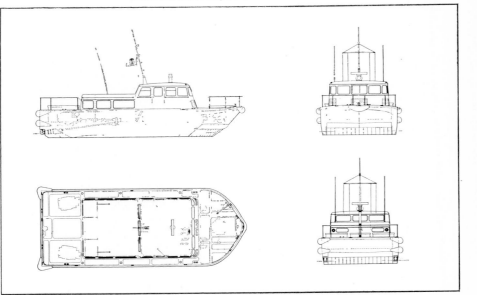

Hovermarine-Merryweather Fire Tender

HM.2 Surveymarine, a complete hydrographic survey system produced by Hovermarine working
in conjunction with the Decca Navigator Company

surfaces are treated with fire retardant paint.
The sidewalls act as twin keels, and apart
from any tendency to drift in a cross wind,
they also offer considerably more resistance
than a conventional hull to thrust from the
monitors when they are operating on the
beam.

Fire-fighting equipment will include six
sets of breathing apparatus, four sets of
protective clothing, an 'Aquator' suction lift
fitting for salvage work, a searchlight and
portable VHF radio.

HOVERCAT

The Hovercat is a 5/6 seat light ACV
evolved from the Parkhouse Scorpion.
Redesign of the craft was started by Hovermarine in September 1967 after the company
had taken over the Manx Hovercat prototype.

The craft will be built in two versions with
different propulsion engines. Mk 1 will have
a 54 bhp Volkswagen engine and Mk 2 will
have 90 bhp Porsche. Tooling for production started in April 1968.

Two Mk 2 Hovercats are on order, one for
East Pakistan and one for Sarawak.

LIFT AND PROPULSION: Lift is provided
by a VW 1584 cc single carburettor unit,
rated at (max) 46 bhp at 3,600 rpm, driving
a Rotafoil 43 in (1,104 mm) diameter
centrifugal fan. Cushion pressure is 16·4
lb/sq ft. Propulsive thrust for the Hovercat
Mk 1 is supplied by a VW 311 100 025F

1584 cc twin-carburettor unit rated at 54
bhp, and driving a 6 ft 6 in (1·98 m) diameter
Hoffman fixed-pitch propeller.

Propulsion engine on the Mk 2 is a Porsche
912 1582 cc of 90 bhp.

A single fuel tank with a max capacity of
15 gallons is located beneath the lift fan in
the gearbox support structure. The refuelling neck is sited behind the cabin inboard of
the transport joint.

CONTROLS: Craft direction is controlled by
two aerodynamic rudders operating in the
airscrew slipstream. Pitch is trimmed by
ballast, and yaw is controlled both by puff
ports and rudders.

HULL: The hull is built up from four glass-
reinforced plastic mouldings—the lower hull;
the upper hull, including the cabin; the
empennage and the two fins, and the sponsons.
A continuous peripheral skirt is fitted and
this has a depth of 2 ft 0 in (0·6 m). Worn
or damaged areas can be easily replaced.

ACCOMMODATION: The cabin seats an
operator and either three or four passengers.
There are two bucket seats forward and a
bench type seat at the rear.

Access is through two cabin entry doors, one
port and one starboard. Emergency "knock-
out" window exits are provided in the cabin.
Safety equipment can include a life raft, life
jacket and a hand fire extinguisher piped to
the lift engine.

AIR CUSHION VEHICLE MANUFACTURERS
HOVERMARINE: United Kingdom

SYSTEMS:
ELECTRICAL: 12 volt, 450 Watt generator, dc, for starting, instrumentation and lighting.
HYDRAULICS: Manual single-line constant volume system for rudders and throttle controls. Limiting pressure 1,000 psi.
COMMUNICATIONS AND NAVIGATION: Supplied to customer's requirements as extras.

DIMENSIONS, EXTERNAL:

Length overall	27 ft 2 in (8·28 m)
Hull length	26 ft 10½ in (8·18 m)
Width	12 ft 11 in (3·93 m)
Height to top of cowling	7 ft 4 in (2·23 m)
Skirt depth	
2 ft (0·6 m)-1 ft 8 in (0·5 m) below landing strake	
Cushion area	262 sq ft (24·3 m²);

CABIN DIMENSIONS:

Length	7 ft 0 in (2·13 m)
Floor area	35 sq ft (3·2 m²)

DOOR SIZES:
27 in (686 mm) high × 44 in (1,127 mm) wide (one each side)

WEIGHTS:

All-up weight	4,500 lb (2,039 kg)

Normal capacity
4 persons, or driver plus 540 lb (244 kg)
Overload
5 persons, or driver plus 720 lb (326 kg)

PERFORMANCE:
Hovercat Mk. 2:
Normal cruising speed 30 knots (55 km/h)
Duration   2 hours at full throttle
Max wave capability on scheduled runs
3 ft 0 in (0·9 m)

Hovercat Mk. 1
Normal cruising speed 25 knots (47 km/h)
Duration   2·5 hours at full throttle
Max wave capability on scheduled runs
3 ft 0 in (0·9 m)

PRICE:

Mk. 1	£7,500
Mk. 2	£8,500

HM.4

A 125 ton ferry craft, the HM.4 is designed to carry a mixed payload of 40 tons of passengers and cars, or alternatively 60 tons of freight. Production of the HM.4 is scheduled to start in 1971.

It will offer the same work capacity as many medium size ferryboats, but will operate at treble the service speed.
LIFT AND PROPULSION: Propulsive power will be provided by either high speed diesels or marinised gas turbines housed within the lower part of the sidewall. The centrifugal fans providing cushion lift together with their powerplant will be mounted in the bracing structure between the hulls.

The propulsion system envisaged employs a direct shaft line running from the engine to the propellers, which will be completely enclosed within the sidewall and fed by a flush intake.
HULL: Like its predecessors, the craft will be built in glass reinforced plastic or aluminium alloy.

Since the area above the bracing structure will not carry any considerable load apart from the lift fans and their powerplant, it will be little more than a flexible surface to carry the cushion lift load over to the sidewalls.
ACCOMMODATION: The payload is carried within the sidewalls together with the

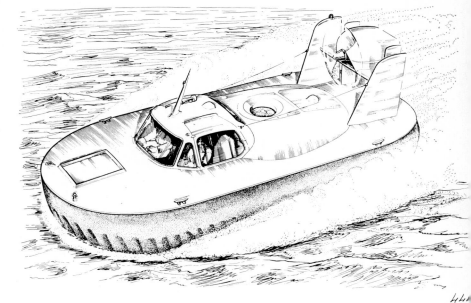

Artist's impression of the Hovermarine Hovercat Mk 2

A Hovermarine Hovercat Mk I in use as a development vehicle for the Hovercat Mk 2 which will be i production by mid-1969. Lift engine is a 1,600 cc Volkswagen developing 46 bhp and the prop ulsion engine is a 1,600 cc Porsche developing 54 bhp.

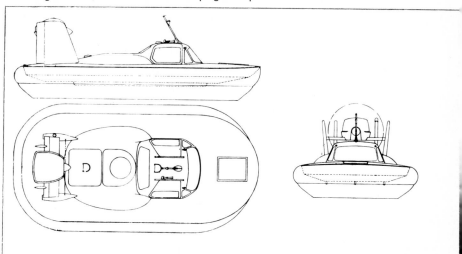

Hovermarine Hovercat Mk 2

propulsion system and fuel. As a result it is possible to raise the bracing structure above the cushion, providing a much greater over-wave clearance with a negligible effect on the centre of gravity height. Direct end loading of the passenger/car ferry version will be facilitated by a tail door, and for an all-freight application, an additional nose door will permit freight to be driven straight on and straight off.
DIMENSIONS:

Length overall	160 ft 0 in (48·77 m)
Beam overall	68 ft 0 in (20·73 m)
Height above hovering waterline	
	30 ft 0 in (9·14 m
Draught hovering	2 ft 0 in (0·61 m
Draught floating	4 ft 0 in (1·22 m

WEIGHTS:
Gross weight, normal 125 tons (127,000 kg)
Payload, passengers and/or cars
40-45 tons (40·6-45·8 kg
Payload freight   60 tons (60·9 kg

PERFORMANCE:
Service speed in 3 ft (0·914 m) waves
40 knots (74 km/h

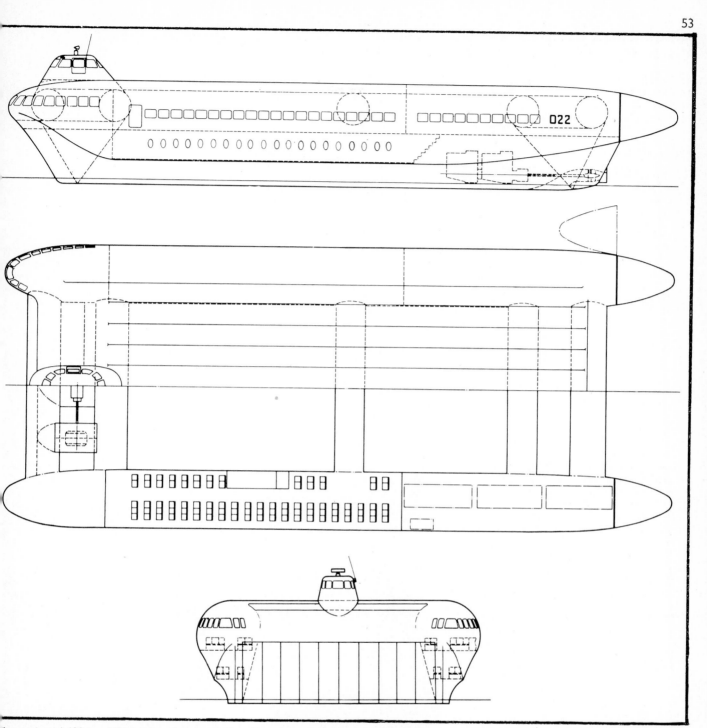

The projected 120-ton HM.4 sidewall ferry craft. Propulsive power will be provided by either high speed diesels or gas turbines housed within the sidewalls. Lift fans and their powerplant will be mounted on the bracing structure between the hulls. The HM.4 is designed to carry a payload of 40 tons of passengers and cars or up to 60 tons of freight within the two sidewalls. It will have a service speed in 3 ft waves of 40 knots

Hoversports
HOVERSPORTS

HEAD OFFICE:
389b Durnsford Road, London SW19

TELEPHONE:
01-947-2953

PROPRIETOR:
Henry Pooley

Hoversports supplies engines, component and spares for amateur air cushion vehic builders and also produces in kit form lightweight sports craft, the Hovercart.

Vosper Thornycroft
VOSPER THORNYCROFT (HOVERCRAFT DIVISION)

HEAD OFFICE:
Vosper House, Southampton Road, Paulsgrove, Portsmouth, England

TELEPHONE: Cosham 79481
TELEX: 86115
CABLES: Repsov, Portsmouth

DIRECTORS:
Vosper Ltd

Sir David Brown, MIMechE, MIAE, Chairman

Commander Peter Du Cane, CBE, RN, MRINA, MIMechE, AFRAeS, Deputy Chairman

John Rix, MBE, AMRINA, MIMarE, Managing Director

Commander C. W. S. Dreyer, DSO, DSC, RN, Sales Director

A. A. C. Griffith, OBE, BSc, MRINA, Assistant Managing Director

J. W. Thornycroft, CBE, MIMechE, MRINA, MIMarE

John I Thornycroft & Co Ltd

Sir David Brown, MIMechE, MIAE

Commander Peter Du Cane, CBE, RN, MRINA, MIMechE, AFRAeS

John Rix, MBE, AMRINA, MIMarE

Commander C. W. S. Dreyer, DSO, DSC, RN

T. E. P. Thornycroft, MA, AMIMechE

Vosper Thornycroft Uniteers Ltd

Commander C. W. S. Dreyer, DSO, DSC, RN

R. G. Bennett (Deputy Chairman)

J. A. Wilde, MRINA, Managing Director

E. St J. Berrill, Director and Secretary

DIRECTORS:
E. J. Walker
D. Arnott
T. E. P. Thornycroft, MA, AMIMechE

SENIOR EXECUTIVES:
John Rix, MBE, AMRINA, MIMarE, Managing Director

A. A. C. Griffith, OBE, BSc, MRINA, Assistant Managing Director

Commander C. W. S. Dreyer, DSO, DSC, RN, Sales Director

R. D. Hunt, BSc, MSc (Illinois), Manager, Hovercraft Division

J. S. Watford, Sales Manager, Hovercraft Division

A. E. Bingham, BSc (Tech.), AIMMechE, AFRAeS, Chief Hovercraft Designer

In March 1966, the merger of two famous South Coast shipbuilding companies—Vosper Ltd, Portsmouth, and John I. Thornycroft & Co, Ltd, Southampton—brought about the formation of the Vosper Thornycroft Group. The Group specialises in the design and building of all types of patrol craft and frigates and also provides comprehensive ship repair and engineering services. It is a subsidiary of the David Brown Corporation Ltd.

John I. Thornycroft & Co Ltd, of Southampton, was founded in 1864 and Vosper Ltd, at Portsmouth, in 1871. Vosper Ltd had become a subsidiary of the David Brown Corporation prior to the merger and in 1966 received the Queen's Award to Industry both for their export achievement and for their technological innovations. In April, 1967, the Singapore subsidiary, Thornycroft (Malaysia) Ltd, became Vosper Thornycroft (Far East) Ltd, now Vosper Thornycroft Uniteers Ltd.

The Group has four main operating divisions, Shipbuilding, Repairs, Hovercraft and Engineering Products; the latter comprises four sub-divisions.

Assessment of the future ACV market in both commercial transport and high speed military craft, led to the application in late 1965 by Vosper Ltd to the NRDC for a design and construction license. This was granted in late 1967 and the original ACV

design team was then rapidly expanded Details of the 76-ton VT1, the first Vospe Thornycroft ACV design, were announced February 1968 concurrently with the placin of the first order for this hoverferry.

VT 1

The VT 1 is a 76 ton semi-amphibious AC designed for fast, low-cost passenger/ca freight operation. Power is supplied by tw Avco Lycoming TF20 marine gas-turbine each driving four fixed-pitch lift fans and o controllable-pitch water propeller.

Cruising speed is 40 knots (75 km/h) and th craft will operate in complete safety in wav heights up to 10-12 ft (3-3·7 m). The VT can be operated from existing termina where full advantage can be taken of roll-on/roll-off through-loading faciliti Alternatively, simple low-cost slipways pontoon terminals can be established beaches.

Forward and aft loading doors of the VT1 are both 17 ft (5·18 m) wide × 9 ft 9 in (2·97 m) hi To simplify the control and positioning of cars a guide track is provided for each lane of cars and r the full length of the bay

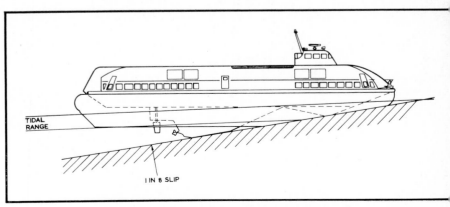

TIDAL RANGE

1 IN 8 SLIP

Tidal range acceptable by VT1 during turn-round

he first VT 1 has been ordered by Hover-
vel Limited and there is an option on the
ond. The prototype is scheduled for
ipletion in April 1969.
RIANTS: Typical car and passenger
outs include a standard version for 148
sengers and 10 cars (with further propor-
ial variations); a commuter version for
passengers, and a cruise version for 260
sengers.
ilitary and fully-amphibious types are
ig developed but details had not been
ased at the time of going to press.
'T AND PROPULSION: Motive power
provided by two Avco Lycoming TF20
ine gas-turbines, with power ratings
veen 1,675 and 2,000 hp for ambient
peratures between 60-80°F. These are
ted in separate engine rooms, located
dships, port and starboard. Each engine
irectly coupled via a transfer gearbox to
5 ft diameter centrifugal g.r.p. lift fans
thence to a skeg-mounted water propeller
a Vee-drive gearbox.
ie eight fans deliver air to the cushion via
ontinuous peripheral HDL segmented
made in lightweight neoprene-proofed
n material with full cushion depth
ients. There are neither stability skirts
other compartmentation arrangements.
skirt provides an air cushion depth of
it 5½ ft (1·68 m).
ie propellers are Stone KaMaWa 3-bladed
rollable-pitch units and have a diameter
1 ft (640 mm).

Fuel is contained in four integral tanks,
located two each side in the raft structure
amidships, beneath the lift fan rooms. Total
fuel capacity is 3,480 Imp gallons (15,820
litres). One pressure refuelling point is
fitted, on the starboard side forward. Types
of fuel recommended are: Kerosene, AVTUR
and Widecut; Diesel, gas Oil.

CONTROLS: The control cabin is located
above the port side of the superstructure and
provides a 360° view. Provision is made for
two craft control positions abreast of each
other forward, with radar located at a third
seat position behind. Engine controls are
on a central console within easy reach of both
front seat positions.
    The main driving controls for course and
attitude are positioned in front of the port
seat, and duplicated in front of the starboard
seat. Directional control is provided by
power-operated twin water rudders, controllable-pitch propellers and twin skegs. Longitudinal and lateral skirt shift control craft
attitude in trim and heel when underway.
A water ballast system is provided for C of G
adjustment.

OPERATING TECHNIQUE: The design of
the VT 1 allows normal ship-type operation
at sea and at existing terminals. It also
offers the advantage of being able to operate
from simple concrete ramps or slips, laid on
any reasonably steep beach having a minimum off-shore depth of water of about 4½ ft
(1·4 m). Recommended beach gradients are

between 1 in 8 and 1 in 12. Using this
technique, ferry routes can be set up with
relatively cheap facilities at high block speeds
and low operating costs.
    When beaching, the VT 1 is driven slowly
towards the slip by pitch adjustment on the
controllable-pitch propellers, at constant
power turbine speed. As the bow clears the
water's edge, it begins to rise up the slip, and
the craft slows due to the incline. On a
rising tide, the craft can be brought in on the
hover until the resilient pads on the main
skegs touch the ramp. On a falling tide,
the bows of the craft should just clear the
water's edge before settling. Reduction of
engine speed (and therefore lift fan speed),
allows the craft to settle firmly on to the slip
on its four landing pads.
    In the beaching mode, the craft can accept
a change in water level due to tide of about
3 ft (0·9 m) on a 1 in 8 slip, and 1 ft (0·3 m)
on a 1 in 12 slip. At such a stop, the hull
is 2 ft (0·6 m) clear of the calm water surface;
surf of about 5 ft (1·5 m) height would only
just touch the hull, therefore the risk of craft
pounding is minimal.
HULL: Construction is mainly in marine
corrosion-resistant aluminium alloys. Both
the bottom and deck structures are of conventional stiffened plate. The craft bottom
is designed to resist water impact pressures
arising from 6 ft (1·8 m) seas encountered at
service speed, with closed-up framing in the
bow where higher impact pressures are likely
to be encountered. The deck structure in

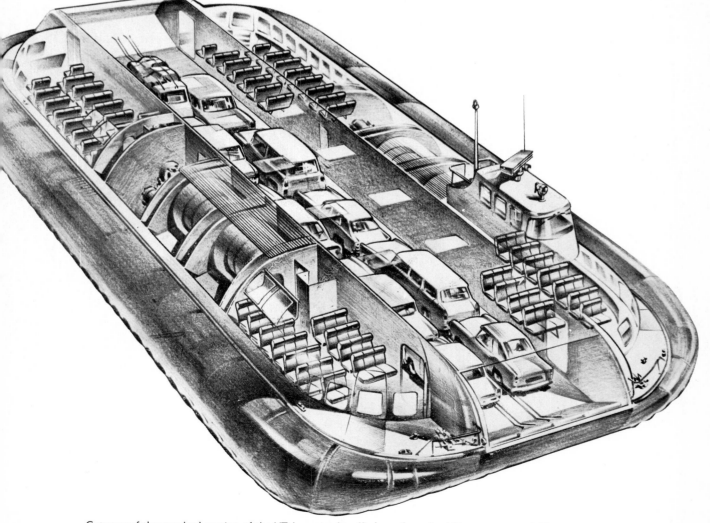

Cutaway of the standard version of the VT 1, a mixed traffic hoverferry for 148 passengers and 10 cars

AIR CUSHION VEHICLE MANUFACTURERS
VOSPER THORNYCROFT: United Kingdom

the central car bay will support axle loads up to 4,000 lb (1,814 kg)—an approximate gross vehicle weight of 3 tons (3·1 tonnes)—with lighter structure in the deck's side bays where only foot traffic is anticipated. Alternatively, standard ISO 20 ft (6·1 m) containers of average weight (up to ½ ton per ft run) can be carried, using the car guide tracks. The containers would be mounted on weight distributing rollers.

The bottom and deck structure are separated by longitudinal and transverse web frames which form a buoyancy raft of 31 separate watertight compartments including oil and fuel tanks. The raft provides the entire torsional strength of the craft. Reserve buoyancy is approximately 200%.

Two main longitudinal vertically stiffened bulkheads run the length of the craft separating the central car bay from the outer machinery and the passenger bays. These provide the craft's resistance to overall longitudinal bending and shear. The outer bays are subdivided by four transverse bulkheads of similar construction linked across the central car bay by beams to provide the overall transverse strength of the craft.

The superstructure covering is of light gauge sheet with longitudinal swedge stiffening. It is supported on transverse roof and vertical side beams which are designed to resist aerodynamic loading in airspeeds up to 80 knots. The hull is designed for a maximum disposable load of 35 tons and a normal payload of 21 tons.

LANDING SKEGS: These are of stiffened plate construction similar to that of the buoyancy raft bottom. Loads due to beaching are diffused into the craft's longi-

tudinal bulkheads via several main transverse frames.

ACCOMMODATION: The standard version has four passenger saloons, one at each corner of the craft, and seats a total of 148 passengers. Each saloon has a toilet/washroom and steward's post. There are two main entrances to each saloon. For operations from a beach, passengers enter over the main ramp or may use the external superstructure doors via mobile embarkation steps, similar to those in aircraft.

The car bay, designed for 10 cars, has full width doors at the bow and stern, which become access ramps for loading and unloading. The craft always beaches bows-to, and cars must be driven off in reverse. To simplify the control and positioning of cars a guide track is provided for each lane of cars and runs the full length of the bay. Vehicles can be disembarked quite satisfactorily with no hands touching the steering wheel. If normal terminal facilities are available at one end of the route, cars can be driven on and off in the forward direction. As an alternative to cars, up to three ISO 20 ft containers can be carried.

Each passenger saloon has a sufficient number of approved emergency exits according to the numbers carried. A full range of safety equipment is carried, including first-aid kits, axe and asbestos gloves in each saloon. Both main engine rooms have individual fire warning and extinguishing systems monitored and are controlled from the control cabin. The control cabin and each passenger saloon have hand-operated extinguishers.

One inflatable lifejacket of approved type

is stowed under each seat in the passenger saloons, and in addition, liferafts cater for at least 100% of passengers and crew stowed in external compartments within superstructure.

HEATING AND VENTILATION: Fresh heating and ventilating is provided for four passenger saloons and control cabin on The heating plant is a separate oil burner a blower unit of approved commercial desi It supplies fresh air at ambient or hig temperatures and is thermostatically contr led. Complete air conditioning can be fit if required.

SYSTEMS:

ELECTRICAL: 240 volt 50 HZ single-ph AC; 115 volt 400 HZ single-phase AC; volt DC.

Provision for shore supply.

The 240 volt 50 HZ AC supplies are deri from air-cooled diesel-driven alternators ra at 15·625 kVA continuous, giving 12·5 kW 0·8 power factor, lagging. Other supp are those met from transformer/rectifiers solid state inverters. The medium volt service supplies the following: lighting heating; pumps for the fuel, prope blade pitch and bilge systems; the tra former/rectifiers for the 115 volt sin phase AC and main 24 volt DC supplies. 115 volt 400 HZ AC provides power for following control systems; horizontal longitudinal skirt shift, steering, sp (propeller blade pitch-adjustment, turb power (throttle controls).

The transformer/rectifiers supply the na gation and communications requiremen systems controls and fire detection/supp sion equipment, and are backed up by bat

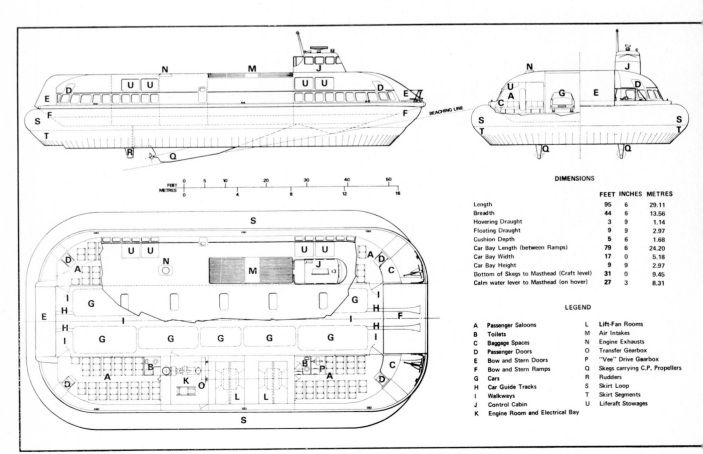

DIMENSIONS	FEET	INCHES	METRES
Length	95	6	29.11
Breadth	44	6	13.56
Hovering Draught	3	9	1.14
Floating Draught	9	9	2.97
Cushion Depth	5	6	1.68
Car Bay Length (between Ramps)	79	6	24.20
Car Bay Width	17	0	5.18
Car Bay Height	9	9	2.97
Bottom of Skegs to Masthead (Craft level)	31	0	9.45
Calm water level to Masthead (on hover)	27	3	8.31

LEGEND

A	Passenger Saloons	L	Lift-Fan Rooms
B	Toilets	M	Air Intakes
C	Baggage Spaces	N	Engine Exhausts
D	Passenger Doors	O	Transfer Gearbox
E	Bow and Stern Doors	P	"Vee" Drive Gearbox
F	Bow and Stern Ramps	Q	Skegs carrying C.P. Propellers
G	Cars	R	Rudders
H	Car Guide Tracks	S	Skirt Loop
I	Walkways	T	Skirt Segments
J	Control Cabin	U	Liferaft Stowages
K	Engine Room and Electrical Bay		

Vosper Thornycroft VT 1 semi-amphibious passenger/car hoverferry

when needed. Batteries start the main
turbine engines and the diesel AC
erators.

YDRAULICS: A 3,000 lb/sq in (14,647
/m²) hydraulic system is installed to
erate the skirt-shift, rudders, bow and
rn doors and ramps. Propeller pitch is
uated by a separate system.

MMUNICATIONS AND NAVIGATION:
andard equipment includes the following:
IF and standby VHF radio; crew intercom
d public address system.

AVIGATION: Decca 202 radar, Sperry
.2 gyro compass and two repeaters, stand-
magnetic compass, waterspeed indicator
d log, Brooks and Gatehouse echo sounder.
Decca Navigator and Flight Log is optional.
ternative equipment can be fitted to
stomer specification.

MENSIONS, EXTERNAL:

ength overall	95 ft 6 in (29 m)
3eam	44 ft 6 in (13·5 m)
Height overall	32 ft 0 in (9·8 m)
Skirt depth	5 ft 6 in (1·67 m)
Draft afloat	9 ft 9 in (2·97 m)
Draft hovering	3 ft 9 in (1·14 m)
Cushion area	34,870 sq ft (3,240 m²)

MENSIONS, INTERNAL:

Four passenger cabins with toilets, each
with the following dimensions:

Length	24 ft 0 in (7·3 m)
Max width	13 ft 6 in (4·1 m)
Max height	7 ft 6 in (2·3 m)
Floor area	320 sq ft (29·8 m²) app

Vehicle bay (may also be used for passenger
accommodation):

Length	79 ft 6 in (24·2 m)
Width, clear	16 ft 0 in (5·18 m)
Height, clear	9 ft 8 in (2·95 m)
Max axle load	4,000 lb (1,820 kg)

SIZE AND POSITION OF DOORS:
Forward and aft loading doors, 17 ft (5·1
m) wide × 9 ft 8 in (2·97 m) high. Four
passenger external access doors to saloons,
four further doors from saloons to car bay.

WEIGHTS:

Empty weight	50 tons
Normal operating weight	76 tons
Normal disposable load	26 tons
Normal payload	21 tons
Max disposable load	35 tons

PERFORMANCE (At maximum continuous
power and normal operating weight), at
ambient temperatures of 60°F:

Speed in calm conditions	48 knots (88 km/h)
Normal service speed	40 knots (74 km/h)
Turning circle diameter at 30 knots entry speed	1,150 ft (351 m)
Water speed in 4 ft waves and 15 knot headwind	36 knots (66 km/h)
Max wave capability at 15 knots	12 ft (3·6 m)
Max wave capability on scheduled runs	8 ft (5·48 m)

Still air range and endurance:

at cruising speed	160 miles, 4 hours
at maximum fuel load	350 miles, 9½ hours

PRICE AND TERMS:
Approximately £390,000—Standard Version VT 1, subject to negotiation.

VT 1(M)

This is a manned scale model of the VT 1,
built by Vosper Thornycroft for both
research and sales demonstrations. Design
began in February 1968 and the craft was
completed in July.

Thirty-seven feet long, it is powered by two
Volkswagen and two Porsche engines and
carries a crew of two.

LIFT AND PROPULSION: Two 50 hp

Volkswagen engines located amidships, port
and starboard, each drive four 2 ft diam
centrifugal lift fans. The fans supply air to
the cushion via a continuous peripheral
HDL-type segmented skirt manufactured
from neoprene-proofed nylon. Thrust is
provided by two 130 hp Porsche Type 2000
automotive engines, driving two 10 in
diameter Michigan Wheel Company water
propellers mounted on skegs.

CONTROL: Directional control is provided
by water rudders. Comprehensive trim and
heel facilities are provided by a skirt shift
system.

HULL: The hull is an all-wooden structure
of resin-bonded laminations and sheet marine
ply. Design loads are as required by the
Provisional British ACV Safety Regulations.

ACCOMMODATION: In the experimental
role, a crew of two is carried. Dual control
is provided. Entry is via a representative
forward ramp.

SYSTEMS:
ELECTRICAL: 12 volt dc for all control
systems.

HYDRAULICS: System for skirt shift
control 1,650 lb/sq in.

COMMUNICATIONS:
RADIO: VHF for distress and internal
company communications only.

DIMENSIONS, EXTERNAL:

Length overall	37 ft 4 in (11·3 m)
Beam overall	17 ft 5 in (5·3 m)
Skirt depth	2 ft 4 in (0·7 m)
Draft afloat	4 ft 0 in (1·2 m)
Draft hovering	1 ft 6 in (0·3 m)
Cushion area	556 sq ft (51·8 m²)

WEIGHT:
Normal all-up weight 4·8 tons (10,700 lb)

PERFORMANCE:
Max speed in calm (ISA) conditions
40 knots (74 km/h)

The 4-ton VT I(M) a manned model of the VT I. Powered by two Volkswagen and two Porsche engines it carries a crew of two and is used for research and demonstrations

THE UNITED STATES OF AMERICA

Aeroglide
AEROGLIDE SYSTEMS, INC

HEAD OFFICE:
120 Broadway, New York 10005

TELEPHONE:
Cortlandt 7-0941

DIRECTORS:
Jean Bertin
R. M. Dubois
Fowler Hamilton
Leon Kaplan
Mark Millard

EXECUTIVES:
R. M. Dubois, President and Treasurer
Daniel S. Shapiro, Secretary

Aeroglide is a jointly held subsidiary of Bertin & Cie and Société de l'Aerotrain, and was incorporated in Delaware in December 1966 with a capital of $20,000.

It is at present studying the application of tracked air cushion vehicles of various capacities, speeds and modes of propulsion for fast passenger services between cities, central metropolitan areas and airports, and between airports in the USA.

The studies are part of a marketing programme initiated by Aeroglide with object of solving ground transportation problems in the USA through the use of tracked air cushion vehicles.

During 1967-8, Aeroglide has been under contract to the Office of High Speed Ground Transportation, Department of Transportation, Washington, D.C., to prepare a "Definition and Evaluation of Air Cushion Guided Ground Transportation System" a study which is now nearing completion.

Aero-Go
AERO-GO, INC

HEAD OFFICE:
2447 Sixth Avenue South, Seattle, Washington 98134

TELEPHONE: (206) MA 4-226

OFFICERS AND DIRECTORS:
Stanley B. McDonald, President
Kenneth G. Wood, Executive Vice President
Fred Kimball, Treasurer
Wheeler Grey, Secretary
M. Lamont Bean
Robert J. Behnke
William Caswell
Robert Halliday
Rogers P. Holman
William S. Leckenby
Gregg C. MacDonald
Philip S. Padelford
Richard C. Philbrick
James C. Pigott
Hugh A. Smith
T. Evans Wyckoff

Aero-Go was founded in April 1967 to commercialise the developments of the Boeing Company in the field of air film and air cushion devices. It holds the exclusive world-wide licence to Boeing's proprietary products, experience and patent rights in this field. The first air cushion vehicle built by Aero-Go is the Terra Skipper, brief details of which are given below.

TERRA SKIPPER Mk. 1

Terra Skipper is an experimental single-seat sports ACV, which will undergo further development before being marketed by the company. A single 10 hp 2-cycle engine drives a single fan for lift and propulsion. The hull upper structure is in fibreglass and the craft weighs 180 lb (82 kg). A speed of 30 mph (49 km/h) has been reached on beaches and motor racing tracks. A powered retractable centre wheel assists hill climbing and parking. Length overall is app 9 ft (2·7 m) and width is app 4 ft 6 in (1·37 m). The craft will be amphibious.

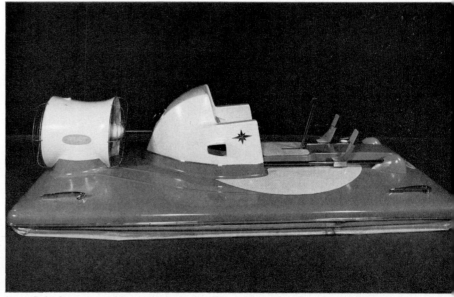

Aero-Go's first air cushion vehicle is the Terra Skipper, a fibreglass hulled single-seater. experimental sports machine built to evaluate power plant and control configurations, it reached 30 mph during tests

Aerojet
AEROJET-GENERAL CORPORATION
(Subsidiary of the General Tire and Rubber Co)

HEAD OFFICE:
9100 East Flair Drive, El Monte, California 91731

TELEPHONE:
(213) 288-7250

DIRECTORS:
M. G. O'Neill, Chairman
W. E. Zisch, Vice-Chairman

D. A. Kimball, Chairman, Executive Committee
R. I. McKenzie, President
A. H. Rude, Honorary Chairman
T. E. Beehan
F. W. Knowlton
L. A. McQueen
J. O'Neill
T. F. O'Neill

SENIOR EXECUTIVES:
L. W. Mullane, Executive Vice-President
W. L. Gore, Senior Vice-President, Sales
A. L. Antonio, Senior Vice President, Research and Technology
W. C. House, Vice President, Preliminary Design
J. M. Farrin, Asst. Division Manager Surface Effect Ships
R. D. Waldo, Manager, Surface Effect Ships Programmes
W. J. Eggington, Manager, Air Cushion Vehicles

Aerojet-General began research and development programmes on both captured bubble and amphibious skirted air cushion configurations in June 1966.

n 1967, Aerojet-General won its first ntract from the Joint Surface Effect Ships gramme Office to make a design study a less than 100-ton SES test craft. Addi- nal contractual programmes have been cerned with obtaining fundamental data surface effect ships of up to 4,000-5,000 ns. The company is currently operating US Navy XR-3 as a research tool.

Aerojet-General has evaluated the feasi- ity of amphibious ACVs for US Navy nphibious Assault and Inshore Warfare, Army Combat and Logistics and US rine Corps applications. Advanced velopment of the multiple cushion con- uration have resulted from analysis and del-test programmes. An experimental cushion vehicle, MANTA RA, will be in eration in the autumn of 1968.

The company's laboratory facilities for the earch and development of captured air bble and air cushion vehicles has been veloped extensively. They include hydro- namic, aerodynamic, dynamic response, d flexible and rigid material testing boratories.

ANTA-RA

Aerojet-General's first full-scale research vehicle is the Manta-RA, a 25 ft long amphib- ous 3-seater employing a multiple cushion system.

The craft was due to be completed in mid- September 1968.

LIFT AND PROPULSION: Cushion lift is provided by a 425 hp Chevrolet 427D driving two centrifugal, 3 ft 2 in diameter, steel lift fans. The airflow is ducted to eight indi- vidual skirts, each 2 ft high. These are in turn surrounded by a single peripheral skirt of neoprene filled dacron open weave cloth, 1,602 yd². Cushion pressure is 34 lb sq ft.

Aft of the lift fans is a second 425 hp Chevrolet 247D driving two 3-bladed 5 ft diameter Hartzell variable and reversible pitch shrouded propellers for propulsion.

Fuel—premium gasoline—is carried in four tanks, two forward, two aft, with a total capacity of 266 gal. The filler neck is in the centre of the top deck.

CONTROLS: Craft direction is controlled by differential pitch of the propellers and by two aerodynamic rudders operating in the slip- stream.

HULL: Built in GRP (glass-fibre reinforced plastics) foam sandwich with an aluminium centre keel.

ACCOMMODATION. The cabin, which is heated and ventilated, seats 3—a driver, test engineer and one passenger. Entry doors are provided on each side of the cabin. Emergency exits and safety equipment are as specified by the US Coast Guard.

COMMUNICATIONS AND NAVIGATION: Standard marine radio is carried, radar is optional. A gyro compass is also fitted.

DIMENSIONS:

Length overall	25 ft 6 in (7·7 m)
Beam overall	10 ft 0 in (3 m)
Height overall on landing pads	
	8 ft 0 in (2·4 m)
Skirt depth	2 ft 0 in (0·6 m)
Draft afloat	6 in (0·15 m)
Cushion area	204 sq ft (18·9 m²)

WEIGHTS:

Normal all-up weight	6,500 lb (2,945 kg)
Max payload	1,500 lb (680 kg)

PERFORMANCE:

Cruising speed, calm water	40 knots
Turning circle dia at 30 knots	
	1,500 ft (457 m)
Still air range and endurance at cruising speed	8 hours
Max gradient, static conditions	1 in 6·4
Vertical obstacle clearance	18 in (458 mm)

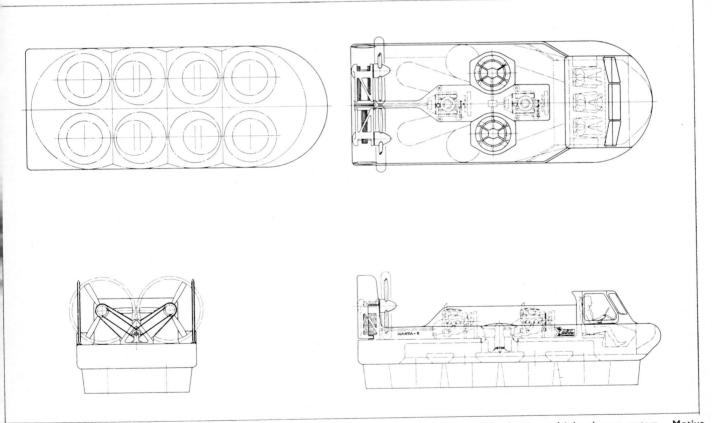

Aerojet-General's new research vehicle, the Manta-RA, is a 25 ft long amphibious 3-seater employing the Bertin multiple plenum system. Motive power is provided by two 425 hp Chevrolet 427Ds and the cruising speed is 40 knots

AIR CUSHION VEHICLE MANUFACTURERS
AEROMAR: United States of America

Aeromar
AEROMAR CORPORATION
HEAD OFFICE:
567 Fairway Road, Ridgewood, New Jersey
PRESIDENT:
E. K. Liberatore

Aeromar Corporation was formed in 1964 on the initiative of E. K. Liberatore, the engineering consultant, who has been active in the ACV field since 1958. He was responsible earlier for initiating the ACV programmes at Bell Aerosystems and at the Electric Boat Division of General Dynamics Corporation. He has also directed ACV activities at Bell and Curtiss Wright Corporation.

Aeromar's activities during the past four years include:

The design of a commercial ACV free of NRDC patents.

The securing of Maritime Administration Title XI Mortgage insurance coverage for ACVs.

The establishment of a US Coast Guard ACV Certification programme.

The completion of engineering studies on sidewall configurations directed at the 90-4,000 ton Maritime Administration and US Navy CAB programmes.

AEROMAR A-1
Aeromar's first commercial design is the model A-1, a gas-turbine powered, amphibious passenger ferry with a cruising speed of 44 knots. A freight carrier version is being planned with a gross weight of 30,000 lb and a maximum payload of 9 tons.

LIFT AND PROPULSION: Power is provided by two separate lift/propulsion units, each comprising a Garrett 331 shaft turbine, a propeller, drive system and lift fan. The propellers are of standard, variable-pitch Hartzell type and the fans, which are driven through a right angle gearbox and shafting, are specially designed, solid fibreglass units and have a variable-pitch control.

The powerplant cowls are completely sealed to avoid water seepage into the nacelles. Engine air intake is from the pressurized duct plenum. The air makes a turn through the cushion fan, providing momentum separation of particles, then flows up the pylon to the turbine. On the way up it passes through a filter.

The fuel system consists of four flexible cells in the wall of the passenger well, one in each quarter. This permits balancing the craft with fuel, augmenting the ballast boxes provided fore and aft in the hull.

CONTROL: The operator uses a wheel for roll, column movement for pitch and rudder pedals for yaw. Two hydraulically-actuated aerodynamic rudders, operating in the airscrew slipstream, provide directional control. The horizontal stabilisers are used to balance out pitching moments in forward flight. Pitch and roll control are provided by raising the flexible skirt on the appropriate side. A novel feature of the skirt design provides for some cushion pressure relief, to reduce accelerations in waves. Hovering yaw control is produced by differential pitch of the propellers, and a slight amount of additional yaw can be produced by the impingement of exhaust gas on the rudders. An optional feature is an aircraft-type tricycle landing gear. This permits taxiing with positive ground control.

Aeromar's A-I circular planform, amphibious ACV will be powered by two 600 shp Garrett 331 shaft turbines. Seating 45—56 passengers the craft will cruise at 50 mph

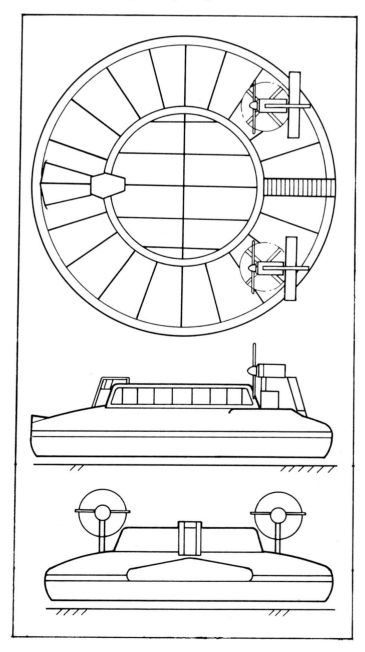

ULL: The craft is of circular planform with o integrated lift/propulsion units at the r. Passengers are accommodated in a itral well which is covered by a glazed erstructure. Forward of the well and set ghtly above the passenger compartment erstructure is the pilothouse.

he passenger well is a double wall cylinder aluminium sheet, open at its upper end, l covered by a sheet aluminium structure taining plexiglass windows. Both the f and the passenger floor are flat aluminium eycomb structures built up from standard els. The walls and floor are divided by kheads into watertight compartments.

he air duct around the passenger compart- nt is doughnut-shaped, and built from -assembled segments which are attached und the passenger well. Upper and er parts of the duct are made in sandwich terial and the core of the lower part is watertight to provide additional buoyancy.

The flexible structure consists basically of a peripheral skirt and dividing members across the base.

ACCOMMODATION: Entrance to the pass- enger compartment, which will seat from 44 (standard) to 56 (maximum) depending on the operator's requirements, is from the rear, through a double doorway and down a flight of steps. The compartment can be converted to a cargo hold by removal of the roof and seats.

The pilothouse, which provides a 360° view, is located forward of the passenger well and accommodates a crew of two. Access is normally from inside the passenger com- partment; a side door is provided for on-deck activities.

Standard marine equipment is carried to meet US Coast Guard requirements.

DIMENSIONS:

Length overall	42 ft 0 in (12·80 m)
Width overall	42 ft 0 in (12·80 m)
Height	22 ft 6 in (6·86 m)
Cushion area	1,260 sq ft (117 m²)

WEIGHTS:

Gross weight	25,200 lb (11,500 kg)
Empty weight	12,000 lb (5,450 kg)
Useful load	13,200 lb (6,000 kg)

PASSENGERS:

Maximum	56
Normal	44
Crew	2

PERFORMANCE:

Max hover height (daylight clearance)	1 ft 0 in (0·305 m)
Max negotiable wave height	6 ft 0 in (1·83 m)
Max speed (calm water)	74 knots (137 km/h)
Cruising speed	44 knots (50 mph)

AIR CUSHION VEHICLE MANUFACTURERS
AIR KINETICS / AMERICAN AEROCAR: United States of America

Air Kinetics
AIR KINETICS INC

HEAD OFFICE:
5555 NW 5th Street, Miami, Florida 33126
WORKS:
6225 SW 8th Street, Miami, Florida
DIRECTORS:
Barry H. Palmer, President
James P. Eder, Secretary/Treasurer

Formed in November 1966 as Paraplanes Inc, this company was originally engaged in the development of light, flexible wing aircraft for sports and other applications. The company has recently expanded its activities to cover ACV research and its first craft, the Smuggler, will be used to evaluate a 2-seat sports ACV of similar configuration. A smaller machine is also under consideration.

SMUGGLER

First ACV to be designed and built by Air Kinetic is the Smuggler, a two-seat amphibious craft of glass-fibre covered plywood construction, powered by a single 45 hp Volkswagen automotive engine and capable of 35 mph overwater   During trials in July 1968, Smuggler successfully negotiated typical Florida Everglades terrain with brush and grass 3-8 ft high. A moulded fibreglass version is planned and it is possible that drawings of the present craft in its developed form will be made available to home builders. Design and construction of the Smuggler started in March 1968, it was completed in June, and is currently undergoing tests. The craft is registered

as a recreational boat by the Florida Department of Conservation.

LIFT AND PROPULSION: Power for the integrated lift/propulsion system is supplied by a single Volkswagen 1500 cc automotive engine delivering 45 hp at 3000 rpm. This drives via vee belts a 42 in diameter 11 blade axial flow fan for lift and a 54 in diameter fixed-pitch, 2 blade propeller. Both fan and propeller are of fibreglass covered wood.

HULL: The basic structural member is a strong boatlike hull constructed in plywood covered with glass fibre. Operator and passenger sit forward in an open cockpit which contains a single push-pull rudder control with twist grip throttle and engine instrumentation. Under the cockpit seat is a 12-gal (USA) steel gasoline tank. An automotive type filter neck is located outboard and ahead of the lift fan. Fuel recommended is 100 octane gasoline. A simple 10 in deep skirt is fitted across the bow and amidships and a bag type skirt is fitted aft.

CONTROLS: Two air rudders operating in the airscrew slipstream provide directional control. Pitch and roll control are provided by raising the flexible skirt on the appropriate side.

Safety equipment includes a fire extinguisher, flotation cushions, paddle and a length of styrofoam log.

DIMENSIONS:
Length overall	13 ft 4 in (4·06 m)
Beam overall	7 ft 0 in (2·13 m)
Height overall on landing pads	7 ft 0 in (2·13 m)

Skirt depth	10 in (0·25
Draft afloat	6 in (0·15
Cushion area	78 ft² (7·2

DIMENSIONS, INTERNAL:
Cabin/cockpit length	5 ft 8 in (1·7
Max width	4 ft 0 in (1·2
Floor area	23 ft² (2·1

WEIGHTS:
Normal gross weight	1,126 lb (510
Normal payload	412 lb (186

PERFORMANCE:
Max speed over calm water (nominal pow
35 mph (57 km/h)
Cruising speed   30 mph (49 kmh/)
Still air range and endurance at cruis speed
180 miles (111 km), 6 hours at 30 m (49 km/h)
Max gradient, static conditions   1 in
Vertical obstacle clearance   8-10

The Air Kinetics Smuggler is being used evaluate a 2-seat sports ACV of similar c figuration. Powered by a 45 hp Volkswa engine it has reached 40 mph over land dur tests

American Aerocar
THE AMERICAN AEROCAR COMPANY

HEAD OFFICE AND WORKS:
411 Park Drive, Norristown, Penna, USA
ZIP CODE:
19401
TELEPHONE:
215-272-4110
DIRECTORS:
Ronald G. Moyer, President and Chairman
Charles V. White, Secretary/Treasurer
SENIOR EXECUTIVES:
Ronald G. Moyer, General Manager
James Reardon, Chief Designer, Propulsion
Thomas Emory, Chief Designer, Controls

The American Aerocar Company was founded in May 1965 and the Aerogem is the company's first ACV design.

AEROGEM 1A

The Aerogem is designed to incorporate the advantage of ram-wing, ground effect and blown wing concepts.

LIFT AND PROPULSION: The craft is of modified plenum design and has a high lift section hull. Designed static hover height capability is about 4 in, increasing with the aid of lift developed by the aerodynamic hull to around 12 in at 60 mph. Power for the integrated lift/propulsion system is

provided by a 60 hp, 4-cycle 2-cylin Dyna-Panhard air-cooled engine driving f 10-bladed 21 in diameter, axial-flow fa The fans are of ILG Multi-Wing type a are located immediately aft of the nose intake. Posi-drive belts drive three f off the primary fan shaft, which is V-jo coupled to the engine crankshaft. Thr is provided by the ejection cushion horizontally from the rear section of the h Forward and reverse thrust and turning controlled by two electrically-operated thr vents. Rudders and elevators prov directional control and longitudinal trim speed is increased. A small amount of

The Aerogem 1A built by the American Aerocar Co.

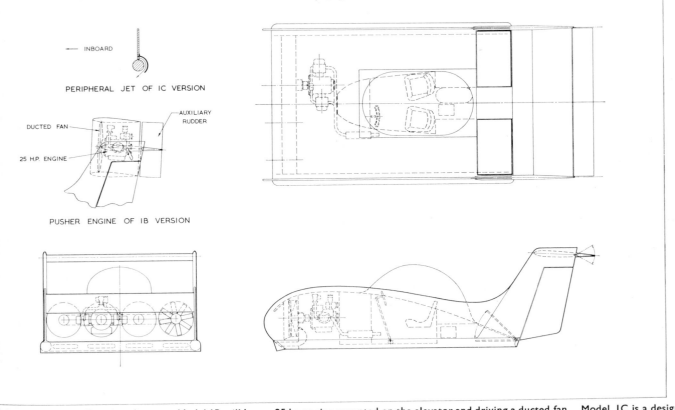

INBOARD

PERIPHERAL JET OF IC VERSION

DUCTED FAN

AUXILIARY RUDDER

25 H.P. ENGINE

PUSHER ENGINE OF IB VERSION

The American Aerocar Company Aerogem Model IB will have a 25 hp engine mounted on the elevator and driving a ducted fan.   Model IC is a design modification to permit a comparison of peripheral jet and open plenum configurations

control is provided by the use of internal deflector foils.

HULL: The hull is of Fibreglass-Styrofoam-Fibreglass sandwich construction. At the base of each of the two hull endplates is a circular section flotation chamber. A simple bop-type skirt in neoprene impregnated nylon is fitted across the bow.

ACCOMMODATION: Side-by-side seats are provided for an operator and one adult passenger plus two children. Access is through a sliding plexiglass cockpit canopy. Safety equipment includes a fire extinguisher.

SYSTEMS:

ELECTRICAL: One 12 volt battery for starter, lights and controls.

NAVIGATION: One magnetic compass.

DIMENSIONS, EXTERNAL:

Length overall	16 ft 3½ in (5·26 m)
Beam overall	7 ft 11½ in (2·42 m)
Height overall on landing pads	
	4 ft 1 in (1·24 m)
Draft afloat	6 in (154 mm)
Cushion area	100 sq ft (9·29 m²)

DIMENSIONS, CABIN:

Length	5 ft 3 in
Max width	3 ft ½ in
Max height	4 ft
Floor area	6 sq ft (0·55 m²)

WEIGHTS:

Normal all-up weight	700 lb (317 kg)

Normal gross weight	1,150 lb (521 kg)

PERFORMANCE (Design):

Max speed over calm water, max power	
	50 mph (80·4 km/h)
Cruising speed, calm water	
	45 mph (72·4 km/h)
Still air range at cruising speed	
	100 miles (160·9 km)
Max gradient, static conditions	5%
Verticle obstacle clearance	
	3 in (77 mm) without skirt

AEROGEM 1B

Model 1B will have a separate 25 hp tail-mounted propulsion engine powering a ducted fan and a rudder operating in the slipstream.

Bartlett

BARTLETT FLYING SAUCER

HEAD OFFICE AND WORKS:

PO Box 3234, Scottsdale, Arizona 85257

OWNER:

Herbert, L. Bartlett

The first Bartlett Flying Saucer was test flown during the spring of 1960. This machine had a diameter of 10 ft and used a 3 hp Briggs & Stratton lawn mower engine for lift. It was equipped with a tractor inner tube beneath the deck structure which also served as a buoyancy chamber for over water operation. Although its lift characteristics were good, it proved unstable in forward flight and this necessitated further development of the hull design.

Twelve models have been built and tested since 1960. The hull dimensions have remained essentially the same except for a 7 ft diameter model which lacked sufficient area to lift a load of 200 lb. A 12 ft hull was tested in 1962 (6 hp Airboy) and showed good flight characteristics, but proved to be

An inexpensive lightweight craft, the M-8 Flying Saucer can be constructed in about 16 hours. It has a forward speed of 12-25 mph, depending on the skill and weight of the operator

AIR CUSHION VEHICLE MANUFACTURERS
BARTLETT / BELL: United States of America

too large to transport. Various hull modifications have been made to improve lift, forward speed, stability and torque control.

The prototype of the present M-8 was constructed in the autumn of 1962.

M-8 FLYING SAUCER

The M-8 was designed as an inexpensive, lightweight machine featuring ease of assembly (this takes approximately 16 hours), operator safety and readily obtainable building materials. Twenty have been built.

HULL: The hull is built mainly of plywood sheet. The hull frame comprises 16 spruce rib formers set radially from a central propeller well and secured above and below by two central deck rings of $\frac{1}{2}$ in plywood. The framework is covered in doped, unbleached muslin, and the propeller well is lined with sheet aluminium. An 18 in deep polyvinyl skirt is secured around the hull by a perimeter moulding. A vertical stabiliser is fitted and this is hinged for limited arc to counter engine torque in forward flight. Control linkage can be fitted if required.

POWERPLANT: Lift is supplied by a 3 hp Briggs and Stratton lawn mower engine mounted above the central plenum well and driving a 2-bladed Banks-Maxwell Mod 30-14 30 in diameter pusher propeller. A protective screen is attached to the top of the well above the propeller. The throttle lever is carried on a simple braced structure ahead of the operating position.

CONTROL: The craft is designed for a single operator standing on footboards at the centre of the craft, where the overall centre of gravity coincides with the centre of lift. It is controlled kinesthetically and when, from a position of neutral balance (hovering) the operator leans forward the craft will move forward.

The operator stands on the floorboards either side of the engine with engine at idle. Engine speed is gradually increased until the machine is cushion borne. There is a slow rotation about the lateral axis, which is caused by torque and may be trimmed out by adjusting flow straighteners. The

transition from hover to forward or si[de]ways motion is gradual and requires o[n]ly a very slight weight displacement. Flig[ht] is restricted to a smooth, level surface.

DIMENSIONS:

Diameter	9·5 ft (2·8
Skirt depth	2 ft (0·6

WEIGHTS:

Machine weight	150 lb (68 k
Normal all-up weight	350 lb (159 k
Normal payload	200 lb (91 k
Maximum payload	250 lb (113 k

PERFORMANCE:

Speed

Forward speed is 12-25 mph (19·40 km [...] depending upon weight and skill of t[he] operator

Price

(complete kit, including engine a[nd] matched propeller), f.o.b., Scottsda[le] Arizona $350·00

Terms   Cash with ord[er]

A comprehensive plan packet is availab[le] Price is $3·00 overseas, plus 50c for posta[ge]

Beardsley
BEARDSLEY AIR CAR CO

HEAD OFFICE:
40, Windward Drive, Severna Park, Maryland

PRESIDENT:
Melville W. Beardsley

The Beardsley Air Car Co is basically a research and development operation con-

ducted by Melville Beardsley. Details [of] the Fan-Jet Skimmer, the Beardsley [Wheel]barrow and Flying Carpet can be fou[nd] under the entries for Skimmers Incorporat[ed] the company marketing these products.

Bell
BELL AEROSYSTEMS COMPANY

HEAD OFFICE:
Buffalo, New York 14240

TELEPHONE:
Area Code 716 297-1000

OFFICERS:
William G. Gisel, President

Dr. Richard M. Hurst, Executive Vice President

Robert S. Ames, Vice President, Manufacturing

Clifford F. Berninger, Vice President, Research

Joseph E. Conners, Secretary and Chief Counsel

John F. Gill, Vice President, Products Assurance

Ramon J. Hartung, Vice President, Project/Systems Management

Lawrence P. Mordaunt, Vice President, Marketing

Con R. Ostrander, Vice President, Planning

Joseph R. Piselli, Vice President, Engineering

John M. Schweizer, Vice President, Western Region

William M. Smith, Assistant to the President and Chief Scientist

John H. van Lonkhuyzen, Vice President and Manager, Minuteman Programme

Edward W. Virgin, Vice President, Eastern Region

Peter J. Wacks, Vice President, Industrial Relations

Norton C. Willcox, Vice President, Finance

SENIOR ACV EXECUTIVES:
Angelo V. Palermo, ACV Programme Director

Joseph A. Cannon, ACV Product Mana[ger]

Colin Faulkner, Assistant ACV Produ[ct] Manager

John B. Chaplin, Technical Director, A[CV] Programmes

Peter J. Mantle, Chief of Advanced A[CV] Development

Owen Q. Niehaus, Project Director, Advan[c]ed ACV Development

John A. Mullen, Project Manager, US Na[vy] ACV Programme

Harry W. Peterson, Project Manager, U[S] Army ACV Programme

Thomas J. Comer, Director, ACV Operatio[n]

Emanuel Paxhia, Product Engineer, A[CV] Marketing

Theodore W. Musser, Product Engine[er] ACV Marketing

E. Vernon Griffith, Manager and Te[ch] Director, ACV Laboratory

The US Army has taken delivery of three Bell SK-5 (model 7255) which were put into service in Vietnam in 1968. In its AACV (Assault Air Cushio[n] Vehicle) form the craft is armed with a ·50 machine gun in each of two roof positions, a 7·6 mm machine gun in the two rear cabin windows, port an[d] starboard, and a remotely controlled 40 mm M5 grenade launcher. Maximum speed is 60 knots

Bell Aerosystems Company began its air cushion vehicle development programme in 1958. Craft built by the company range in size from the 18 ft XHS3 to the US Navy's ft, 27-ton SKMR-1 Hydroskimmer, largest and most powerful ACV built to date in the USA.

Additionally, the company has rights to manufacture and sell in the United States machines employing the hovercraft principle through a licencing arrangement with the British Hovercraft Corporation and Hovercraft Development Ltd. It has imported seven BHC SR.N5s, which have been re-engined with 7LM-100PD101 gas turbines and designated SK-5s. Three of these have been sold to the US Navy and the others are being used in military training programmes and in Bell's technical and marketing efforts. The company's current activities in this field include technical and field support for the Bell SK-5 PACVs operated by the US Navy and 3 SK-5s operated by the US Army in Vietnam. In addition, Bell has completed its ACV Technology Laboratory adjacent to Niagara Falls International Airport. Development of the 25-ton SK-9 is being deferred pending further market assessement.

K-5 (Model 7232)
A re-engined version of the BHC SR.N5, the SK-5 (Model 7232) has demonstrated its many capabilities during a series of evaluation and operational programmes in the USA and Canada. These included an eight-week 220 mile demonstration tour along the Gulf Coast from Houston, Texas, to Florida; operational evaluation by the Canadian Coast Guard; the first ACV passenger service in the USA in the Oakland-San Francisco Bay Area of California, and a 500 mile round trip in extreme conditions of winter ice from Buffalo, N.Y. to Pelee Island, Ontario.

Three military SK-5s were successfully employed by the US Navy for eight months in Vietnam, where they patrolled the coast-line and the monsoon-flooded interior. As weapons platforms, each craft normally mounted a single or twin .50 machine guns or grenade launchers on the cabin roof. Similar weapons were sometimes mounted in the front and sides of the cabin or on the outer decks.

The three craft, with 40 officers and men, were formed into PACV (Patrol Air Cushion Vehicle) Division 107. In an effort to make the Navy's designation pronounceable, personnel called their craft "Pak-Vees". The Division's main task was the surveillance of coastal traffic to prevent the movement of Viet Cong contraband and to facilitate efforts by the friendly populace to carry their goods to the cities. The craft operated for some time at sea from a 9,000 ton LSD. A gate at the end of the hull opened to permit the craft to leave or enter.

The three craft were employed for ship-to-shore logistics, river patrol, junk and sampan interception, reconnaissance, rescue and ambulance craft. They logged a total of 1,063 hours of operation during their service. None suffered serious damage from enemy action or the extremely difficult terrain.

Experiences from the operations in Vietnam led to modifications of these machines after their return to the United States in late 1966.

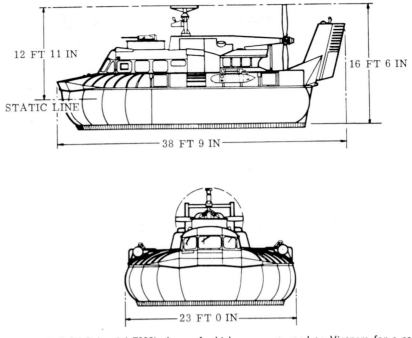

12 FT 11 IN
16 FT 6 IN
STATIC LINE
38 FT 9 IN

23 FT 0 IN

The U.S. Navy Bell SK-5 (model 7232) three of which were returned to Vietnam for a second combat tour in October 1967

These craft were returned to combat in Vietnam in November 1967 and are now operating from a new base.

At the present time only military versions of the SK-5 are being built. Details of a projected commercial version, Model 7250, are given below.

Model 7250
DIMENSIONS, EXTERNAL:

Length	38 ft 10 in (11·84 m)
Beam (inflated trunks)	23 ft 9 in (7·24 m)
Height	15 ft 11 in (4·85 m)

DIMENSIONS, INTERNAL:
Cabin floor area
 12 ft 0 in × 7 ft 8 in (3·66 × 2·34 m)
Door opening
 5 ft 9 in × 5 ft 7 in (1·70 × 1·75 m)

WEIGHTS:

Basic craft empty	9,857 lb (4,470 kg)
Gross weight normal	17,000 lb (7,710 kg)
Gross weight (max overload)	20,000 lb (9,070 kg)

ACCOMMODATION:

Number of crew	1
Seated passengers	16

PERFORMANCE (at 17,500 lb (7,940 kg)):

Maximum speed	60 knots (110 km/h)
Range at 50 knots	175 nautical miles (3·25 km)
Endurance at 50 knots	3·5 hr
Maximum gradient, static conditions	1 in 7·5
Max gradient 50 yd (46 m) capability at 25 knots	1 in 3
Wave clearance at 40 knots	4 ft 6 in (1·37 m)

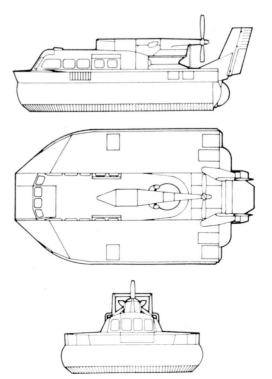

The BELL SK-5 (MODEL 7250) commercial hovercraft which is now in production in the United States. Accommodation is for 16 passengers and an operator

AIR CUSHION VEHICLE MANUFACTURERS
BELL: United States of America

OBSTACLE CLEARANCE:

Solid wall	3 ft 6 in (1·07 m)
Earth mound	5 ft 0 in (1·5 m)
Vegetation	5 ft-6 ft (1·5 m-1·8 m)

Ditches up to 12 ft (3·66 m) wide and 8 ft (2·44 m) deep can be crossed at 20 knots

SK-5 Model 7255

Built under a US Army Aviation Material Command Contract, the SK-5 Model 7255 is Bell's first production craft and the first combat ACV to be produced exclusively in the US to a military specification.

Design started in July 1966 and the first craft left the assembly line in February 1968. Acceptance testing was completed at the end of March and the US Army took delivery of three in April.

The three craft were airlifted to Bien Hoa, Republic of Vietnam, during May 1968 and are now taking part in river operations in the Mekong Delta.

Compared with earlier SK-5 7232, Model 7255 differs in basic design as follows:

In place of the 1,000 hp 7LM-101 PD 101 the more powerful 1,250 shp 7LM-100 JP-102 has been installed.

Puff ports have been added to improve low speed manoeuvrability.

The bow loading door and ramp has been widened to 5 ft 7 in to ease access and permit the entry of a jeep-size vehicle, and the cabin area has been increased by extending the floor of the cabin by 29 in.

A self-contained auxiliary power unit and a split hydraulic system have been added.

Other modifications include the redesign of the electrical system to assist maintenance; the provision of hinged bow door windows and side access doors, and the addition of armour plate protection for the crew and engine.

Although the three US Army SK-5s are identical in design and construction two which are assault air cushion vehicles (AACVs), are more heavily armed than the third, which is a transport air cushion vehicle (TACV).

The two AACV models are equipped with a ·50 machine gun in each of the roof mountings and a 7·6 mm machine gun in both port and starboard rear cabin windows. In addition a remotely controlled 40 mm M5 grenade launcher, capable of firing 225-230 rounds per minute, is mounted on the port bow.

The TACV model will accommodate twelve or more combat-ready troops and substantially more cargo and/or equipment than the assault version. Armament comprises a bow-mounted ·50 machine gun and two 7·62 mm machine guns operated from positions at the two rear cabin windows.

LIFT AND PROPULSION: Power for the integrated lift/propulsion system is provided by a single General Electric LM100 JP102 free turbine engine with a maximum continuous rating of 1,250 hp at 50°F. The output is absorbed by a three-bladed Hamilton Standard variable-pitch propeller of 9 ft diameter and by a 7 ft diameter centrifugal lift fan.

The lift fan and propeller are linked mechanically and the power output of the engine can be apportioned between the propeller and the lift fan allowing speed and hoverheight to be varied to suit prevailing operating conditions.

CONTROLS: Steering is by means of two aerodynamic rudders hinged to the rear of the tail fins. Directional control is also assisted by a hydraulically-operated skirt lift system and, below 15 knots, by puff ports.

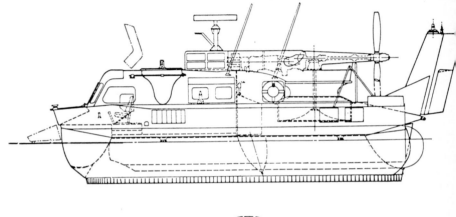
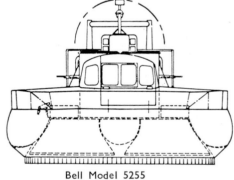

Bell Model 5255

US Navy Bell SK-5s (model 7232), which had successfully completed one eight-month tour of Vietnam, were returned to the USA for modifications and overhaul in January 1967 and are now back in service in Vietnam. Modifications included the installation of auxiliary fuel tanks, additional communications equipment, new segmented skirts and puff ports for improved directional control.

wo electrically actuated elevators give
ch trim at cruising speed.

LL: The hull and superstructure are built
onventional aircraft light alloys. 6061T6
minium has been used in the fabrication of
as susceptible to corrosion. The basic
icture comprises a centre section and two
board sections. The centre section includ-
he cabin, fuel tank, lift fan bays and a
tform which carries the tail unit. A
yancy tank is incorporated in the extreme
position of this platform.

xtending below the static waterline the
in also contributes to buoyancy, and for
ed safety, the double-skinned cabin floor
lled with foam plastic. Immediately aft
he cabin is a bay housing a 304 US gallon
-sealing fuel tank, and above this bay is
ubular structure supporting the engine
reduction gearboxes.

ach of the two outboard sections incorpor-
s a buoyancy tank in addition to support-
the flexible skirts. To ensure maximum
ty, the buoyancy tanks are each divided
twelve watertight compartments.

EL AND OIL: Fuel capacity is 304 gal-
s. Oil capacity, main system, 5·4 US
ons; auxiliary system, 1·7 gallons. The
elling point is situated amidships on the
t side cabin top.

EL: JP-4 or JP-5 spec. MIL-T-5624G.

COMMODATION: In the assault role
del 7255 has a crew of seven, comprising
operator, navigator/radar operator, M5
ner, two turret gunners and two 7·62 mm
chine gunners. In the transport role, the
ft requires only an operator and a navigat-
:adar operator.

Entrance to the cabin is through the bow
door/ramp and two side doors at the aft end.
Side doors and turrets provide exits in an
emergency.

SYSTEMS:

ELECTRICAL: Nominal voltage is 28 volts
The main generator is a Westinghouse Type
FA14, 140 amps, 28 volts, driven by the
main engine. Auxiliary generator is an
Onan Model 205 DUA-224R, 88·6 amps,
24-30 volts. Three volt 34 Ah BB433 Nickel
Cadmium batteries are carried. During
engine cranking one battery is removed from
parallel bank to provide stable voltage for
the engine control and instrument circuit.

INSTRUMENT POWER: 115 volt, 400
cycle, 3-phase rotary inverter, dc-driven.

HYDRAULICS: Hydraulic jacks lift the
peripheral skirts at four points and operate
the fore and aft puff ports for directional
control at slow speed. The hydraulic system
is separate from the engine system but uses
the same oil. Pressure is 3,000 psi.

APU: 1-cyl Onan diesel, employed to keep
standard batteries charged and to operate
certain electrical systems when main engine
is not running.

RADAR: Decca 202.

RADIO: Equipment classified.

NAVIGATION EQUIPMENT: Gyro compass, Decca Navigator.

ARMAMENT: single ·50 calibre machine
guns on ring mountings in each of two topside
turrets; single 7·62 mm machine guns on
pintle mounts at side doors, aft cabin, port
and starboard; M5 40 mm grenade launcher,
port bow.

DIMENSIONS, EXTERNAL:
Length overall   38 ft 10 in (11·8 m)
Beam, skirt inflated   23 ft 9 in (7·2 m)
Height, skirt inflated 15 ft 11 in (4·8 m)
DIMENSIONS, INTERNAL:
Cabin floor 12 ft (3·6 m) × 8 ft (2·4 m)
Door opening
    5 ft 9 in (1·75 m) × 5 ft 7 in (1·7 m)
WEIGHTS:
Basic craft, empty   10,200 lb (4,620 kg)
Gross weight   17,000 lb (7,701 kg)
    (Crew, fuel weapons, ammunition)
Maximum overload   4,000 lb (1,812 kg)
Max gross weight   21,000 lb (9,151 kg)
PERFORMANCE (at normal gross weight):
Max speed   60 knots
Range   175 n. miles at 50 knots
Endurance   3·5 hours at 50 knots
Max gradient, static conditions   1 in 7·5
Max gradient (50 yd) capability at 50 knots
                                    1 in 3
Wave clearance at 40 knots   4·5 ft (1·3 m)
OBSTACLE CLEARANCE:
Solid wall   3·5 ft (1·0 m)
Earth mound   5 ft (1·5 m)
Vegetation   5-6 ft (1·5-m-1·8 m)

BELL SK-6

This is a re-engined licence-built version of
the BHC SR.N6. It can seat 33 in a roomy,
soundproofed and air-conditioned cabin, or
alternatively, the passenger seats can be
removed to convert the craft into a freight
carrier with 164 sq ft (15·2 m²) of floor space.
Completely amphibious, it can operate from
relatively unsophisticated bases for search
and rescue missions, firefighting, harbour and
river patrol, high-speed public transport and
as a logistic transport or utility freight carrier.

BELL's SK-6 cruises at 35 knots and accommodates 33 passengers in its soundproofed and air conditioned cabin.   Removal of the passenger
seats will convert it into a high speed freight carrier with a 3½ ton payload

AIR CUSHION VEHICLE MANUFACTURERS

BELL: United States of America

A proposed military, logistics support version, is the SK-6C. This would have a cargo compartment 7 ft 9 in wide by 22 ft long, and carry a 4-ton payload.

The integrated lift/propulsion system is powered by a General Electric 7LM-100 PJ-102 marinised gas turbine, rated at 1,250 hp on a standard day. Maximum speed is 56 knots. Structural details can be found in the UK section.

DIMENSIONS, EXTERNAL:

Length	48 ft 6 in (14·78 m)
Beam (inflated trunks)	23 ft 9 in (7·24 m)
Height	15 ft 11 in (4·85 m)

DIMENSIONS, INTERNAL:

Cabin floor area
 21 ft 8 in × 7 ft 8 in (6·70 × 2·34 m)
Door opening
5 ft 9 in high × 5 ft 7 in wide (1·75 × 1·70 m)

WEIGHTS:

Basic craft empty	11,463 lb (5,200 kg)
Gross weight (normal)	22,000 lb (9,980 kg)
Gross weight (max overload)	25,000 lb (11,340 kg)

ACCOMMODATION:

Crew	1
Seated passengers	33

PERFORMANCE:

Max speed	56 knots (104 km/h)
Range	160 nautical miles (300 km)
Max gradient, static conditions	1 in 10
Max gradient 50 yd (46 m) capability at 25 knots	1 in 3·5
Cruising speed in 4·5 ft (1·2-1·5 m) waves	30-35 knots
Endurance at 50 knots	3·5 hr

OBSTACLE CLEARANCE:

Solid wall	3 ft 6 in (1·07 m)
Earth mound	5 ft 0 in (1·52 m)
Vegetation	6 ft 0 in (1·83 m)

Ditches up to 16 ft (4·9 m) wide and 8 ft (2·4 m) deep can be crossed at 22 knots

BELL SK-9

A twin-engined "stretched" derivative of the SK-5/6 series, the Bell SK-9 uses many of the basic structural components of the earlier craft, and the same powerplants, fan and propeller systems, but will accommodate up to 90 passengers and two crew members, plus two tons of baggage or cargo.

Passenger loading doors are located in the bows and on each side of the cabin to reduce turn-round time. Power is provided by two GE LM100 PJ102 marine shaft-turbines of 1,250 shp, driving two four-bladed 9 ft (2·74 m) diameter propellers, and two 7 ft (2·13 m) diameter centrifugal lift fans. Fuel capacity is 680 US gallons (2,573 litres).

DIMENSIONS, EXTERNAL:

Length	55 ft 8 in (1·73 m)
Width	32 ft 10 in (10·00 m)
Height	16 ft 6 in (5·03 m)

DIMENSIONS, INTERNAL:

Cabin floor
 29 ft 0 in × 17 ft 8 in (8·84 × 5·38 m)
Door opening (bow)
7 ft 4 in × 6 ft 4 in (2·23 × 1·93 m) (plus auxiliary doors)

WEIGHTS:

Normal gross weight	47,000 lb (21,300 kg)
Overload gross weight	52,000 lb (23,600 kg)
Normal payload	17,600 lb (7,980 kg)
Normal useful load	22,750 lb (10,320 kg)

ACCOMMODATION:

Seated passengers	90
Crew	2

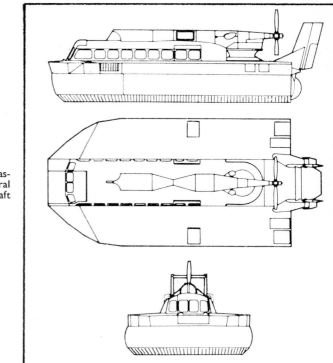

BELL SK-6, 33-seat passenger ferry and general purpose hovercraft

Above: A twin-engined derivative of the Bell SK-5/6 series, the SK-9 will accommodate up to 90 passengers, two crew members and two tons of baggage or cargo

The 90-seat BELL SK-9 has passenger loading doors in the bow and each side of the cabin to reduce turnround time

PERFORMANCE (at normal operating weight):

Max speed	61 knots (113 km/h)
Max gradient, static conditions	12%
Cruising speed in 4·5 ft (1·2-1·5 m) waves	39 knots (72 km/h)

OBSTACLE CLEARANCE:

Solid wall	3 ft 6 in (1·06 m)
Earth mound	5 ft 0 in (1·5 m)
Vegetation	6 ft 0 in (1·8 m)

Ditches up to 18 ft (5·5 m) wide and 8 ft (2·4 m) deep can be crossed at 22 knots (40 km/h)

SK-9B

A freight carrier version of the SK-9, the Bell SK-9B has a bow loading ramp measuring (2·13 m) high by 6 ft (1·83 m) wide, and a ft × 7 ft (2·13 × 2·13 m) hatch in the to permit alongside loading. In addition auxiliary doors are located on either side of the cargo compartment, which accommodates 10 tons of low density freight. The basic design and powerplant arrangement, dimensions and obstacle clearance performance, are all identical to those of the SK-9.

WEIGHTS:

Normal gross weight	43,350 lb (20,560 kg)
Overload gross weight	52,000 lb (23,600 kg)
Normal payload	17,700 lb (8,030 kg)
Normal useful load	22,850 lb (10,370 kg)
Max payload	24,000 lb (10,890 kg)

ACCOMMODATION:

Crew	2

PERFORMANCE:

Max speed at 45,350 lb	65 knots (120 km/h)
Cruising speed in 4·5 ft (1·2-1·5 m) waves	43·5 knots (80 km/h)
Range	195 nautical miles (360 km)
Max gradient, static conditions	12%

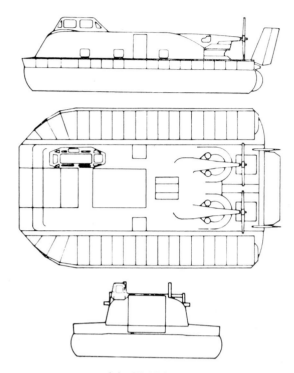

The cargo compartment of the SK-9B freight carrier will accommodate up to 10 tons of low density freight

BELL SK-10

The SK-10 is an assault landing craft for use in conjunction with the US Navy's LSDs (Landing Ships Dock), LPDs (Amphibious Transport Dock), and probably the planned FDL and LHA ships.

Providing almost ten times the working capacity of the SK-6C, it is designed to transport personnel, supplies and equipment through the surf to an appropriate debarkation zone.

The 80 ft long BELL SK-10 ASSAULT LANDING CRAFT will transport personnel, supplies and equipment to a debarkation zone at speeds up to knots. The 60-ton payload can range from a main battle tank—about the heaviest single item of the US Army equipment—to 500 fully armed troops

AIR CUSHION VEHICLE MANUFACTURERS

BELL: United States of America

A 60-ton payload can be carried over stage lengths of up to 100 nautical miles (185 km) at 60 knots in Sea State 3, or 80 knots in Sea State 1. A flexible skirt extends 5 ft 0 in (1·52 m) beneath the hard structure.

The open well-deck space of the craft is sufficiently large to accommodate almost any item of US Army equipment, including a main battle tank. Bow and stern ramps expedite loading and unloading, which can take place in a dry LPD well deck.

A total of 160 troops can be carried in the port and starboard superstructure, with 320 additional troops on the deck when no cargo is carried.

Power is provided by two 12,000 shp gas-turbines driving two 12 ft (3·66 m) diameter centrifugal lift fans, and two 14 ft 6 in diameter four-bladed variable-pitch propellers.

Directional control is provided by the twin propellers, and twin rudders provide yaw control. A "puff port" air bleed system similar to that used on SK-5 and SK-6 provides lateral control.

DIMENSIONS, EXTERNAL:

Length	80 ft 0 in (24·38 m)
Width	48 ft 0 in (14·63 m)
Height	23 ft 0 in (7·01 m)

DIMENSIONS, INTERNAL:

Cargo area	1,300 sq ft (121 m²)
Bow ramp	21 ft 6 in wide (5·65 m)
Stern ramp	13 ft 0 in wide (3·96 m)

WEIGHTS:

Basic weight	133,000 lb (60,300 kg)
Normal gross weight	295,000 lb (133,800 kg)
Normal payload	120,000 lb (54,400 kg)
Normal useful payload	162,000 lb (73 500 kg)

ACCOMMODATION:

Crew	3-4
Troop capacity	up to 500

PERFORMANCE (at normal gross weight):

Max speed	80 knots—Sea State 1
	60 knots—Sea State 3

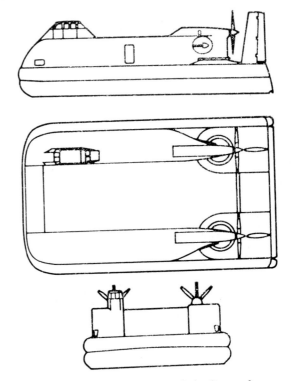

BELL SK-10, 80-knot assault landing craft

Cruising speed	60 knots

ENDURANCE:

60 ton payload	3-4 hours
20 ton payload	12 hours
Max gradient, cont	10%
Vertical obstacle clearance	4 ft 6 in (1·22 m)
Range	100 nautical miles at 60 ton payload
	400 nautical miles at 25 ton payload

BELL SES

Bell engineers are making a number of design studies of trans-ocean AVCs. This artist's impression is of an SES (Sur Effect Ship) configuration with a crui speed of 80 knots. It would have an ove length of 420 ft (128 m), beam of 14 (42·7 m) and weigh 4,000 tons. Lift propulsion would be provided by marin gas-turbines developing 140,000 shp. air cushion is contained by solid sidew with flexible rubber bow trunks to allow craft to pass over water obstacles with damaging the hull.

Artist's impression of a 4,000 ton, sidewall type SURFACE EFFECT SHIP, based on a Bell feasibility study. Overall length of the craft would 420 ft and it would cruise at 80 knots. Marinised gas turbines developing an output of 140,000 hp would power the lift and propulsion system

rtelsen

RTELSEN MANUFACTURING COMPANY NC

AD OFFICE:
343, 18th Avenue, Rock Island, Illinois 61201

LEPHONE:
Area Code 309, 894-2041

RKS:
13 Commercial Street, Neponset, Illinois 61345

LEPHONE:
rea code 309, 894-204

RECTORS:
Villiam R. Bertelsen, President and Chairman of the Board
. W. Bertelsen, Vice President
lberta M. Bertelsen, Secretary-Treasurer
. C. Redebaugh
red Russell

ECUTIVES:
Villiam R. Bertelsen, Designer
. W. Bertelsen, Co-ordinator
Villiam Wirges, Plant Manager
rlo Reck, Field Engineer

r William R. Bertelsen, a general prac-
oner and talented engineer, was one of the
t to build and drive an air cushion vehicle.
is interest was largely inspired by the
ficulties he faced when trying to visit
ients by car over icy roads. Having
covered that a helicopter would be too
ensive to be a practical solution, he set
work to develop a vehicle that could be
ed free of the ground by air pumped
eath its base. Dr Bertelsen designed
first Aeromobile air cushion vehicle in
50, and has since built and tested thirteen
-scale vehicles, ranging from simple

plenum craft to ram-wings. One, the 18 ft long Aeromobile 200-2, was a star exhibit at the US Government's Trade Fairs in Tokyo, Turin, Zagreb and New Delhi in 1961. Construction of the prototype Aeromobile 13, first design to be marketed by the Bertelsen Manufacturing Company, started in 1967. It was completed in early 1968 and trials are under way.

AEROMOBILE 13

A light, amphibious air cushion vehicle of moulded fibreglass construction, Aeromobile 13 introduces a new form of propulsion-control, aimed at giving the operator precise directional control under all normal operating conditions.

The basic vehicle carries an operator and four passengers, but it can also be used for a variety of alternative light utility roles, from cargo carrying to crop dusting.

LIFT/PROPULSION AND CONTROLS: Twin engines drive two 8-bladed fans of identical diameter mounted in two gimballing spherical ducts—one sited forward, one aft—which are selected as needed to provide lift, propulsion and control. The duct units can be rotated throughout 360 degrees to provide variable lift and thrust. Full power can be used for lift by tilting both ducts downwards or to provide thrust by raising them both to the horizontal position when the vehicle is operating in the displacement mode. The system is designed so that the operator has the maximum control over the power available, permitting him to utilise it to the best advantage to cross obstacles,

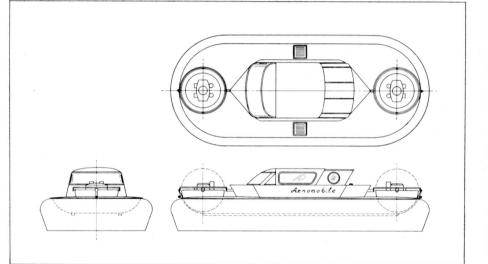

The Aeromobile 13, built by Bertelson Manufacturing Company

Bertelsen's Aeromobile 13 introduces a completely new lift/propulsion system.   Twin engines drive two 8-bladed fans of identical diameter mounted in two gimballing spherical ducts, one forward, one aft, which are rotated as needed to provide lift, propulsion and control

climb sloping terrain or maintain the desired direction in strong winds.

POWER PLANT: Both engines provide lift and thrust through 8-bladed lift fan/propellers constructed by Bertelsen Mfg Co. Engines specified for the Aeromobile 13 are two 40 hp JLO-L594, two 72 hp McCulloch 4318AX or two 90 hp McCulloch 4318G. The JLO-L594 drives 36 in diameter fans, and the McCulloch engines 48 in diameter fans. One 30 gallon fuel tank is located at the rear of the cabin with the filler cap outside the rear window. Additional tanks are optional. Fuel is automotive gasoline with two-cycle oil mixture 10 : 1.

HULL: Moulded fibreglass.

SKIRT: Urethane nylon inflated toroid, with skirt extensions below.

ACCOMMODATION: Entry to the cabin is through a sliding canopy, which gives access to both the operator's and passengers' seats. The operator has a single bucket seat well forward. All instruments and controls are within his reach. Passengers sit three abreast on a single seat which is removable for cargo carrying. The cabin may be heated or air-conditioned if required. A fire extinguisher is mounted inside the cabin and in emergencies the windshield or windows may be kicked out.

SYSTEMS: Electrical, 12 volt alternator, one on each of the engines, voltage control and 12 volt storage battery.

COMMUNICATIONS AND NAVIGATION: Radio equipment is optional. A magnetic compass is standard.

DIMENSIONS, EXTERNAL:

Length, power off	20 ft	(6·1 m)
skirt inflated	21·5 ft	(6·5 m)
Width, power off	8 ft	(2·4 m)
skirt inflated	9·5 ft	(2·8 m)
Height overall, power off, on skids	4 ft	(1·2 m)
skirt inflated	5 ft 6 in	(1·65 m)
Skirt depth	1 ft 6 in	(0·5 m)
Draft afloat, power off	3 in	(77 mm)
Draft, hovering	2 in	(51 mm)
Cushion area	160 sq ft	(14·8 m²)

DIMENSIONS, INTERNAL:

Cabin		
Length	12 ft 0 in	(3·6 m)
Width	5 ft 0 in	(1·5 m)
Height	3 ft 10 in	(1·1 m)
Floor area	60 sq ft	(5·57 m²)
Freight hold (if converted for cargo)		
Length	8 ft 0 in	(2·4 m)
Width	5 ft 0 in	(1·5 m)
Depth	3 ft 10 in	(1·1 m)
Baggage compartment, rear of passenger seats		
Length	2 ft 0 in	(0·6 m)
Width	5 ft 0 in	(1·5 m)
Depth	2 ft 6 in	(0·75 m)

DOORS:
Sliding canopy opens over full 5 ft width, sliding back 4 ft

WEIGHTS:

Normal empty weight	1,700 lb	(771 k
Normal gross weight	2,700 lb	(1,225 k
Normal payload	1,000 lb	(454 k
Max payload	1,200 lb	(544 k

PERFORMANCE (with 180 hp installe normal gross weight):

Max speed over calm water		
60°F	70 knots	(128 km
100°F	60 knots	(110 km
Max continuous speed		
60°F	65 knots	(118 km
100°F	55 knots	(101 km
Cruising speed, calm water	50 knots	(92 km
Turning circle at 30 knots	approx 100 ft	(30
Water speed, 4 ft waves, 15 knot headwi	approx 10 kn
Max wave capability on scheduled ru	4 ft	(1·2
Still air range	130 miles	(210 k
Endurance at cruising speed	2½ ho
Range and endurance in 4 ft waves, 15 knot headwind 25 miles (40 km) 2½ ho
Max gradient, static conditions	15
Vertical obstacle clearance	18 in (458 m

Price (USA) $4,995·00 f.o.b. Neponset, Illinois

Terms 25% in advance, balance on acce tance

Delivery 90 days from firm order specifyi equipment and accessories.

Cushionflight
CUSHIONFLIGHT CORPORATION

HEAD OFFICE AND WORKS:
23700 Sunnymead Blvd., Sunnymead, California 92388

TELEPHONE:
682-5704 (Area Code 714)

EXECUTIVES:
Ralph P. Maloof, President
William Maloof, Jr, Vice-President
Russell L. Hopf, Secretary/Treasurer/Chief Design Engineer
Robert E. Wall, Manufacturing Manager
Joseph E. Wall, Manager of Dicron Division
J. Bruce Frenzinger, Sales Manager

World-wide marketing of the Airscat air cushion vehicle is handled by Revmaster Inc. 930N, Main Street, Riverside, California.

TELEPHONE:
(714) 686-6638

Cushionflight Corporation was founded in California in August 1966 to succeed Aerosphere, an earlier ACV design partnership. The Corporation's Airscat 240, a lightweight, amphibious two-seater, can be licensed by the United States Coast Guard as a special purpose power boat for use over navigable waters.

Airscat 240, a fibreglass-hulled, amphibious two-seater, is capable of speeds up to 35 knots ov calm water

AIRSCAT 240

One of the most successful light air cushion vehicles to date, Airscat 240 is an amphibious two-seater powered by a 52 hp Volkswagen engine and capable of speeds up to 35 knots over calm waters.

Eight years of configuration experiments and component development preceeded the

design of the Model 240, which is now in production.

The production prototype was complet in February 1968, and trials ended in ea May. As of June 1st, 4 units were complet 25 were in production, and firm orders h been received for 514.

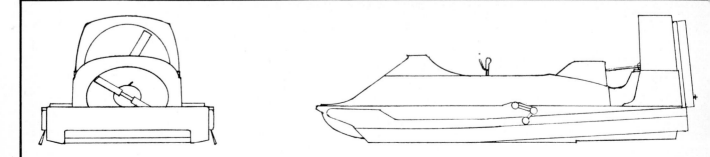

[H]LL: Built in moulded reinforced fibre-
[gla]ss, the hull is of planing sidewall configur-
[ati]on. Steel skids are fitted to the base of
[eac]h sidewall to prevent wear. A retrac-
[tab]le skirt, consisting of a flexible sub-
[str]ucture of the bristle-and-membrane type,
[ena]bles the operator to convert the craft
[qui]ckly from rigid sidewall to simple plenum
[mo]de for beaching and overland operation.
[AC]COMMODATION: Operator and passen-
[ger] are seated side-by-side in a central, open
[coc]kpit. The company is developing a
[win]dshield and cockpit cover which will be
[ava]ilable to owners towards the end of 1968.
[LIF]T AND PROPULSION: Immediately
[aft] of the cockpit is a single, internally-
[mo]unted 45 hp, 4-cyl, 4 cycle Volkswagen
[eng]ine which drives, via a belt and shafting,
[two]-blade axial lift fan, and a ducted two-
[bla]ded, fully-variable, reversible-pitch
[thr]ust fan. Both fans are of metal construc-

tion and adequate protection is provided by
nylon mesh guards.
FUEL: A single 4·7 gallon fuel tank with a
visual supply guage is standard. Regular
automotive gasoline is used.
CONTROLS: Eight vanes aft of the thrust
fan provide directional control. Vanes and
fan pitch are controlled by the movement of a
single column on which is mounted the
throttle lever and skirt retraction switch.
SYSTEMS: Electrical: An engine operated
generator supplies 12 volts to an aircraft
type battery for the operation of the skirt
actuator, running lights and engine starting.
DIMENSIONS, EXTERNAL

Length overall	14 ft 6 in (4·4 m)
Beam overall	6 ft 6 in (1·98 m)
Height	4 ft 8 in (1·42 m)
Draft afloat	6 in (0·15 m)
Draft hovering	variable to cushionborne
Cushion area	84 sq ft (7·8 m²)

DIMENSIONS, INTERNAL

Seat width	3 ft 10 in (1·16 m)
Cockpit length	3 ft 9 in (1·14 m)

WEIGHTS:

Normal gross weight	1,020 lb (462 kg)
Normal empty weight	580 lb (263 kg)
Max payload	440 lb (200 kg)

PERFORMANCE:

Speed (calm water)	35 knots (64 km/h)

Turning circle diameter at 30 knots
400 ft (120 m) on water
Max wave capability
2 ft (0·6 m) waves crest to trough, 20 knot
wind
Max range
50 miles (80 km) with 4 gallon tank
Max gradient, static conditions (at 750
lb (340 kg)) 22%
Vertical land clearance (base of sidewalls)
2-3 in (52-77 mm)
Price $2,995·00, f.o.b., Riverside, California

[D]obson
[DO]BSON PRODUCTS CO
[HE]AD OFFICE:
[5]18 Roxbury Road, Corona del Mar,
California
[TE]LEPHONE:
[7]14 673-6438
[W]ORKS:
[S]anta Ana, California
[DI]RECTOR:
[F]ranklin A. Dobson

[D]obson Products Co was formed by
[Fr]anklin A. Dobson in 1963 to develop and
[m]arket small ACVs either in complete,
[fa]ctory built form, or as kits for private use.
[H]is first model, the Dobson Air Dart, won
[th]e first ACV race in Canberra in 1964.
[Cu]rrent Dobson designs are the single-seat
[Ai]r Car Model B and a higher powered two-
[se]at version, Model D.

[AI]R CAR MODEL B
[The] Air Car Model B is a lightweight, amphib-
[io]us ACV being sold in increasing numbers
[in] the USA to private owners. It normally
[se]ats one person (160 lb) but two may be
[ca]rried at a reduced operating height.
[It] will operate over any reasonably smooth
[an]d level surface—dirt, gravel, grass, snow,
[ic]e, mud or water—at 30-35 mph (48-56 km/h).
[H]ULL: The hull structure is of waterproof
[pl]y. Built in floats provide buoyancy in
[ca]se of engine failure over water. In dis-
[pl]acement condition the craft may be used
[a]s a boat for fishing or wildfowl hunting.
[LI]FT AND PROPULSION: The craft is of
[m]odified plenum type, with straight-through
[fl]ow and has an integrated lift-propulsion-
[co]ntrol system.
[E]NGINE: Normally a Chrysler West Bend
[8]20 two-stroke developing about 7½ hp,
[b]ut a number of alternative engines can be
[fit]ted ranging from 5-20 hp.
[C]ONTROLS: An aircraft-type control
[co]lumn operates two control vents at the
[re]ar to vary thrust and an aerodynamic
[ru]dder for directional control. Forward
[m]ovement of the column opens the vents
[t]o give forward thrust, while moving it aft
[o]pens them in the opposite direction for
[b]raking. Sideways movement operates the
[v]ents differentially for control at low speed
[an]d also turns the rudder for control at high
[s]peed. Centering the column gives maximum

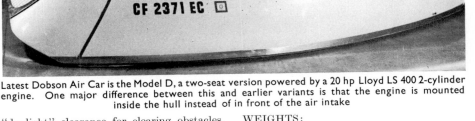

Latest Dobson Air Car is the Model D, a two-seat version powered by a 20 hp Lloyd LS 400 2-cylinder engine. One major difference between this and earlier variants is that the engine is mounted inside the hull instead of in front of the air intake

"daylight" clearance for clearing obstacles.
Extreme forward movement gives maxi-
mum thrust.
DIMENSIONS:

Length	13 ft 0 in (3·96 m)
Width	7 ft 0 in (2·13 m)
Height	5 ft 0 in (1·52 m)

WEIGHTS:

Normal payload	160 lb (72 kg)
Max overload	300 lb (136 kg)
Empty weight	115 lb (52 kg)

PERFORMANCE:
Max speed over land or water
30-35 mph (48-56 km/h)
Endurance About 3 hrs at ¾ throttle
Obstacle clearance
Will clear solid obstacles up to 3 in (75
mm) and waves up to 6 in (150 mm)
Max gradient, static conditions About 10%

AIR CAR MODEL C
Larger and more powerful than the Model
B Air Car, Model C is fitted with a flexible skirt.
By mounting the engine, a 15 hp McCulloch
MC-101 single-cylinder 2-stroke, within the
body, it has been possible to introduce an
air inlet of improved design for the fan.
DIMENSIONS:

Length	14 ft 0 in (4·28 m)
Width	7 ft 10 in (2·39 m)
Height	5 ft 6 in (1·67 m)

WEIGHTS:

Normal payload	160 lb (72 kg)
Max overload	300 lb (136 kg)
Empty weight	140 lb (63 kg)
Fuel capacity	3 US gals (11·5 litres)

PERFORMANCE:
Max speed over land or water
30-35 mph (48-56 km/h)
Endurance About 2 hours at ¾ throttle
Obstacle clearance
Will clear solid obstacles up to about
6 in (150 mm) and waves up to 12 in
(300 mm)
Gradient capability About 20%

AIR CAR MODEL D
Air Car Model D has been developed in
response to a demand for a two-seat machine
in kit form. Design started in 1967 and the
prototype was completed in 1968. The new
machine follows the general lines of previous
models but has a number of refinements.
Performance has been improved and the kit
has been carefully designed for straight-
forward construction with simple tools.
Only woodwork and a small amount of
fibreglassing is necessary.
As with Model C the engine is mounted
internally, affording better protection and
giving the operator easier access in an
emergency.

E

AIR CUSHION VEHICLE MANUFACTURERS
DOBSON / EGLEN-CULL: United States of America

Another feature is a 10 in skirt, a patented combination of flexible and rigid members. The lift and propulsion system is identical to that employed on its predecessors.

ENGINE: A 20 hp Lloyd LS400E drives a single 3 ft diameter aluminium alloy, axial-flow fan. Because of the rugged construction of the fan and its low tip speed (300 ft second) it is not severely affected by water impact should the craft encounter a large wave unexpectedly. The effect of partially submerging the fan in water is to increase the propulsive efficiency and lift the nose. The low tip speed also ensures a very low noise level as well as increasing efficiency.

ACCOMMODATION: Operator, passenger

FUEL CAPACITY: 5 gallons (US) gasoline with oil 40 : 1.

ELECTRICAL SYSTEM: 75 watt generator for battery, lights, starter

DIMENSIONS, EXTERNAL:

Length overall	14 ft 0 in (3·15 m)
Beam overall	7 ft 10 in (2·3 m)
Height overall on landing pads	5 ft 0 in (1·5 m)
Skirt depth	10 in (0·25 m)
Draught afloat	6 in (0·15 m)
Cushion area	75 sq ft (6·9 m²)

WEIGHTS:

Normal all-up weight	630 lb (286 kg)
Normal payload	400 lb (181 kg)

PERFORMANCE (at normal operating weight):

Max speed over calm water (max power)	35 mph (57 km/h)
Max wave capability	1 ft (0·3 m)
Still air range and endurance at cruising speed	50 miles (81 km)
Max gradient, static conditions	20%
Vertical obstacle clearance	1 ft (0·3 m)

Price and terms:
Approximately cost of craft f.o.b. US $985 for kit; $2,350 complete, f.o.b. Los Angeles.

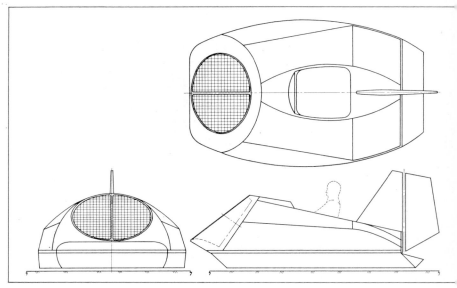

Model D is a larger add more powerful Air Car variant. Maximum speed over land and water about 35 mph (57 km/h)

Dobson Air Car Model D

Eglen-Cull
EGLEN-CULL AIR CUSHION VEHICLES INC

HEAD OFFICE AND WORKS:
214 Wabash Avenue, Terre Haute, Indiana 47801

TELEPHONE:
812-232-2455

DIRECTORS:
Jan Alan Eglen, President
Woodrow S. Nasser, Secretary-Treasurer and Corporate Attorney
Joseph D. Cull, Vice President

BOARD MEMBERS:
M. Hoesman
J. Malooly
N. George Nasser
F. Couch
W. Nickel
W. Thomas
F. Shahady
O. Nasser
G. Kassis
M. Kassis

Eglen-Cull was founded in May 1966 and is a registered corporation in the State of Indiana. The firm acquired patents for a completely new ACV lift-guidance-propulsion

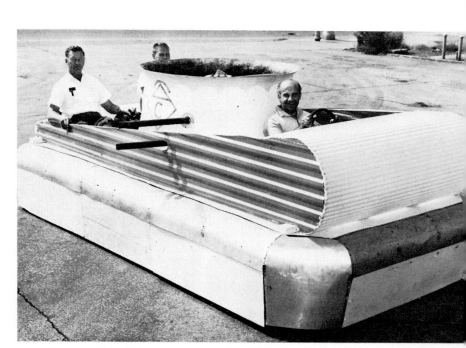

The Eglen-Cull ECX-1 4-6 seat research craft, powered by a 125 hp Lycoming engine

em, and then constructed a prototype
rporating the system. The company has
 active in pursuing the legislation of
's in the USA and has also investigated
 possibility of using ACVs on inland
erways which have hitherto been consider-
unnavigable.

glen-Cull's current research vehicle is the
X-1, preliminary details of which are
en below. The company is now complet-
 the prototype of a 2-3 seat sports ACV
ch if successful will be made available
mercially.

X-1

his is a testbed designed to furnish
rmation for a commercial ACV which is
 in the planning stage. Construction of
craft began in June 1966 and the proto-
e was completed in April 1968.

t the time of going to press the vehicle had
cessfully completed overland trials, but
 not undergone water trials.

T AND PROPULSION: Motive power
 the integrated lift/propulsion system is
plied by a 125 hp Lycoming aero-engine
ving a 4 ft 0 in diameter Arrow Propeller
al impeller. Lift air is fed from the
num chamber in the form of a peripheral
tain. Thrust is provided by bleeding
num air through a diffuser and nozzle
tem.

JLL. The hull structure is built in marine
, aluminium and fibreglass.

ACCOMMODATION: Seats are provided for
an operator and 4-5 passengers.

DIMENSIONS:

Length overall	18 ft 0 in (5·48 m)
Beam overall	7 ft 6 in (2·28 m)
Height overall on landing pads	
	5 ft 0 in (1·52 m)
Daylight clearance	1 ft 0 in (0·30 m)

WEIGHTS:

Weight empty	1,500 lb (679 kg)

EGLEN-CULL TWO-SEAT ACV

The prototype of this elegant 2-3 seat sports
craft was nearing completion at the time of
going to press. Fully amphibious, the craft
is powered by two 20 hp engines and has a
designed cruising speed of 35 knots (65 km/h).

HULL: The hull has a marine ply covered
pine frame with curved sections in fibreglass
and aluminium. Integral with the hull
structure is a slab of polyurethene foam to
provide reserve buoyancy. Skirt is a
peripheral fingered bag with an inflated depth
of 12 in.

POWER PLANT: Mounted immediately aft
of the cockpit are two 20 hp engines driving
two 24 in diameter centrifugal lift fans which
draw air through flush intakes for the
integrated lift/propulsion system. Fan air is
expelled through two rear thrust apertures.
A pusher propeller with its own engine can
be installed for additional thrust.

ACCOMMODATION: Operator and either
one or two passengers are seated side-by-side
in a central open cockpit. Aft of the cockpit
along the cg line is a rectangular box structure housing batteries and the fuel tank.
Cockpit instrumentation includes an air speed
indicator, tachometer, fuel indicator, ammet-
er and roll indicator.

CONTROLS: Flaps facing the rear thrust
apertures are opened differentially for turning.
In addition, the rudders and stabilisers are
mounted directly in the path of the propulsive
air jets to provide directional control at low
speeds. Roll is controlled by a valve which
reduces the air supply to the side skirts and
pitch is similarly controlled by limiting air
to either the bow or stern skirt. Bow puff
ports, port and starboard, will be installed
while the craft is undergoing trials. Steering
mechanism is a combination of yoke and
heel-and-toe pedals.

DIMENSIONS:

Length overall	13 ft 10 in (4·21 m)
Width overall	8 ft 0 in (2·43 m)
Height	5 ft 0 in (1·52 m)

WEIGHTS:

Payload	2-3 passengers plus 150 lb (68 kg)
of baggage, stowed in hold ahead of cockpit	

PERFORMANCE:

Cruising speed over water (estimated)	
	35 knots (65 km/h)
Vertical obstacle clearance	12 in (305 mm)

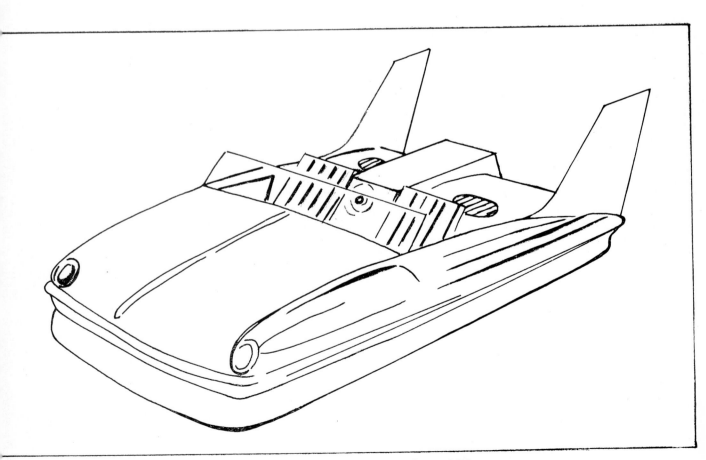

Artist's impression of the Eglen-Cull Sports ACV

AIR CUSHION VEHICLE MANUFACTURERS
GENERAL DYNAMICS: United States of America

General Dynamics

GENERAL DYNAMICS CORPORATION, ELECTRIC BOAT DIVISION

HEAD OFFICE:
   One Rockefeller Plaza, New York, NY
   10020, USA
WORKS:
   1 Eastern Point Road, Groton, Connecticut,
   06340
TELEPHONE (Works):
   203 446-5960
LONDON OFFICE:
   General Dynamics, 54 Grosvenor Street,
   London, W1, England
PARIS OFFICE:
   General Dynamics, Rue de Bassano, Paris
   8e, France
BRUSSELS OFFICE:
   General Dynamics, 23 Rue De La Lois,
   Brussels 4, Belgium
OFFICERS:
   R. Lewis, President and Chairman of the
   Board
   W. C. Bolenius
   H. S. M. Burns
   S. C. Coleman
   E. B. Finucane
   J. M. Laddon
   M. T. Moore
   D. Packard
   J. A. Sargent
   L. D. Welsh
   J. F. Floberg
   D. N. McDonnell
   E. A. Walker
   J. D. Pierce, General Manager
   Dr H. E. Sheets, Programme Development
   Director
   D. E. Kidder, Director of Long Range
   Planning and Marketing
   V. T. Boatwright, Jr., Director of Research
   and Development
   A. G. Anderson, Surface Effect Ships (SES)
   programme Manager

General Dynamics has been active in the
air cushion vehicle field since 1960, when the
Convair Division participated in some early
theoretical work on internal aerodynamics
and model testing under contract to the US
Navy's Bureau of Ships.

In 1962, reponsibility for coordination of
activity in this field was vested in the
Electric Boat Division, and a concentrated
research and development programme was
established.

In 1962-1963 Electric Boat Division was a
participant in the Navy's Hydroskimmer
(SKMR-1) programme, through the design,
construction, and testing of the four cushion
lift fans, and naval architectural consulting
services.

Company-funded work in SES development
has been conducted in the areas of internal
and external aerodynamics, stability and
control, flexible understructures, systems
analysis of the shipyard fabrication of large
Surface Effect Ships, parametric studies
applied to the design and performance of
SES, theoretical performance, and extensive
tow tank testing to define optimum configurations including combinations of rigid
sidewalls and flexible skirts.

Late in 1964, the decision was made to build
a man-carrying research craft, the SKIP-1,
to serve as a test bed of sufficient scale to
provide experimental verification of theoretical work.

General Dynamics is continuing and
amplifying the technical tasks established by
the objectives of the US Government's Joint
Surface Effect Ships Programme Office.
Studies have been conducted under contract
in the areas of resistance in waves, structural
loading criteria, design specifications, lift
system analysis, and design studies of large
SES and assault craft. Recently a proposal
was submitted to the JSESPO in Washington,
DC for the design, construction and testing
of a 100 ton SES Test craft which will

contribute to the determination of
feasibility of larger (500-4,000 ton) SES cr

SKIP-1

This comparatively small ACV incorpora
new concepts in flexible nozzle and b
design. It is basically a research vehicle a
was built in 1965 to verify laboratory theo
of design and performance. The cont
system has been designed to permit maxim
latitude of operation. The design will a
permit future variations of periphe
appendages, lift systems and bow configu
tions.

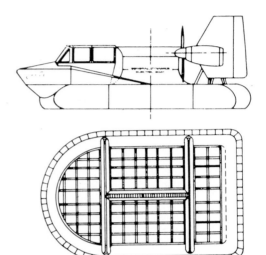

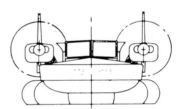

SKIP-1 employed by General Dynamics Electric Boat Division to verify
laboratory theories on design and performance   Completed in 1965,
it has been operated at speeds up to 60 knots and overload gross weights
up to 6,100 lb

The General Dynamics SKIP-1 (Skimmer Investigation Platform) employed to verify laborat
theories on design and performance

KIP-1 has logged over 250 hours, has
achieved speeds in excess of 60 knots over
water and has operated in waves up to 4 ft
(1·21 m) high.

LIFT AND PROPULSION: A 180 hp
Lycoming IVO-360-A1A drives a 64 in
diameter wood and monel propeller fan with
radial diffuser for lift. Two 115 hp Lycoming
0-235-C1Bs, drive two 61 in (1,550 mm)
diameter twin bladed Hartzell variable pitch
propellers for thrust. The craft utilises a peripheral jet with cross-jet compartmentation,
dividing the platform into three athwartship
compartments. The largest, central compartment is also divided down the centre line by a
fore and aft flexible skeg. The flexible nozzles
are made of a composite of airmat and
polyurethane coated neoprene/nylon fabric.
CONTROLS. Control is achieved through
the use of spoilers in the peripheral and
compartmentation jets, air rudders and the
variable-pitch propellers.

HULL: The structure consists primarily of a
welded aluminium alloy raft-like frame, with
glass fibre panels top and bottom, overlaid
with honeycomb above the distribution
plenum chamber.

ACCOMMODATION: The cabin accommodates either four people, or two with instrumentation. Access to the cabin is through a
sliding plexiglas canopy. The driver's station is located forward at the port side of the
cabin. The seat is adjustable fore-and-aft.
A similar seat is provided on the starboard
side for an observer.

A centre console is located between the
two seats and provides a simple presentation
of all essentials required to operate SKIP-1,
including engine condition instruments,
switches and gauges for system operation
and monitoring and levers for the thrust
engines. Lift engine controls are located on
the driver's left side. All directional and
attitude controls are readily accessible to the
driver. Two rudders located in the propeller
slipstream are controlled by a foot-operated
rudder bar to provide directional control.
Throttles on the centre console control speed
and provide additional directional control.
Roll vanes actuated by the control wheel
provide lateral translation. Pitch vanes
actuated by the control wheel provide pitch
trim.

Safety and Marine Equipment:
Life Jackets (AR) and life raft
Seat Belts
Portable fire extinguisher and axe

Roll bar
Anchor and rope
Signal pistol and cartridges, shark repellent
SYSTEMS:
ELECTRICAL SYSTEM: Two 25 amp 28
volt DC generators are installed on the
propulsion engines. Two 12 volt batteries
provide for engine starting, secondary 24 volt
power and 12 volt power for instruments.
FUEL SYSTEM: Fuel for the lift engine is
carried in two tanks forward. Twin tanks
aft supply fuel for the propulsion engines.
Electrical boost pumps and engine driven
pumps are incorporated in each fuel system.
HYDRAULIC SYSTEM: A pump driven by
the port engine supplies pressure to the
hydraulic system which is located on the aft
deck. Hydraulic pressure for pitch change
actuation is supplied to servo valves mounted
on the propellers.
APU: 2,650 watt, 115 volt Sears Alternator
supplies 60 cycles 115 volt direct and 400
cycle 115 volt through inverter for instrumentation power.
COMMUNICATIONS AND NAVIGATION:
Bendix two-way marine radio including test
and marine band frequencies. Navigation
lights. Magnetic compass.
DIMENSIONS, EXTERNAL:

Length overall	22 ft 6 in (6·8 m)
Breadth overall	13 ft 0 in (3·9 m)
Height overall	10 ft 2 in (3·09 m)
Skirt depth	20 in
Cushion area	212 sq ft (19·6 m²)
Draft afloat	2 ft 0 in (0·6 m)

WEIGHTS:

Overload	6,000 lb (2,718 kg)
Basic operating	4,580 lb (2,079 kg)
Empty weight	3,850 lb (1,748 kg)

Artist's concept of a 90 ton surface effect testcraft, resulting from a recently completed conceptual
and parametric design study by the Electric Boat division of General Dynamics. The craft uses a
modified captured air bubble (CAB) concept in which the air cushion is contained between two
sidewalls with flexible seals at bow and stern

PERFORMANCE:

Maximum speed calm water	60 knots (84 km/h)
Cruise speed	45 knots (78 km/h)
Turn radius at 35 knots	360 ft (109·7 m)
Max wave height at 45 knots	1 ft 6 in (0·15 m)
Range	100 miles (160 km)
Endurance	2 hours
Max gradient	1 in 6
Obstacle clearance	1 ft 8 in (0·50 m)

90-TON SURFACE EFFECT SHIP TEST CRAFT

A $200,000 contract extension has been
awarded to the Electric Boat division of
General Dynamics for the continuing development of a 90-ton Surface Effect ship test
craft.

The Joint Navy-Maritime Surface Effect
Ship (SES) Programme Office made the award
following the recent completion of a conceptual design study by the Electric Boat
division. Three other divisions, Convair,
Quincy and Electro Dynamics participated
in the design study.

The goal of the study was to achieve a craft
with a calm water speed of at least 80 knots
and capable of operating in 6 ft (1·8 m)
waves.

The craft proposed in the study uses a
modified captured air bubble (CAB) concept,
with the air cushion contained between two
sidewalls, with flexible seals at bow and stern.

4,000-TON SES

Preliminary design studies are continuing
on an ocean-going 4,000 ton SES capable of
operation at speeds of 80-100 knots (148-298
km/h).

AIR CUSHION VEHICLE MANUFACTURERS
GUNDERSON: United States of America

Gunderson

GUNDERSON HOVERCRAFT CO

HEAD OFFICE:
Twin Valley, Minnesota, 56584

TELEPHONE:
216-584-2185

PROPRIETOR:
Thomas M. Gunderson

Tom Gunderson designed the first of his "Flying Plywood Disks" in 1965 and the prototype successfully completed its trials the following year. His company now produces four designs; two ACV crop sprayers, one propeller-driven, one wheel-driven; a low price Styrafoam runabout, and a high speed vehicle designed for traversing ice and snow.

FLYING SAUCER CROP SPRAYER

The Flying Saucer Crop Sprayer has been designed specifically for agricultural use. First air cushion vehicle in the USA to be licenced for crop spraying it was in use throughout 1967 in the State of Minnesota.

HULL: Basically this is a circular plywood platform, 12 ft in diameter, with a 24 in rubber-covered Nylon skirt attached to the periphery. The central section carries the powerplant, control position and a 30-gallon chemical tank. The two outer sections are hinged to fold upwards to facilitate transport. Beneath the hull are 4 × 8 boat trailer wheels to allow the craft to be towed as required, without the need for a special trailer. The wheels are about 6 in above the ground when spraying.

Spray booms mounted beneath and on each side of the hull enable the vehicle to spray a 32 ft swath.

LIFT AND PROPULSION: The craft is of

Operating speed of the Gunderson Flying Saucer Crop Sprayer is 15 mph. It can spray all p[ ] crops not more than 6 in and will cover 8 acres on 20 gallons of spray.

simple plenum design, with two 6-7 hp Tegumseh engines driving two horizontally-mounted 30 in (750 mm) diameter propellers for lift, and a single 15 hp Hirth driving a twin-bladed propeller for propulsion.

Steering is by means of an aerodynamic rudder sited in the propeller slipstream and operated by a steering wheel. The only other controls are the throttle levers for the three engines.

The latest model of the Saucer Sprayer is a combined ground effect machine and wheeled vehicle, and rides on three wheels, two at the rear and one at the front. The front wheel provides steering and the rear wheels propulsion, throttling of the lift engines allowing the selection of weight transference to the wheels as required. During normal spraying operation the wheels carry around 15% of the total load.

DIMENSIONS (standard model)
Diameter   12 ft 0 in (3·6
Height overall on landing pads
                                      3 ft 0 in (0·9
Skirt depth   2 ft 0 in (0·6
Draft afloat   6 in (0·15
WEIGHTS:
Normal all-up weight   600 lb (272
PERFORMANCE:
Max speed over land   20 mph (32 km[ ]
The craft normally operates over land [ ] 15 mph (24 km/h) and at this speed [ ] cover 8 acres with 20 gallons of chemic[ ] While the craft is amphibious in the se[ ] that it can cross waterlogged fields, it is [ ] designed for traversing lakes and rivers.
Price: f.o.b. Twin Valley, Minnesota: $2,450 Air Drive model, $1,850·00 Ground Dr[ ] Model.
Terms by arrangement.

Research Affiliates
RESEARCH AFFILIATES INC

HEAD OFFICE:
12401 River Road, Potomac, Maryland
20854

DIRECTORS:
William H. Dunham, President and Chairman of the Board
Dr F. Harding, Treasurer
Dr R. A. Cowley, Secretary
Dr R. K. Thompson, Vice-President

Research Affiliates Inc was founded in 1961, and has since been engaged on a research and development programme for combined aerodynamic lift and ground effect machines (CAL-GEMS). A report on the concept is being completed for the US Navy. Work is being undertaken in conjunction with John J. McMullen Associates of New York, and a prototype model is nearing completion.

All military rights for the patents associated with the design have been assigned to the US Government, and all commercial rights are retained by William H. Dunham, who began research and experimental work on craft of this type in 1959.

The CAL-GEM concept is seen as an aerodynamically stable craft which promises to exceed the cruising efficiency of present ACV designs, and will at the same time provide ample capacity for cargo and passengers. It is being designed to carry large loads at speeds up to 100 knots over flat or rolling surfaces at heights ranging from several inches to several feet, and smaller loads up to a height of three thousand feet.

Two methods are used for producing lift. The first, as a combined aerodynamic lift and ground effect machine (CAL-GEM) and the second by aerodynamic lift as a GETOL or a GESTOL (ground effect take-off and landing or ground effect short take-off and landing craft).

Up to a height of about six inches, or when there is little or no forward motion, all lift is provided by the air cushion. As the forward velocity and altitude are increased, the aerodynamically-shaped hull augments the cushion lift. At about 25 ft, the pilot has a choice between providing all the lift by the aerodynamically-shaped hull, or augmenting it by means of a jet flap.

Use of the jet flap will allow the vehicle to maintain altitude at a lower forward velocity as well as augmenting the forward thrust, but the air cushion is destroyed when the jet flap is used. The air cushion or two inflated balloons may be used to eliminate or sharply reduce the landing shock.

At low altitudes the vehicle is trimmed in pitch by changing the flow of air over the forward trailing edge. At higher altitudes it can also be trimmed in pitch by changing the jet angle.

Two designs are being developed. RAM 1 for long range operation in open areas, and RAM 11 for short range operation in more confined surroundings.

80

AIR CUSHION VEHICLE MANUFACTURERS
US ARMY AVIATION MATERIAL LABORATORIES / SKIMMERS INCORPORATED: United States of America

Skimmers
SKIMMERS INCORPORATED

HEAD OFFICE:
PO Box 855, Severna Park, Maryland,
21146
TELEPHONE:
301-647-0526
DIRECTORS:
M. W. Beardsley, President and General
Manager
H. L. Beardsley
W. D. Preston

Skimmers Inc was formed in April 1966 to produce plans and components for use by homebuilders in constructing the Fan-Jet Skimmer sport ACV. It is affiliated with the Beardsley Air Car Co.

Overseas Representation
United Kingdom: The Hydro Marina, St. Osyth, Essex.

FAN-JET SKIMMER

Fan-Jet Skimmer is one of the world's first practical solo sport ACVs. It was designed by Col. Melville Beardsley, a former USAF technical officer, and one of the pioneers in ACV development in the United States.

The Fan-Jet Skimmer was designed to be the simplest and cheapest one-man ACV that could be devised. Some twenty craft of this type have been built to date.

HULL: The main structural component is a tractor inner tube, giving 700 lb of buoyancy, around which is an aluminium framework of square tube, and L girders. The topside bow profile is in plywood. The structure is decked in vinyl-coated nylon fabric, which is also used for the self-extending skirt system.

LIFT AND PROPULSION: Power for the integrated, lift/propulsion system is provided by a Chrysler 2-cycle 6 hp engine, driving an 18 in axial flow fan. The fan has a marine plywood hub with 9 sheet metal formed blades. The primary air flow, used for direct thrust is ejected through a propulsive slot control flap located aft of the fan duct. The area of the slot can be varied by a hinged-flap controlled by a lever. This and the throttle lever and ignition switch are the only controls. The secondary air flow, for cushion lift, passes into a rearward plenum chamber.

CONTROL: The craft is steered by kines-thetic control (body movement) which the designer feels is the ideal method of control for a craft of this size.

DIMENSIONS:
Length overall	9 ft 8 in (2·9 m)
Beam overall	6 ft 2 in (1·8 m)
Height overall on landing pads	36 in (0·9 m)
Skirt depth	9 in (0·2 m)
Draft afloat	5 in (0·12 m)
Cushion area	44 sq ft (4·0 m²)

WEIGHTS:
Normal all-up weight	250 lb (113 kg)
Normal payload (operating)	150 lb (68 kg)
Maximum payload	180 lb (397 kg) app

PERFORMANCE:
Max speed, calm water	18 mph (29 km/h)
Cruising speed, calm water	18 mph (29 km/h)
Max wave capability	6 in app (153 mm)
Still air range	35 miles app (56 km)
Max gradient, static conditions	5° app
Vertical obstacle clearance	5 in (127 mm)

For full over-the-hump performance with an operator weighing more than 175 lb the installation of two power plants is reco-mmended—each identical with the standard

singe power unit. With an operator wei-ing up to 225 lb the speed of the twin approx 20% greater than the standa single engine.

With the overall length of the twin-eng model increased to 11 ft 2 in, it will carry useful load of 350 lb at maximum speeds approximately 35 mph over smooth land a 22 mph over calm water.

Price: USA, f.o.b. Severna Park, Maryla
$1,200·00 for complete vehicle
$600·00 for kit
Terms of payment   50% do

The Fan-Jet Skimmer

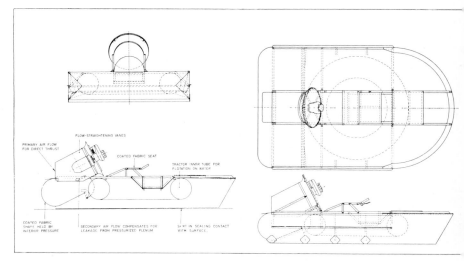

The Fan-Jet Skimmer, designed by Melville Beardsley

US Army Aviation Laboratories
US ARMY AVIATION MATERIAL LAB-ORATORIES

HEADQUARTERS:
Fort Eustis, Virginia, USA 23604

OFFICERS:
Col Edwards M. Soler, Commanding Officer
Larry M. Hewin, Technical Director
Charles D. Roach, Director of Research
William E. Sickels, ACV Project Engineer

The US Army Aviation Material Labora-tories is responsible for supporting research in Army aviation related areas, including air cushion vehicles, which were studied first in 1958. The object of the unit is, primarily, to provide a technological base that will support development of vehicles to extend Army mobility.

The unit is concerned with the developme of off-road vehicles like the SK-5, which a capable of operating over open areas of deser mud flats, snow, tundra or organic soil. Tw small vehicles developed by the unit are th Gemulance, an air cushion borne stretch unit, and the Mine Search Head Carrie described in the 1967-68 edition.

ESPO

nt Surface Effect Ships Program Office

AD OFFICE:
JS Naval Research and Development
Center, Carderock, Maryland

ECUTIVES:
Marvin Pitkin, Program Manager
ames L. Decker, Deputy Program Manager
Robert L. von Gerichten, Commander US
  Navy, Director, Plans and Program
Dr. Alfred Skolnick, Commander US Navy,
  Director, Technology
R. C. Taruax, Director System Engineering
Robert L. von Gerichten (acting), Director
  Requirements

The term "Surface Effect Ships (SES)",
is first used several years ago by the
aritime Administration, in studies perform-
by them.   As used in the current context,
ES simply implies a "large" or "ship" size
  cushion vehicle (ACV), regardless of
ecific configuration.

n the United States, both the Department
the Navy and the Maritime Administra-
n, under the Department of Commerce,
onsored and participated in early and
lependent studies and experimental efforts
 Air Cushion Vehicles (ACV) or Surface
fect Ships. These early efforts clearly
dicated the great potential that these type
aft have for both commercial and military
oplications.

Realizing the common interest involved,
nd reinforced by a Presidential Directive to
udy Surface Effect Ships jointly, both
epartments entered into an agreement in
id-1960 to establish the basis for accom-
lishing a cooperative research program
hich would provide basic technological
nowledge and data sufficient to determine

the feasibility of building and operating large
fast surface effect ships in the order of
4,000-5,000 tons and capable of 80 knots or
higher speed.

This joint agreement initiated a joint
program involving broad governmental
laboratory and industry participation. The
objective is to advance the state of technology
of SES up to a point where design parameters
and technological problems can be predicted,
identified and measured with reasonable
confidence. The engineering and technical
framework is thus laid for later and independent development of naval and commercial
ships.

A Joint Steering Committee was established
to provide policy and technical guidance to
the Program Manager. Representing the
Department of Commerce are the Deputy
Assistant Secretary for Science and Technology and the Acting Chief, Office of Research and Development, Maritime Administration. Representing the Department of
the Navy are the Director, Air, Surface and
Electronic Warfare Division, Office of the
Deputy Chief of Naval Operations (Development) and the Technical Director, Ship
Concept Design Division, Naval Ship
Engineering Centre.

Mr Marvin Pitkin, an industrial executive
with a broad background in research and
engineering in government and industry, was
appointed Program Manager. The Joint
Surface Effect Ships Program Office under
his direction is currently quartered at the
US Naval Research and Development
Center, (formerly the David Taylor Model
Basin), Carderock, Maryland.

The program itself follows a paralleling
technology and system engineering approach.
The technology portion will investigate and

solve the crucial problems in such areas as
aero-hydrodynamics, propulsion, structures,
and related technologies, thus forming a
sound and fundamental basis in depth for
advancing the program. The paralleling
system engineering portion will serve to
combine the necessary technologies into an
overall system—the ship. Also falling under
the system group will be the actual verification of the studies, analysis and technological
developments by use of experimental test
craft including operations, test, reporting and
the preparation of design manuals for future
SES.

Included in the overall program is the
coordination and development of various
environmental, applications, and trade-off
studies and analysis

Recently, contracts were negotiated with
three different contractors for conceptual and
parametric design studies for a high speed
SES test craft of less than 100 gross tons.
The craft will be expected to meet or improve
upon the following major design requirements
or characteristics.

Gross weight	less than 100 short tons
Maximum speed	
80 knots acceptable; 100 knots preferred	
Sea state	operation in 6-foot waves
Propulsion	2 gas turbine engines and supercavitating propeller or equivalent systems

The three contractors—Aerojet-General
Corp, Bell Aerosystems and General Dynamic's Electric Boat Division—are to submit
their studies within five months. JSESPO
is currently negotiating for the design
construction and test of a 100-ton test craft
which is expected to be completed during the
fiscal year 1971.

Two CAB (Captured Air Bubble) test craft, the 51 ft 6 in, 15-ton XR-1A and the 26 feet, 1½-ton XR-3, are being used by the Joint Surface
Effect Ships Program Office as basic technology experimental tools

THE UNION OF SOVIET SOCIALIST REPUBLICS

Krasnoye Sormovo
KRASNOYE SORMOVO
ADDRESS:
   Gorky

This shipyard began work in the ACV field by building a five-passenger air cushion river craft known as the Raduga (Rainbow). It has completed the prototype of a 50-passenger ACV, the Sormovich, and is now producing the 48-passenger Gorkovchanin sidewall craft, designed for service on narrow, winding rivers. Under development are the Opytny and the Zarya, two air-lubricated-hull craft for service on particularly shallow waterways, and the Taiga, a 26 knot utility craft designed for work at timber felling centres.

GORKOVCHANIN

The Gorkovchanin is a 48-seat rigid sidewall ACV designed for water-bus services on shallow winding rivers. The craft is now in series production and the prototype was demonstrated at Gorky in October 1968. Like the Opytnyi "glissyor" type craft, the Gorkovchanin runs bow-on to flat sloping banks to embark passengers.

LIFT AND PROPULSION: A 180 hp engine mounted at the stern drives a centrifugal fan for the plenum lift system and a waterjet unit for propulsion. The fan normally absorbs about 30 hp. A simple bag skirt is fitted across the bow. At the stern the sidewalls are submerged to a depth of 0·72 in (30 cm).

CONTROL: Rudders located in the waterjet stream provide directional control. Reversing is achieved by waterflow deflectors.

HULL: Similar appearance to that of the

The Gorkovchanin, a 48 seat rigid sidewall waterbus, propelled by a waterjet system. At po of call the craft runs bow-on to a flat sloping bank to pick up passengers

Opytnyi, the hull is built in corrosion-resistant marine light alloy.

ACCOMMODATION: Seats are provided for 48 passengers and a crew of two. Access to the passenger saloon is through a single door

located at the bow in the centre of wheelhouse.

PERFORMANCE:
   Normal service speed
                        19-22 mph (30-35 kr

The Gorkovchanin rigid sidewall waterbus is powered by a 180 hp diesel engine and has a service speed of 30-35 km/h

The experimental AVP-4XAL, designed and built by students at the Kharkov Aviation Institute

KHARKOV AVIATION INSTITUTE

An experimental disc-shaped ACV, the AVP-4XAI, has been designed and constructed by students at the Kharkov Aviation Institute.

A single engine at the rear drives a horizontally mounted lift fan to provide a peripheral curtain, and two shrouded propellers one located each side amidships, for propulsive thrust. The driver sits in a small cabin at the forward end of the craft. Directional control is provided by two aerodynamic rudders, one attached at the rear of each of the shrouds, and operating in the propeller slipstream. Small wheels are fitted on either side of the hull to facilitate handling and parking. Max speed of the craft is 9·3 mph (15 km/h).

OPYTNYI

Experiments with high-speed "aeroglisseur" (literally air-slider) water buses, capable of navigating the many shallow waterways in the Soviet Union, began in 1963.

The object was to develop a vessel for services on shallow waters, with depths of only 20 in (0·5 m), at speeds of at least 21·5 knots (40 km/h). The first operational prototype is the Opytnyi (experimental) waterbus, which is of lightweight, aluminium construction, and propelled by a waterjet. A localised ram-air cushion, introduced by an upswept nose and contained on either side by shallow skegs, lifts the bows clear of the water as the craft picks up speed.

The hull has a flat bottom and this, combined with the elevated bow, and the absence of a water propeller, allows the vessel to run bows-on to any flat sloping bank, to load or off-load passengers and freight.

Opytnyi, which is powered by a 900 hp diesel, carries 83 passengers and a crew of two. It draws only 16 in (40 cm) and has a speed of 24 knots (45 km/h) in deep water; the reduction of speed in shallow water does not exceed 10%.

In 1964-5, the vessel went into experimental service on two shallow rivers in Central Russia—the Volkhov and Msta. In 1967 it travelled 160 miles (250 km) down the Sukhona in Northern Russia and easily negotiated logs being rafted on the river.

The Raduga experimental ACV equipped with a fingered bag type skirt

AIR CUSHION VEHICLE MANUFACTURERS
KRASNOYE SORMOVO: The Union of Soviet Socialist Republics

RADUGA

This experimental amphibious ACV was completed at the Krasnoye Sormovo shipyard in the summer of 1962 and is reported to have attained a speed of 100 km/h (62 mph) during trials.

Built originally as a peripheral jet type, it is now being used to develop control techniques, and provide amphibious experience and data on skirt design.

LIFT AND PROPULSION: The craft is powered by two 220 hp air-cooled riadal engines. One, mounted amidships, drives a 5 ft 11 in (1·8 m) 12-bladed lift fan; the second, mounted on a pylon at the stern, drives a two-bladed propeller for propulsion. The fan delivers air to the cushion via a continuous peripheral skirt, the bow and side sections of which are of the fingered bag type.

HULL: Riveted aluminium construction.

ACCOMMODATION: The cabin seats five.

CONTROLS: Directional control is provided by an aerodynamic rudder operating in the propeller slipstream.

DIMENSIONS:

Length	30 ft 10 in (9·40 m)
Beam	13 ft 6 in (4·12 m)

WEIGHTS:

Operating weight	3 tons

PERFORMANCE:

Maximum speed	75 mph (120 km/h)
Endurance	3 hours

SORMOVICH

Launched in October 1965, the Sormovich is a 50-passenger ACV designed by Mr Valery Schoenberg, Chief Constructor of the Krasnoye Sormovo Shipyard, with the assistance of the N. E. Zhukovski Central Institute of Aerodynamics.

In general layout, the craft represents a "scale-up" of the configuration tested with the Raduga.

LIFT AND PROPULSION: All machinery is located aft behind a sound-proof bulkhead to keep down the noise level in the passenger compartments. A single 1,800 shp Ivchenko AI-24 shaft-turbine, at the extreme stern, drives the integrated lift/propulsion system. Its output shaft passes first to a differential gearbox from which shafts extend sideways to the two four-blade ducted variable-pitch propellers. A further shaft runs forward from the differential to a bevel gearbox from which a drive-shaft runs vertically upward to the 12-blade lift-fan mounted under the intake on the rear of the roof of the vehicle. Cushion pressure is 41 lb/sq ft (200 kg/m²).

CONTROLS: Each propeller duct contains two hydraulically-actuated rudders, working in the slipstream.

HULL: Light alloy buoyancy type, with peripheral slot for the air curtain. There is a fore and aft stability slot on each side parallel to and about 5 ft (1·50 m) inboard of the peripheral slot.

ACCOMMODATION: The crew compartment at the front contains two seats and is separated from the main cabin by a partition containing a door. The front two rows of seats in the cabin are only four-abreast to facilitate entry through the forward door on each side. The remaining 42 seats are six-abreast, in three-chair units with centre aisle. Aft of the cabin is a wardrobe on the port side, with a buffet opposite on the starbo[ard] side. Then comes the main entry lo[bby] with a passenger door on the port side [and] service door opposite, followed by a t[oilet] (port) and baggage hold (starboard).

An unusual feature of the Sormovich is [that] it is fitted with retractable wheels which [can] be lowered to avoid damage to the hull w[hen] the craft operates over uneven ice or ro[ugh] country. The wheels are carried on ligh[tly] sprung legs, enabling them to ride easily [over] obstructions.

DIMENSIONS:

Length	87 ft 0 in (26·5[0]
Beam	32 ft 9½ in (10·0[0]
Height	19 ft 8½ in (6·0[0]
Cushion area	1,775 sq ft (165

WEIGHTS:

Max loaded weight	21·75 [t]

PERFORMANCE:

Max speed	75 knots (140 k
Hover height	8-12 in (20-30
Range	215 nautical miles (400

TAIGA

This ACV, which has a cargo payload of [ ] tons, has been designed for work at tim[ber] felling centres. It will carry supplies [and] equipment to logging camps and will be [used] to tow small barges in shallow water.

The 12 in (30 cm) air cushion is produce[d by] a gas-turbine engine, driving two lift f[ans.] Taiga is 42 ft 8 in (13 cm) long and 1[9 ft] 8 in (6·00 m) wide and has a speed of 26 kn[ots.]

ZARYA

A smaller version of the Opytnyi, Zar[ya] is generally similar to the earlier craft, [but] has accommodation for only 65 passen[gers]

The SORMOVICH 50-seat ACV passenger ferry.   A single 1,800 shp Ivchenco AI-24 shaft turbine drives the integrated lift-propulsion syst[em.]
Top speed is 75 knots

AIR CUSHION VEHICLE OPERATORS

EUROPE

FRANCE

SOCIETÉ NAVIPLANE COTE d'AZUR

Services with the SEDAM N 300-01 and 02 Naviplanes, both seating 90 passengers, will begin on the Côte d'Azur in June 1969.

ITALY

AERONAVE, NAPLES

Three SR.N6 Winchesters are operating a passenger ferry service between Naples, Ischia and Capri.

SWEDEN

An experimental postal delivery service is being conducted by the Swedish Post Office using a Hover Air Hover Hawk.

SOVIET UNION

MINISTRY OF THE RIVER FLEET

The 50 seat Sormovich ACV is operating eight return trips daily between Gorky on the Volga and Pavlovo on the Oka river, a distance of 60 nautical miles (96 km). During 1968 the new Gorkovchanin sidewall ACV was introduced on services on the Irtysh river.

UNITED KINGDOM

BRITISH HOVERCRAFT CORPORATION

Four craft, one Warden and three Winchesters, are used by the British Hovercraft Corporation for development, training, demonstrations and short term charters.

BRITISH RAIL HOVERCRAFT LTD (SEASPEED)

REGISTERED OFFICE:

222 Marylebone Road, London, NW1

EXECUTIVE HEADQUARTERS:

Marine Court, The Parade, Cowes, Isle of Wight

British Rail Hovercraft Ltd opened a cross-Channel service for passengers and cars with the prototype SR.N4 Mountbatten on August 1st, 1968, and up to mid-October, when the craft was withdrawn from service for modifications, 27,000 pasengers and more than 3,000 cars had been carried between Dover and Boulogne.

The craft is being fitted with a deeper skirt, further sound-proofing and ventilation, and will re-open the service in April 1969. In the summer of 1969 with five trips in each direction at the peak holiday period, British Rail expects to carry up to 2,500 passengers daily between Dover and Boulogne (Le Portel). The company is currently negotiating the purchase of a second SR.N4 hovercraft which would enable 10 trips to be operated in each direction during the summer. They are also negotiating an option on a third SR.N4.

The SR.N4 carries up to 254 passengers and 30 cars at a speed of 70 knots and crosses the Channel in 35-40 minutes. Purserettes sell duty-free cigarettes, wines and spirits on board.

The world's first major international Hovercraft Terminal at Dover is capable of handling up to four hovercraft in international service.

To build the Terminal, engineers reclaimed six and a half acres of land from Dover harbour using chalk dug out locally during the widening of the A2 trunk road.

Over 200,000 cubic yards of chalk with retaining walls were used to form a base for the 500 foot wide Hovercraft ramp and operating apron.

British Rail is the world's biggest operator of commercial hovercraft, and since the company was formed in 1966, more than four million passenger miles have been logged.

On the Solent, British Rail carried 225,000 passengers up to November 1968 on its all the year round routes, an increase of 30 over the 1967 total.

The Southampton-Cowes and Portsmouth Cowes services are operated by the Winchester class SR.N6 hovercraft, with seats and a journey time on each route 20 minutes.

A new service between Portsmouth and Ryde began in 1968 using the HM.2 65-seat ACV. Two HM.2 hovercraft are in use for the 10 minute crossing at speeds in excess of 35 knots.

HOVERLLOYD LTD

ADDRESS:

The Hoverport, Ramsgate, Kent

In July 1965 two shipping companies Swedish Lloyd and the Swedish American Line ordered two SR.N4 Mountbatten hovercraft at a cost of £3½ million from BHC to be delivered in 1968.

Hoverlloyd Ltd was formed by the two companies to operate a cross Channel car and passenger ferry service between Ramsgate and Calais.

During 1966 and 1967, Hoverlloyd leased two 38-seat SR.N6s from BHC with which they operated a passenger service between Ramsgate and Calais. This service, though not commercially viable provided crew and operating experience for the SR.N4 service.

In 1968, the company was unable to begin the service because planning permission had not been granted for the hoverport, so they leased an SR.N6 for the year and operated pleasure cruises from Ramsgate Harbour Building permission was given in June 196

Hoverlloyd will offer frequent ferry service for cars and passengers. The crossing between Ramsgate and Calais will take minutes and there will be fourteen return

Hoverlloyd's International Hoverport at Pegwell Bay, Ramsgate

...s a day in summer, and three a day in
...ter. Additional services will be introduc-
...at Christmas and Easter.

...assengers will be able to buy tickets from
...vel agents, or by making a booking
...ectly with Hoverlloyd or at the hoverport.
...hose travelling with a car will be paying
...y for their car, according to its length.
...e car charge covers all the occupants.

...here will be two tariffs; 'A' and 'B'. 'A'
...ff will be slightly more expensive and is
...plied to approximately nine hundred peak
...e departures, in either direction, according
...a detailed traffic analysis. 'B' tariff is
...aper and accounts for the balance of the
...00 departures listed in the first six months
...operation. The tariffs have been designed
...as to encourage a balance in the origin of
...ss Channel traffic. The company esti-
...tes it will fill nearly 800,000 seats and al-
...st 100,000 car spaces in the summer of
...9.

...he company's hoverport will cover 12½
...es below the cliffs at the north end of
...gwell Bay, Ramsgate. The site is raised
...t above the level of the beach, so that
...erations will not be affected by tides. It
...l consist of a group of long low buildings
...ning parallel to the cliffs. Between the
...ildings and the cliffs will be a car park and
... car reception area which will be joined
...the main Ramsgate-Sandwich road by an
...ess road built up the cliff face.

...n front of the buildings will be a large
...uare concrete apron with a ramp at both
...ners leading down into the sea. The
...N4 will come up one ramp, park on the
...ron in front of the buildings while it loads
...d unloads and then leave down the other
...mp.

...hese buildings will contain the main
...ssenger and car terminal area which will
...clude the inspection halls for Customs and
...migration, shops, cafes, banks and other
...ssenger facilities. Next to this area will
... the administrative offices.

OVERSPEED LTD

...Hoverspeed was formed in January 1968,
...itially to provide a service in the Bahamas
...tween Nassau and The Current, Spanish
...ells and Harbour Island on the island of
...leuthera.

...Two HM.2s will operate in the Bahamas,
...d these are being equipped with air-
...nditioning and refreshment dispensing
...cilities.

OVERTRAVEL LTD

...DDRESS:

...Easton House, 12 Lind Street, Ryde, Isle
... of Wight

...Hovertravel Limited was formed in 1965
...nd is a £120,000 company whose main
...tivity has been the operation of two
...Vinchester SR.N6 hovercraft in the Solent;
...rimarily between Ryde and Southsea. The
...ervice has gained in popularity and the total
...umber of passengers carried between April
...nd October 1968 exceeded 325,000. The
...aximum number of passengers carried in
...ne day (using both craft) was over 3,660.
...On October 8th, 1968, Hovertravel carried
...neir one millionth passenger on the Solent
...ervice since its inauguration in July
...965. The hovercraft in use had accumulat-

At the end of May 1968 a joint demonstration and sales tour was undertaken by Hoverwork Limited in Trinidad, Venezuela, Guyana, Brazil and Argentina. The Winchester used on the tour operated

ed over 10,020 operating hours by the end of
October 1968.

During the winter of 1968/1969, Hovertravel continue to operate their schedule
with eleven return crossings per day
between Ryde and Southsea. The average
crossing time throughout the year is less than
7 minutes for the 4 mile route and the
reliability of the Winchesters has been over
90%.

Hovertravel Limited is now the most
experienced, profit-making ACV operator in
the world, and employs a staff of some 40
including 6 captains, and 5 maintenance
engineers. In association with their subsidiary company, Hoverwork Limited, over 1½
million passengers have been carried—an
estimated 68% of all hovercraft passenger
traffic to date.

In July 1969, Hovertravel Limited will be
announcing their new UK route over which
their first Vosper Thorneycroft VT1 Hoverferry will be introduced.

HOVERWORK LIMITED

ADDRESS:

Easton House, 12 Lind Street, Ryde, Isle
of Wight

Hoverwork Limited is a subsidiary of
Hovertravel Limited and was formed in
1966. The company provides crew training
and charter facilities for all available types of
ACVs, thus bridging the gap between the
operators and manufacturers.

Hoverwork have trained over 30 hovercraft
captains and received some 32 charter contracts, including film sequences and the
operation of two Winchester class SR.N6
hovercraft at Montreal's Expo '67 when
366,633 passengers were carried in 180 days.

The Royal Navy's SR.N6 Winchester fast amphibious communications craft, operating with Naval Party 9802 in the Faulkland Islands in support of Royal Marine Units

As a direct result of the success of the Expo operation, Hoverwork Canada Limited was established as a separate company.

During 1968 Hoverwork's operations have included the successful cold weather trials at Fort Churchill, Manitoba for the Canadian Department of Transport when the average ambient temperature during operations was —25°F and the lowest recorded was —43°F; two demonstration/sales tours jointly with the British Hovercraft Corporation up the Amazon and in Trinidad, Venezuela, Guyana, Brazil and Argentine; the scientific "Amazonas" expedition sponsored by the Geographical Magazine, comprising the first journey by a powered craft up the Rio Negro, through the Casiquiare Canal, down the Rio Orinoco and on to Trinidad in the Caribbean. Hoverwork has also supplied captains for the operation of Winchester hovercraft servicing offshore oil rigs in Brunei, North Borneo.

The company, jointly with Hovertravel Limited, offers a route feasibility investigation service and the companies are actively looking to the expansion of their overseas operations on a permanent route basis. Negotiations are currently being pursued in a number of countries in four continents.

HUMBER HOVERCRAFT SERVICES
ADDRESS:
Union Bank Chambers, Rigby Square, Grimsby, Lincs.

This company was formed in 1968 to operate between Grimsby and Hull.

The service will be provided by two HM.2s, numbers 002 and 008, in standard 60 seat form.

Length of the route is 17 nautical miles (30·5 km), journey duration will be 35 minutes, and the block speed, 30 knots (55 km/h).

MARINE MASTER
ADDRESS:
4 Buxton Road, Weymouth, Dorset

Marine Master is proposing to operate two SR.N4 Mountbattens between Weymouth and Cherbourg starting in 1970. The company has received planning permission to construct a hoverport at Newton's Cove, inside Portland harbour, near Weymouth.

INTERSERVICE HOVERCRAFT UNIT
ADDRESS:
HMS Daedalus, Lee-on-Solent, Hampshire

The Interservice Hovercraft Unit at Lee-on-the-Solent is responsible for the assessment of hovercraft in various military roles, although some pure performance assessments are made. The unit is directed jointly by the Ministries of Defence and Technology, and currently operates one Winchester, three Wardens and an SR.N3.

NOR'WEST HOVERCRAFT
ADDRESS:
City Gate House, Finsbury Square, London EC2

A subsidiary of Denny Hovercraft, this company operates a passenger srevice with a Denny D2 between Fleetwood, Morecambe and Barrow.

ROYAL CORPS OF TRANSPORT, 200 SQUADRON
The operational role of this unit is high speed amphibious logistic support. The squadron was on "shake down" trials in Singapore at the time of going to press. equipment comprises a BHC Warden a three Winchesters.

ROYAL NAVY: NAVAL PARTY 8902
Naval Party 8902 was commissioned September 1967, and is the Royal Nav first hovercraft unit. It is equipped with 27th production SR.N6 which has be specially adapted for the role of fast cc munications in the Falkland Islands, off coast of Argentine. The unit's compleme is two pilots, Lt Cdr V. R. Phillips a Lt C. S. Stafford; two navigators and maintenance ratings. The craft, wh operates in all weathers by day and nig has internally fitted overload fuel tanks a has an endurance of 7 hours. It can ca 30 men with a reduced fuel load or 12 n with maximum load.

TOWNSEND CAR FERRIES
ADDRESS:
c/o P & A Campbell, 4 Dock Chamb Bute Street, Cardiff

Townsend Car Ferries operates one W chester, which was on charter to Hoverlle for pleasure trips out of Ramsgate harb during the summer of 1968.

YUGOSLAVIA
GLOBTOUR
Globtour—the Yugoslavian tour firm planning to operate SR.N6 Winchesters supplement its Kometa hydrofoils for spe excursions and resort link work from Sp

The craft will be leased from the mana ment of Split airport, which like all Yugosl ian airports, is responsible for tour development within its area.

WEST INDIES

WEST INDIES
JAMAICA HOVERCRAFT LTD
Jamaica Hovercraft Ltd was due to take delivery of the Denny D2 002 at the end of 1968. The Company will operate a service in Kingston harbour between Kingston and Palisadoes.

The AMERICAS

ANADA

PARTMENT OF TRANSPORT

ne SR.N5 Warden is operated by the
partment of Transport on coastguard and
cue duties. The craft is based at Sea
nd Airport, Vancouver.

OVERWORK CANADA LTD

ee entry for Hoverwork Ltd (UK)

CIFIC HOVERCRAFT, LTD, VAN-
OUVER

Pacific Hovercraft Ltd has been awarded
first licence granted by the Canadian
partment of Transport for a regular
mmercial ACV service. The company will
erate two 36-seat SR.N6 Winchesters, one
which will be employed on a service bet-
en Vancouver and Victoria, the other
ween Vancouver and Nanaimo. Six
urn trips daily are planned between
ncouver and Victoria, and seven return
ps each day on the Vancouver-Nanaimo
..

NITED STATES

LL AEROSYSTEMS

Bell Aerosystems is operating four SR.N5
ardens on technical marketing, develop-
nt and training programmes. The craft
e based at Buffalo, New York and Alameda
lifornia.

NITED STATES ARMY

The first three SK-5s produced by Bell are
odel 7275s for the US Army. The three
aft were airlifted to Bien Hoa, Republic of
etnam on May 8/9 1968 and are being
ployed on Riverine operations in the
ekong Delta. Two configurations are being
aluated during a six month operation:
ssault ACV (AACV) and Transport ACV
ACV), which carries an infantry squad.
oth models are equipped with machine guns

A Winchester class (SR.N6) hovercraft at the first 'lift-off' at Fort Churchill, Manitoba, Canada, in January 1968. This was the start of 2½ month cold weather trails conducted by Hoverwork Limited for the Canadian Department of Transport when operations were carried out over open sea, broken floes, muskeg and land at an average ambient temperature of —25°F. The lowest temperature recorded while operating the craft was —43°F. This hovercraft had come straight from Montreal's Expo 67 where Hoverwork had carried 366,633 passengers in 180 days

firing from the cabin sides and twin roof mountings, but the two AACV models have additional armament in the form of an M5 grenade launcher on the port bow, capable of firing 225-230 rounds per minute.

UNITED STATES NAVY

Three Bell SK-5s (Model 7232), which were put into combat-service against Viet Cong guerillas in South Vietnam for eight months in 1966, were returned to the United States

for modification, overhaul and crew training in January 1967. Modification to the three SK-5s included the installation of auxiliary tanks; new fingered-bag skirts for improved directional control; additional communications equipment and heavier armament.

The craft now equip Coastal Division 17, a patrol and assault unit assigned to the US Pacific Fleet's Amphibious Force and operating from Da Nang and Tan My. The unit's Vietnam assignment is for one year.

ASIA

RUNEI

HELL (BRUNEI) LTD

This company is operating one SR.N6
Winchester for off-shore oil-rig support.

RAN

MPERIAL IRANIAN NAVY

BHC Winchesters and Wellingtons are being
perated by the Imperial Iranian Navy for
oastal patrol. It is reported that eight
R.N6s and two BH-7s have been ordered.

APAN

ITSUBISHI

A modified SR.N6 Winchester (SR.N6-M),
aported by Mitsubishi as part of the Com-
any's marketing and technical development

programme, was operated on a commercial basis by the Kyushu Shosen Line in Kyushu, between Kumamoto and Hondo from September 1, 1967 to May 1, 1968. This was the first attempt at operating a hovercraft passenger ferry service in Japan. Between September 20 and November 10, 1968, the craft was used for pleasure trips on Lake Biwa, in the Shiga Prefecture during the Biwa-ko (lake) Grand Exhibition.

EAST PAKISTAN INLAND WATER
TRANSPORT AUTHORITY

One of the responsibilities of the Authority

is the hydrographic survey of the East Pakistan Delta. It will employ a Hover-marine Surveymarine and a Hovermarine Hovercat Mk.2 to speed the completion of surveys in this area.

THAILAND

THAILAND CUSTOMS DEPARTMENT

A Mitsui MV-PP1, Custom Hovercraft 1, has been operated by the Thailand Customs Department since August 1967. The craft is in service in the Menam Chao Phya estuary and adjacent waters.

AUSTRALIA

PORT JACKSON HOVERTRAVEL PTY,
LTD
ADDRESS:
No. 2 Jetty, Circular Quay, Sydney, NSW

This company was formed in 1968 by Hovertravel Limited of Ryde, Isle of Wight, England, and the Port Jackson & Manly Steamship Co Ltd of Sydney.

During 1969, the company will start operating ACVs in Australasia. Initially services will be based on Sydney.

AIR CUSHION ASSISTED LOAD CARRIERS

UNITED KINGDOM

BHC
BRITISH HOVERCRAFT CORPORATION

HEAD OFFICE:

Yeovil, Somerset

DIRECTORS:

See ACV Section

AIR CUSHION HEAVY LOAD TRANSPORTER

The development of this equipment was prompted initially by the Central Electricity Generating Board, which is constantly faced with route-planning problems caused by the high weights of laden transporters.

Transformer units now going into service weigh between 195 and 250 tons and 300 ton units are in prospect. On occasion the CEGB has been involved in the heavy expense of strengthening and even rebuilding bridges to accept these loads when no alternative route has been available.

The use of air-cushion equipment, however, provides a practical and economic alternative. By providing an air-cushion under the centre section of an existing transporter it is possible to support a high proportion of its gross weight. More even distribution over the whole length of the transporter reduces the bending movements and shear force imposed on bridges so that these heavy transformers can be transported without damage over existing bridges.

The investigation into and development of this air-cushion transporter has been supported by the CEGB with the co-operation of the Ministry of Transport and the road haulage companies that operate the transporters.

The transporter illustrated has a length of 90 ft (27·4 m) and a maximum width of 16 ft 10 in (5·13 m). The payload is normally supported between two bogies each of which may have up to 48 wheels.

The air cushion container is between the two main frames of the transporter and measures 32 ft (9·75 m) × 14 ft (4·26 m). It is constructed largely of nylon/neoprene sheet extending across the underside of the load platform and formed into a bellows around its periphery. To the bottom of the bellows is attached a series of plates, each about 1 ft (0·30 m) long, which make contact with the road surface. Thus, the only escape route for air from the cushion is through the small gap formed between the plates and the ground by the roughness of the surface.

Any general unevenness of the surface, such as the camber of a road or the hump of a

The CEGB Heavy Load Transporter crossing Felin Puleston Bridge, Wrexham, with a 155-ton load

bridge, causes the bellows of the 'skirt' to flex so that the plates can remain in contact with the road.

The cushion is capable of a 155-ton lift, when the cushion pressure reaches 5·4 pounds per square inch. At this pressure, when moving over the roughest road surfaces, the volume of air escaping from underneath the shoes may be as much as 13,200 cu ft/min (373·5 m³/min) (free air volume flow).

The power to maintain the air cushion is provided by four Rolls-Royce B81SV petrol engines delivering 235 hp (gross) at 4,000 rpm. Each engine drives, through a gearbox, its own centrifugal compressor, with engine, gearbox and compressor mounted together on a steel underbed as a complete working unit. The four units supplying the power are contained within a soundproofed bodywork built onto a road vehicle chassis. This vehicle, which also contains stowage space for the folded cushion container, is attached to the rear of the transporter train whenever it is required for a bridge crossing. It is connected to the air cushion through four, 1 ft diameter air ducts, each connected to a power unit. The ducts are connected by sections of flexible hose to allow for relative movement between the vehicles.

From a position in the driver's cab of t compressor vehicle an operator controls aspects of the operation, such as the starti and adjustment of engines, and the selecti of cushion pressures. The raising a lowering of the skirt is controlled by t trailer steersman.

Should one power source fail, it is au matically sealed off. In normal operatic 25% of the air supply is blown to waste but the event of a power unit failure, this automatically diverted into the cushion, th maintaining a constant cushion pressu The whole system is sound-proofed to satis stringent limitations on noise level laid do by the Ministry of Transport, and the cushion does not affect other road users.

The equipment can be fitted in the vicin of the bridge requiring its use. When t crossing has been made the skirt can either removed or raised and could be taken aw for use on another vehicle.

The advantage gained by the air cushion very much a function of the lift provide With increasing lift, the load on the transpo er wheels is relieved, so that the weight more evenly distributed, but there is a poi beyond which the bending moments creat by the cushion exceed those due to the bogi

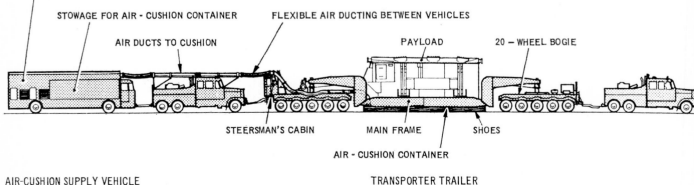

COMPARTMENT CONTAINING ENGINES AND BLOWING EQUIPMENT

STOWAGE FOR AIR - CUSHION CONTAINER

FLEXIBLE AIR DUCTING BETWEEN VEHICLES

AIR DUCTS TO CUSHION

PAYLOAD

20 - WHEEL BOGIE

STEERSMAN'S CABIN

MAIN FRAME

SHOES

AIR - CUSHION CONTAINER

AIR-CUSHION SUPPLY VEHICLE

TRANSPORTER TRAILER

CEGB Air-cushion Heavy Load Transporter

…ere is, therefore, an optimum cushion …essure, which has been determined by …mputer for a wide range of single and …ultiple span bridges. For many bridges, …e optimum pressure is reached when the …shion is lifting about 40% of the trans-…orter's laden weight, so that it may well …ove unnecessary to vary the cushion …essure from bridge to bridge.

The first commercial load carried by the …ansporter was a 155-ton transformer for …livery to the Central Electricity Board's …b-station at Legacy, near Wrexham, from …e A.E.I. Transformer Division Works at …ythenshawe, Manchester. The route …volved crossing the Felin Puleston Bridge …hich, under normal circumstances, was …capable of withstanding the combined …eight of the transporter and the transformer. …y using the air cushion to relieve the load …n the transporter's wheels the stress on the …ridge was reduced by about 70 tons.

…Had a conventional transporter been used …e bridge would have had to be strengthened …t a cost equal to about half the cost of …eveloping and equipping the transporter.

…IR-CUSHION OFF-THE-ROAD CARRIER

The Air-Cushion Load Carrier is designed to …arry materials over farmland to construction …ites without damaging the soil. Convention-…l trucks generally compact clay soil and …hurn up soft, damp land through the …epeated use of a track from a road access …oint.

It is hauled across the farmland by a low …round loading tractor or winched across …vhen the ground is extremely soft.

The vehicle is designed to carry loads of up …o 9 tons. It then has a gross laden weight of …5 tons of which only 2 tons is supported by …he eight ground stabilising wheels.

It comprises a flat aluminium platform of …27 ft 6 in (8·38 m) × 9 ft 2½ in (2·80 m) …overall dimensions. The rear 20 ft 6 in …(6·24 m) of the platform is a loading area …large enough to take a truck weighing 9 tons; …this is the largest single load anticipated. …Forward of the loading area is the air cushion …blower unit comprising a double-sided centri-…fugal fan and Rolls-Royce V-8 petrol engine,

the driver's cab and an auxiliary power unit. The latter provides power for the winches, wheel springing and steering. A flexible rubber/fabric skirt is fitted around and below the edge of the Carrier platform.

STRUCTURE: A basic load bearing struc-ture, running the full length of the Carrier, is built up from 12 in (305 mm) deep extruded aluminium channel. The rear 20 ft (6·09 m) of the structure forms a freight area and is covered with plywood. The underside of the freight area is open to the air cushion and carries four skids upon which the Carrier rests when the cushion and suspension system are discharged.

A driver's cab and the various power units are mounted as individual items on the forward area of the basic structure.

AIR CUSHION SYSTEM: A Rolls-Royce V-8 Type L.841 engine drives a double-sided impeller centrifugal fan through a direct coupling; both units are mounted fore-and-aft alongside the driver's cab.

Apart from a deflector sheet which prevents any stones and water which might be thrown up by the air cushion from striking the engine and transmission, the lower part of the engine compartment is open to atmosphere. A water radiator is fitted in the conventional manner ahead of the engine and air passing over the engine enters the forward impeller of the fan; air enters the rear impeller direct from atmosphere. The fan volutes discharge directly into the cushion space below the platform. The space below the platform is enclosed by a flexible skirt and is used to provide the air cushion.

Steel shoes on the lower edge of the skirt are arranged to ride over grassland and the depressions left by the tractor and are articulated to follow ground contours. For movement on the road the skirt is manually strung up against the underside of the platform by a series of straps with suitable handgrips.

Cushion pressure is controlled by a variable

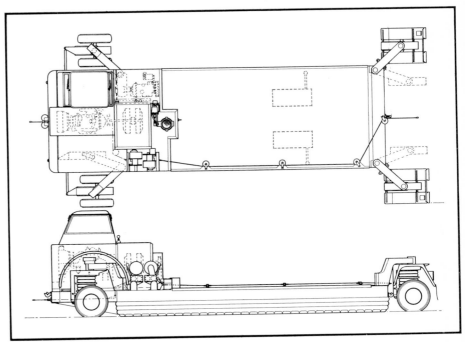

BHC Air-Cushion Off-the-Road Carrier

BHC's Air-Cushion Off-the-Road carrier is a special purpose vehicle capable of carrying a 9 ton load over soft ground. It is currently used for carrying trucks engaged in the construction of overhead power lines

AIR CUSHION ASSISTED LOAD CARRIERS
BHC: United Kingdom

setting discharge valve coupled to a controller in which the required setting is selected by the driver.

WHEEL SUSPENSION: Four separate units each carrying two wheels, support the whole Carrier weight on the road and stabilise the Carrier when on the air cushion.

The wheel pairs are mounted by trailing arms and pneumatic springs onto a swan neck which can be rotated about vertical pintles so that the track of the wheels can be varied to give increased stability.

A Ford Type 122E engine drives a pneumatic compressor for the suspension system and the cushion air spill actuator; the system also includes an air storage reservoir, pressure reducing valves, and the necessary indicators.

The driver controls the system pressure for road and off-the-road travel by a two-position setting control.

A conventional hydraulic braking system is fitted to all wheels; a pneumatic override to this system provides the parking brake.

A hydraulic circuit connects the front road wheels to the cab steering lever, using components already developed for another purpose. Front wheel steering only will be fitted initially, but the possible requirement of steering on the rear wheels is recognised and this can be fitted later if necessary. To assist in manoeuvring in a restricted space, each wheel pair can be rotated through angles up to 90 degrees by hand.

WINCH SYSTEM: Two winches taking 2 ton $\frac{5}{16}$ in dia. cable and take-up reels are mounted to the rear of the driver's cab. Pulleys are disposed so that the Carrier may be winched either forward or backward. In addition the cable can be arranged to enable the Carrier to winch itself between two ground tethering points. Up to 250 yards (228·6 m) of cable can be used on each winch.

The winches and take-up reels are driven hydraulically by the Ford auxiliary engine.

POWER UNITS: The two engines are each fitted with separate ignition systems, hand throttles, revolution counters and other instruments.

A common fuel system provides a total capacity of 36 gallons, which is considered to be adequate for a half day's operation.

OTHER SERVICES: The Carrier is fitted with lights and markings for use as a trailer on the road.

DIMENSIONS:

Length	35 ft 6 in (10·8 m)
Width:	
minimum track	9 ft 2½ in (2·80 m)
maximum track	14 ft 3 in (4·34 m)
Height (on road)	9 ft 6 in (2·89 m)
Ground clearance (on road)	1 ft (0·30 m)
Wheelbase	29 ft (8·83 m)
Load platform:	
Length	20 ft 6 in (6·24 m)
Width	9 ft (2·74 m)
Cushion	
24 ft 6 in (7·46 m) × 8 ft 4 in (2·54 m)	

WEIGHTS:

Tare weight, plus driver and fuel
13,440 lb (6·0 to⬤

Maximum payload 20,160 lb (9·0 to⬤
Gross weight 33,600 lb (15·0 to⬤

PERFORMANCE (Up to maximum freig⬤ load of 9 tons):

Normal ground load:
Air cushion 144 lb sq⬤
Wheels 600 lb (272 kg) per wh⬤

Transient wheel load when passing over bump, or the Carrier rolling
1,500 lb (680 kg) per wh⬤

Wheel ruts after repeated runs over t⬤ same track:
Less than 1 in (0·03 mm) deep over s⬤ grass
Less than 3 in (0·12 mm) deep over ve⬤ wet grass
Up to 4 in (0·15 mm) deep over grass⬤ very wet sandy loam (20% moist⬤ content)

Over dry loose soil or gravel the air cushi⬤ disturbs the ground considerably and t⬤ performance is doubtful

Maximum slide slope (a stability consider⬤ tion) Up to 1 in 12 depending upon t⬤ resistance of the ground to slipping si⬤ ways

Towing speed (on cushion)
10 mph (17 km⬤

Winching speed (on cushion)
5 mph (8 km⬤

Towing speed (on the road)
20 mph (33 km⬤

TRACKED
AIR CUSHION VEHICLES

TRACKED AIR CUSHION VEHICLES
SOCIÉTÉ DE L'AEROTRAIN

FRANCE

SOCIÉTÉ DE L'AEROTRAIN

HEAD OFFICE:
  42 Avenue Raymond Poincarré
  Paris 16 éme
TELEPHONE:
  704.51.10
TELEX: 26 778 Bertrain
TELEGRAMS:
  Trainair, Paris
PRESIDENT DIRECTOR GENERAL:
  Leon Kaplan
DIRECTOR GENERAL:
  Guy Du Merle
INTERNATIONAL DIVISION:
  Jean M. Berthelot

Originally named "Société d'Etudes de l'Aerotrain", this company was formed on April 15, 1965 to develop a high speed transportation system based on air cushion support and guidance principles conceived by Bertin & Cie.

The Aerotrain has completed its experimental phase as far as the air cushion technique is concerned. The 01 half-scale prototype, after nearly three years of test runs at speeds up to 215 mph (346 km/h), has successfully attained its phased design requirements, namely the verification of dynamic behaviour, the development of integrated suspension systems, and the accumulation of data for the design and costing of full-scale operational vehicles.

The new 02 half-scale prototype is now undergoing similar tests in order to produce data for vehicles at speeds above 210 mph.

There are two families of Aerotrain systems —intercity and suburban. Intercity vehicles designed for medium-range services will have a speed of 160-200 mph (257-322 km/h) and those designed for long-range services will operate at speeds above 200 mph (322 km/h). The guideway is to be standard for both medium and long-range vehicles. The speeds selected will be based on economic considerations. Suburban systems will cover a variety of routes from city centres to airports and city centres to satellite towns and suburban areas. The size, speed and control system of each vehicle will be decided according to the route.

Current studies are aimed primarily at developing associated techniques including propulsion modes for the various speeds and environments, controls, signals and stations.

A mathematical model has been developed in order to computerise the various parameters for both families of applications. This will enable operating costs to be obtained,

The experimental Aerotrain 01 running at 215 mph over its 4·2 mile long test track, located sou west of Paris, near Gometz-la-Ville.

Turntables are installed at each end of the present Aerotrain test track, but they will not be u normally on operational lines. In service Aerotrains will be able to manoeuvre independently the flat floor surfaces of stations

in an optimized form, for given traffic requirements.

All these programmes, completed or under way, represent a financial development effort of roughly $14 million. The French Government has extended its support at every stage by means of various loans, subsidies and orders, the balance being covered by the funds of Société de l'Aerotrain.

EXPERIMENTAL AEROTRAIN 01

An experimental, half-scale prototype, this vehicle operates along a test track 4·2 miles (6·7 km) long. The track has an inverted T cross section, the vertical portion being 1 ft 10 in (55 cm) high and the horizontal base 5 ft 11 in (1·80 m) wide. A turn-table is fitted at each end.

The vehicle is of light alloy construction. The slender body has seats at the front for

six people, and an engine compartment at rear. Lift and guidance are provided two centrifugal fans, driven by two 50 Renault Gordini motor car engines, linl by a shaft. The fans supply air to guidance and lift cushions at a pressure about 0·35 lb/sq in (25 gr/cm²), the maxim airflow being 350 cu ft/sec (10 m³/se Propulsion is provided by a 260 hp Contine al aero-engine, mounted at the top of a 3 11 in (1·20 m) tail pylon and driving a reve ible-pitch propeller, which is also used normal braking. There are brake pads the rear of the vehicle which grip the verti track section like a disc brake.

The first test run on the track was made December 29, 1965. The prototype v intended to evaluate and demonstrate t Aerotrain principle on a small scale, and v

Close-up of a model of the Orleans Aerotrain showing the shrouded propeller and the seating arrangement at the rear of the passenger saloon.

odel of the suburban Aerotrain variant which is now under construction.   The vehicle will seat 44 passengers and cruise at 112 mph (180 km/h.)
e dark structure at the side of the vehicle represents the level of passenger platforms at the stations.   Also seen in this photograph is the aluminium
induction rail for linear motor propulsion

e Aerotrain 02, a research vehicle built for tests up to and above 250 mph on the No. 1 track at
Gometz

veloped with the active support of the
ench Government and French Railways.
Although the vehicle was designed for a
aximum speed of 125 mph (200 km/h),
sts have been undertaken at higher speeds
th the help of booster rockets to supple-
ent the propulsive airscrew.   In December
67, the vehicle reached the top speed of
5 mph (345 km/h) several times with a jet
gine assisted by two booster rockets.

DIMENSIONS:

Length overall	32 ft 10 in (10·00 m)
Width overall	6 ft 7 in (2·00 m)
Height overall	12 ft 2 in (3·70 m)
Height to top of body	5 ft 3 in (1·60 m)

WEIGHTS:

Basic weight	5,500 lb (2,500 kg)

PERFORMANCE:

Cruising speed	125 mph (200 km/h)
Top speed	188 mph (303 km/h)

XPERIMENTAL AEROTRAIN 02

Aerotrain 02 is an experimental half-scale
rototype designed for high speed tests on
e same track at Gometz as used by the first
rototype.

Due to the track's relatively short length, a
more powerful thrust engine, a Pratt &
Whitney JT 12, is installed in order to maintain high speeds over a distance of 1·3 miles
(2 km) for performance measurements.

During its first series of test runs, the
Aerotrain 02 attained 235 mph (378 km/h).
Auxiliary power will be added later on to
increase the acceleration for further experiments at higher speeds.

The air cushions for lift and guidance are
provided by fans driven by a Turbomeca
Palouste gas turbine.   At high speed, the
dynamic pressure is sufficient to feed the air
cushions.

The internal space has been devoted in the
main to test instrumentation.   Seats are
provided only for the pilot and a test engineer.

Aerotrains 01 and 02 are both equipped
with propulsion engines which were readily
available from the aviation market and are
capable of giving high speed on a short test
track.   Operational vehicles will use quieter
power arrangements.

THE ORLEANS INTERCITY PROJECT 80-SEAT AEROTRAIN

This medium range intercity vehicle (the
Orleans-Paris line will be 70 miles (113 km)
long) is designed for speeds of 155-185 mph
(250-300 km/h) and is currently under construction.   The standard model will carry
80 passengers in airliner comfort in an air-
conditioned and sound-proofed cabin.

The lift and guidance air cushions are fed
by two axial fans driven by a 400 hp Turbomeca Astazou gas turbine.   At high speeds,
they will be fed by dynamic intake pressure.

Propulsion is provided by a shrouded
propeller, driven by either of two 1,500 hp
Turmo 111 gas turbines. The power required
for cruising will be about 700 hp, less than
half the total available output.

Hydraulically retractable tyred wheels are
incorporated to help to achieve silent operation near and in stations, and also to assist
in manoeuvring and switching the vehicle
on station floors.   The vertical rail of the
inverted T track is unnecessary at low speeds.

A very low empty-weight-to-payload ratio
has been possible because of the lack of
concentrated loads inherent in the vehicle.
This permits the use of lightweight supporting
structures—tracks and stations.

The vehicle does not represent a standard
size for any project.   The capacity and speed
will be selected according to traffic requirements.   Vehicles will not be coupled, so that
very high frequency services can be offered.
Coupling will not be necessary with this
vehicle since the headways can be kept below
one minute for heavily loaded lines at peak
hours.

DIMENSIONS:

Length overall	84 ft (25·60 m)
Beam	10 ft 6 in (3·20 m)
Height	10 ft 10 in (3·30 m)

WEIGHTS:

Empty weight	24,800 lb (11,250 kg)
Loaded weight	44,000 lb (20,000 kg)

PERFORMANCE:

Cruising speed	155 mph (250 km/h)
Top speed	185 mph (300 km/h)

TRACKED AIR CUSHION VEHICLES
SOCIÉTÉ DE L'AEROTRAIN: France

Prefabricated beams of the Aerotrain guidew being lowered into position by mobile cran

Model of the 80 passenger Orleans Aerotrain which is now under construction

THE GUIDEWAY

The first leg of the future Orleans to Paris line—a track 11·5 miles (18·5 km) long—is under construction. It includes turntables at both ends and a central platform for manoeuvring and switching.

The track has been designed for a service speed of 250 mph (402 km/h). It is mounted on pylons along the entire route. The prefabricated concrete beams, of 67 ft (20 m) span, have a minimum ground clearance of 16 ft (4·90 m). This allows the track to be constructed across roads and cultivated land.

Due to the low stresses produced by the Aerotrain vehicles it has been possible to design a lightweight elevated track structure, which is less expensive than an equivalent ground track. Local ground subsidence will be countered by adjusting the pylon heads.

The radii of curves and gradient angles will depend upon the accelerations admissible without causing discomfort to passengers.

44 PASSENGER AEROTRAIN

A full-scale 44 passenger suburban vehicle is under construction. The prototype is equipped with a linear induction motor. Later, an alternative propulsion system will be fitted, using an automotive engine and transmission and driving tyred wheels, which will exert just sufficient pressure on the track to provide the propulsive power required.

In both versions the power for the lift fans will be provided by a V-8 car engine. Practically silent operation will be possible since there will be no noise of rolling wheels or any vibration.

An electrical linear motor developed by Merlin Gerin will provide a thrust of 18.000 N

Aerotrain guideway track beams can be adjust at the heads of the pylons in the event initial ground subsidence

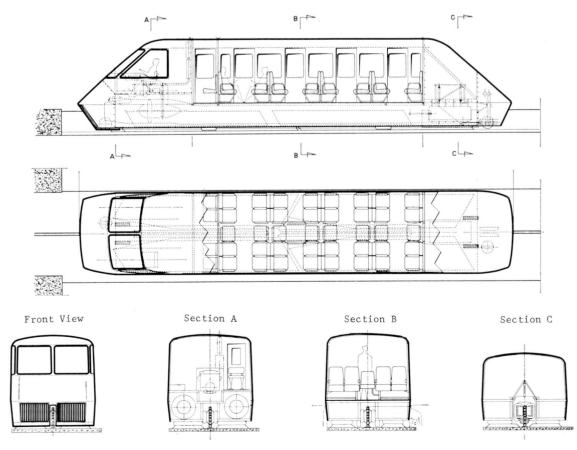

Front View   Section A   Section B   Section C

The 44 passenger Aerotrain for suburban operation. Two versions will be built; one with a linear induction motor, the other with tyred wheel driven by an automobile engine.

85 mph (137 kmh) and 13·000 N at 112 h (180 km/h). A cruising speed of 112 h will be attained with an average rate of mph/sec (5·6 km/h/sec).

raking performance is expected to be ticularly efficient. It will utilise electrical tor inversion, combined with linear disc kes which will grip the track vertically. tomatic doors are provided on both sides of h passenger compartment which will help reduce stopping time. On multistop urban lines average speeds as high as 95 mph (137-153 km/h) will be possible ere the distances between stations are n 2-5 miles (3·2-8 km). The coupling of

several of these vehicles will be possible, but this should only be necessary at peak hours for heavy commuter traffic.

DIMENSIONS:
Length	47 ft 0 in (14·4 m)
Beam	9 ft 4 in (2·75 m)
Height	10 ft 2 in (3·10 m)

WEIGHTS:
Loaded weight:
linear motor weight	25,000 lb (11,500 kg)
automotive version	22,000 lb (10,000 kg)

PERFORMANCE:
Cruising speed	112 mph (180 km/h)

A lower speed system is being designed for urban lines with stations only ½ mile apart.

THE GUIDEWAY

In this programme the track will be at ground level. The horizontal support is an asphalt carpet and the upright is an aluminium beam, which will be used for both guiding the vehicle and as an induction rail for the linear motor. A 1·8 mile (3 km) long track is being constructed at the company's base at Gometz and is nearly complete.

Operational suburban lines will generally be supported on pylons in order to leave the ground free. The use of an elevated track will reduce the construction time and avoid costly tunnelling.

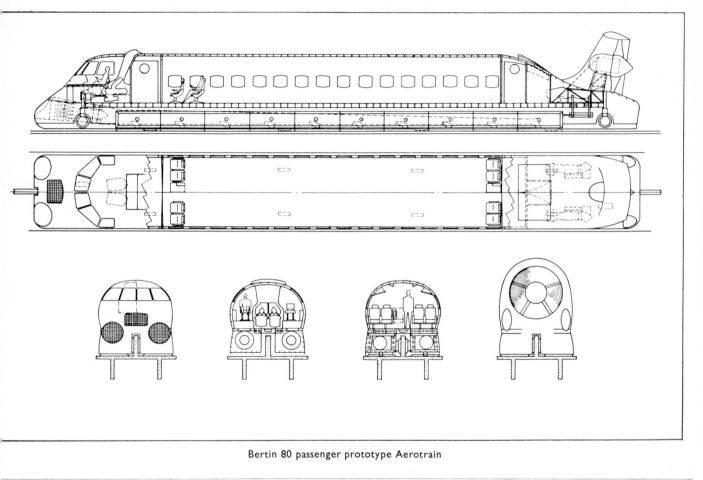

Bertin 80 passenger prototype Aerotrain

RBA

mpagnie d.Energetique Lineaire mb
AD OFFICE:
Rue Monge, 92 Vanves, France
ICERS:
. E. Barthalon, ScMMIT, Ecole Poly-
technique, President Director General
REPRESENTATIVE:
Bn Powercels Ltd,
25 Bedford Row, London WC1
. Watson, BA, MIMarE, Managing
Director.

. Maurice Barthalon has invented a new n of suspended monorail for mass public nsportation. The vehicle is suspended n its track by an air lift system in which pressure is sub-atmospheric. The proto-e, designated URBA 4, was demonstrated Lyon in March 1968. The company is w constructing the prototype URBA 100, ich is expected to reach a speed of 65 mph 5 km/h) on a 1 km (0·6 mile) length of ck.

URBA 4

A prototype urban and suburban monorail transport vehicle, the URBA 4 consists of a rectangular-framed cabin seating up to twelve passengers and suspended from three Dyna-vac air bogies running in an experimental 30 m (98 ft) track. The track section is like a flattened inverted U. Inward facing flanges are formed on the bottom outer edges of the sides of the U, on which the bogies sit when at rest. Each Dynavac air bogie has four suction fans and when these operate, they draw air from the space between the track and the top of the bogie, so producing a pressure difference which causes the air bogie to lift off the flanges. Special sealing arrangements provide a controlled leak into the lift chamber which decreases as the weight of the vehicle increases, so increasing the pressure difference. The air bogies therefore remain in a stable, floating condition without being in contact with the track. Lateral

guidance of the air bogies is provided by similar but smaller Dynavac cushions between the sides of the bogie and the sides of the track.

PROPULSION: Propulsion and normal braking is by a Merlin Gerin linear motor of 25 kW, weighing 176 lb (80 kg) and providing a thrust of 220 lb (100 kg) at starting (66 lb (30 kg) at normal service speed. Supply is from 380 volt, 3-phase, 50 cycle mains. The motor is the first to be designed as an industrial unit for vehicle propulsion. An aluminium conductor fin runs down the centre of the track and a set of coils is mounted in each bogie. Conductor rails for current supply to the linear motor and lift fans are in the base of the fin.

CABIN: The cabin is rectangular and measures 14 ft 10 in (4·5 m) long, 5 ft 3in (1·6 m) wide and 4 ft (1·2 m) high. It is built from 4 cm square section tube and diecast corners of a type normally used for the framework of holiday bungalows.

TRACKED AIR CUSHION VEHICLES
URBA: France

The floor is of light alloy and the sides are perspex. Suspension between the cabin and the three air bogies is by rubber cord springs and hydraulic automobile shock absorbers.

Tests have demonstrated that the air bogie concept is suitable for sharp curves, can climb steep slopes and provides good acceleration and braking. It cannot be derailed.

The company's future programme includes the construction of an extended 820 ft (250 m) track with curves, an incline and points, and the demonstration of a 100 passenger prototype along a 1 km track at speeds up to 65 mph in August 1969. The first commercial installation is due to be opened in January 1971.

URBA 20

An enlarged version of the URBA 4, this model will seat 20 passengers in a cylindrical cabin and have a top speed of 45 mph (72 km/h). More efficient lift fans will be employed on this model which will require a total of 12 kW for lift power. All-up weight will be 10,470 lb (4,750 kg).

URBA 30

This model is similar to URBA 20, but has a "stretched" cabin to seat 30 people.

URBA 100

A 100-seat variant, the URBA 100 will use 60 kW for lift, 100 kW on level lengths of track and 500 kW when climbing a 17% incline. Its cabin will be 36 ft 2 in (11 m) long, 8 ft 3 in (2·5 m) wide and 8 ft 7 in (2·6 m) high, and will be supported by five air bogies, each 6 ft 11 in (2·1 m) long and 4 ft 8 in (1·4 m) wide. The cabin is likely to by based on a stressed skin, single-deck bus body with a strengthened roof.

It will weigh 8 tons empty, 15 tons loaded and will have a service speed of 50 mph (80 km/h). Preliminary estimates indicate that overhead track for this model will be in the region of £400,000 to £500,000 per mile of double track, excluding wayleaves.

The URBA 4 prototype seats 6/12 passengers and has a cruising speed of 50 mph (80 km/h)

URBA 20, a light urban transport vehicle with a service speed of 45 mph (72 km/h) and seating passengers

Cabin of the 100 seat URBA 100 may be based on a stressed skin single-deck bus or coach body with a strengthened roof

UNITED KINGDOM

acked Hovercraft

ACKED HOVERCRAFT LIMITED

AD OFFICE:
O Box 235, Kingsgate House, 66/74
Victoria Street, London SW.1

LEPHONE:
1-828-3400

MBRIDGE OFFICE:
O Box 28, Cambridge

LEPHONE:
aversham, Cambridgeshire, 3111

RECTORS:
. Hennessey, Chairman
. G. Fellows, Managing Director
I. W. Innes, Director
rof. J. Diamond, Director

ECUTIVES:
. S. Bliss, Chief Engineer
. L. E. Spier, Commercial Manager

racked Hovercraft Ltd., a subsidiary of
National Research Development Cor-
ration, was formed in September 1967 to
velop and promote the use of tracked
vercraft. A major component of the
mpany's development programme is the
nstruction and testing of a substantially
l-scale vehicle on a 20-mile site running
rough the counties of Cambridge and
rfolk. The design of the test vehicle and
track is now in progress.

n support of this programme further
eoretical and experimental technical work
ll be undertaken, and economic evaluation
dies pursued.

Artist's impression of the Tracked Hovercraft Ltd test vehicle

The company's first full-size test vehicle
is in the design stage.

Accommodation will be provided for crew,
instrumentation and up to 16 passengers.

Length, approx	50 ft (15 m)
Height, approx	10 ft (3 m)
Width, approx	10 ft (3 m)
Design speed	250 mph (403 km/h)

PROPULSION SYSTEM: Linear induction motor

LIFT SYSTEM: Separate peripheral jet
hovercraft pads for lift and guidance,
incorporating a second suspension.

POWER SUPPLY: Current collection from
track-side conductors.

TRACK DESIGN: Pre-stressed concrete
construction, T section.

THE UNITED STATES OF AMERICA

Aeroglide

HEAD OFFICE:

Aeroglide Systems, Inc, 120 Broadway, New York 10005

DIRECTORS:

R. M. Dubois, President

Aeroglide is a subsidiary of the Société de l'Aerotrain and Société Bertin et Cie. It is at present undertaking various marketing studies and a performance evaluation contract for the Office of High Speed Ground Transportation of the Department of Tra portation in Washington. The company not at present building ground effect vehic in the United States.

General Electric
GENERAL ELECTRIC COMPANY
TRANSPORTATION SYSTEMS DIVISION

HEAD OFFICE:

2901 East Lake Road, Erie, Pennsylvania 16501

TELEPHONE:

(814) 455-5466

The General Electric Company's Transportation Systems Division, Erie, Pa, has been awarded a contract by the Department of Transportation's Office of High Speed Ground Transportation to make a preliminary design study of a tracked air cushion research vehicle. A $100,000 subcontract to assist in the development of the vehicle has been awarded to LTV Aerospace Corporation, which will undertake design studies for selected parts of the vehicle. These will include aerodynamic shapes, structural aerodynamic loads, propulsion systems installation and design problems related to human factors.

The vehicle will be designed to travel speeds up to 300 mph (483 km/h) in h traffic-density areas between cities. It travel at about ¾ in (19 mm) above between a fixed guideway.

LTV Aerospace Corporation, a L Temco-Vought subsidiary, will be concer mainly with the utility module, the par the vehicle containing the passenger comp ment, fuel tanks, air breathing engines related subsystems.

Impression of General Electric's tracked air cushion research vehicle which will be capable of operating at speeds up to 300 mph (483 km/h) in h traffic density areas between cities

AIR CUSHION APPLICATORS, CONVEYORS and PALLETS

AUSTRALIA

Federated Engineers
FEDERATED ENGINEERS LTD
HEAD OFFICE:
PO Box 21, Artarmon, N.S.W., Australia

Federated Engineers manufacture Jet-stream conveyor systems under licence from Jetveyors Incorporated of San Francisco.

The systems are described in the entries the USA section for Jetveyors Incorporat and the Jetstream Systems Company.

FRANCE

Bertin
SOCIETE BERTIN ET CIE
OFFICE AND WORKS:
BP No. 3, 78—8 Plaisir, France
PRESIDENT DIRECTOR GENERAL:
Jean Bertin
DIRECTOR GENERAL:
Benjamin Salmon

The Bertin principle of separately fed, multiple plenum chambers surrounded by flexible skirts (see entries for SEDAM and Societe de l'Aerotrain) is being applied to materials handling.

Specially constructed conveyors, pallets and applicators are being built by the company for tasks for which conventional handling equipment has proved unsuitable, either for economical or practical reasons. The company designs equipment for moving heavy or fragile loads and for precise or intricate positioning and handling sequences.

None of the examples described below are standard items for "off-the-shelf" delivery. They have been selected from the company's designs to illustrate what has been achieved so far by applying the Bertin multiple plenum principle in this field.

HOVER PALLET 800 KG

Designed for handling of fragile goods within factory workshops, this self-contained hover pallet carries payloads of up to 1,800 lb (800 kg) on a loading surface measuring 65 in (1,652 mm) × 39 in (991 mm). Lift is supplied by a compressor driven by a 5 hp electrical motor and feeding six low pressure cushions. In order to prevent dust being raised by the cushion air, the leakage gap has been kept as low as possible. The surface over which it operates must therefore be comparatively smooth. Floors with poor surfaces can be cleaned, smoothed or sealed before using the pallet. The platform height has been kept low so as to ease loading and unloading.

HOVER PALLET 10,000 KG

This pallet is designed to carry loads of up to 22,000 lb (10,000 kg) along concrete tracks. Cushion lift is provided by four compressors driven by 5 hp electric motors. The leakage gap is less than 1/10 mm. The tracks are treated with silicone surfacing material.

HOVER PALLET 18,000 KG

The biggest Bertin hover pallet introduced so far has been used for the positioning of exceptionally heavy machinery within a

A Bertin pallet designed for the movement of machinery units weighing up to 40,000 lb (18,120 in old buildings where the floors do not permit the use of conventional lifting devices

Bertin multiple cushion handling table for handling heavy sheet metal

Bertin airliner food container unit

xtile factory. The problem was to position
w machinery weighing over 40,000 lb
8,160 kg) within old buildings. The floor
as too weak to support the load had it been
ncentrated on wheels, and the ceilings were
o low to permit the use of a temporary crane
idge. Moreover, precise positioning was
actically impossible with any traditional
andling system.

The machinery was successfully moved by
e hover pallet over a temporary surface of
noleum and manoeuvred into its exact
osition without the assistance of any lifting
evice. This pallet has also been employed
o move a machinery unit across deep ditches
mporarily filled with sand.

The pallet comprises two sets of four hover-
allets, one set being fitted on either side of
e machinrny being moved.

Leakage gap	0·004 in (0·10 mm)
Ground pressure	2·32 lb/sq in (0·163 kg/cm²)
Total loaded weight	47,000 lb (21,000 kg)

HEET METAL HANDLING TABLE

A number of custom-built metal sheet
ables have been built by Bertin. The
ultiple air cushion units ease the handling
f heavy metal sheets up to 33 sq ft and 0·6 in
nick. The system allows for bends in the
etal surface, and can be applied to most
andling tables and conveyors. Curves and
oints can be designed for intricate conveyor
ystems.

Capacity: steel sheets
9 ft 10 in × 3 ft 3 in (3·0 m × 1·0 m)
Thickness   0·63 in (16 mm)

Number of cushions	28
Size of cushion	7·87 in (200 mm)
Effective diam of each air film unit	6·3 in (160 mm)
Max loaded capacity of each air cushion	31 lb (14 kg)

Air supply: two units, each including 2
compressors and driven by a 5·5 kW motor
The cushions are fed in four separate units,
of seven cushions each.

AIRLINER FOOD CONTAINER

Food containers for airliners are normally
required to be loaded and off-loaded quickly,
and an airliner floor can be damaged from the
wheels of a heavily loaded trolley. To solve
this problem Bertin has introduced a range of
air cushion container units. Brought near
to the airliner by a conventional truck, the
units are then hovered into position in the
airliner's kitchen.

This factory hover pallet has been designed by Bertin for payloads of up to 22,000 lbs (10,000 kg)

Bertin workshop hover pallet with a load capacity of 1,800 lb (800 kg).

Neu

ÉTABLISSEMENT NEU

HEAD OFFICE:
Sac Postal No. 28, Lille, France
Etablissement NEU is a licencee of Jet-
veyors Incorporated of San Francisco.
Details of the Jetstream Conveyor System
built by the company can be found in the
entries in the USA section for Jetveyors
Incorporated and the Jetstream Systems
Company.

GERMANY

Stöhr
STOHR FORDERANLAGEN & CO

HEAD OFFICE:
  Sprendluiger Landstrasse 115, Offenbach/
  Main
DIRECTORS:
  Dipl Ing Gert Salzer
  H. C. Felder
  A. Hartmann

STOHR AIR TABLE
Stöhr of Offenbach specialises in the construction of junction tables for closed conveyor systems. The table tops normally house ball bearings to support the transfer of packages or piece goods from one conveyor to another, but the standard "spherical" tables cannot always be used. In the case of piece goods with a soft bottom—surface-cellulose, pulp bales, stacked paper and corrugated board, for example—the ball bearings press into the goods and the resistance to sliding is too great. For goods of this nature, and for very heavy loads, air tables have been developed.

The ball bearings are replaced by ball valv sunk into a table shaped container. In the container, compressed air is introduce the pressure depending on the weight of t material being conveyed. As the mater arrives on the table it depresses the valv and slides across it to be turned and mov with the minimum exertion even if it weig 1,100 lb (500 kg).

Stöhr tables are produced in a wide ran of sizes and heights to meet custome requirements.

Neu
NEU GmbH

HEAD OFFICE:
  5132 Ubach-Palenburg, Schwalbenstrasse,
  Germany

NEU GmbH manufactures Jetstream Conveyor Systems under licence from Jetveyors Incorporated of San Francisco. Details of the system can be found in the entries in t USA section for Jetveyors Incorporated a the Jetstream Systems Company.

JAPAN

Ebara
EBARA MANUFACTURING COMPANY

HEAD OFFICE:
  11 Haneda Asahicho, Otu-Ku, Tokyo

This company produces Jetstream conveyor systems under licence from Jetveyors Incorporated of San Francisco. Details of the systems can be found in the entries in USA section for Jetveyors Incorporated a the Jetstream Systems Company.

UNITED KINGDOM

BHC
BRITISH HOVERCRAFT CORPORATION

HEAD OFFICE:
  Yeovil, Somerset
DIRECTORS:
  See ACV section

FLOATALOAD (1 Ton)
The 1-ton Floataload hoverpallet consists of a load-carrying, steel and plywood sandwich platform with four easily removable rubber diaphragm assemblies underneath and a peripheral skirt. Air is supplied through a 1 in BSP connector and control valve.

Designed for moving loads of up to 1 ton on smooth floors, the hoverpallet can also be used in conjunction with standard fork lift trucks, pallets and stillages, which can easily be modified for this purpose. Single man operation of the loaded pallet is easily effected.

Loads may be placed directly on to the platform of the Floataload hoverpallet, but a simple bridge system allowing the units to be slid under the load is more economical.

When this is done the centre of pressure should be approximately under the centre of the load.

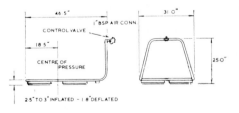

BHC 1-ton Floataload hoverpallet

Operation is by opening the control valve until the load is airborne. The load can then be pushed, pulled or spun with minimum effort, the valve being closed and Floataload withdrawn when the load reaches the required position.

Floataload will operate satisfactorily over any smooth non-porous surface. Sheet metal, linoleum, vinyl, sealed concrete, plywood, smooth asphalt, and similar surfaces are suitable.

On smooth surfaces the pressure requi at the air inlet connection is 8 lbf/in² mi mum and the airflow approx 20 sq ft per m Under these conditions a load of 1 t requires approximately 6 lbf effort initiate movement.

The size of airline required will depend the pressure of air available and length hose. Thus a 15 lb sq in (1·05 kgf/cm compressor will require a 1 in bore h whereas a 100 lb sq in (7·03 kgf/cm²) compr sor needs only a ½ in bore hose.

DIMENSIONS:
Max length of pallet   3 ft 10 in (1·16
Width of pallet   2 ft 8 in (0·81

AIR PRESSURE:
Working air pressure for 100 lb (45·3 l
  load   3 lb sq in (0·21 kgf/cm
Working air pressure for 1,000 lb (453·5 l
  load   6 lb sq in (0·42 kgf/cm
¾ in BSP connection, 1 ton load
                          8 lb sq in (0·56 kgf/cm

...ATALOAD (5 ton)

...his hoverpallet consists of aluminium
...y corrugated web with 12 swg aluminium
...s bonded top and bottom to form a
...ng platform. It has a tubular steel
...dle, with control valve on the handle.
...orporating six easily removable flexible
...phragms and a peripheral skirt round the
...form, the unit can move loads and
...tainers up to 5 tons gross weight on
...oth floors. Spherical castors on the
...erside of the platform allow it to be easily
...under a container. Flat-bottomed con-
...ers or fork lift-pallets can be easily
...lified for use with the hoverpallet.
...ration is identical in method to that
...ployed with the 1-ton version.

...n smooth surfaces the pressure required
...the air inlet connection is 15 lbf/in²
...imum and the airflow approximately
...scfm. Under these conditions a load of
...ns requires approximately 18 lbf effort
...nitiate movement.

...e size of airline required will depend on
...pressure of air available and the length
...ose required. For most applications a
...bore hose will be sufficient.

...IENSIONS:

...ngth of pallet	7 ft 5¼ in (2·26 m)
...idth of pallet	5 ft 6 in (1·67 m)

...PRESSURE:

...orking air pressure for 1,000 lb load
    8 lb sq in (0·56 kgf/cm²)
...orking air pressure for 1 ton load
    11 lb sq in (0·77 kgf/cm²)
...in BSP connection), 5 ton load
    15 lb sq in (1·05 kgf/cm²)

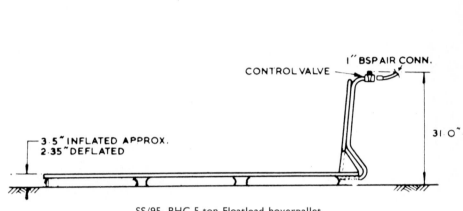

SS/95 BHC 5-ton Floatload hoverpallet

...stream
...STREAM AIRVEYORS LTD

...D OFFICE:
...ameside Industrial Estate, Factory Road,
...ilvertown, E.16

...ECTORS:
  H. S. Green
  S. Stafford
  G. White, Managing Director
  H. Wall

...t Stream Airveyors Ltd is a subsidiary of
...dley Page Ltd and has the licence to
...ufacture and market Jet Stream Convey-
...n the United Kingdom and Scandinavia.
...company is currently building conveyor
...ems for carrying cartons and flat-bottom-
...oods, granular products and paper and
...al trim.

...ods are conveyed on air emitted through
...l orifices in the top of a plenum or duct.
...disposition of these orifices is varied to
...the commodity being conveyed. Damp-

...ers may be incorporated in the plenum to
vary the pressure along its sections and so
control the speed or boost commodities up
gradients.

Air pressures used do not generally exceed
5 in wg (127 mm). For the heavier type of
commodity, pressures of 12 in wg (305 mm)
or more are used where the conveyor's other
advantages may outweigh this increased
power consumption. For light or empty
carton conveying pressures of 0·5 in wg
(12·7 mm) are usual.

Further details of the Jetstream conveyor
can be found in the entries in the USA
section for Jetveyors Incorporated and the
Jetstream Systems Company, USA.

Jetstream conveyor for handling empty cartons
in a large confectionary firm in the United
Kingdom

AIR CUSHION APPLICATORS, CONVEYORS AND PALLETS
NATIONAL ENGINEERING LABORATORY / NPL: United Kingdom

NEL
NATIONAL ENGINEERING LABORATORY MACHINERY GROUP

HEAD OFFICE:
East Kilbride, Glasgow, Scotland
TELEPHONE:
20222
TELEX:
77588

The National Engineering Laboratory Machinery Group has developed an air bearing system for moving heavy loads.

The system consists of a platform supporting a total load of approximately 2,050 lb (929 kg) carried on three air bearing pads. The effective diameter of each pad is $3\frac{5}{8}$ in (91 mm) and the specific loading on the pads under these conditions is 66 psi. The total air consumption is 6·4 cu ft per minute at 100 psi. The pads have porous stainless steel surfaces which operate through the air

bearing film created under the porous surface against a compliant layer laid on top of the floor. In this case, the compliant layer was $\frac{1}{4}$ in (6·2 mm) thick neoprene on top of a typical concrete floor, in the same condition as would be found in many factories. The system is capable of crossing relatively large gaps between the mats of compliant material,

A National Engineering Laboratory air pallet. The three air bearing pads have porous stainless steel surfaces

NPL
NATIONAL PHYSICAL LABORATORY HOVERCRAFT UNIT

HEAD OFFICE:
St John's Street, Hythe, Southampton
TELEPHONE:
Hythe 3065

The activities of Hovercraft Development Ltd in this field were transferred to the National Physical Laboratory in April 1967.

INDUSTRIAL SEGMENTED SKIRT SYSTEMS

A specialist section of the NLP Hovercraft Unit was formed in August 1966 to study industrial application of the air cushion principle.

The industrial skirt system under development has individual sections constructed in neoprene-nylon fabrics. The object to be moved is equipped with a skirt round its lower periphery. Provided the base of the object is airtight and of sufficient strength, air can be pumped into the skirt and allowed to percolate beneath the object until sufficient pressure is built up to raise it. Once lifted onto its air cushion, the object may be towed or manoeuvred to its new position using any standard method.

The air flow and pressure will depend on the size and weight of the object to be moved and the terrain to be traversed. An oil tank 50 ft (15·24 m) diameter by 30 ft (9·14 m) high, with an all-up-weight of 60 tons, requires 45,000 ft³ (1,274 m³) per min at 65 lb/ft² (320 kg/m² per min) for traversing a compacted earth surface.

Standard ventilating centrifugal fans are satisfactory where pressures do not exceed 90 lb/ft² (440 kg/m²). Drive may be supplied by an electric or internal combustion engine, depending on the application and power sources available.

A tank used in one trial was 21 ft (6·4 m) diameter, 10 ft (3·04 m) high and weighed 12 tons. A segmented skirt was fitted to the bottom of the tank, and air was supplied to the skirt by a mobile centrifugal fan and power unit.

Once on cushion, movement was provided by two vehicles, one to tow, and the other to

A large oil storage tank being resited with the help of an industrial skirt. A skirt is fitted round the lower periphery of the object to be moved. Air is pumped into the skirt and once lifted its air cushion the object can be towed or manoeuvred to its new position

provide a restraining force. For convenience, the motorised fan unit was carried in one of the vehicles. Obstacles in the path of the tank, such as curbs, gullies, etc may be traversed without trouble as long as the height of the obstacles does not exceed 75% of the available hover height.

The basic hover height is a design function of the skirt, and can be regulated within reasonable limits. In the recent experiments 12 in (305 mm) was taken as a datum, and lift within this height regulated by changes in fan speed.

In operation it was found that the tank was very stable; the changes in the centre of cushion pressure obtained from the skirt design being sufficient to provide the necessary righting movement to maintain the tank in a stable condition.

During trials a variety of different ground surfaces were covered, including roadway, rough open ground, and a railway crossing.

For the railway crossing, a bed of sleep was laid on the rails to bring the level up the approximate height of the adjacent ro and this bed was then covered with sheet to provide a simple air seal.

Other large objects, e.g. containers, can moved by the air cushion method provid that the ratio of weight to cushion a available does not exceed about 90 lb sq ft (439 kg/m²) and that the skirt segme maintain an adequate cushion seal with surface.

HOVERPALLETS

A number of applications of air cush technology for industrial purposes are be assessed and developed by the Hovercr Unit of the National Physical Laboratory.

Industrial hoverpallets and hoverpads move heavy loads over surfaces too weak withstand high wheel loads, and awkward delicate loads over relatively uneven surfac overpads have been developed that can be ...ped under a loaded pallet. The air ...hion seal is made from a lightweight ...ofed fabric, formed into segments designed ... operate at pressures up to 10 psi and ...rances of the order of 2 in (51 mm). ...s clearance height enables the loaded ...let to negotiate obstacles normally ...ociated with warehouse and industrial ...rs, and ships decking.

...allets with loads of 1 ton have been lifted ... moved quite easily over a normal ...ustrial floor surface, using a 36 in (915 mm) ...side diameter mono-cushion with air ...plied by an industrial blower. At a 2 in ...er height the area for a cushion of this ... is 800 sq in (5,161 cm²). Work is at ...sent being undertaken on a multi-cushion ...et that remains stable due to the inherent ...ness of each cushion.

...further adaptation of the air cushion ...nciple is lifting much heavier loads than ...se associated with pallets. For instance ...overpad system is being developed for ...ng and moving 20 ton containers in the ...ls of ships. This system consists of two ...ble cushion pads with a total cushion area ...ome 600 sq in (3,871 cm²) mounted under ...0 ft × 8 ft platform. A 20 ton load has ...n lifted using two compressors of 25 hp ...h and moved by three men over a concrete ...r. Roll stiffness is improved by a valve ...ch controls the airflow to each cushion. ...ave oscillation can occur in some conditions ... can be radically reduced by controlling ... amount of airflow to the air cushion. ...periments are being carried out to elimin... the heave with no loss of lift height. ...ts are also being carried out to find a light ...ght material with good wear properties.

Hoverpad system for lifting and moving 20 ton containers in the holds of ships. The system consists of two double cushion pads with a total cushion area of some 600 sq ins mounted under a 20 ft × 8 ft platform

THE HOVERBED

The Hoverbed consists of a rigid framework inside which is hung a fabric bag made from a light nylon coated with a synthetic rubber of the kind normally used for anoraks and light mackintoshes. The top of the bag consists of two rows of pockets based on the segmented skirts of Hovercraft. Warm sterile air at low pressure ($\frac{1}{4}$ to $\frac{1}{3}$ lb per sq in) is pumped into the bag, inflates the pockets which meet along the centre.

The first Hoverbed, with a rigid top, was constructed by the National Engineering Laboratory of the Ministry of Technology. The later, flexible models have been built by Hovercraft Development Limited.

When the patient is placed on the bed the pockets form a seal along the side of the body, and fall away beneath it. The body is left solely supported on air, though normally the head is supported on a pillow. The seal automatically conforms to any size of patient and follows any movement of the patient.

The air supply unit is housed in a four-wheeled trailer outside the ward.

After the treatment is concluded the fabric of the Hoverbed can be removed, suitably wrapped, and sterilised.

The first two patients have been successfully treated on the Hoverbed, and the results have been sufficiently encouraging for the National Research Development Corporation to decide to sponsor the construction of a two-bed clinical trial unit by Allen & Hanbury (Surgical Engineering) Ltd.

One patient had petrol burns over one third of his body, front and back. The other patient was burning waste paper in a gale force wind when his oily clothes caught fire and he received burns on his right side. The first patient was on the Hoverbed for six hours and the second for 15½ hours.

In both cases, the doctors report, the weeping areas of the burns dried very rapidly— that is the reason for using a Hoverbed—and it proved easy to nurse the patients.

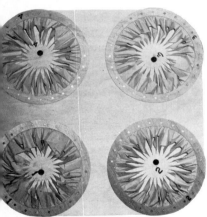

...erside of one of the NPL Hovercraft Unit's multi-cushion pallets

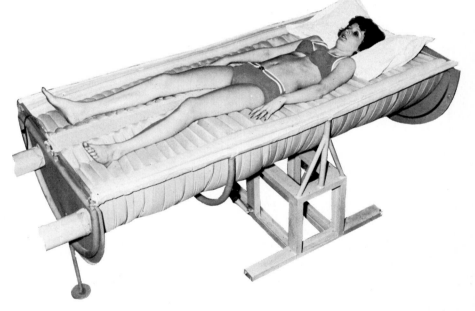

The Hoverbed's air pockets, inflated by an air supply unit in a four-wheeled trailer outside the ward, form a seal at the patient's sides and collapse beneath it, so that the body is wholly supported on a cushion of air, with the head supported by a pillow

AIR CUSHION APPLICATORS, CONVEYORS AND PALLETS
SPENCER (MELKSHAM): United Kingdom

Spencer (Melksham)
SPENCER (MELKSHAM) LTD

HEAD OFFICE AND WORKS:
  Melksham, Wiltshire
TELEPHONE:
  Melksham 3481;
TELEX:
  44392
TELEGRAMS:
  Spencer, Melksham
DIRECTORS:
  Major-General A. T. de Rhe-Philipe
  G. A. Bisset
  F. S. Winkworth
  J. T. Ayre
  G. Meggison
  A. J. Ball
SENIOR EXECUTIVES, AEROGLIDE SECTION:
  G. A. Bisset, Director
  J. Smith, Project Engineer
  C. Jefferson, Sales and Design Engineer

Spencer (Melksham) Ltd is a member of the Elliott-Automation Group. The company's Aeroglide section was formed to design and develop air cushion conveyors for handling 56 lb (25 kg) and 112 lb (50 kg) paper and polythene bags containing powders and granular materials, and also float tables for handling flat metal plate, glass, plywood and specially designed pallets.

At present, a road vehicle is being fitted with an Aeroglide bed in order to conduct experimental work on loading and unloading vehicles. The company is also working with industry and air freight services with the object of introducing Aeroglide aircraft floors.

AEROGLIDE FLOAT TABLE
The float table's conveying surface is of metal or formica faced plywood construction, made in two units to give a load carrying area of 8 ft (2·44 m) × 8 ft (2·44 m), with valves spaced at 6 in (152 mm) pitch.

The unit can carry a 3 ft (0·91 m) square metal-faced loaded pallet, paper and polythene bags, or flat objects such as steel and glass sheets. Air supply is via narrow blade centrifugal fan or Rootes type positive displacement type blowers, remote from the unit and feeding the valve chambers via a flexible hose. The unit can be installed as a false floor in warehouses, in aircraft, and in road vehicles for pallet and bag handling.

Aeroglide float table in operation at the ICI plasterboard factory at Severnside near Bristo

Load and pressure requirements:

Load	Pallet Size	Working Pressure	Blower Horse Po
100 lb	2 ft × 2 ft	0·35 psi	$\frac{1}{3}$ (Narrow Fan)
(54·3 kg)	(0·6 × 0·6 m)	(0·025 kg/cm²)	
1,000 lb	3 ft × 3 ft	0·78 psi	1$\frac{1}{4}$ (Narrow Fan)
(453 kg)	(0·9 × 0·9 m)	(0·055 kg/ cm²)	
1 ton	4 ft × 4 ft	2·00 psi	2 (Positive
(1·016 kg)	(1·2 × 1·2 m)	(0·14 kg/cm²)	displacement)

AEROGLIDE CONVEYOR
The Aeroglide air cushion conveyor is made up from nodules ranging from 2 ft (0·6 m) × 4 ft (1·21 m) to 4 ft (1·21 m) × 8 ft (2·42 m). Decking is of formica-covered plywood, with a support frame of hollow square mild steel tube. Power supply is a $\frac{1}{3}$ hp fan type blower supplying air via a flexible hose to a valve chamber directly below the centre of the conveyor.

Thé system will handle materials in pa and polythene bags; flat metal, glass plywood sheet, and specially designed pal Blower/fan hp requirements are depend upon the application.

THE UNITED STATES OF AMERICA

Aero-Go
AERO-GO INC

HEAD OFFICE AND WORKS:
2447, 6th Avenue South, Seattle, Washington 98134

Aero-Go was founded in April 1967 to commercialise air film and air cushion devices developed by the Boeing Company. It holds the exclusive world licence for the products and patent rights of Boeing in this field.

A major part of the company's current activity relates to engineered materials handling systems based on special Aero-casters. Another development is the Compass Rose Aero-Caster Turntable which will "float" the finished Boeing 747 airplane during the calibrating of its compasses. The capacity will be 500,000 lb and the diameter will be 50 ft (15·2 m). Eighteen 48 ft (14·6 m) diameter Aero-Casters will support this load.

Beyond this the company is working on the development of high-pressure large-diameter Aero-Casters for very large industrial loads. Performance tests are currently underway on individual casters of up to 85 tons working capacity.

AERO-CASTER MODEL K21

Aero-Go casters operate from pressurised air. Their air supply ranges from vacuum cleaner blowers to high pressure plant air. In effect the Aero-Caster is an open ended piston with a lift area of 250 sq in. At 1 psi 250 lb (113 kg) can be lifted on one caster, and at 10 psi the same caster will lift 2,500 lb (1,132 kg).

In operation, air first inflates the caster to lift the load clear of the floor and force the peripheral seal into positive ground contact.

Air, escaping in a thin self-regulating film under this seal, lubricates the bearing and allows it to float freely. As the caster moves across floor surfaces the flexible seal automatically contours to provide a constant gap and thus maintain a uniform air flow. When the air supply is shut off, the captured air bubble within the caster escapes slowly, lowering the load gently to the ground. Deflated, the caster lies flat.

Ideally, the casters are mounted beneath loads in a way that the total weight is equally divided. For stability it is recommended that three or more casters are arranged in a triangle, or four in a square pattern. The centre of gravity of the load should be as close as possible to the geometric centre of the caster pattern. An optional mounting flange can be used to attach the caster to the load.

Sources of air supply can be 100 psi plant air, portable piston type compressor/accumulator, low pressure centrifugal blower or air bottle, depending on the load and floor surface. The casters are self pressure-regulating systems that may be operated without separate line regulators.

Typical coefficient of friction between an inflated Aero-caster and a smooth level surface is under 1%. For example, a 2,000 lb (908 kg) load can be moved with a push of less than 15 lb (6·8 kg). On inclined or undulating surfaces, free floating casters will tend to drift to the lower level.

Base plate and mounting flange are in mild steel. The casters which are replaceable are of hypalon or neoprene impregnated nylon.

DIMENSIONS:

Diameter	2 ft 5 in (0·73 m)
Height	3 in (unpressirused)
Lift	1½ in (inflated maximum)

TRANSPORTER AIR PALLET

Lifting capacities of the standard Transporter Air Pallet loading platforms range from 4,000-60,000 lb (1,816-2,7240 kg) and the dimensions from 3 ft (0·9 in) × 3 ft (0·9 m) to 12 ft (3·6 m) × 8 ft (2·4 m). The platforms are rectangular, and built of mild steel, or in the case of the smaller ones, metal-clad plywood. Six air casters are mounted beneath the assembly. Moving wheels and fork lift cut-outs are optional.

AERO-GO TURNTABLE

Aero-Go, a Boeing subsidiary, has produced an air-bearing turntable which will be used to calibrate the compasses of Boeing 747 superjets. The turntable, 46 ft (14 m) in diameter, will support loads up to 500,000 lb. The Boeing 747, empty, weighs 320,000 lb. Five air-bearing platforms will raise the turntable about 3 in (77 mm) above ground level. One air bearing unit will be placed beneath each of the four main undercarriage units, and a smaller unit will be placed beneath the dual-wheel nose gear. A fixed king post in the centre of the turntable will supply service connections to operate the air bearings and the plane's systems. Electronic devices used for the calibrations are accurate to 1°.

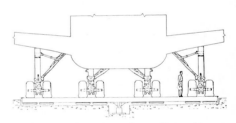

Compass Rose Aero-Caster Turntable

Airfloat
AIRFLOAT CORPORATION

HEAD OFFICE:
R.R. 3 Box 300C, Decatur, Illinois 62526, USA

TELEPHONE:
Area Code 217, 963-2234

SALES MANAGER:
C. A. Braver

In February 1967, Vega Enterprises, a partnership, acquired a licence from General Motors Corporation to produce and market air bearing devices previously manufactured by Inland Manufacturing Division of General Motors Corporation, and sold by them under the trade name of Hovair and later Invisalift.

In October 1967, the partnership of Vega Enterprises was dissolved to form Airfloat Corporation to manufacture and market air bearing devices under the name of Airfloat.

Airfloat air castor pads normally incorporate a rigid platform for supporting the load. The perimeter of a flexible plastic diaphragm is attached with an air-tight seal to the periphery of the platform, and the centre of the diaphragm is attached to the platform also. Compressed air is fed to the space between the platform and the diaphragm, passing through one or more holes near the centre of the diaphragm to its underside.

The air causes the diaphragm to inflate, lifting the platform off the ground, and finally escapes around the periphery of the pad, through the narrow gap between the underside of the diaphragm and the ground plane.

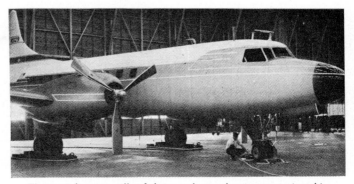

Three air bearing cells of three pads are shown supporting this 46,000 lb aircraft to ease-in-hanger handling

AIR CUSHION APPLICATORS, CONVEYORS AND PALLETS
AIRFLOAT: United States of America

In an early application of the air bearing cell at the Airfloat Research Laboratories two identical pads with independent air supply sources were use to handle a station wagon. The separate air sources overcame a problem associated with the unequal distribution of weight between front and re pads. A top view of one of the air bearing cells is shown in the photograph on the right

The Airfloat cell has the omni-directional capability, low ground pressure, and the extremely low friction of other air cushion systems plus the flexibility of the diaphragm to overcome the extreme intolerance of the air castor to irregularities in the ground plane.

At the same time the air flow rate is sufficiently low to avoid the clouds of dust sometimes encountered with the peripheral jet.

The airflow rate required at a fixed load and supply pressure is dependent on the nature of the ground plane. If the ground plane is a flat, smooth metal plate the airflow requirement is minimal. Airflow needs are normally low over smooth cement, resiliant tile or linoleum floors. If, on the other hand, the surfaces are of a non-continuous nature, such as unsealed wood block factory floors, or hard tile floors with recessed grout or cement joints, the airflow requirements are large.

These surfaces can of course be improved by cleaning, smoothing, caulking, sealing or covering.

One solution for dealing with off-centre loads, when it is evident that if a single pad is used the platform will come into contact with the ground, is to install wheeled castors at intervals around the periphery of the platform. In the case of excessive tipping, the contact of one or more small wheeled castors with the ground provides a restoring movement without sacrificing omni-directional capability.

Flotation by air bearing cells permits the sensitive adjustment and positioning needed to assemble the fuel section to the rocket motor section of the Saturn V launch vehicle. The complete assembly tool has a capacity of supporting approx 200,000 lb

Airfloat cells are being used by major aircraft manufacturers such as Boeing Company, McDonnell-Douglas Corporation, Lockheed, and Fairchild Hiller-Corporation. The applications include moving sub-assemblies as well as complete airframes in their plants.

Airfloat Corporation has also designed and fabricated a conveyor for the movement of air cargo pallets and containers. Typical conveyor sections measure 7 ft 4 in (2·23 m) × 10 ft 5 in (3·17 m) and can carry up to 12,000 lb (5,436 kg). In this application the

smooth pallet or container bottom pass over inverted stationary air bearing cell The practicality of this design was prove after weeks of successful operation of th prototype at the American Airlines termina in San Francisco, California. The fir Airfloat air cargo conveyor was due to b installed at American Airlines Boston freigl terminal in the autumn of 1968. The majc advantages of this conveyor include one-ma movement of loaded containers, omn directional movement, and reduced damag to the underside of the containers.

This large air bearing cell supports a 40,000 lb load for a two-dimensional simulation of space docking within the laboratory

This standardised track container has built-in air bearing cells. It was developed by Airfloat Styling to demonstrate the feasibility of moving cargo from flat-bed trucks onto warehouse docks

A three pad air bearing cell used as a practic platform by astronauts. Battery-powered, th cell eliminates friction in one plane which hel the astronaut to develop a "feel" for spac walking

hlen

HLEN MANUFACTURING COMPANY

DRESS:

O Box 569, Columbus, Nebraska, USA

LEPHONE:

02-564-3111

ehlen Manufacturing Company is develop-
a steel stadium system in which large
tions can be repositioned quickly and with
atively little effort by air lubrication.

he company believes that the development
large air lubricated seating sections is
essary before stadiums can be adapted to
t a wide variety of sporting events.

A prototype section recently completed by
company measures 24 ft (7·3 m) wide ×
ft (10·97 m) deep and weighs 12 tons.
ethene rubber Invisalift pads, developed
General Motors Corporation, are fitted to
el pads at the base of four supporting
umns. The stadium section floats when
pads are inflated to a pressure of 2-5
unds per sq in and a thin layer of air
apes from beneath. The volume of escap-
g air is so small that it is difficult to detect
d no dust problem exists. Air pressure
uld be supplied by a portable turbine
mpressor.

It requires approximately 50 to 100 pounds
lateral push per flotation pad to move the
adium. In use, a section many times the
ze of the prototype would be manoeuvered
rubber-wheeled tractors. In a matter of
urs, a seating arrangement could be shifted
om football to horse racing.

The company is examining the possibility
using air flotation to move a 1,000 ft (305
) span arched roof in situations where an
door-outdoor sports facility is considered
sirable.

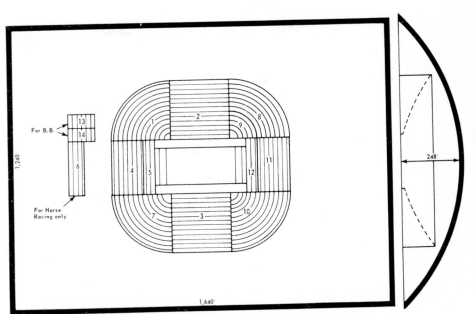

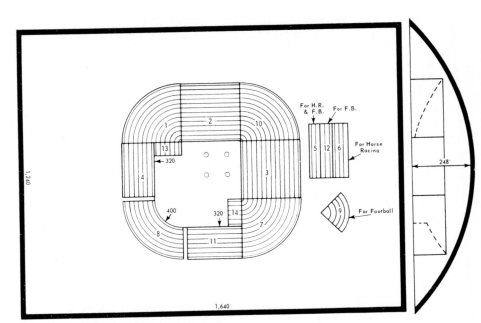

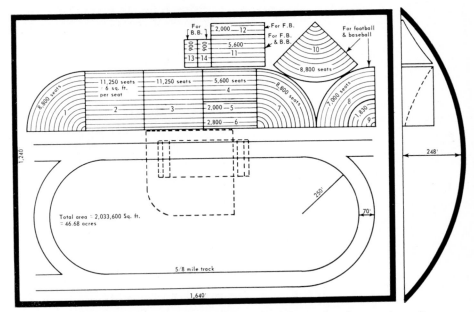

Seating arrangements possible with Behlen air lubricated stadium seating units

AIR CUSHION APPLICATORS, CONVEYORS AND PALLETS
BEHLEN / CLARK: United States of America

A 12-ton section of stadium seating being moved by man power. Behlen Manufacturing Company is planning air-lubricated seating units, many ti the size of this prototype, which will be repositioned by tractors to convert a stadium's seating from football to horse racing layout in a matter of ho Air pressure would be supplied by portable turbine compressors

Clark
CLARK EQUIPMENT COMPANY
INDUSTRIAL TRUCK DIVISION
HEAD OFFICE:
  PO Box 1320, Battle Creek, Michigan
  49016, USA
OFFICERS:
  George Spatta, Chairman
  Walter E. Schirnier, President
  B. E. Phillips, Executive Vice-President
  John R. Wood Jr, Senior Vice-President—
    Finance and Treasurer

Clark Equipment Company is one of the world's largest manufacturers of air lubricated handling systems. The current range of Load Glide air bearing systems includes the CAP-60-H, with a 6,000 lb (2,768 kg) load capacity and the CAP-450, with a 45,000 lb load capacity.

CLARK AIR PALLET CAP-60-H
The Air-in-Pallet (AIP) system employs one or more inflatable air pads attached to the underside of a load-carrying structure. These pliable air pallets of almost any size or shape, bleed a continuous low pressure, 1 to 20 psi (0·7 to 1·41 kg/cm²), volume of air between the pad and the reaction surface thus creating an air film.

View of the world's first air pallet assembly line at the Westinghouse distribution plant at Shai Pennsylvania. The complete transformers, which weigh up to 8,000 lb (3,632 kg), are each b up on air pallets and moved from station to station manually. The dozens of Clark air pa employed in this operation float along gently along the floor in a specially constructed networ air pallet channels. The transformers shown here have travelled almost the entire network are complete apart from painting and final fittings

he air pads are in several shapes and
es—round, oval and square—and can be
d singly or in multiple. The load support
se may be a piece of plywood, a freight
ntainer, a truck frame or a custom-designed
lding fixture.

ow pressure air is used at moderate
lume flow rates. For example, the air
m a household vacuum cleaner type
wer is sufficient to move a 2,000 lb (900 kg)
d over a good surface.

The equipment can be supplied in the form
pallets, turntables or mobile industrial
ucks. The power source can be an in-plant
supply system or a self-contained air
nerating unit mounted on the truck or
llet and powered by industrial batteries,
petrol engine or main electrical current.

The air pads will operate over most surfaces
t the rougher the surface the greater the
lume of air required to float the load
ressure remaining constant). Large gaps
t the entrances to elevators, for example)
ust be bridged with rubber mats to ensure
od load translation. Open floor drains,
rge cracks or unsealed wood blocks cause
r loss and possible grounding of the air
ds, but most surfaces are compatible.

The Clark CAP-60-H (a standard size is
) in (1·02 m) long by 48 in (1·22 m) wide)
as four air pads and a 6,000 lb (2,720 kg)
apacity. The load capacity to weight ratio
60:1.

ONSTRUCTION: The frame is of ply-
etal panel, consisting of 1 in (25·4mm)
xterior grade AC plywood faced both sides
ith 0·050 in (1·3 mm) mill finished 3003-H12
luminium.

The air distribution system is a combina-
ion of metal tubing and plastic hose, with
ntegral pressure reduction, fastened to the
ame with "U" clips.

The air pads are dual metal round sections,
7 in (432 mm) outside diameter, mated with
n inflatable diaphragm made from a plastic
ubber compound. A metal pedestal in the
entre of the pad supports the load when the
iaphragm is deflated.

The air pad diaphragms are repairable and
eplaceable.

IR SUPPLY: Air pallets are designed to
perate on clean compressed air in the
ressure range of 80/100 psi, (5·6 to 7·7
g/cm²) and flow rate of 30 to 50 cu ft
0·85-1·42 m³) per minute delivered by 0·5 in
13 mm) air hose to the inlet. The perform-
nce will change if the air supply differs from
hese values. Low pressure input air models
re available.

PERATION: High pressure air is intro-
uced into the pallet and reduced to a lower
pressure of 5 to 10 psi (0·35-0·70 kg/cm²).
Lower pressure air is evenly distributed
within the air pad assemblies and allowed to
escape in a continuous flow through communicating holes in the diaphragm. The
diaphragm inflates like a balloon raising the
pallet. A film of air 0·005 to 0·015 in
(0·13 to 0·38 mm) thickness caused by the
airflow forms between the peripheral edge
of the air pad and floor surface to "free float"
its load. Best operation is obtained if load
is centred on pallet; reduced performance
may result from off-centre loading.

The Clark CAP-60-H has four air pads and a 6,000 lb (2,724 kg) load capacity

STABILITY: On some surfaces the pallet
may vibrate vertically when empty, but a
light load will eliminate vibration. The
pallet is stable with all low centre of gravity
loads up to its 6,000 lb (2,720 kg) capacity.
A high C.G. load may induce an oscillating
motion on some surfaces.

CAP-450

This is a new addition to the Clark Air
Pallet Line. It is designed specifically to
handle containers weighing up to 45,000 lb
(20,385 kg) in the holds of ships. The
container is placed by crane onto the air
pallet which is then moved into position by a
fork lift truck. The forks slide into openings
in the pallet's welded steel frame. Approximately 3 lb (1·36 kg) of moving force are
required to move each 1,000 lb (454 kg) load.
Only 150 lb (68 kg) of moving force is required
to move the maximum 45,000 lb load.

AIR PADS: The CAP-450 has six large air
pads mounted on its undersurface. These
have metal plate backing sections, 36 in
(916 mm) by 44 in (1,118 mm), mated with
an inflatable diaphragm made from a
urethane compound. They will operate over
surfaces having temperatures up to 150°F

and can be removed easily for repair or
replacement. Off centre loads are handled
by an air manifold system controlled by a
four-way valve. This enables the operator
to compensate for off-centre loads by sending
varying amounts of air to each air pad to
level the pallet so that the load is handled
efficiently.

The air inlet to the manifold distribution
system is a 1 in NPT female fitting to accept
a standard air nose system.

AIR SUPPLY: The pallet is designed to
operate on clean compressed air in the
pressure range 80-110 psi and flow rate
approximately 200 cu ft per minute, delivered
by a 1 in air hose to inlet. Manifold system
is contained with the platform structure.

FLOOR SURFACES: The area over which
a load is floated must have a surface capable
of maintaining an air film between the pad
diaphragm and floor. A smoothness equal
to steel-trowelled concrete, vinyl tile or steel
plate is best. Pallet performance will
decrease in proportion to an increase in
surface roughness. The pallet will not float
over brick, wood blocks, coarse macadam or
equivalent surfaces.

AIR CUSHION APPLICATORS, CONVEYORS AND PALLETS
CLARK / JETSTREAM: United States of America

The pallet will negotiate an undulating surface and will move from one surface to another in different elevation providing the two are connected by a smooth gradual slope not greater than 1% incline.

Sealing various porous surfaces as recommended will result in more efficient operation. Concrete treated with an epoxy, paint or wax is better than untreated concrete. Large floor cracks may be filled with a plastic floor repair compound.

POSITIONING POWER: Since the load is lifted by the air pallet, power is required only to move and manoeuvre the load. The truck should be equipped with a reel and an adequate length of 1 in (26 mm) hose for air supply to pallet. An electric or gas truck equipped with an automatic transmission is recommended because of the high-cycle manoeuvering capabilities demanded.

DIMENSIONS:

Width	10 ft 4 in (3·14 m)
Length	8 ft 2 in (2·48 m)
Height (deflated)	$5\frac{3}{4}$ in (146 mm)
Height (inflated, fully loaded)	$6\frac{7}{8}$ in (175 mm)
Weight	1,800 lb (816 kg)

Clark CAP-450 air pallet, designed to handle containers weighing up to 45,000 lb (20,430 k

Jetstream
JETSTREAM SYSTEMS COMPANY

HEAD OFFICE:
3486 Investment Boulevard, Hayward, California 94545

OFFICERS:
Stanley Lenox, President
Warren P. Landon, Vice-President, Marketing
Eugene S. Batter, Vice-President, Operations
Rudolph Futter, Vice-President and Technical Director

Jetstream Systems Company has the Jetstream rights for North America. The company is currently producing and developing Jetstream conveying and processing equipment and Jetsweep storage and drying systems.

Jetstream uses low-pressure air delivered to a plenum by a fan or fans and introduced to the conveyor surface through various types of orifices along the full length of the conveyor, to maintain a belt of air flowing close to the conveyor surface. It conveys granular materials, such as sand, iron pellets, grain, etc; paper and metal trim and scrap; cartons; webs or sheets of paper or metal; and practically any other material within reason.

The air can be heated or cooled to condition the product while it is being conveyed. Extremely good results have been attained, especially in the heating, cooling and drying field. Longer or shorter dwell time can be obtained by using different configurations of the conveyor.

Objects are moved along a succession of angularly disposed conveyors with a change of direction of movement. They are placed

Jetstream conveyor removing trim from underneath a modern die cutter in an Oakland, Califor box plant

or dropped in an extended collecting zone and carried into a common stream in a take-off conveyor. The objects can be moved upwards along an inclined conveyor and can be discharged into a hopper or other receptacle. The conveyor membrane may be used for moving solid objects by air-jet action and as a support and walkway for workmen while adjusting, operating or maintaining an associated machine.

POWER SUPPLY: Pressure of air necessary: $\frac{1}{10}$ inch water gauge to $\frac{1}{2}$ psi. Air ducting

and centrifugal fans are generally fitted as integral part of the conveyor.

CONVEYOR SYSTEM: Units are design to suit product. The length can run 1,000 ft or more and the width from 1 in 10 ft or more as necessary.

PALLET SIZES: 1 in (25·4 mm) × 1 (25·4 mm) to 6 ft (1·8 m) × 6 ft (1·8 m) larger if required.

BLOWER H/P: Power requirements loadings up to 7 lb sq ft (34·17 kgt/r $\frac{1}{100}$ hp/sq ft—$\frac{1}{10}$ hp sq ft.

veyors

VEYORS INCORPORATED

AD OFFICE:
347-17th Avenue, San Francisco, California 94122

FICERS:
. E. Futer, President
Lenneth L. White, Secretary

Jetveyors Incorporated is the holder of foreign patents for Jetstream conveyors. The concept was first developed in 1960 by Engineers Associated of Berkeley, California, for removing corrugated trim from beneath a high speed folder-gluer in box plants. Jetstream has subsequently been adapted to a great many applications, and conveying corrugated trim is now one of the minor uses.

Jetveyors Incorporated is purely a licencing body handling the international licencing arrangements.

In 1967, Engineers Associated was acquired by merger with Bangor Punta Operations, and the company name was changed to Jetstream Systems Company, who have the Jetstream rights for North America. The Jetstream conveyor system is described under the entry for the Jetstream Systems Company.

immers

MMERS INCORPORATED

AD OFFICE:
O Box 855, Severna Park, Maryland

RECTORS:
. W. Beardsley
. L. Beardsley
J. D. Preston

YING CARPET

he standard Flying Carpet is designed for iding operator who sits or stands at a ation which causes the over-all centre of vity to coincide with the centre of lift. is controlled kinesthetically. If, from a ition of neutral balance (hovering), the rator leans forward, the Flying Carpet move forward. If he leans to the right, machine will turn to the right.

specially designed inflatable structure ws the carpet to lie flat on the ground en the machine is not operating. When ver is applied by the operator's hand-held ottle control, the resulting air flow causes body to inflate and rise from the ground, ing the carpet to a height of about 15 hes. The bottom extremity of the ated structure, though not readily visible ler the fringed edge of the carpet, clears ground by a height of about 3 in when operator's weight is about 120 lb (54 kg). ads as great as 400 lb (180 kg) can be lifted moved over the ground at reduced rance height.

speed of 20 mph (32 km/h) can be attained

The Flying Carpet, an inflatable ACV devised by Skimmers Incorporated for Stores promotions. It can also be used as an "air barrow" or air cushion stretcher

by a 40-second acceleration run over level ground. With a 120 lb (54 kg) riding operator, it will climb slopes of up to 3·3% (1 in 30); but will drift downhill on surfaces having greater inclination.

The craft can be controlled by a remote operator, through the manipulation of connected cords or by radio equipment. Machines for use with remote control require individual design consideration to assure proper balance and controllability.

As an "air barrow" the craft which has a lifting area of 6 ft × 8 ft (1·83 × 2·44 m),

would carry over 400 lb (180 kg). Barrow handles would be attached to the base of the housing for the lift engine. Another application envisaged is that of an air cushion stretcher.

DIMENSIONS:
Length of rigid tubular frame
                          7 ft 0 in (2·13 m)
Width of frame   5 ft 0 in (1·52 m)
Weight   70 lb (31·75 kg)
Inflatable body material
                    Vinyl-coated Nylon fabric
Engine   2 cycle, 5 hp West Bend

HYDROFOIL MANUFACTURERS

CANADA

De Havilland
THE DE HAVILLAND AIRCRAFT COM-PANY OF CANADA, LIMITED

HEAD OFFICE AND WORKS:
Downsview, Ontario, Canada
TELEPHONE:
633-7310 Area Code 416
TELEGRAMS:
Moth Toronto
DIRECTORS:
A. S. Kennedy, Chairman
Sir Harry Broadhurst
W. B. Boggs, President
P. C. Garrett
F. A. Stanley, Vice-President Finance and Secretary Treasurer
D. B. Annan, Vice-President, Operations
A. J. MacIntosh QC, Legal Counsel
SENIOR EXECUTIVES:
W. B. Boggs, President, Chief Executive Officer
P. Y. Davond, Vice-President, Marketing
W. T. Heaslip, Vice-President, Engineering
F. H. Buller, Engineering Chief Designer

In 1947-49, a 45 ft craft powered by a 1,200 hp Rolls-Royce Merlin was designed by Phillip Rhodes for Cdr D. M. Hodgson RCNR of Montreal for an attempt on the existing water-speed record. At about this time, the Canadian Defense Research Board became interested in the potential operational employment of hydrofoils and Cdr. Hodgson's craft, named the R-100 Massawippi (after Lake Massawippi, Quebec, the site of its construction and initial tests) was built under the Board's direction. Success of the Massawippi, which displaced 7·5 tons and could reach 55 knots, led to an extensive experimental programme involving Massawippi and two subsequent craft, the Bras d'Or and RX. The Bras d'Or, designed and built by Saunders Roe for the Defense Research Board, was delivered in 1957. The RX is a fully instrumented test bed for testing a wide range of new foil designs. De Havilland have used the craft extensively during their design development programme for the FHE-400.

The extensive test experience, together with that gained from the US programmes, led the Naval Research Establishment to prepare proposals for a 200-ton ASW hydrofoil capable of all-weather operation in the North Atlantic. At a tripartite conference in January 1960, a group of specialists from the US and Britain reviewed these proposals and concluded that the extension of NRE's work to a prototype craft was desirable. This led to the design and construction of the FHE (fast hydrofoil escort) 400 by De Havilland Aircraft of Canada as design agent for the Canadian Government.

FHE-400

In early 1961 the Canadian Department of Defence contracted De Havilland Aircraft of Canada Ltd for a feasibility and engineering study, based on the NRE ASW hydrofoil report, which could lead to detailed design and construction of a full-scale craft. The company's recommendations were approved in April 1963. The FHE-400 programme

has two fundamental objectives: (a) to establish in practice the feasibility of an ocean-going hydrofoil of the proposed size and characteristics (b) to evaluate the prototype as an ASW system.

It is intended that the prototype shall be capable of being developed into a warship. For operational evaluation the fighting equipment is likely to include variable depth sonar for submarine detection, homing torpedoes for armament and the necessary facilities for navigation, communication, radar, command and control. Tactical use of the FHE-400 is based upon variable depth sonar as the prime means of submarine detection.

Launching was planned for mid-1968 and completion by mid-1970 after contractor's sea trials, weapon systems installation and systems evaluation.

After commissioning as HMCS Bras d[...] in Quebec City, an RCN crew will oper[...] the ship during contractor's acceptance tri[...] Rough water and operational trials will t[...] be conducted by the Hydrofoil Evaluat[...] team at Halifax, N.S.
FOILS: The foil system is a canard configu[...] tion of the surface piercing type and n[...] retractable. The steerable foil is supercavi[...] ing and designed for good response in[...] seaway. The subcavitating main foil car[...] 90% of the static weight and is a combinat[...] of surface-piercing and submerged foils. [...] centre high speed foil section is protected fr[...] ventilation by the struts and the dihed[...] foils have full-chord fences to inhibit vent[...] tion. Anhedral foils provide reserve lift[...] take-off and their tips provide roll restor[...] forces at foilborne speeds.

FHE prototype on slipway

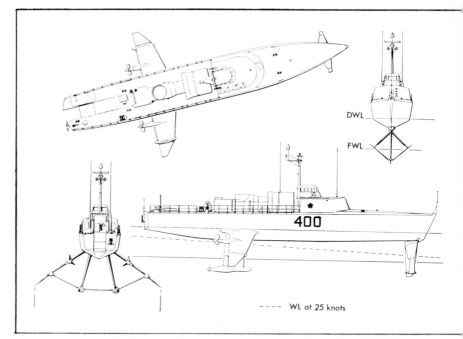

De Havilland FHE-400 ocean going ASW warship

The struts are a compromise to provide
e optimum fin effect in yaw in conjunction
th the steerable bow foil. The foils are
nstructed in maraging steel.

ULL: Hull and superstructure are fabricat-
from ALCAN D54S, and extensive use is
ade of large extrusions with integral
ringers for the plating.

Strain gauges are attached to critical points
the hull and foil system so that predicted
ress levels can be monitored and recorded
oscillograph charts or magnetic tape for
alysis ashore.

A crew of twenty will be carried, comprising
ght officers and twelve men. In order to
aintain crew alertness at all times, comfort-
le crew quarters and good messing facilities
ere considered essential features. Both
ere intensively studied by the Institute of
viation Medicine. The study included the
sting of crew bunks on a motion simulator
NCR Ottawa, and the use of a simulator
assess crew efficiency under foilborne
onditions.

OWER PLANT: Continuous search for a
seful period demands economical operation
any sea state at displacement speeds and
he ability to attack at high speeds. For
his reason there are two propulsion systems
—the foilborne "free" marinized gas-turbine,
22,000 shp Pratt & Whitney FT4A-2, and a
,000 bhp Davey-Paxman 16YJCM diesel
ngine for hullborne power. The maximum
oilborne speed is expected to be about 60
nots and the hullborne speed about 14
nots. The KWM controllable-pitch dis-
lacement propellers of 7 ft (21·33 m)
iameter are novel, since they will be feather-
d when the craft is foilborne so as to
inimize the appendage drag penalty. Slow
peed manoeuvring will be effected by a
ontrol of individual propeller pitch settings.

Thrust is provided by twin 4 ft (1·22 m)
iameter supercavitating propellers fitted in

pods at either end of the main foil's fully
submerged centre section.

The FT4A-2, a marine version of the shaft-
turbine engine developed from the JT4 and
5 gas turbine, is enclosed by a protective
cowling aft of the bridge.

Shaft power is transmitted to the inboard
gearbox directly aft of the engine exhaust
elbow and is then transmitted via dual
shafts through each of the two inner struts
to the outboard gearboxes in the streamlined
pods at the intersection of the struts and foils.
The dual shafts are combined at the outboard
gearboxes into a single drive, taken through
an over-running clutch to each of the two
fixed-pitch supercavitating propellers.

A governor prevents overspeed if the
propellers leave the water in rough seas.

A Paxman Ventura 16YJCM diesel-engine
is sited in the engine room, on the ship's
centreline. Power is transmitted to the
variable pitch hullborne propellers through a
dual output gearbox and thence through
shafts to gearboxes located in the pods.

CONTROLS: Diesel power, propeller pitch,
main gas turbine speed and individual
displacement propeller pitch are all normally
controlled by lever from the bridge. Dual
wheels are provided to steer the bow foil.
An engineer's console is located in the
operation room and starting and stopping of
all engines is undertaken from this position.
Engine and propeller pitch controls duplicat-
ing those on the bridge are provided on the
console.

SYSTEMS

AUXILIARY POWER: An auxiliary gas
turbine, A United Aircraft of Canada ST6A-
53 rated at 390 hp continuous at 2,100 rpm
is used to power electric generators, hydraulic
pumps and a slat-water pump. It can also
be used to increase the available displacement
propulsion power and for emergency propulsion power at reduced speed.

EMERGENCY POWER: The emergency
power unit is an AiResearch GTCP-85-291
shaft-coupled turbine rated at 190 hp
continuous. In the event of the auxiliary
gas turbine becoming unserviceable or being
in use for the displacement propulsion, this
turbine will power the ship's system. Alternatively bleed air may be drawn from the
compressor for main turbine starting.

ARMAMENT: The FHE 400 will be equipped
with a specially designed detection, data
processing and weapon delivery system.
Primary sensor will be a towed sonar and the
armament consists of lightweight homing
torpedoes. Canadian Westinghouse Co is the
main contractor to the RCN for the weapons
system which will be installed on the completion of sea trials. The sonar towed body is
being built by Canadian Westinghouse to a
design developed as part of the Naval
Research Establishment's long term high
speed towed sonar programme. Handling
gear is a compact, lightweight mechanism
developed by Fleet Manufacturing.

DIMENSIONS, EXTERNAL:

Length overall, hull	151 ft 0 in (45·9 m)
Length waterline, hull	147 ft 0 in (44 m)
Hull beam	21 ft 6 in (6·5 m)
Beam across foils	66 ft 0 in (20 m)
Draft afloat	23 ft 6 in (7·16 m)
Freeboard	11 ft 0 in (3·3 m)

WEIGHTS:

Gross tonnage (normal)	212 tons
Light displacement	165 long tons
Max take-off displacement	235 long tons
Useful load (fuel, crew and military load)	over 70 tons

PERFORMANCE:

Cruising speed, foilborne
50 knots rough water 60 knots calm water
Cruise speed, hullborne   over 12 knots
Sea state capability
        Sea State 5 significant wave height 10 ft

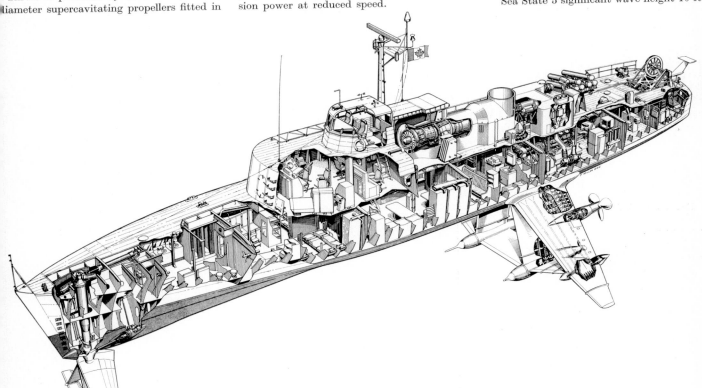

Cutaway of the De Havilland FHE-400

HYDROFOIL MANUFACTURERS
WATER SPYDER: Canada

Water Spyder
WATER SPYDER MARINE LTD

HEAD OFFICE AND WORKS:
157 Richard Clark Drive, Downsview, Ontario

TELEPHONE:
244 5404

DIRECTORS:
J. F. Lstiburek, President
G. A. Leask, Secretary/Treasurer
A. Lstiburek, Vice President

SENIOR EXECUTIVES:
L. Civiera, Sales Manager
J. F. Lstiburek, Designer

Water Spyder Marine Ltd is a wholly-owned Canadian company operating under charter issued by the Government of the Province of Ontario. It produces two fibreglass-hulled sports hydrofoils, a two-seat sports model and a six-seat family model. Both are available either ready-built or in kit form. Canadian Department of Transport plates were issued in 1966 for both models.

WATER SPYDER 2-B

The Water Spyder 2-B is a two-seat sports hydrofoil powered by a long-shaft outboard of 20-35 hp.

FOILS: The foil system comprises a split W-type surface piercing main foil supporting 98% of the load and an adjustable outrigged trim tab which supports the remaining 2%. The foils and the trim tab assembly are retracted manually for docking and beaching. The main foils are of polished 65ST aluminium and the trim tab is of steel.

HULL: This is a two-piece (deck and hull) moulded fibreglass construction and incorporates buoyancy chambers. Standard fittings include a curved Perspex windshield and regulation running lights, fore and aft.

ACCOMMODATION: The craft seats two in comfortably upholstered seats. Foils and the trim tab assembly are adjustable from inside the cockpit.

POWER PLANT: Any suitable outboard engine of 20-35 hp (Mercury 200L or 350L or Evinrude) with long-shaft extension. Total fuel capacity is 5 gallons.

CONTROLS: Controls include steering wheel with adjustable friction damper, single-lever throttle and gearshift control, and trim tab control.

DIMENSIONS:
Length overall, hull   12 ft 0 in (3·6 m)
Beam overall, foils retracted
                            5 ft 4 in (1·6 m)
Beam overall, foils extended
                            7 ft 4 in (2·2 m)

WEIGHTS:
Weight empty   220 lb (99·7 kg)

PERFORMANCE:
Max speed   up to 40 mph (64 km/h)
Max permissible wave height in foilborne
    mode   1 ft 6 in
Turning radius at cruising speed
                            10 ft (3 m) app
Number of seconds and distance to take-off
    (theor app)   4-6 sec, 15 ft (4·5 m)
Number of seconds and distance to stop
    craft (theor app)   4-6 sec, 15 ft (4·5 m)
Cost of standard craft and terms of payment: US$970. Terms: Cash. Delivery: 3 weeks from date of order, fob Toronto.

Water Spyder 2-B, a two seat, fibreglass-hulled hydrofoil pleasure craft powered by a 20-30 hp long shaft outboard motor. The retractable W main foil system carries 98% of the total load

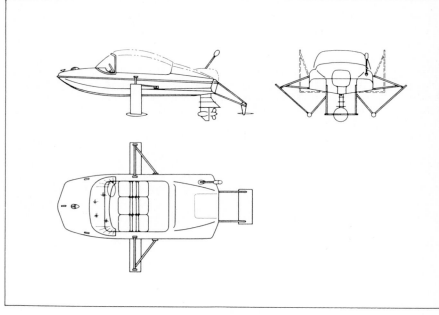

Water Spyder 6-A

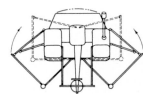
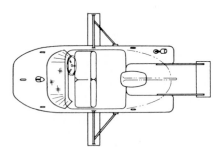

Water Spyder 2-B

WATER SPYDER 6-A

An enlarged version of the Water Spyder 2, Model 6-A is a six-seat family pleasure hydrofoil boat, with a two-piece moulded fibreglass hull. The foil system is identical to that of the earlier craft except that the foils are retracted with the aid of a crank and winch.

The seats, located immediately over the main foil, are arranged in two rows of three abreast, one row facing forward, the other aft.

Power is supplied by a long-shaft outboard motor of 60-115 hp. Total fuel capacity is 6 gallons.

DIMENSIONS:

Length overall, hull	19 ft 0 in (5·79 m)
Beam overall, foils retracted	8 ft 3 in (2·5 m)
Beam overall, foils extended	13 ft 0 in (3·96 m)
Height overall, foils retracted	4 ft 6 in (1·37 m)
Floor area	30 sq ft (2·78 m²)

WEIGHTS:

Gross tonnage	1 ton app
Weight empty	980 lb (444 kg)

PERFORMANCE:

Max speed	35-40 mph (56-64 km/h)
Cruising speed	32 mph (51 km/h
Max permissible wave height in foilborne mode	2 ft 6 in (0·76 m)
Turning radius at cruising speed	20 ft (6·09 m)
Number of seconds and distance to take-off (theoretical, app)	4-6 sec, 15 ft (4·57 m)
Number of seconds and distance to stop craft (theoretical, app)	4-6 sec, 15 ft (4·57 m)

Cost of standard craft and terms of payment: $US2,200. Terms: cash. Delivery: Three weeks from date of order f.o.b. Toronto.

Water Spyder 6-A is a six-seat hydrofoil. The main foil, trim-tab support and engine fold upward so the craft can be floated on and off a trailer

GERMANY

Blohm & Voss
BLOHM & VOSS AG

HEAD OFFICE:
D 2000 Hamburg 1, Postfach 720

TELEPHONE:
0411-3061

DIRECTORS:
Joseph H. Van Riet
Ernst Christian Frh v. Werthern
Dr. Heinricht V. Prinz Reuss

SENIOR EXECUTIVES:
Erich Schneider, General Manager
Albert Schütt, Shipbuilding Manager
Egbert Müller, Engineering Manager

Under partnership arrangement with Grumman Engineering Corporation, Blohm & Voss undertook the final development and construction of the Grumman Dolphin.

From January 1965 the company's engineers have worked together with Grumman's design staff. The Dolphin prototype was completed in October 1966. The second Dolphin was due for completion in the autumn of 1968 and has been sold to an operator in the United States.

The company is now planning to build the 325-ton Neptune, a passenger/car ferry similar in design and construction to the AG(EH) experimental hydrofoil designed by Grumman.

NEPTUNE

The Neptune is a design for a fast, seagoing passenger/car ferry, capable of operating in up to Sea State 6. It will have a maximum take-off displacement of 325 tons and a cruising speed of 50 knots (93 km/h).

The standard design will accommodate 302 passengers on the saloon deck and 37 cars on the vehicle deck beneath, but all-passenger layouts will be available.

Foilborne power will be supplied by two General Electric LM 1500 marine gas turbines each rated at 14,200 hp continuous.

FOILS: The foil system is fully submerged and of "aeroplane" configuration, with 90% of the weight supported by the two bow foils and 10% by the rear foil. The foils are subcavitating and of medium aspect ratio. The stern strut rotates for steering and all three foil struts retract completely clear of the water. Incidence of the three foils is controlled by an autopilot system. Struts and foils will be built in steel.

HULL: The hull will be almost completely built of aluminium and will be of predominantly welded construction. Most of the deck, side and bottom plating will be made from integrally stiffened, aluminium extruded planks.

ACCOMMODATION: The wheelhouse, located forward, provides a 360° view. The first officer and engineer are seated side-by-side, with a third seat for the captain. Immediately aft of the wheelhouse is a chart room/radio cabin. Normally the crew will have ten members, a captain, a first officer, an engineer, an assistant engineer, two deck hands and four stewards.

Passengers are accommodated in three well glazed saloons, a fore compartment seating 68, a central compartment seating 142 and an aft compartment seating 92. Passenger and crew compartments are air-conditioned.

Access to the compartments is through two doors in the forward saloon, port and starboard, or two doors in the aft saloon, port and starboard. Separate doors, port and starboard, are provided for the crew. Four emergency exits are provided, two port, two starboard.

HYDROFOIL MANUFACTURERS
BLOHM & VOSS AG: Germany

A full range of safety equipment is carried, including fire extinguishers and approved life rafts sufficient for the crew and 302 passengers.   Life jackets for adults and children are also provided.

The vehicle deck, designed for up to 37 cars, has two wide doors at the stern which become access ramps for loading and unloading.   A turntable at the forward end permits the vehicle to be turned round so that they can be driven straight off.

POWER PLANT: Foilborne propulsion is supplied by two General Electric LM1500 marine gas turbines of 14,000 bhp continuous rating, connected by Z-drives through the main struts to two stainless-steel, super-cavitating fixed propellers of 4 ft 4 in (1·3 m) diameter at the end of the propulsion pods on the main foils.   The air intake is at the top of the deckhouse.   Four integral fuel tanks will give a total fuel capacity of 35 tons.   Oil tank capacity will be 4 tons.

Hullborne propulsion is supplied by two MB 835 BB, or equivalent diesels, rated at 1,650 hp at 1,500 rpm, driving two waterjet pumps with moveable nozzles.

NAVIGATION AND COMMUNICATIONS: Radio and radar are standard equipment.

SYSTEMS:

AIR CONDITIONING: Type not yet determined.

ELECTRICAL: Diesel generator 100 kW, 125kVA at 0·8 P.F. for auxiliary power,

lighting system, master warning and monitoring system and autopilot.

HYDRAULICS: 210 atu for strut retraction, foil incidence control and auxiliary power.

APU: 1 emergency gas turbine generator, 30kW.

DIMENSIONS, EXTERNAL:

Length overall, hull	212 ft 8 in (64·85 m)
Length waterline, hull	198 ft 7 in (60·9 m)
Length overall, foils retracted	219 ft 8 in (67·0 m)
Length overall, foils extended	223 ft 0 in (67·97 m)
Hull beam, maximum	41 ft 6 in (12·65 m)
Beam overall, foils retracted	82 ft 9 in (25·2 m)
Beam overall, foils extended	70 ft 9 in (21·57 m)
Draft afloat, foils retracted	7 ft 8 in (2·33 m)
Draft afloat, foils extended	26 ft 1 in (7·95 m)
Draft foilborne	6 ft 7 in (2·0 m)
Freeboard	14 ft 1 in (4·3 m)
Height overall, approx	62 ft 6 in (19·0 m)

DIMENSIONS, INTERNAL:

Superstructure interior, including wheelhouse, chart room, radio cabin, passenger cabins, galley, toilets and air conditioning compartment:

Length	167 ft 5 in (51·0 m)
Max width	33 ft 0 in (10·0 m)
Max height	7 ft 5 in (2·3
Floor area, approx	4,951 sq ft (460
Volume, approx	37,432 cu ft (1,060

BAGGAGE HOLDS:

Racks for hand luggage in passenger cab
baggage holds in forepeak.

WEIGHTS:

Light displacement	205 t
Normal take-off displacement	320 t
Max take-off displacement	325 t
Normal deadweight	115 t
Max deadweight	120 t
Normal payload	73 t
Max payload	78 t

PERFORMANCE:

Max speed foilborne	58 knots (106 km
Max speed hullborne	20 knots (38 km
Max permissible wave height in foilbo mode	14·7-16·4 ft (4·5-5
Cruising speed foilborne	50 knots (93 km
Cruising speed, hullborne	18 knots (32 km
Design range at cruising speed	325 n.m. a
Turning radius at cruising speed	1,148 ft (350
Number of seconds and distance to take-	35 sec/1,312 ft (400
Number of seconds and distance to s craft	16 sec/656 ft (200
Fuel consumption at max speed	250·5 gallons per h
Fuel consumption at cruising speed	255 gallons per h

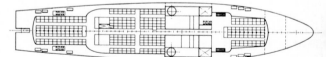

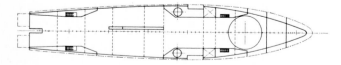

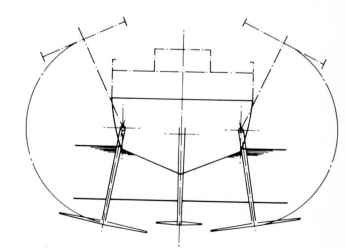

General arrangement of the Neptune hydrofoil passenger/car ferry showing outboard profile, passenger and car decks

hlichtingwerft
ILICHTINGWERFT

AD OFFICE:
ecklenburger Landstrasse, Lubeck-Trav-
emunde

NAGING DIRECTOR:
nwick Harmstorf

hlichtingwerft is constructing the proto-
e of a 160-ton hydrofoil patrol craft of
ramar design for the Federal German
vy (Bundesmarine). It is generally simi-
in construction to the proposed gas-turbine
ered version of the PT 150.

Details of the gas-turbine version of the
PT 150, a 300-seat passenger ferry for routes
up to 250 nautical miles, were released by
Supramar in 1963. To facilitate calls at
smaller ports, the crossing of shallows,
docking and slipping, the foils, rudders and
propellers are retractable.

A combined surface piercing and submerging foil configuration is employed with two
surface piercing foils forward and two submerged foils aft. Initially the gas turbine
powered PT 150 was to be fitted with
hydraulically-operated stability augmentation flaps on the front foils to give improved

performance in a seaway, and the new
Supramar air stabilisation system was to be
fitted at a later stage.

The two 4,250 bhp Marine Proteus turbines
are located aft, and each transmits power
through a mechanical right-angle drive
transmission to a propeller at the aft end of a
strut-and-pod assembly. For manoeuvring
in displacement condition there is an independent 200 hp gas-turbine with its own
propeller.

Designed maximum speed of the craft was
given as 48 knots, and the cruising speed
45 knots.

ITALY

vance Marine Systems
VANCED MARINE SYSTEMS—
LINAVI S.p.A.

AD OFFICE:
ia Gramsci 24, Rome, Italy

EPHONE:
79 204

RECTORS:
r. Publio Magini (Boeing), President
iro M. Gonnella (Boeing)

W. J. Kane (Boeing)
Brantz Mayor (Boeing)
Ing. Riccardo Baldini (Finmeccanica)
Ing. Giorgio Bettini (Finmeccanica)
Cav. del Lav. C. Rodriquez (Rodriquez)

EXECUTIVE:
Ing. Francesco Cao, Chief Engineer

This company was formed in 1964 to develop
military and commercial advanced marine
systems, primarily in Europe and the

Mediterranean areas. Local manufacturing
and marketing support will be given to
technology from Boeing. At present the
company's major activities are confined to
the sale and production of military hydrofoil
boats and research into hydrofoil design, and
advanced marine propulsion systems. The
company is jointly owned by The Boeing
Company (60%), Finmeccanica (30%) and
Carlo Rodriquez (10%).

opoldo Rodriquez
OPOLDO RODRIQUEZ SHIPYARD

AD OFFICE:
Molo Norimberga 24, Messina

LEPHONE:
4801 (PBX)

LEX:
8030 Rodrikez

RECTORS:
Cav Del Lavoro Carlo Rodriquez, President
Leopoldo Rodriquez
Franco Rodriquez

NIOR EXECUTIVES:
Dott. Ing. Leopoldo Rodriquez, General
Manager
Capt. Franco Rodriquez, Sales Director
Dott. Ing. Giovanni Falzea, Yard Director
Ing. Frederick Leobau, Design Office
Director

The Leopoldo Rodriquez Shipyard was the
st in the world to produce hydrofoils in
ries, and is now the biggest hydrofoil
ilder outside the Soviet Union. On the
itiative of the company's president, Carlo
odriquez, the Aliscafi Shipping Company
is established in Sicily to operate the world's
st scheduled seagoing hydrofoil service in
ugust 1956 between Sicily and the Italian
ainland.

The service was operated by the first
odriquez-built Supramar PT 20, Freccia
l Sole. Cutting down the port-to-port
ne from Messina to Reggio di Calabria to
e-quarter of that of conventional ferry
ats, and completing 22 daily crossings, the
aft soon proved the commercial viability
Supramar designs. With a seating cap-
ity of 75 passengers the PT 20 has carried
tween 800-900 passengers a day and has
nveyed a record number of some 31,000 in
single month.

The prototype PT 20, a 27-ton craft for 75
assengers, was built by Rodriquez in 1955
nd the first PT 50, a 63-ton craft for 140
assengers, was completed by the yard in
958.

Since 1956 the company has built forty-one
PT 20s and twenty-three PT 50s. Sales
have been made to 21 countries. Under
construction at the yard at the time of going
to press are seven PT 20s, six PT 50s and
one PT 150. Apart from building the
standard range of Supramar designs (see
Supramar, Switzerland) the company also
produces a number of variants, including the
PAT 20 fast naval and police patrol craft,
the PT 20/59 Caribe and the PT 50/S which
are described below.

PAT 20

Two PAT 20 fast patrol hydrofoils, Cami-
guin 72 and Siquijor 73, have been built by
Rodriquez for the Phillipine Navy. The
craft carry one, bow-mounted 12·7 machine
gun and have been employed on contraband
patrol and coastguard duties since June 1965.
Their main patrol area is between the island
of Mindanao and the NW coast of Borneo.

FOILS: Bow and rear foils are of surfacing
piercing V configuration and identical to
those of the standard PT 20. About 59%
of the total weight is borne by the bow foil
and 41% by the rear foil. The foils are of
hollow ribbed construction and made from
medium Asera steel.

Total foil area is 112 sq ft (10·4 m²). The
angle of incidence of the forward foil can be
varied during flight by means of a hydraulic
ram acting on the foil strut supporting tube.

HULL: The hull is of riveted light alloy
construction with Peraluman (aluminium
and magnesium alloy) plates and Anti-
corrodal (aluminium, magnesium and silicon
alloy) profiles.

ACCOMMODATION: The crew comprises a
captain, two officers and eight NCO's and
ratings. The pilot's position is on the left of
the wheelhouse, with the principal instrumentation; and the radar operator sits on
the right with the auxiliary instrumentation.
The pilot is provided with an intercom
system connecting him with the officer's

cabin, engine room and crew cabin. The
internal space has been divided as follows:

(a) The forward or bow room, subdivided
into two cabins, one for the captain, the
other for two officers, and including a
WC with washstand and a storeroom
with a refrigerator.

(b) The stern room, with eight berths for the
NCOs and ratings, a WC with washstand
and a galley equipped with a gas stove
and an electric refrigerator.

(c) The deck room, aft of the wheelhouse,
with tilting sofa and table for R/T
equipment.

Air conditioning is installed in the captain's
and officer's quarters.

POWER PLANT: Power is supplied by a
supercharged 12-cylinder Mercedes-Benz
MB820 Db with a max continuous output of
1,350 hp at 1,500 rpm. Engine output is
transferred to a 3-bladed bronze aluminium
propeller through a Zahnradfabrik BW 800/S
reversible gear. Fuel (total capacity 2,800
kg) is carried in ten cylindrical aluminium
tanks located in the double bottom beneath
the bow room and the stern room. Dynamic
and reserve oil tanks in the engine room give
a total oil capacity of 120 kg. An auxiliary
engine can be fitted in the stern for emergency
operation.

ARMAMENT AND SEARCH EQUIP-
MENT: Single 12·7 machine-gun mounted
above well position in bow, and two
searchlights.

SYSTEMS:

ELECTRICAL: 220v, 10 kW, diesel generat-
or with batteries. Supplies instruments, radio
and radar and external and internal lights,
navigation lights and searchlights.

HYDRAULICS: 120 kp/cm² pressure hydraulic system for steering and varying
forward foil incidence angle.

APU: Onan engine for air conditioning when
requested.

HYDROFOIL MANUFACTURERS
RODRIQUEZ: Italy

A Rodriquez PAT 20 fast patrol hydrofoil under test off Messina. Two are employed by the Philippine Navy on contraband patrol and coastgu
duties.

DIMENSIONS:

Length overall, hull	68 ft 6 in (20·89 m)
Hull beam	15 ft 8¾ in (4·79 m)
Beam overall	24 ft 4 in (7·4 m)
Draft afloat	9 ft 1 in (2·76 m)
Draft foilborne	4 ft 0 in (1·20 m)
Height overall:	
hullborne	21 ft 0 in (6·44 m)
foilborne	26 ft 3 in (8·00 m)

WEIGHTS:

Net tonnage	28 tons
Light displacement	26 tons
Max take-off displacement	32·5 tons
Useful load	7·6 tons
Max useful load	8·1 tons

PERFORMANCE:

Max speed foilborne	38 knots
Max speed hullborne	13 knots
Cruising speed foilborne	34 knots
Cruising speed hullborne	12 knots
Max permissible sea state foilborne mode	Force 4
Designed range at cruising speed	540 miles (869 km)
Number of seconds and distance to take-off	20 secs, 328 ft (100 m)
Number of seconds and distance to stop craft	12 secs, 164 ft (50 m)
Fuel consumption at cruising speed	145 kg/h
Fuel consumption at max speed	180 kg/h

PT 20/59 CARIBE

This version of the PT 20 was designed originally for services in tropical waters. The bridge and engine room have been arranged in the foreship to give maximum forward vision in areas where there is an influx of driftwood. Tropical conditions have also been taken into consideration in the design and installation of the powerplant.
FOILS: Bow and rear foils are of standard Schertel-Sachsenburg surface-piercing Vee configuration, with about 66% of the weight supported by the bowfoil and 34% by the rear foil. Submerged foil area when foilborne is 67 sq ft (6·2 m²). Each foil, together with its struts and horizontal girder forms a rigid framework which facilitates the ex-

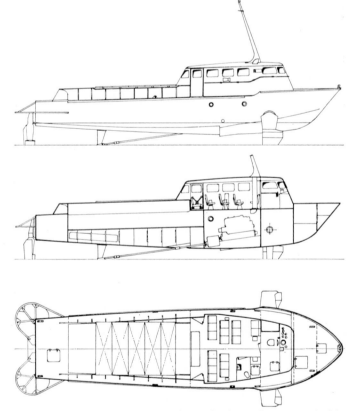

Mixed passenger cargo version of the Caribe with a cargo deck in place of the main passenger cabin

change of the foil structure. The foils are of hollow-ribbed construction and fabricated from medium Asera type steel. The incidence angle of the forward foil can be adjusted hydraulically during operation to counter the effect of large variations in passenger loads.
HULL: The hull is of riveted light metal alloy and framed on a combination of longitudinal and transverse formers. Watertight compartments are provided in the bow and stern and beneath the passenger decks. Some are filled with foam plastic which makes these boats practically unsinkable.

POWER PLANT: The engine is a sup charged Mercedes-Benz MB 820 Db, with maximum continuous output of 1,100 hp 1,500 rpm. Engine output is transferred a 3-bladed, 27·5 in (700 mm) diameter bro aluminium propeller through a Zahnradfab BW 800 H reversible gearbox.
ACCOMMODATION: Fifty-one passeng can be accommodated in the main cabin a fifteen in the small forward cabin. Acc to the forward and main compartment through either of two doors, located port a starboard, to the rear of the wheelho superstructure. Steps from the forw

e Rodriquez Caribe, a special class of the PT 20 designed for commercial service in tropical conditions. Fifteen passengers are accommodated the forward cabin above the engine room and fifty-three in the main cabin. Powered by an MB 820Db diesel rated at 1,350 hp continuous, the craft cruises at 34 knots

mpartment lead down to the main cabin. t the aft end of the main cabin is a WC and emergency exit.

A mixed passenger/cargo version is avail-le, with seats for 19 in a cabin immediately t of the wheelhouse and a cargo deck in ace of the main passenger cabin.

YSTEMS:

LECTRICAL: Single phase generator 220 lts, 7·1 kW, 50 c/s and batteries. Supplies struments, radio, radar and internal and terior lights.

YDRAULICS: 120 kp/cm² pressure hy-raulic system for rudder and varying cidence angle of bow foil.

PU: Onan engine for air conditioning, when ecified.

OMMUNICATIONS AND NAVIGATION: adio: VHF radio-telephone, to customer's quirements.

adar: Decca, Raytheon, etc., to customer's quirements.

IMENSIONS:

Length overall, hull	64 ft 0 in (19·5 m)
Hull beam	16 ft 7 in (5·06 m)
Width over foils	24 ft 2 in (7·38 m)
Draft afloat	9 ft 1 in (2·77 m)
Draft foilborne	3 ft 10 in (1·16 m)
Height overall, hullborne	20 ft 4 in (6·18 m)
Height overall, foilborne	27 ft 11 in (8·5 m)

VEIGHTS:

Net tonnage	43·31 tons
Light displacement	25·8 tons
Normal take-off displacement	33 tons
Max take-off displacement	33·5 tons
Useful load (fuel, water, passengers, baggage and crew)	7·2 tons
Max useful load	7·7 tons

ERFORMANCE (with normal payload):

Max speed, foilborne	34·5 knots
Max speed, hullborne	12 knots
Cruising speed, foilborne	31 knots
Cruising speed, hullborne	11 knots
Max permissible sea state in foilborne mode	State 5

Designed range at cruising speed
250 n miles

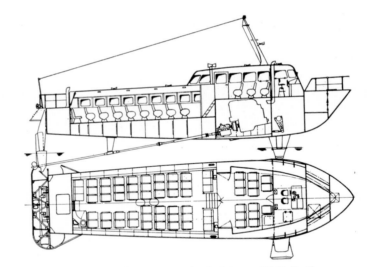

Inboard profile and plan of the Rodriquez PT 20 Caribe

Fuel consumption at max speed	396 lb/h (180 kg/h)
Fuel consumption at cruising speed	320 lb/h (145 kg/h)

PT 50/S

The PT 50/S differs from the standard PT 50 in having the bridge arranged in the foreship. Immediately aft of the wheelhouse is a belvedere (viewing) saloon with seats for 14 and a bar. Companies operating this particular variant include the Port Jackson and Manley Steamship Co of Sydney, Australia, and the Hong Kong-Macao Hydrofoil Co.

FOILS: Bow and rear foils are of surface-piercing vee configuration identical to those of the standard design. About 60% of the total weight is borne by the bow foil and 40% by the rear foil. Hydraulically-operated flaps are fitted at the trailing edge of the bow foil to balance out longitudinal load shifting, assist take-off and adjust the flying height.

HULL: This is of riveted light alloy construction and framed on a combination of longitudinal and transverse formers.

ACCOMMODATION: The PT 50/S carries a crew of 6 and 125 passengers. The main compartment, aft, seats 65, the forward compartment seats 46, and the belvedere saloon, located above the engine, seats 14. Either a dry ice or electric refrigerator of about 150 litre capacity can be fitted in the bar, together with a stainless steel wash basin served with running water. Both the forward and aft saloons have a WC/washbasin unit. Access to the passenger saloons is through either of two doors on the main deck, port and starboard. Separate doors, on either side of the wheelhouse, are provided for the pilot and crew.

POWER PLANT: Power is supplied by two 12-cylinder supercharged MB 820 Dbs, with a maximum output of 1,350 hp at 1,500 rpm. Reverse and reduction gears are manufactured by Zahnradfabrik. The reverse clutches are solenoid operated from the bridge.

SYSTEMS:

AIR CONDITIONING: Genefrigor Genoa, where requested.

ELECTRICAL: Air cooled MWM type AKD412E or similar diesel driving a single

HYDROFOIL MANUFACTURERS
RODRIQUEZ: Italy

phase generator of 220 volts, with batteries. Supplies instruments, radio and radar and external and internal lights.

HYDRAULICS: System to operate rudder and flaps on bow foil, 120 kp/cm².

DIMENSIONS:

Length overall, hull	95 ft 2 in (29 m)
Length waterline, hull	80 ft 1 in (24·8 m)
Hull beam	20 ft 1 in (6·1 m)
Width over foils	33 ft 6 in (10·2 m)
Draft afloat	11 ft 6 in (3·5 m)
Draft foilborne	4 ft 11 in (1·5 m)

Height overall, hullborne	29 ft 7 in (9 m)
Height overall, foilborne	36 ft 2 in (11 m)

WEIGHTS:

Net tonnage	82 tons
Light displacement (with fuel, oil and water)	51·5 tons
Max take-off displacement	64·5 tons
Useful load (fuel, water, passengers, baggage and crew)	13·5 tons
Max useful load	14 tons

PERFORMANCE (with normal payload):

Max speed foilborne	37 knots

Max speed hullborne	18 kn
Cruising speed foilborne	34 kn
Max permissible sea state in foilborne m	Stat
Designed range at cruising speed	250 n. mi
Number of seconds and distance to take- (theor app)	25 secs, 164 yd (150
Number of seconds and distance to st craft	18 secs, 88 yd (80
Fuel consumption at max speed	360 kg
Fuel consumption at cruising speed	330 kg

Flying Flamingo, a Rodriquez-built 125-seat PT 50/S, operated by the Hong Kong Macao Hydrofoil Company.   Cruising speed is 34 knots.

aflight
AFLIGHT S.p.A.

AD OFFICE:

ia della Munizione 3, Messina

LEPHONE: 46100

CHNICAL OFFICE:

illaggio Torre Faro, Messina

LEPHONE: 50200

he Seaflight series of hydrofoils use a foil
tem introduced by Guiseppe Guiffrida,
o joined this company in 1961. The foil
omatically assumes the best angle of
idence in relation to the flow of water.
this way it always produced the same
ount of lift, whether the speed varies, or
foils' submerged surface varies in a wave
st or cavity.

eaflight is backed by a group of Messina
ustrialists. Construction of the Seaflight
d on the beach at Torre Faro began in
vember 1962, and the prototype Seaflight
s launched in January 1964. The yard
capacity for the production of fifteen
rofoils a year.

AFLIGHT P.46

esigned for off-shore and inter-island
senger ferry services, the Seaflight P.46
ts 32 in its roomy passenger saloon and
ises at 32-35 knots (60-65 km/h).

ILS: The craft incorporates a foil system
which the foil automatically assumes the
t angle of incidence in relation to the wave
dition.

lever attached to the hydrofoil bearing
embly is connected by springs to the hull,
hat a reaction force rotates the lever and
ring assembly, together with the foil, in
irection opposite to that in which it would
d to be rotated by lift forces exerted on
foil. The spring reaction force may be
nually adjusted.

Seaflight P46 showing the rear foil assembly and the split bow foil which combines a horizontal submerged centre section with inclined surface piercing areas

aflight P46 (two Cummins VT8N-370-M) is available as a 30-32 seat passenger ferry, luxury yacht or fast coastal patrol boat. A mechanically operated system of incidence control is fitted to the bow foil

HYDROFOIL MANUFACTURERS
SEAFLIGHT: Italy

The Seaflight H57 (two 650 hp Fiat-OM) seats 60 passengers and has a maximum speed of 39 knots (72 km/h)

The bow foil is of the split-type and combines a horizontal, submerged centre section, with inclined, surface-piercing areas. The configuration is stated by the company to offer a good compromise between the fully submerged foil, with its horizontal lift surfaces, and the surface piercing foil with its oblique surfaces. The Seaflight's horizontal foil surfaces produce about two-thirds of the lift required.

POWER PLANT: Power is provided by two Cummins VT8N-370-M marinised, turbo-charged V8 engines, each developing 370 hp.

HULL: The hull is riveted, light alloy construction and the foils are of specially strengthened corrosion-resistant steel.

DIMENSIONS:

Length overall	45 ft 11 in (14·00 m)
Breadth over foils	16 ft 5 in (5·00 m)
Draught afloat	5 ft 9 in (1·75 m)
Foilborne draught	2 ft 6 in (0·75 m)

WEIGHTS:

Displacement	12·50 tons

PERFORMANCE:

Max speed	40 knots (74 km/h)
Range	270 nautical miles (500 km)

SEAFLIGHT H.57

This is a larger and more powerful development of the C.46 seating 60 passengers. Hull construction is in riveted light alloy and its foils are in specially strengthened corrosion resisting steel. Power is supplied by two 650 hp Fiat Carraro diesels

DIMENSIONS:

Length overall	57 ft 1 in (17·50 m)
Breadth over foils	26 ft 3 in (8·00 m)
Draught afloat	8 ft 1 in (2·47 m)
Draught foilborne	3 ft 8 in (1·12 m)

WEIGHTS:

Max displacement	26·00 tons

PERFORMANCE:

Cruising speed	32-35 knots (60-65 km/h)
Max speed	39 knots (72 km/h)
Range	270 nautical miles (500 km)

SEAFLIGHT L.90

The prototype of the L.90, latest passenger ferry hydrofoil in the Seaflight series, is under construction at the company's yard at Tor Faro, Messina. Powered by two 1,350 CRM 18/DS diesels, it will accommodate 100-120 passengers, and have a cruising speed of 35 knots.

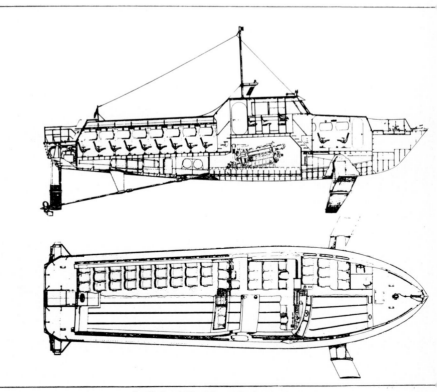

Seaflight L90 side and plan view

ILS: The foil system is of the fixed surface
rcing type. The split bow foil combines
orizontal submerged centre section with
lined surface piercing areas and incorpor-
s the Seaflight mechanically operated
tem of incidence control. The geometry
the foils is such that it is possible to beach
e vessel on a falling tide on a nearly flat
dy bottom, the hull remaining stable.
JLL: The V-bottom hull is mainly in
rine corrosion resistant aluminium alloys.
el is used for highly stressed parts.
CCOMMODATION: In the standard ver-

sion, passengers are accommodated in three
compartments, a forward saloon seating 18;
an observation or belvedere deck in the wheelhouse superstructure seating 22, and a main
aft saloon seating 60. The forward compartment contains two toilet/washbasin units.
Access is through either of two doors, port
or starboard in the forward cabin, or two
doors either port or starboard in the wheelhouse superstructure.
POWER PLANT: Power is provided by two
CRM type 18/DS diesels with a maximum
output of 1,350 hp at 2,075 rpm, and normal

output of 950 hp at 1,950 rpm.   Each engine
drives a three-blade fixed propeller through
an inclined shaft.
DIMENSIONS:

Length overall	69 ft 3 in (21·10 m)
Width across foils	28 ft 9 in (8·80 m)
Draft afloat	9 ft 3 in (2·81 m)
Draft foilborne	4 ft 0 in (1·21 m)

WEIGHTS:

Maximum take-off displacement	37 tons

PERFORMANCE:

Cruising speed	35 knots (64 km)
Cruising range	270 nautical miles (499 km)

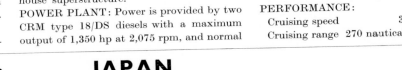

JAPAN

**TACHI SHIPBUILDING & ENGINEERING
.O**
EAD OFFICE:
47 Edabon 1-chome, Nishi-ku, Osaka, Japan
YDROFOIL SHIPYARD:
Kanagawa Shipyard, 1 Mizve-cho, Kawa-
saki-City, Kanagawa Prefecture
IRECTORS:
Yosomatsu Matsubara, Chairman of the
Board of Directors
Takao Nagata, President
Hideo Fukuda, Managing Director and
General Manager of Shipbuilding Division

Yoshio Kinoshita, Director and Manager of
Product Development Department
Isao Yoshimura, Director and Manager of
General Affairs Department (including
advertising sect):
Hitachi, the Supramar licencee in Japan,
has been building PT 3, PT 20 and PT 50
hydrofoils since 1961.   The majority of these
have been built for fast passenger ferry
services across the Japanese Inland Sea,
cutting across deep bays which road vehicles

might take two-to-three hours to drive
round, and out to offshore islands. Other
PT 20s and 50s have been exported to Hong
Kong and Australia for ferry services.
Specifications of the PT 3, PT 20 and PT 50
will be found under Supramar (Switzerland).
The Hitachi-built craft are identical apart
from minor items.
In 1962 Hitachi, in conjunction with Eidai
Sangyo Co Ltd, introduced two small
hydrofoil runabouts equipped with Supramar

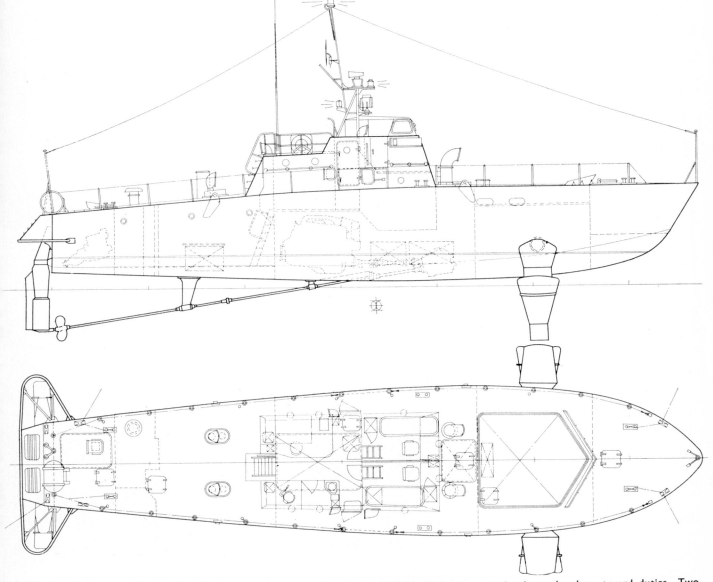

General arrangement of the PT 32 fast patrol hydrofoil developed for the Philippine Navy for contraband patrol and coastguard duties. Two
craft of this type were delivered by Hitachi in November 1965. Armament comprises a twin .50 calibre machine gun mounted above the forward
deck well and a single .50 calibre machine gun on the aft deck. Cruising range is 360 miles and the cruising speed is 32 knots

HYDROFOIL MANUFACTURERS
HITACHI: Japan

foils. The foils can be retracted and folded close to the sides of the hull by means of a lever operated from the cockpit.

A special military hydrofoil, based on the Schertel-Sachsenburg foil system, and designated PT 32, has been designed and built by Hitachi for the Philippine Navy.

PT 32

This craft was specially designed as a fast patrol boat. Two have been delivered to the Philippine Navy for contraband patrol and general Coast Guard duties in coastal waters. The PT 32 is powered by a 1,350 hp Mercedes-Benz-Ikegai diesel, which gives a maximum speed of 35 knots. The hull is of light alloy, riveted construction and accommodation is provided for three officers and twelve NCOs and ratings. The armament comprises a twin ·50 cal machine gun mounted above the forward deck well, and a single ·50 cal machine gun on the aft deck.

DIMENSIONS:

Length overall	69 ft 0 in	(21·0 m)
Length over deck	56 ft 9 in	(20·0 m)
Beam over deck	15 ft 9 in	(4·8 m)
Width over foils	25 ft 7 in	(7·8 m)
Depth from top of keel to deck at side, amidships	9 ft 10 in	(3·0 m)
Draft, hullborne, from base of foils	9 ft 2 in	(2·8 m)
Draft, foilborne from base of foils	4 ft 3 in	(1·3 m)

WEIGHT:

Fully loaded displacement   approx 32 tons

PERFORMANCE:

Cruising speed	approx 32 knots
Maximum speed	35 knots
Cruising speed	360 miles
Speed with auxiliary engine	approx 4 knots

Main engine Licence built:
Mercedes-Benz-Ikegai MB 820 Db supercharged diesel engine

MB 820 Db supercharged diesel engine

Maximum output	1,350 hp × 1,500 rpm
Continuous full output	1,100 hp × 1,400 rpm
Fuel consumption	0·364 lb/hp/h (165 g/hp/h)

Auxiliary propelling power:

Diesel engine	60 hp

Complement:

Officers	3 persons
Enlisted personnel	12 persons
Total	15 persons

AT-FOIL

In addition to their range of Supramar-designed commercial passenger craft, Hitachi also manufactures retractable foils for the YODO-14 and -16 hydrofoil runabouts, substantial numbers of which have been sold throughout Japan and South East Asia.

CONSTRUCTION: Built by Eidai Sangyo Co Ltd, of 33 Hirabayashi Minamino-cho, Sumiyoshi-ku, Osaka-City, and constructed in marine ply, the craft are powered by standard 40-70 hp marine outboards.

FOIL DESIGN: The front foil is of the surface-piercing split type, and the rear foil is a fully submerged type. Both front and rear foil systems fold upwards for retraction.

ACCOMMODATION: YODO-14 is a 14 ft craft seating 3-4 passengers, and uses AT-40 foils; YODO-16, a 16 ft craft. seats 5-6 and is fitted with AT-75 foils.

Hayate 2, one of the two Hitachi PT 20s operated by Kansai Kisen Co. between Osaka and Takamat

Wakashio, a Hitachi PT 50 (two 1,350 hp MB 820 Db diesels) which has been operated betwee Enosima and Atami by Nihon Kosokusen since 1963.

YODO-16, a 5-6 seat, 34 knot sports hydrofoil built by Eidai Sangyo Co. and fitted with Hitach Supramar retractable AT-foils

DO-14

DIMENSIONS:

Length	13 ft 6 in (4·1 m)
Beam	5 ft 1 in (1·55 m)
Width across foils:	
Foils extended	9 ft 5 in (2·87 m)
Foils retracted	7 ft 4 in (2·24 m)
Draught foilborne	1 ft 8 in (0·50 m)
Draught afloat:	
Foil extended	2 ft 10 in (0·85 m)
Foils retracted	9 in (0·23 m)
Complement	4 persons

WEIGHT:

Weight displacement	905 lb (410 kg)

PERFORMANCE:

Max speed:	
2 passengers	32 knots (60 km/h)
fully loaded	30 knots

Max permissible wave height in foilborne condition	(1 ft 0·30 m approx)
Take-off performance:	
It takes about 30 sec with engine at 1,000 rpm to reach max speed	
Landing:	
About 10 sec with engine at 4,500 rpm to stop the boat. Distance about 60 m	
Turning radius	329 ft (100 m approx)
Complement	4 persons
Outboard engine	40 hp × 1

YODO-16

DIMENSIONS:

Length	15 ft 2 in (4·7 m)
Beam	6 ft (1·85 m)
Width across foils:	
Foils extended	11 ft (3·23 m)
Foils retracted	8 ft 5 in (2·62 m)
Draught foilborne	1 ft 8 in (0·50 m)
Draught afloat:	
Foils extended	3 ft (0·90 m)
Foils retracted	11 in (0·26 m)
Complement	5 persons
Outboard engine	75 hp × 1

WEIGHT:

Light displacement	1,234 lb (560 kg)

PERFORMANCE:

Max speed:	
2 passengers	37 knots
full load	34 knots
Max permissible wave height in foilborne condition	1 ft 6 in (0·40 m approx)
Take-off performance	as for YODO-14
Landing	as for YODO-14
Landing radius	329 ft (100 m approx)

Ishikawajima-Harima
ISHIKAWAJIMA-HARIMA HEAVY INDUSTRIES

HEAD OFFICE:
, 2-Chome, Fukagawa-Toyosu, Koto-Ku, Tokyo, Japan

TELEGRAMS:
ISHITOYOSU TOKYO

OFFICERS:
Kenzo Taguchi, Director
. Itoh, Manager, Development Department, Research Institute

The Technical Development Department of Ishikawajima-Harima has been conducting a hydrofoil research and development programme since 1960. This has led to the construction of a series of small hydrofoil sportscraft and the IHF-3 waterbus. Two larger craft, the 23-ton IHF-8 and the 70-ton IHF-25 are in the planning stage.

IHF-3

A 15-seat multi-purpose transport, the IHF-3 was the first production craft to use IHI's retractable and folding foil system, which permits the craft to operate in displacement mode and go alongside piers and other vessels without damaging the foils. Applications include sightseeing, high-speed water-taxi, fire, harbour police and lifeguard patrol and pilot boat.

HULL: The hull is constructed in anti-corrosive aluminium alloy. The cabin seats a maximum of 13 passengers and a crew of 2.

FOILS: Front and rear foils are of the split, surface-piercing type, the front foil being fully foldable. When retracted the forward foil assembly is up above the water line. The power for this operation is supplied by a hydraulic pump driven by the main engine. Folding and unfolding is controlled by a lever sited by the helmsman's seat and can take place when under way at low speed.

POWER PLANT: Power from a 280 hp Chrysler (or similar engine) is transmitted to the propeller through a vertical shaft with bevel gears. The power strut also serves as the support for the aft hydrofoil, and is extended upwards in order to support a small auxiliary propeller which is driven through the same vertical shaft. The whole integral assembly, including the aft hydrofoil and the two propellers at the opposite ends of the power strut, is rotated hydraulically through 180° about a horizontal axis in an athwartship

The IHF-3's foil system is retracted hydraulically. The forward foil assembly is folded and swings aft above the waterline. The complete aft foil assembly is rotated through 180° bringing the hullborne propeller into position.

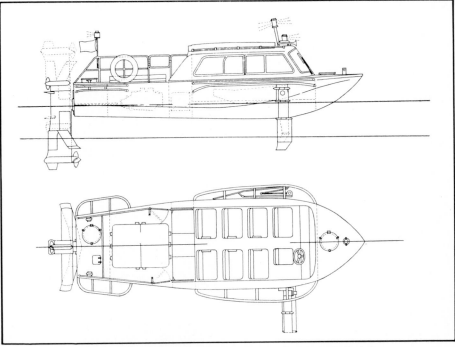

IHF-3, 15-seat passenger ferry and general purpose hydrofoil

plane. It is so arranged that in the inverted position the auxiliary propeller is set at the correct position to propel the craft at minimum draught.

DIMENSIONS:

Length overall, hull	26 ft 3 in (8·00 m)
Length waterline, hull	23 ft 7½ in (7·20 m)
Hull beam	8 ft 2½ in (2·50 m)
Length overall, foils retracted	29 ft 9 in (9·06 m)
Length overall, foils extended	29 ft 9 in (9·06 m)
Max beam, foils retracted	12 ft 5 in (3·78 m)
Max beam, foils extended	16 ft 9 in (5·09 m)
Draught, foils retracted	1 ft 2 in (0·66 m)
Draught, foils extended	6 ft 1¼ in (1·86 m)
Freeboard	1 ft 0 in (0·61 m)

WEIGHTS:

Gross tonnage	4½ tons
Light displacement	3¼ tons
Max take-off displacement	4 tons
Useful load (fuel, water, passengers, baggage and crew)	1⅛ tons

PERFORMANCE:

Max speed, foilborne 36 knots (66 km/h)

The IHF-3, a 13 seat multi-purpose hydrofoil for services in lakes, bays and estuaries. Cru speed is 35 knots

Cruising speed foilborne, (30 knots 55 km/h)
Cruising speed, hullborne
7 knots (12·8 km/h)
Max permissible wave height in foilborne mode 3 ft 5 in-4ft 6 in (1·0-1·4 m)

Turning radius at cruising speed
1,640 ft (50(
Fuel consumption at cruising speed
0·53 lb sh
Cruising range approx 156 miles (250

Mitsubishi
MITSUBISHI HEAVY INDISTRIES LTD

HEAD OFFICE:
10, 2-chome Marunouchi, Chiyoda-ku, Tokyo, Japan
TELEPHONE:
(212)-3111
WORKS:
1130 Hikoshima Shimonoseki, Yamaguchi-Pref
TELEPHONE:
(66) 2111
CABLES:
Dock Shimonoseki
DIRECTORS:
F. Kono
K. Kita
SENIOR EXECUTIVES:
S. Katsumata, General Manager
T. Kaneko, Sales Manager
Y. Kaneko, Chief Designer

Mitsubishi entered the hydrofoil field in 1960 and built the prototype of the 38-ton MH30, the first large Japanese-designed hydrofoil, in 1962. Five MH30s have so far been delivered for passenger services. The company has also built the MH03, a 20-passenger water-bus and has prepared designs for the 168-seat MH60. In 1964 Mitsubishi built the MH3 fully submerged foil test craft and in 1966 the company completed a waterjet propelled test craft which has reached a speed of 42 knots (77 km/h).

MH30

Designed for rough water operation around the Japanese Islands, the Mitsubishi MH30 seats eighty passengers and has a crew of four. Power is supplied by a Mitsubishi 12 WZ or Maybach MD655/18 high speed diesel. The cruising speed is 33 knots (61 km/h).

FOILS: The foil configuration is a combined surface-piercing and submerged system and is non-retractable. The split-Vee bow foil supports 65% of the load and the single, fully-submerged rear foil, which carries the propeller pod, supports the remaining 35%. The bow foil is in welded mild steel plate, and the rear foil is constructed in solid high tensile steel. Twin rudders, which act individually for port or starboard turns, are fitted to the trailing edges of the aft foil struts.

HULL: The hull is an all welded, aluminium structure of the high speed type with hard chine sections for performance as a planing hull in waves.

ACCOMMODATION: Accommodation is on two levels. Passengers board the craft through single doors located amidships, port and starboard, leading to a 19-seat central saloon. Companion ladders lead down to the fore and aft saloons, with seats for 37 and 24 passengers respectively. Each cabin is fully air conditioned. Separate entrances, port and starboard, are provided for the pilot and crew. There is a toilet in the aft saloon. Two emergency exits are provided and a full range of safety equipment is carried, including life rafts.

POWER PLANT: Power is supplied by a Mitsubishi 12WK-AK high-speed diesel developing 1,500 hp at 1,600 rpm maximum; and 1,350 hp at 1,500 rpm normal. The output is transmitted through a mechanical right-angle drive transmission to a 0·76 m diameter, aluminium bronze, subcavitating propeller.

SYSTEMS:
AIR CONDITIONING: Daikin air condit ing unit.
ELECTRICAL: APU-driven 15 KVA volt ac generator.
AUXILIARY POWER UNITS: Mitsu 22 Ps and 11.5 Ps diesels.
COMMUNICATIONS AND NAVIGATI Marine radio-telephone and radar stand

DIMENSIONS, EXTERNAL:

Length overall, hull	69 ft 0 in (21·
Length waterline, hull	64 ft 4 in (19·
Hull beam	15 ft 9 in (4·
Beam across foils	41 ft 6 in (12·6
Draft afloat	10 ft 9 in (3·2
Draft foilborne	4 ft 8 in (1·
Freeboard	5 ft 0 in (1·4
Height overall	38 ft 5 in (11·

WEIGHTS:

Max take-off displacement	37·2
Light displacement	27·13
Net tonnage	30
Max payload	7·2

PERFORMANCE:

Max speed foilborne	38·2 knots (70·8 k
Max speed hullborne	14 knots (25·7 k
Cruising speed	33 knots (61·6 k

Powered by a Mitsubishi 12WZ-AK high-speed diesel developing 1,500 hp, the Mitsubishi seats 80 passengers and cruises at 33 knots. Five are in service with Japanese operators.

Max permissible wave height in foilborne
mode   6 ft 6 in (2 m)

Designed range at cruising speed
       200 n. miles (37 km)

Turning radius at cruising speed
       820 ft (250 m) app

Number of seconds to take-off (theor app)
       40 sec

Number of seconds to stop craft   40 sec

Cost of standard craft:
       Approx 100,000,000 Yen

WATERJET RESEARCH CRAFT

Research into waterjet propulsion systems
led to the construction of a four-seat test craft
powered by a GE T58 gas turbine. The craft
was completed in January 1966, and has since
been used to evaluate waterjet systems and
provide performance information.

FOILS: The foil configuration is a combined
surface piercing and submerged system and
non-retractable. The Vee bow foil supports
% of the load, the split-Vee foils slightly
aft of amidships support 40%, and the fully-
submerged, 8 ft span rear foil supports the
remaining 42%. Total foil area is 22 sq ft
(2·075 m²) and the foil loading is 3·3 ton/m².
Bow and rear foils are in solid mild steel and
the midship foils are in welded mild steel
plate. An adjustable flap is fitted to the
trailing edge of the rear foil to assist take-off
and adjust the flying height. Side and
reverse thrust from the main waterjet nozzle
provides directional control.

HULL AND ACCOMMODATION: The
flat-bottom hull is of metal construction.
Welded aluminium alloy is employed throughout for frames and plating. The cabin
accommodates a crew of two and two
technicians.

Mitsubishi's waterjet research craft. The
waterjet is generated by a double-section
centrifugal pump powered through a reduction gearbox by a General Electric T58

POWER PLANT: The waterjet is provided
by a double-suction centrifugal pump powered through a reduction gearbox by a General
Electric LM100 (formerly T58) gas-turbine,
rated at 1,250 hp. Propulsion water enters
a ram scoop at the base of the rear foil strut
and is ducted upwards to the pump.

SYSTEMS:
ELECTRICAL: One 24 volt, 150 Ah battery.
HYDRAULICS: 1,000 psi pressure hydraulic
system to operate waterjet steering system;
3,000 psi system to operate tail foil flap.

DIMENSIONS, EXTERNAL:
Length overall, hull	37 ft 5 in (11·4 m)
Hull beam	11 ft 4 in (3·4 m)
Beam across foils	21 ft 11 in (6·7 m)
Draft foilborne	2 ft 2 in (0·65 m)
Height overall	11 ft 9 in (3·6 m)

WEIGHTS:
Normal take-off displacement   7·6 tons

PERFORMANCE:
Max speed foilborne	42 knots (77 km/h)
Cruising speed foilborne	38 knots (71 km/h)

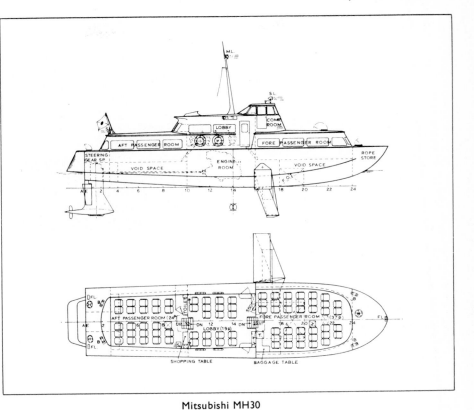

Mitsubishi MH30

Mitsubishi waterjet test craft

Max permissible wave height in foilborne
mode   3 ft 4 in (1 m)
Turning radius at cruising speed
       329 ft (100 m)

M3 SUBMERGED FOIL TEST CRAFT

This craft is basically a Mitsubishi M3
adapted as a test craft for the company's
submerged foil research programme, and
fitted with a Mitsubishi autopilot system.

FOILS: The foil system is fully submerged
and non-retractable. It comprises two forward foils located forward of the centre of
gravity and supporting 64% of the load and
a single auxiliary foil, supporting the remaining 36%, located aft as a tail assembly. Foils
and struts are in welded mild steel plate.
Total foil area is 1·226 m² and the loading is
3·5 T/m². The autopilot system input is
received from a sonic ranging probe in the
bow which senses the height above the water
of the bow in relation to a fixed reference,
from rate gyros, which measure pitch, roll
and yaw, from accelerometers, and from a
vertical gyro which senses the angular
position of the craft in pitch and roll. This
information is processed by the autopilot
computer and fed to the foil control surfaces.

HYDROFOIL MANUFACTURERS

MITSUBISHI / WESTERMOEN: Japan / Norway

HULL AND ACCOMMODATION: The craft has a Vee-bottom high speed hull of metal construction. Welded aluminium alloy is used throughout for frames and plating. The cabin accommodates the crew of two plus the bulk of the autopilot system and data gathering equipment. Entry is via either of two hinged hatches, port and starboard, each measuring 50 cm × 50 cm.

POWER PLANT: Propulsion is provided by a GM automotive engine rated at 280 hp at 4,000 rpm. Power is transmitted through a mechanical right-angle drive transmission to a 0·3 m diameter aluminium bronze-subcavitating propeller at the aft end of a strut and pod assembly.

DIMENSIONS, EXTERNAL:

Length overall, hull	26 ft 1 in (8·0 m)
Length overall, foils extended	32 ft 0 in (9·7 m)
Hull beam	7 ft 3 in (2·2 m)
Beam across foils	14 ft 9 in (4·5 m)
Draft foilborne	2 ft 4 in (0·72 m)
Height overall	10 ft 6 in (3·2 m)

WEIGHTS:

Light displacement	4·3 tons

The Mitsubishi M3 submerged foil test craft

PERFORMANCE:

Max speed, foilborne	38 knots (70 km/h)
Cruising speed, foilborne	33 knots (61 km/h)
Max permissible wave height in foilborne mode	1 ft 6 in-2 ft 6 in (0·5-0·8 m)
Turning radius at cruising speed	328 ft (100 m)
Number of seconds and distance to take (theoretical, approx)	20
Number of seconds to stop craft (theoret approx)	20

NORWAY

Westermoen

WESTERMOEN HYDROFOIL A/S

HEAD OFFICE:
  Hollendergt, 1 Mandal, Norway:
    Postboks 143
CABLES:
  Hydrofoil
TELEPHONE:
  2981
TELEX:
  6514 Hydrofoil ML
MANAGING DIRECTOR:
  Toralf Westermoen

Westermoen Hydrofoils A/S was founded in 1961 by Toralf Westermoen and Kr Haanes with the object of building hydrofoils and fast naval patrol vessels. The company, a Supramar licencee, completed the first PT 150, a 150 ton mixed car/passenger ferry, for Gothenburg-Friedrikshaven Line in June 1968. The craft is now operating on the route Gothenburg, Aalenburg, Friedrikshaven.

The PT 150 was the fifteenth craft to be built at the Westermoen shipyard, which employs a staff of 150. The company has previously built four PT 20 and three PT 50 hydrofoils.

Specifications for the PT 20, PT 50 and PT 150 will be found under Supramar (Switzerland).

H/S Expressan, built by Westermoen Hydrofoil A/S and operated by Gothenburg-Fredrikshavn L

At the end of 1966 a PT 50 (ex Westfoil) was returned to the yard to be fitted with a Schertel-Supramar fully submerged, air-stabilised rear foil in place of the normal surface-piercing unit. Renamed Flipper, it was the first craft to be fitted with an air stabilised foil and it was demonstrated marine authorities in February 1967. Flip is now on charter in Scandinavian wate

A description of the Flipper hydro appeared in the 1967-8 edition of Jan Surface Skimmer Systems.

POLAND

dansk

ANSK SHIP RESEARCH INSTITUTE

DRESS:
echnical University, Gdansk

LEPHONE:
1-47-12

RECTORS:
. Kobylinski
. Krezelewski

Research on problems connected with drofoil design and construction have been ducted by the Department of Theoretical val Architecture at Gdansk Technical liversity since 1956.

Experience with various dynamic test dels led to the construction of the K-3 ar-seat runabout which, powered by an C Lublin converted auto-engine, has a top ed of 27 knots (50 km/h).

In 1961 the Department was invited by the ntral Board of Inland Navigation and ited Inland Shipping and River Shipyards lansk, to design a hydrofoil passenger ferry service in the Firth of Szczecin. Designat-ZRYW-1 the craft seats 76 passengers and uises at 35 knots. It was completed in 65. A second craft, the W-2, intended for assenger services in the Baltic, is under velopment.

During 1966 the Ship Research Institute esigned two hydrofoil sports craft, the WS-4 mor and the WS-6 Eros. The prototypes ere completed in 1967 and both types will put into series production during 1969.

RYW-1

The ZRYW-1 was completed in May 1965, nd sea trials were initiated the following onth. On scheduled passenger services etween Szczecin and Swinoujscie, a distance f 36 nautical miles (67 km), the average perating speed has been in excess of 39 nots (73 km/h). The journey has been overed successfully in Sea States 2-4, with vave heights up to 5 ft 0 in (1·5 m).

OILS: The foil configuration is a combined surface piercing and submerging type. The foils are welded assemblies fabricated from 0·2 to 0·28 in (5·7 mm) thick stainless steel. The configuration is subcavitating and is designed to be inherently stable in any expected combination of heave, pitch, roll and yaw.

HULL: This is a light alloy structure of almost fully welded construction, riveting being applied mainly to the joints of the longitudinal and transverse framings with the outer plating of the vessel's roof, and also the joining of steel elements, such as the foil foundations and stern tube, with light alloy members.

POWER PLANT: Provided by a single Russian-built M-50F4 diesel, rated at 1,000 hp continuous and 1,200 hp maximum, driving a fixed-pitch, three-blade propeller.

The engine room, sited amidships, houses the main engine together with reversible gear, auxiliary set, tanks, and pumps serving the engine room system.

ACCOMMODATION: Forty passengers are carried in the forward passenger saloon, and thirty-six passengers in the aft saloon.

Comfortable, upholstered seats are fitted and the floors are covered with vinyl.

The wheelhouse, crew cabin and toilet are situated forward. Passenger entrance doors are provided on both sides of the craft and lead to a small vestibule forward of the crew's cabin. The two passenger compartments are provided with heat and accoustic insulation, and are electrically heated when stationary (shore supplied) and when in motion.

DIMENSIONS:

Length overall, hull	90 ft 7 in (27·60 m)
Length waterline, hull	75 ft 6 in (23·00 m)
Hull beam	14 ft 6 in (4·40 m)
Width across foils	24 ft 10 in (7·56 m)
Draft afloat	8 ft 1 in (2·45 m)
Freeboard	4 ft 3 in (1·30 m)

WEIGHTS:

Light displacement	22·7 tons
Max take-off displacement	30·7 tons
Useful load (fuel, water, passengers, baggage and crew)	8·0 tons

The ZRYW-1 (one Soviet-built M-50F 4 diesel) averages more than 39 knots on scheduled services between Szczecin and Swinoujscie, a distance of 36 nautical miles (67 km)

The 76-seat ZRYW-1, first Polish designed passenger hydrofoil to go into service

HYDROFOIL MANUFACTURERS

GDANSK SHIP RESEARCH INSTITUTE: Poland

PERFORMANCE

Cruising speed:
foilborne	35 knots (65 km/h)
hullborne	16 knots (30 km/h)

Sea State max capability   State 3

Design foilborne range   250 miles (460 km)

Fuel consumption at cruising speed
                                176 lb/hr (80 kg/h)

Fuel consumption hullborne
                                330 lb/hr (150 kg/h)

WS-4 AMOR

A four-seat sports hydrofoil designed by E. Brzoska, the WS-4, is of moulded fibreglass construction and powered by an outboard engine.   It will be put into series production in 1969.

FOILS: The foil system is of combined surface piercing and submerging type and non-retractable. It comprises a shallow draft surface-piercing bow foil and a fully submerged rear foil.   Both are made of solid aluminium alloy.   The foil arrangement is tandem in the sense that when foilborne the load is balanced between bow and rear foils.

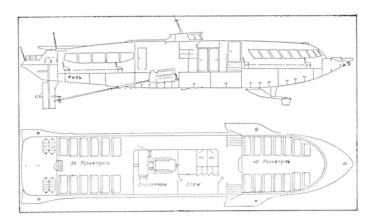

The ZRYW-I 76-seat passenger hydrofoil designed by Gdansk Technical University, Ship Research Institute, High Speed Division

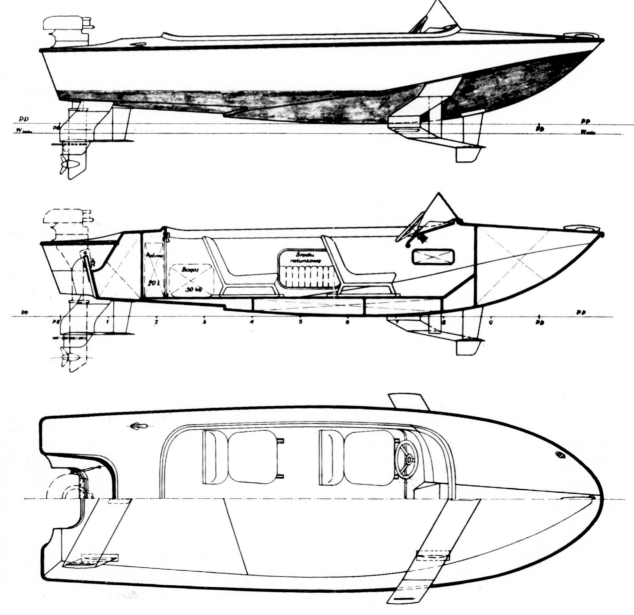

The Gdansk Ship Research Institute WS 4 Amor

OMMODATION: Comfortable upholster-
eats are provided for a helmsman and
e passengers. The hull is of moulded
glass construction and incorporates a
to facilitate take-off.

VER PLANT: The standard model is
pped with a Mercury 350 outboard, with
le lever throttle and gearshift control.
engine propeller unit turns for steering.
l is contained in a 6 gallon tank.

IENSIONS, EXTERNAL:

ngth overall, hull   15 ft 4 in (4·67 m)
ngth waterline, hull   13 ft 2 in (4·0 m)
ull beam   5 ft 0 in (1·5 m)
idth across foils   5 ft 11 in (1·8 m)
raft afloat   1 ft 8 in (·05 m)
raft foilborne   9 in (0·23 m)
eight overall   3 ft 4 in (1·0 m)

MENSIONS, INTERNAL:

ength   7 ft 3 in (2·2 m)
ax width   4 ft 0 in (1·2 m)
loor area   27 sq ft (2·5 m²)

IGHTS:

ight displacement   1,521 lb (686 kg)
ax payload   881 lb (400 kg)

RFORMANCE (with normal payload):

lax speed foilborne   34 mph (55 km/h)
lax speed hullborne   19 mph (30 km/h)
ruising speed foilborne 80 mph (50 km/h)
lax permissible wave height in foilborne
  mode   6 in (0·15 m)
Designed range at cruising speed
                         31 miles (50 km)
Jumber of seconds to take-off (theoretical,
  approx)   15 sec
Number of seconds to stop craft (theoretical,
  approx)   10 sec

S-6 EROS

A six seater hydrofoil runabout, the WS-6
ros was designed by W. Krenicki,, and like
e smaller WS-4 will be put into series
roduction in 1969.

ULL: The prototype is built of marine
lywood, but the hull of the production
odels will be in moulded fibreglass.

OILS: The foil system is similar to that of
he WS-4. It is a combined surface piercing
nd submerged configuration with a shallow
raft surface piercing bow foil central "keel"
nd a fully submerged rear foil. Foils are of
olid aluminium alloy. About 52% of the
oad is carried by the bow foil and 48% by
he rear foil. Total foil area is 11·5 sq ft
1·07 m²).

WS-4 Amor

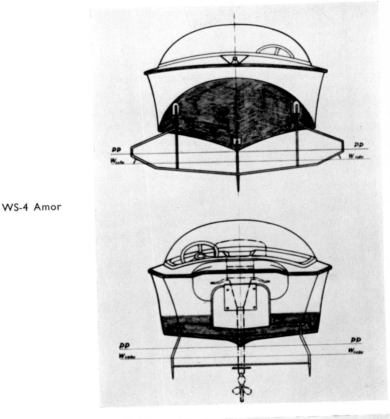

The WS-4 Amor, a four-seat runabout designed by Gdansk Ship Research Institute and powered
by a Mercury 350 outboard motor

A six-seat fibreglass-hulled sports hydrofoil, the WS-6 Eros is powered by a Volvo Penta Aquamatic 110/200 and has a top speed of 30 knots

HYDROFOIL MANUFACTURERS
GDANSK SHIP RESEARCH INSTITUTE: Poland

ACCOMMODATION: Upholstered seats are provided for a helmsman and five passengers.

POWER PLANT: The production model will have a Volvo Penta Aquamatic 110/200. Power is transmitted through a right-angle drive transmission to a 3-blade propeller at the base of a strut-and-pod assembly which rotates for steering. Total fuel capacity is 100 litres.

DIMENSIONS, EXTERNAL:

Length overall, hull	23 ft 9 in (7·25 m)
Length waterline, hull	20 ft 2 in (6·15 m)
Hull beam	7 ft 4 in (2·24 m)
Beam overall, foils extended	
	8 ft 6 in (2·6 m)
Draft afloat	3 ft (0·9 m)
Draft foilborne	1 ft 2 in (0·36 m)
Freeboard	2 ft 2 in (0·65 m)
Height overall	5 ft 1 in (1·55 m)

DIMENSIONS, INTERNAL:

Cockpit length	10 ft 2 in (3·1 m)
Max width	6 ft 7 in (2 m)
Floor area	67·2 sq ft (6·2 m²)

WEIGHTS:

Light displacement	1·05 tons
Normal take-off displacement	1·6 tons
Max take-off displacement	1·75 tons
Normal payload	0·55 tons
Max payload	0·7 tons

PERFORMANCE:

Max speed foilborne	35 mph (56 km/h)
Cruising speed foilborne	31 mph (50 km/h)
Max permissible wave height in foilborne mode	10 in (250 mm)
Number of seconds and distance to take-off	10 sec, 394 ft (120 m)
Number of seconds and distance to stop craft	8 sec 329 ft (100 m)
Turning radius at cruising speed	820 ft (250 m)

REKIN
W-2

The W-2 is a projected hydrofoil ferry designed primarily for operation in the Baltic. Similar to the ZRYW-1, which was

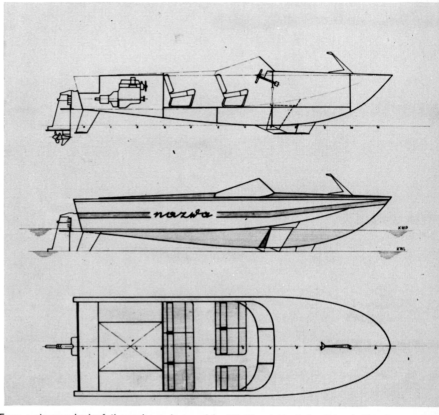

Eros, a six-seat hydrofoil runabout designed by W. Krenicki of the Gdansk Ship Research Institute. The craft has a shallow draft surface piercing bow foil and a submerged rear foil. It [will] go into production in 1969

designed specifically for the relatively sheltered waters of the Szczecin Bay, the W-2 is slightly larger and more sturdily built. It will have a completely redesigned bow, V-foils of revised and deeper configuration and the more powerful Paxman Ventura 12YJXM marine-diesel, rated at 1,020 hp at 1,350 rpm.

Design of the W-2 and tests of the ⅓ scale dynamic model illustrated in Jane's Surface Skimmer Systems 1967-8 edition are now complete.

DIMENSIONS:

Length overall	93 ft 6 in (28·50)
Beam	15 ft 5 in (4·70)
Width across foils	24 ft 7 in (7·50)
Draught afloat	9 ft 1 in (2·75)
Draught foilborne	5 ft 5 in (1·65)

WEIGHTS:

Displacement, loaded	35 t

PERFORMANCE:

Maximum speed	47 mph (75 km)
Cruising speed	40 mph (65 km)

Impression of the W-2 Rekin, a passenger hydrofoil designed at Gdansk for services between ports on the Baltic

SWITZERLAND

ramar
RAMAR AG

D OFFICE:
nkmalstrasse 2, Lucerne

EPHONE:
53 55

EX: 78 228

ECTORS:
anns Freiherr von Schertel, Technical
Director and Vice President
ipl-Ing Karl Büller, Technical Director
einz Muller, lic.oec, Commercial Director

CUTIVES (Design Department):
ipl-Ing Karl Büller
g Volker Jost, Hull Design Division
ipl-Ing Egon Faber, Marine Engineering
Division
ipl-Ing Dietrich Cebulla, Foil Design
Division

earch Department:
anns Freiherr von Schertel
ipl-Ing Ernst Jaksch, Deputy Head of
Research
ipl-Ing Eugen Schatté, Propulsion and
Hydrodynamics
r Ing Hermann de Witt, Propulsion and
Hydrodynamics

upramar was founded in Switzerland in
2 to develop on a commercial basis the
lrofoil system introduced by the Schertel-
hsenberg Hydrofoil Syndicate and its
ncee, the Gebruder Sachsenberg Shipyard.
he co-operation between the companies
rted in 1937 and led to the development
the VS6, a 17 ton hydrofoil, which in 1941
ained 47·5 knots, and the VS8 an 80-ton
ply hydrofoil completed in 1943 which
ained 40 knots. The inherently stable,
id V-foil system used on these and subse-
ent Supramar vessels, stems from experi-
ntal work undertaken by Baron Hanns
n Schertel between 1927-1937.

n May 1953, a Supramar PT 10, 32-
ssenger hydrofoil began the world's first
ular passenger hydrofoil service on Lake
aggiore, between Switzerland and Italy.

August 1956, the first Rodriquez-built
pramar PT 20 opened a service across the
raits of Medina and became the first
drofoil to be licenced by a marine classifica-
n authority for carrying passengers at sea.
Basically a research and design company,
pramar employs a staff of 40, mainly highly
alified scientists and engineers specialising
hydrodynamics, marine engineering, foil
sign and propulsion. The company does
t build hydrofoils but licences shipyards to
oduce its hydrofoil designs. Current
ensees are Cantiere Navale Leopoldo
odriquez, Messina, Italy; Hitachi Ship-
ilding & Engineering Co Ltd, Osaka;
estermoen Hydrofoil A/S, Mandal, Norway;
d the General Dynamics Corp, Quincy
ivision, Quincy, Mass, USA. Hydrofoils
eing built by these companies are referred
elsewhere in this section under the
spective company headings.
The latest Supramar design to be completed
the PT 150 DC, a 150-ton passenger/car
erry, the first of which was built by Wester-
oen Hydrofoil A/S and delivered on June
8, 1968 to Gothenburg-Frederikshavn-Line.
he craft cruises at 35 knots in waves up to

8 ft (2·5 m) in height and will carry 150
passengers and eight cars, or 250 passengers.
A second PT 150 is to be built by Leopoldo
Rodriquez at Messina.

The PT 150 has a partly air stabilised foil
system, stability being maintained jointly by
the inherent stability of the vee-shaped
surface-piercing bow foil and the air-fed,
fully-submerged rear foil.

The company is now developing a fully
submerged foil system with air stabilisation.
First craft to use this system is a 4·9 ton
experimental boat built under a US Navy
contract. During tests in the Mediterranean
it has demonstrated promising stability and
seakeeping qualities and has reached a speed
of 54 knots.

PT 4

A 4·4 ton hydrofoil with applications
ranging from sightseeing and sport-fishing to
fast passenger ferry, the PT 4 is designed for
use on comparatively sheltered waters—
lakes, rivers and bays. Powered by a 300 hp
Chrysler M413D, it has a payload of 1·3 tons
tons and cruises at 32 knots.

The PT 4 was given Board of Trade
approval on completion of sea tests off the
Cornish coast in March 1966. Since the craft
is powered by a gasoline engine, passenger
capacity is restricted to 12 persons in
accordance with international safety regulations.

FOILS: The foil configuration is a combined
surface-piercing and submerged system.
The surface piercing bow foil supports 68%
of the load and the fully submerged rear foil
supports the remaining 32%. Total foil area
is 1·16 m².

The bow foil is made in solid, machined
FB 70 steel, and the rear foil which is partly of
hollow construction, is in FB 70 and MSt
52-3 steel.

Bow and rear foils, together with their
supporting struts and a horizontal guide form
a uniform framework which facilitates the
exchange of the foil structure.

The rudder, of combined hollow and solid
steel construction, forms part of the aft
foil frame.

Angle of incidence of the bow foil can be
adjusted in flight by a hydraulic actuator to
counteract the effect of large variations in
passenger loads.

HULL: Constructed in seawater-resistant
light metal alloy, the V-bottom hull is
longitudinally framed, with web frames
spaced 2·95 ft (900 mm) apart. Joints are
partly welded, partly riveted. Steel is used
for higher-stressed parts such as foil hull
connections and the shaft bracket.

POWER PLANT: Power is supplied by 300
hp Chrysler M413D gasoline engine coupled
to a reverse and reduction gear with a
2 : 1 reduction ratio.

Engine output is transmitted through an
inclined shaft to a three-bladed bronze
propeller located ahead of the rear foil.

SYSTEMS:
ELECTRICAL: 12V, 135 Ah batteries for
electrical services.
HYDRAULICS: 120 kp/cm² pressure hy-
draulic system for operating rudder and bow
foil angle of incidence.
COMMUNICATIONS:
RADIO: Small ship-shore radio-telephone.

DIMENSIONS, EXTERNAL:

Length overall, hull	37 ft 6 in (11·45 m)
Length over deck	36 ft 3 in (11·05 m)
Beam max	10 ft 6 in (3·20 m)
Width over foils	14 ft 2 in (4·32 m)
Draft afloat	4 ft 8 in (1·45 m)
Draft foilborne	1 ft 8 in (0·57 m)

DIMENSIONS, INTERNAL:
Cabin (Pilot stand incl):

Length	15 ft 6 in (4·8 m)
Max. width	8 ft (2·4 m)
Max. height	6 ft 6 in (2·0 m)
Floor area	87 sq ft (8·0 m²)
Volume	813 cu ft (23·0 m³)

WEIGHTS:

Max take-off displacement	4·4 tons
Payload	1·275 tons
Light displacement	3·125 tons

PERFORMANCE:

Max speed foilborne	39 knots
Cruising speed foilborne	32 knots (60 km/h)
Range	155 nautical miles (290 km)

Cost of standard craft: approx $US 40,000

The PT 4 (one Chrysler M413D) is designed for services on lakes and rivers. As a sightseeing
craft it will seat 12 passengers.

HYDROFOIL MANUFACTURERS
SUPRAMAR: Switzerland

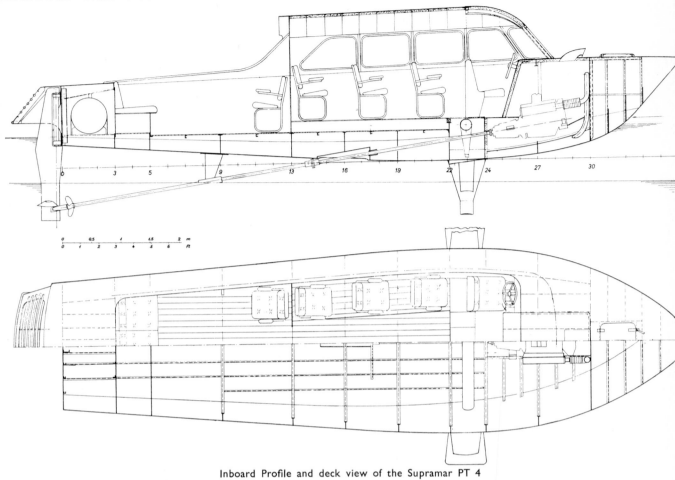

Inboard Profile and deck view of the Supramar PT 4

PT 10

A 13-ton boat for 32-36 passengers, the PT 10 has been designed for commuter and sightseeing services on inland waters and protected bays.

Powered by a single 540 hp Daimler-Benz MB 837 diesel engine, it is of riveted light metal alloy construction and has a cruising speed of 35 knots.

FOILS: Bow foil and rear foil are of standard Schertel-Sachsenberg surface piercing type, with the bow foil supporting 52% of the load and the rear foil supporting the remaining 48%. Both are made from solid high tensile steel, and their struts and fins are of hollow steel design. The two foils together with

their supporting elements form rigid frame units which are easily attached or detached as necessary.

The angle of incidence of the bow foil may be adjusted during flight by means of a hydraulic actuator acting on the foil strut supporting tube.

RUDDER: Hydraulically operated, the rudder is of hollow, welded steel design, and forms part of the aft foil frame.

HULL: The V-bottom hull is of riveted light alloy construction. Transverse framing is employed with 1 ft (300 mm) frame spacing. Foil fittings, shaft brackets and the shaft exit are in high tensile steel.

ACCOMMODATION: A single cabin seats

32 passengers and a crew of 2. Acce[ss] through either of two sliding hat[ches] located forward, port and starboard a[nd] the steering stand. An emergency wi[ndow] exit is provided at the aft end of the com[part]ment. Lifebelts are provided for [each] passenger and the two crew members.

POWER PLANT: Power is supplied [by a] single Daimler-Benz MB 837 Ea 8-cyl[inder] supercharged diesel, rated at 540 hp at [1,600] rpm. Engine output is transferred t[o the] propeller through a V-drive and a sta[inless] steel propeller shaft. A special revers[e-] reduction gear, type BW 200 ES 28, ma[de by] Zahnradfabrik Friedrichshafen, is p[laced] between the engine and the drive shaft.

The Supramar PT10 (one 1,100 hp MB 820 Db diesel), a 32 passenger hydrofoil for sightseeing or commuter services on inland waters and protected

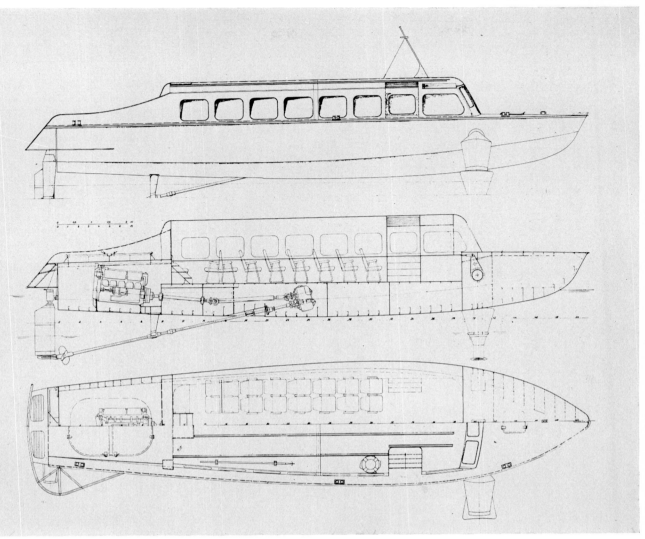

Side and deck views of the Supramar PT 10, 32 passenger hydrofoil

STEMS:

ECTRICAL: 24 volt generator driven by
e main engine; batteries with capacity of
) Ah.

YDRAULICS: 120 kp/cm² pressure hy-
aulic system for steering and bow foil
idence control.

OMMUNICATIONS AND NAVIGATION:
ip-shore radio telephone is fitted; radar is
tional.

MENSIONS, EXTERNAL:

Length overall, hull	53·60 ft (16·34 m)
Length over deck	51·50 ft (15·70 m)
Max beam	11·81 ft (3·60 m)
Width over foils	18·50 ft (5·64 m)
Draft afloat	6·73 ft (2·05 m)
Draft foilborne	2·79 ft (0·85 m)

MENSIONS, INTERNAL:

Cabin (inc pilot stand):

Length	27 ft 7 in (8·4 m)
Width	8 ft 7 in (2·6 m)
Height	6 ft 3 in (1·9 m)
Floor area	234 sq ft (21·8 m²)
Volume	1,449 cu ft (41·0 m³)

EIGHTS:

Light displacement	9·5 tons
Normal take-off displacement	13·3 tons
Normal payload	3·8 tons

ERFORMANCE:

Max speed foilborne	36 knots
Cruising speed foilborne	35 knots
Range at cruising speed	145 nautical miles
Turning radius app.	400 m
Take-off time	30 sec

Fuel consumption at cruising speed 90 kp/h
Cost of standard craft: app $US 160,000.

PT 20

The PT 20, a 27-ton boat for 72 passengers,
is considered by Supramar to be the smallest
size hydrofoil suitable for passenger-carrying
coastal services. The first of this very
successful series was built by the Rodriquez
shipyard at Messina in 1955 and since then
nearly 70 PT 20s of various types have been
built in Sicily, Japan, Holland and Norway.
The design has been approved by almost
every classification society. Fast patrol
boat variants, the PT 32 and the PAT 20,
are described under the entries for Hitachi
(Japan) and Leopoldo Rodriquez (Italy)
respectively.

FOILS: Foils are of standard Schertel-
Sachsenberg, surface-piercing type, with 58 %
of the load supported by the bow foil and the
remaining 42 % by the rear foil. Submerged
foil area in foilborne condition is 5·50 m².
Together with the struts and a horizontal
guide, each foil forms a uniform framework
which facilitates the exchange of the foil
elements. The medium steel foils are of
partly hollow, welded construction. The
angle of incidence of the fore hydrofoil can
be adjusted within narrow limits from the
steering stand by means of a hydraulic ram
operating on a foil support across the hull.
To counteract the effects of large variations
in passenger load and to ensure optimum

behaviour in sea waves the angle of attack
can be adjusted during operation. If
required, the rear foil can be stabilized by
the Schertel-Supramar air feed system. A
fully submerged foil then replaces the standard surface piercing type.

HULL: The hull has a V-bottom with an
externally added step riveted into place.
Frames, bulkheads, foundations, superstructure and all internal construction is in
corrosion-proof light alloy. Platings are of
AlMg 5 and the frames, bars and other
members are made in AlMgSi. Watertight
compartments are provided below the
passenger decks and in other parts of the hull.
Several of these are filled with foam-type
plastic which makes these boats practically
unsinkable.

POWER PLANT: Power is supplied by a
supercharged, 12-cylinder Daimler-Benz MB
820Db with an exhaust turbo-compressor.
Maximum continuous output is 1,100 hp at
1,400 rpm. A BW 800/HS 20 reversible gear,
developed by Zahnradfabrik Friedrichshafen
AG, is placed between the engine and the
drive shaft.

ACCOMMODATION: The boat is controlled
entirely from the bridge which is located
above the engine room. Forty-six passengers
are accommodated in the forward cabin,
twenty in the rear compartment and six aft
of the pilot's stand in the elevated wheelhouse. There is an emergency exit in each
passenger compartment, and the craft is

HYDROFOIL MANUFACTURERS
SUPRAMAR: Switzerland

equipped with an inflatable life raft and life belts for each person. A crew of four is carried.

SYSTEMS:

ELECTRICAL: 24 volt generator driven by the main engine; batteries with a capacity of approx 250 Ah.

HYDRAULICS: 120 kp/cm² pressure hydraulic system for rudder and bow foil incidence control.

COMMUNICATIONS AND NAVIGATION: VHF ship-shore radio is supplied as standard equipment. Radar is optional.

DIMENSIONS, EXTERNAL:

Length overall, hull	68·07 ft (20·75 m)
Length over deck	67·50 ft (19·95 m)
Hull beam, max	16·37 ft (4·99 m)
Width across foils	26·39 ft (8·07 m)
Draft hullborne	10·10 ft (3·08 m)
Draft foilborne	4·59 ft (1·40 m)

DIMENSIONS, INTERNAL:

Aft cabin (inc toilet)	145 sq ft (13·5 m²)
Volume	954 cu ft (27·0 m³)
Forward cabin	280 sq ft (26·0 m²)
Volume	1,766 cu ft (50·0 m³)
Main deck level (inc wheelhouse)	129 sq ft (12·0 m²)
Volume	847 cu ft (24·0 m³)

WEIGHTS:

Gross tonnage	approx 56 tons
Max take-off displacement	32 tons
Light displacement	25 tons
Deadweight (incl. fuel, oil, water, passengers, baggage and crew)	7 tons
Payload	5·4 tons

PERFORMANCE (with normal payload):

Cruising speed, foilborne 34 knots (63 km/h)

Max permissible wave height in foilborne mode 4·25 ft (1·29 m)

Designed range at cruising speed
216 nautical miles (400 k

Turning radius	427 ft approx (130
Take off distance	493 ft approx (150
Take-off time	25
Stopping distance	230 ft (70

Fuel consumption at cruising speed 150 k

SEA TEST: Prototype tests were undertal in the Mediterranean in every kind of condition, and further tests have taken pl off Japan. Acceleration measurements h shown maximum values below 0·5g wh accelerometer had been fitted above the b foil. Maximum lateral acceleration v 0·32g. Measurements were made in wa heights of approx 1·2 to 1·5 m. These the maximum measurements obtained a subsequent tests have seldom equalled th figures.

Cost of standard craft: $US 330,000.

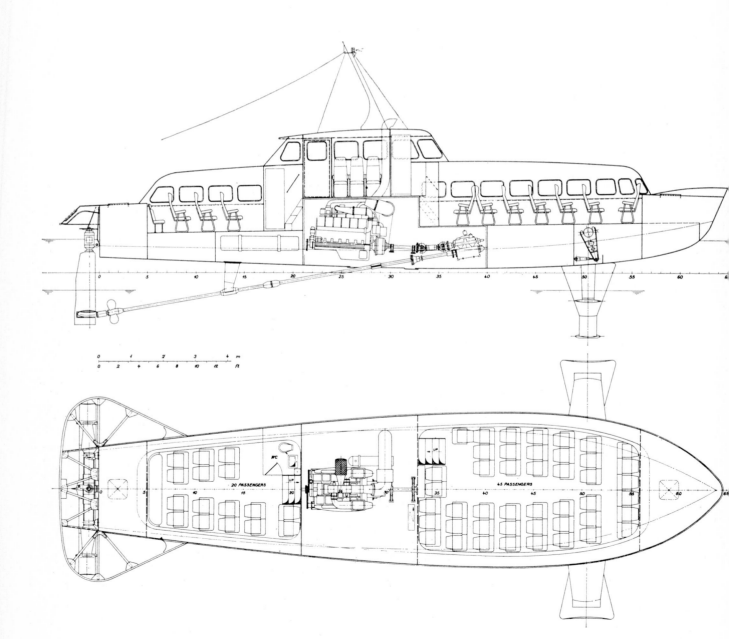

Inboard profile and deck view of the Supramar PT 20

The PT 20, a 72-seat hydrofoil for coastal services, has been in continuous production since 1955.   Nearly 70 are in service in 21 countries

[PT] 20B

In this model of the PT 20, the engine room [an]d bridge are arranged in the foreship. [Th]is improves the pilot's vision in waters [lik]ely to have an influx of driftwood and [pr]ovides a large main passenger cabin with [se]ats for 65 for commuter services.

The first four craft in this series, built for [th]e servicing of offshore drilling platforms on [L]ake Maracaibo, Venezuela, were designated [P]T 27.

[F]OILS: The foil design is similar to that of [th]e PT 20.   About 66% of the total weight [is] borne by the bow foil and 34% by the [re]ar foil.   Submerged foil area in foilborne [co]ndition is 6·2 m².   The forward foil can [be] tilted within narrow limits by means of a [h]ydraulic ram acting on the foil strut [su]pporting tube.   The angle of attack can [th]erefore be adjusted during operation to [a]ssist take-off and to counteract the effect of [la]rge variations in passenger loads.

The rear foil can be stabilized by the [S]chertel-Supramar air feed system with a [fu]lly-submerged foil replacing standard sur-[fa]ce piercing type.

[H]ULL.   This is of riveted light metal alloy [d]esign and framed on a combination of [lo]ngitudinal and transverse formers.   Water-[t]ight compartments are provided below the [p]assenger decks and in other parts of the hull, [a]nd some are filled with foam-type plastic.

[P]OWER PLANT: Power is supplied by a [1]2 cyl Mercedes-Benz Mb 820 Db with a max [c]ontinuous output of 1,100 hp at 1,490 rpm. [A]verage service time between major over-[h]auls is approx 10,000 hours.   Engine [o]utput is transferred to a 3-bladed 700 mm [d]iameter bronze subcavitating propeller [t]hrough a BW 800/H 20 reversible gear made [b]y Zahnradfabrik.   The propeller shaft is

of 3·5 in (90 mm) diameter stainless steel and supported at three points by seawater lubricated rubber bearings.

SYSTEMS:

ELECTRICAL: MWM AKD412E single-phase, 220 volt, 7·1 kVa, 50 c/s generator.
HYDRAULICS: 120 kp/cm² pressure hydraulic system for operating rudder and bow foil angle of incidence control.
ACCOMMODATION: The PT 20B has a crew of 4 and seats 71 passengers.   The main passenger compartment seats 65, and the small cabin behind the pilot's stand seats a further 6.   Access to the main compartment

is through either of two doors, located port and starboard, to the rear of the wheelhouse. An emergency exit is provided at the rear of the main passenger compartment.

A full range of safety equipment is carried, including inflatable rafts and lifebelts for each passenger and crew member.

COMMUNICATIONS AND NAVIGATION: A vhf ship-shore radio is supplied as standard equipment.   Radar is an optional extra.

DIMENSIONS, EXTERNAL:

Length overall, hull	67·50 ft (20·58 m)
Length waterline, hull	67·10 ft (20·45 m)
Hull beam, max	17·05 ft (5·20 m)

Bridge of the PT 20B is located in the foreship to provide improved vision. Sixteen passengers are accommodated in the forward cabin above the engine room and fifty-four in the main cabin Powered by an MB 820Db diesel rated at 1,100 hp continuous, the craft cruises at 34 knots (63 km/h)

HYDROFOIL MANUFACTURERS
SUPRAMAR: Switzerland

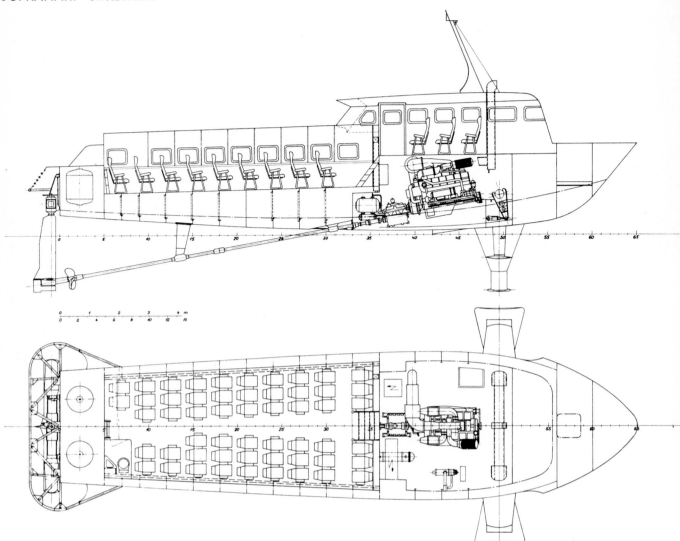

Side and deck views of the PT 20B

Width over foils	26·40 ft (8·05 m)
Draft hullborne	10·04 ft (3·06 m)
Draft foilborne	4·56 ft (1·39 m)

DIMENSIONS, INTERNAL:

Main passenger compartment (inc toilet):

Length	30 ft 7 in (9·3 m)
Width	12 ft 6 in (3·8 m)
Height	6 ft 7 in (2·0 m)
Floor area	379 sq ft (35·3 m²)
Volume	2,489·5 cu ft (70·6 m³)

Main deck compartment (inc wheelhouse):

Length	17 ft 9 in (5·4 m)
Width	13 ft 6 in (4·1 m)
Height	6 ft 7 in (2·0 m)
Floor area	237 sq ft (22·1 m²)
Volume	1,553 cu ft (44·0 m³)

WEIGHT:

Max take-off displacement	32·5 tons
Light displacement	25·4 tons
Deadweight (inc fuel, oil, water, passengers, luggage, crew)	7·1 tons
Payload	5·44 tons

PERFORMANCE (with normal payload):

Cruising speed	34 knots (63 km/h)
Max permissible wave height in foilborne mode	4·25 ft (1·29 m)
Turning radius	426 ft (app 130 m)
Take-off distance	492 ft (app 150 m)
Take-off time	app 30 sec
Stopping distance	231 ft (app 70 m)
Stopping time	app 10 sec

Fuel consumption at cruising speed 150 kp/h
Cost of standard craft, app: $US 330,000

PT 50

The successful and profitable operation of the PT 20 led to the development of the PT 50, a 63-ton hydrofoil passenger ferry designed for offshore and inter-island services. The prototype was completed by Rodriquez early in 1958, and more than thirty are now operating regular passenger services in areas ranging from the Baltic and Mediterranean to the Japanese Inland Sea.

The craft has been approved by almost every Classification Society including Registro Italiano Navale, Germanischer Lloyd, Det Norske Veritas, American Bureau of Shipping and the Japanese Ministry of Transport. The requirements of the SOLAS 1960 convention for international traffic can be met by the type if required.

FOILS: Both rear and forward foils are rigidly attached to the hull but the lift of the forward foil can be modified by hydraulically-operated flaps, which are fitted to assist take-off and turning, and for making slight course corrections and adjustments of the flying height. The foils are of hollow construction using MSt 52-3 steel and GS 22 Cr Mo 4 castings.

The bow foil comprises the following elements:

Two fins, forming connecting links between the foil and the supporting structure which is riveted to the hull.

The hydrofoil which (according to its foil section characteristics) generates the and, with the stern foil, provides transv stability in foilborne conditions.

Two struts, which transmit the main loads to the supporting structure.

The stern foil, also a rigid frame struc is formed by the following:

A supporting structure (stern box) conne the two sides of the frame at the tran

Two struts, forming the connection bet the foil and the supporting structure.

The surface-piercing V-foil.

The rudders, which also transmit the part of the lift into the supporting stru

The rear foil can be stabilised by Schertel-Supramar air feed system, w fully-submerged foil replacing the stan surface piercing type.

HULL: Of hard chine construction, the is of riveted light metal alloy design framed on longitudinal and transverse f ers. Steel is used only for highly str parts such as the foil fittings, and the brackets and exits.

ACCOMMODATION: On long distance ations 105 passengers are carried in saloons, two of which have bars. On sh operations and ferry services the bars omitted and seating can be provided fo to 140 passengers. The crew varies 6-8 members, depending mainly on regulations.

A Rodriquez-built Supramar PT 50, a 63-ton hydrofoil with a cruising speed of 34 knots, and seating up to 140 passengers

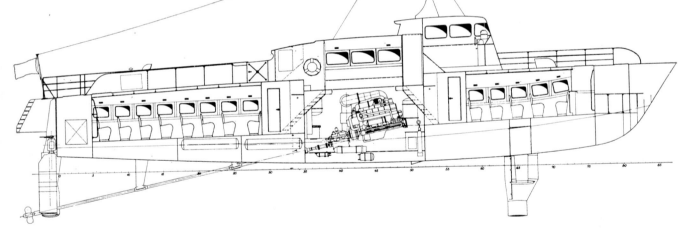

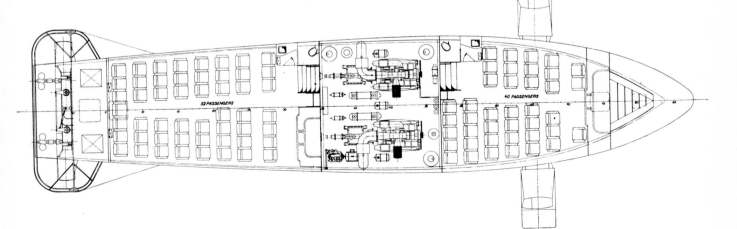

Inboard profile and deck view of the Supramar PT 50

HYDROFOIL MANUFACTURERS
SUPRAMAR: Switzerland

Passenger seats are of lightweight aircraft type and the centre aisle between the seat rows has a clear width of 30 in (0·76 m). Floors and ceilings are covered with light-weight plastic material and the walls, including web frames, are clad in luxury plywood. Toilets are provided in the rear and forward passenger spaces. Each passenger compartment has an emergency exit. Inflatable life rafts and lifebelts are provided for 110% of the passenger and crew capacity.

POWER PLANT: The craft is powered by two Maybach-Mercedes-Banz MB 820 Db diesels each with a continuous output of 1,100 hp at 1,400 rpm. Engine output is transmitted to two 3-bladed 700 mm diameter bronze propellers through two inclined stainless steel propeller shafts, each supported at four points by seawater lubricated rubber bearings. Average operation period between overhauls is 10,000 hours. Electric or pneumatic starting can be provided. Reverse and reduction gear with built-in thrust is manufactured by Zahnradfabrik Friedrichshafen, Germany. The reverse clutches are solenoid-operated from the bridge.

Eight cylindrical fuel tanks with a total capacity of 3,650 litres are located in the aft peak and below the tank deck. Oil capacity is 320 litres.

SYSTEMS

ELECTRICAL: One diesel generator set, Daimler-Benz-Still, type DM 636-DAK 166-2, capacity 24 KVA, 50 cps, 3-phase. Engine-driven 24 V dc generator with 210 AH batteries for emergency lighting and navigation equipment.

HYDRAULICS: 120 kp/cm² pressure hydraulic system for operating twin rudders and front foil flaps.

COMMUNICATIONS AND NAVIGATION: Standard equipment includes UHF and VHF radio telephone. Radar and Decca Navigator is optional.

DIMENSIONS, EXTERNAL:

Length overall, hull	91·55 ft (27·90 m)
Length overall, deck	89·50 ft (27·23 m)
Hull beam, max	20·01 ft (6·11 m)
Width across foils	34·93 ft (10·68 m)
Draft afloat	11·48 ft (3·50 m)
Draft foilborne	4·66 ft (1·42 m)

DIMENSIONS, INTERNAL:

Aft passenger Compartment (incl. bar and toilet):

Length	9·0 m
Width	4·9 m
Height	2·0 m
Floor area	44·1 m²
Volume	88·0 m³

Forward passenger compartment (incl bar and toilet):

Length	7·1 m
Width	5·4 m
Height	2·0 m
Floor area	38·3 m²
Volume	76·6 m³

Main deck passenger compartment (in wheelhouse):

Length	8·0
Width	3·6
Height	2·0
Floor area	28·8
Volume	57·6

WEIGHTS:

Max take-off displacement	63·3 to
Light displacement	49·3 to
Deadweight (incl fuel, oil, water, passenger baggage and crew)	14·0 to
Payload	9·5 to

PERFORMANCE (with normal payload):

Cruising speed	34 knots (63 km)
Range	300 nm (555 k)
Turning radius	1,542 ft (470)
Take-off distance	819 ft (250)
Take-off time	35 s
Stopping distance	264 ft (80)
Time to stop craft	10 s

Fuel consumption at cruising speed 300 kp

SEA TESTS: Location of the most rece test was off the south coast of Norway.

CONDITIONS:

Beaufort	6
Speed of Boat	30 kn
Wave height	3 ft 4 in-5 ft (1-1·5)
Wave-length	65 ft 8 in-166 ft (20-50)

ACCELERATIONS:

Max vertical 0·5g bow foil; 0·37g stern f

Max transverse

0·23g rear section; 0·32g forward sectio

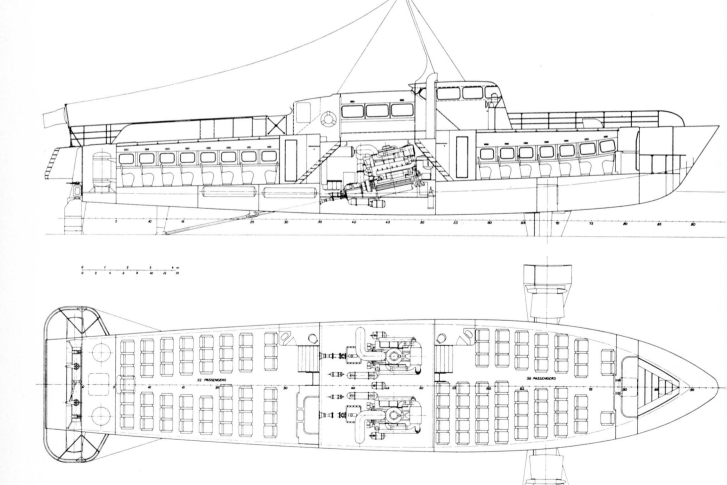

Inboard profile and deck view of the PT 70, a new Supramar hydrofoil passenger ferry designed to seat up to 155 passengers

The test, of 40 minutes duration, was undertaken in all wave directions and the above values were the absolute maximum obtained.

Cost of craft (standard): approx $US 650,000

PT 70

This recent addition to the Supramar design range is basically an enlarged and more powerful PT 50, seating up to 155 passengers. It is almost identical to the PT 50 in most respects but the hull length is increased by 6 ft (1·8 m) and there is a choice of three different twin-diesel power plants. The type has not been constructed so far.

FOILS: As for PT 50.

HULL: A combination of transverse and longitudinal framing has been adopted for the V-shaped hull. The bottom of the craft has transverse frames while the decks and sides are framed longitudinally. Thickness of the corrosion proof light metal alloy sheets is between ·08 in (2 mm) and ·20 in (5 mm). For several of the constructional members high tensile steel is used.

ACCOMMODATION: Normally seating is provided for 120 passengers. If the bars are omitted a further 35 seats can be installed.

POWER PLANT: Three different twin-engine arrangements are available: Two 1,450 hp Maybach-Mercedes Benz MB 835s; two 1,450 hp MB 655/18s, or two 1,500 hp Paxman Ventura 12YJCM. Fuel consumption of each of these engines is approx 170 gHPh or 0·38 lbHPh. Engine output is transferred to two 3-bladed bronze propellers through two inclined stainless steel shafts. Reduction and reverse gears

The first Supramar PT 150, a 150-ton 37-knot passenger/car ferry built by Westermoen Hydrofoil A/S, Mandal, Norway, for Gothenburg-Fredrikshavn-Line. The craft was delivered in June 1968 and is now operating between Sweden and Denmark, calling at Gothenburg, Aalborg and Fredrikshavn

are Zahnradfabrik Type BW 800/H20s with built-in thrust bearings.

SYSTEMS: As for PT 50.

DIMENSIONS, EXTERNAL:

Length overall, hull	96·75 ft	(29·50 m)
Length overall, deck	95·00 ft	(28·93 m)
Hull beam, max	19·80 ft	(6·03 m)
Width over foils	34·95 ft	(10·66 m)
Draft afloat	12·36 ft	(3·77 m)
Draft foilborne	5·28 ft	(1·66 m)

WEIGHT:

Displacement, fully loaded	70 tons

PERFORMANCE:

Cruising speed	35 knots (67 km/h)
Range	260 nm (480 km)

PT 150

In August 1966, Gothenburg-Fredrikshaven-Line placed an order with Westermoen Hydrofoil A/S, Mandel, Norway, for a 150 ton

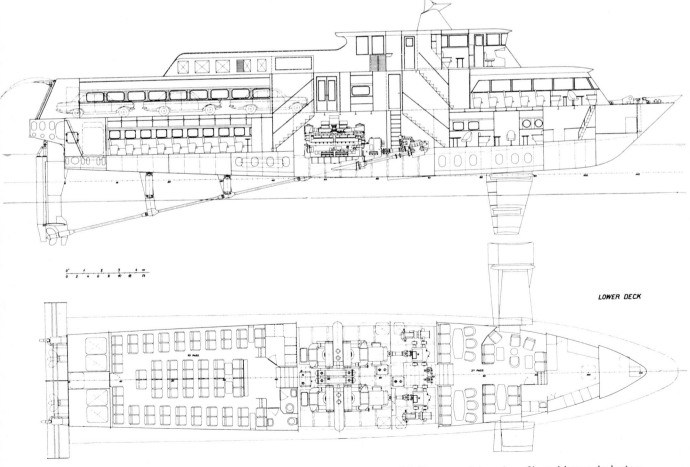

LOWER DECK

The Supramar PT 150 prototype, built by Westermoen Hydrofoil A/S, Mandel, Norway. Inboard profile and lower deck view

HYDROFOIL MANUFACTURERS
SUPRAMAR: Switzerland

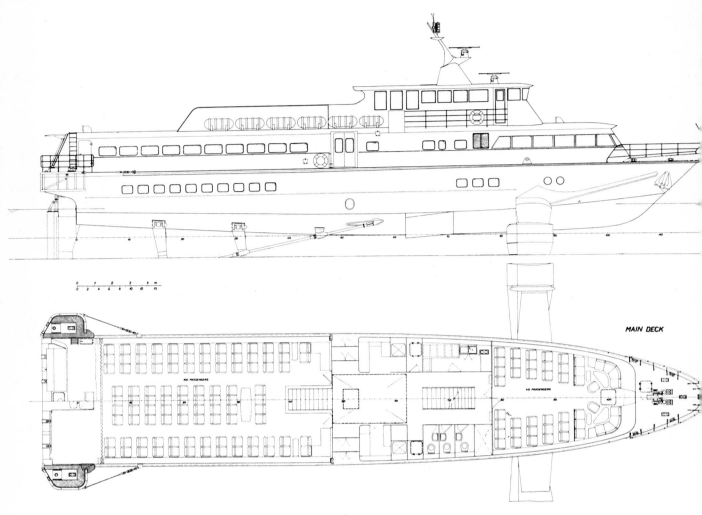

Profile and main deck view of the Supramar PT 150

Supramar PT 150 to operate a fast passenger/car ferry service between Sweden and Denmark, calling at Gothenburg, Aalborg and Fredrikshavn. Originally the PT 150 was intended purely as a 250 seat passenger ferry, but at the request of the operating company, the basic design was modified to allow an alternative payload of 150 passengers and 8 cars to be carried

Close co-operation between Gothenburg-Fredrikshaven-Line, Westermoen and Supramar led to the completion of the first craft within twenty-two months of the order being placed. The prototype PT 150, the world's largest seagoing commercial hydrofoil to date, was delivered to her owners on June 17th 1968.

Building was superintended by Norske Veritas, and the craft was granted the class designation 1A2-Hydrofoil-K.

The second PT 150 is being built at Messina by Leopoldo Rodriquez, Supramar's Italian licencee.

FOILS: The foil configuration is a combined surface piercing and submerged system. The bow foil, which provides the necessary lateral stability, is of the Schertel-Sachsenburg surface-piercing V design and carries 65% of the load. The rear foil, which bears about 35% is of the submerged, Schertel-Supramar air-stabilized type. In foilborne condition the boat is inherently stable.

Hydraulically-actuated flaps are fitted at the trailing edges of the bow foils to balance out larger longitudinal load shiftings, assist take off and adjust the flying height.

The rear foil is fully submerged and makes only a small contribution to lateral stability. It includes the lift-generating sections, rudders and the rear suspension structure which serves as a connecting element with the hull. Struts for the aftermost propeller bearings are also attached to the rear foil, the propellers being sited beneath the foil. The complete assembly is a framed structure which can easily be detached from the transom. The angle of attack of the rear foil can be controlled hydraulically both during take-off and in foilborne operation.

Air stabilisation is fitted to the rear foil for improved passenger comfort under heavy sea conditions. Separate port and starboard systems are installed to stabilise rolling and pitching.

The system feeds air from the free atmosphere through air exits to the foil upper surface (the low pressure region) decreasing the lift. The amount of lift is varied by the quantity of air admitted, this being controlled by a valve actuated by signals from a damped pendulum and a rate gyro. The stabilising moment is produced by decreasing the available air volume for the more submerged side and increasing that of the less submerged one.

The bowfoil centre section is also provided with submergence depth stablization, the quantity of air admitted being varied with the degree of submergence. The submergence depth control is only used in a following sea.

Foils and rudders are made of anti-corrosive

rolled-steel. Front and rear foil are hollow construction and by the extensive of welding, the number of connecting pa requiring screws, bolts or similar means attachment is reduced to a minimum.

HULL: This is of riveted light alloy c struction and framed on longitudinal transverse formers. It has fairly high de rise and hard chine sections for performa as a planing hull and for structural impa in a seaway while foilborne. A step provided to facilitate take-off. While main or structure deck is continuous f bow to stern, the lower deck is interrup by the engine room, sited amidships. superstructure, which is also framed longitudinal and transverse formers, is included in the load bearing structure.

ACCOMMODATION: The forward part the upper deck forms the forward up passenger saloon, and seats 48. The saloon, which seats 100, is designed rapid conversion to carry eight cars or corresponding amount of palletised frei Hydraulically-operated loading ramps at rear of the superstructure are lowered cars to roll on or off over the stern.

Passengers board the craft through dou doors to the single centralized foyer, fr which doors and companion ladders lea the respective passenger saloons on the up and lower decks. The kiosk on the port can be used as a duty-free shop. An o on the starboard side serves as a ticket information office and also as a crew's room.

e lower aft passenger saloon seats 70. A
panion ladder at the centreline leads to
main deck foyer. The lower forward
on has a bar and seats 27.

ovision is made for all passengers to be
ed in their seats with cold meals and
ks as in an airliner.

ssenger seats are of lightweight aircraft
. Floors and ceilings are covered with
weight plastic material and the walls are
in luxury plywood. Each passenger
on has fitted carpets. Each room has
idependent ventilation unit. Six toilets
provided.

e bridge, which is on a separate level
·e the main deck, slightly forward of
ships, is reached by a companion ladder
ie aft of the forward passenger compart-
t. The bridge itself has seating for
her 5 passengers, but these are reserved
/IP guests of the shipping company. All
enger saloons have emergency exits.

e craft carries 12 inflatable RFD life-
. (for 110% of the classified number of
engers and crew) which are stowed along
sides of the superstructure deck, aft of
wheelhouse extension. Lifebelts are
iged beneath the seats.

VER PLANT: Power is supplied by two
ylinder Maybach MD 1081 supercharged
intercooled diesels each rated at 3,400 hp
inuous at 1,740 rpm. To improve torque
acteristics during take-off two engine
nted Maybach torque converters are
ided.

verse and reduction gears are of the
weight Zahnradfabrik BW 1500HS18
aulically-operated type, and incorporate
propeller thrust bearings. They have
· shafts and two gear trains, one of which
in idler. The output shafts rotate either
e same direction as the input shaft or the
site direction, depending upon the gear
igh which power is directed. Selection
pneumo-hydraulic double-plate clutches
he input shafts. A mechanical lock-up
ovided so that the gear can transmit
torque in the event of clutch slip while
·rvice. This takes the form of a dog
h which is effective in one direction, and
only be engaged in the "stop" condition.
gearboxes each have integral oil pumps
ibrication and clutch operation.

e inclined propeller shafts are made of
tensile stainless steel. The propellers
-bladed and of approx. 41 in diameter.

TEMS:

CTRICAL: The total electrical system is
lied by two diesel generators with an
ut of 44 KVA each. An emergency
l generator of 32 KVA output is installed
ie upper deck.

the event of an electrical failure the
gency generator is switched on auto-
cally by a STILL starter to operate the
gency lighting system as well as the
ces and communications system.

A modified ST 3 is being employed by Supramar as a research craft for the Schertel-Supramar fully-submerged, air-stabilised foil system. Powered by a 1,000 hp GE LM100 gas-turbine, the craft has reached speeds in excess of 54 knots during tests in the Mediterranean

HYDRAULICS: Steering, variation of the
front foil flap angle and the angle of attack
of the rear foil are all operated hydraulically.
Each system has its own circuit which is
monitored by a pressure controlled pilot
lamp.

CONTROL: Starting, manoeuvring and
operation of the craft is controlled from the
bridge, but in cases of emergency the main
engines may be controlled from the engine
room.

The two main engines are each controlled
by an operating lever designed for single-
handed control. Propeller reversal is also
by means of these levers, the reverse gear
being actuated by pneumatic remote control
between bridge and main engines.

To start the boat both operating levers
must be put in the "full ahead" position
simultaneously. The engine mounted torque
converter gear is actuated automatically.
Foilborne speed can be regulated by five
adjusting of the operating levers. No other
control devices are necessary for the main
engines.

Levers for variation of the front foil flap
angle and the angle of attack of the rear foil
are actuated only before and after starting.
During foilborne operation these can be used
for trim compensation. All instrumentation
and monitoring equipment is installed on the
bridge.

COMMUNICATION AND NAVIGATION:
Standard navigation equipment of the PT 150
DC includes two Raytheon 2502-3 cm radar
units with IP-33 display panels, one of which
is north-stabilised; an Arma Brown gyro

compass type Mk 1 Mod 5; a Plath T 12
magnetic compass and a Decca Navigator
Mk. 12 with track plotter.

Communications equipment includes a
Fisher F811 coast telephony station, a VHF
telephony transceiver type ME-23C, produced
by SRA Stockholm, and an intercom system
to the engine room and office.

DIMENSIONS, EXTERNAL:

Length overall, hull	123·2 ft (37·55 m)
Length overall, deck	121·8 ft (37·10 m)
Hull beam, max	24·6 ft (7·50 m)
Deck beam, max	24·3 ft (7·40 m)
Width across foils	52·45 ft (16·0 m)
Draft afloat	17·7 ft (5·38 m)
Draft foilborne	8·3 ft (2·53 m)

WEIGHTS:

Displacement, fully loaded	150 tons
Payload	23 tons
As passenger ferry	250 passengers
As passenger/car ferry	
	150 passengers + 8 medium size cars

PERFORMANCE:

Cruising speed at 6,880 hp	39 kt (72 km/h)
Cruising range	300 nautical miles (555 km)
Max permissible wave height in foilborne mode at full power	7 ft 6 in (2·28 m)
Approximate cost	$US 1,500,000

ST 3 FOIL RESEARCH CRAFT

A modified Supramar ST 3 (formerly PT 4)
is being employed to evaluate fully-submerged foils of the Schertel-Supramar air-stabilised
type and provide data to assist the development of this system for larger craft.

The craft is powered by a 1,000 hp LM100
gas turbine and during tests in the Mediterranean has exceeded 54 knots (88 km/h).

UNITED KINGDOM

Airavia
AIRAVIA LTD
HEAD OFFICE:

20 North Road, Shanklin, Isle of Wight

TELEPHONE:

Shanklin 3643

DIRECTORS:

H. H. Snowball, Managing Director

A. Oztemel (USA)

E. Perper (USA)

G. V. Whale, Secretary

Formed in January 1968, Airavia is the sales representative for Sudoimport hydrofoils and air cushion vehicles in the United Kingdom, British Commonwealth countries, Scandinavia and Western Europe. The company will also lease Kometa passenger hydrofoils on wet or dry charters in these areas. Airavia has imported four Volga sports craft and has ordered a Kometa for delivery in early 1969 for service on a route in the United Kingdom, subject to a passenger licence being granted by the Board of Trade.

The Kometa off Tower Bridge

Anglian
ANGLIAN DEVELOPMENT
HEAD OFFICE AND WORKS:

Stephenson Road, Leigh-on-Sea, Essex

TELEPHONE:

Southend 524281

DIRECTORS:

W. H. Holmes, Chairman and Managing Director

G. R. Browne

C. I. Browne

SENIOR EXECUTIVE:

P. A. Nott MA (Cantab)

Development of the Hi-foil started in 1964 and the craft is the company's only product to date. It is the first sports hydrofoil designed in the UK to go into production, and has been sold to private owners in many parts of the world.

Hi-foil 2
FOILS: The foil system is of canard configuration with a fully submerged main foil located at the stern, and bearing 67% of the weight, and a small inverted 'V' emerging foil located at the bow.

The bow foil is mounted at the base of a handle-bar equipped steering head, an arrangement similar to that of a motor cycle. The operator turns the handlebars and leans inwards to match the radius of turn required. The foil system is designed to maintain stability in a turn and prevent 'digging-in' or 'skidding'. If the craft meets a large wave, the increased drag pivots the front foil against a spring and shock absorber to a lower angle of incidence, thus producing less lift and helping to dampen both porpoising and shocks.

HULL: A flat-bottomed planing design, the hull comprises two fibreglass mouldings bonded together to form a single large buoyancy chamber.

The cockpit well is located amidships and fitted with a motor cycle pillion style seat for two. The seat is fitted with a safety ignition cut-out switch and unless the operator is sitting on the seat the motor will not operate.

Hi-Foil 2, a two-seat, fibreglass-hulled sports hydrofoil. Steering is similar to that of a motorc
Top speed is 25-35 mph according to the outboard motor installed

Beneath the seat is a portable 5 gallon fuel tank. A 3-position gear lever—forward, neutral, reverse—is mounted at the side of the cockpit, and a twist-grip controls engine output. The central boss in the steering head will house a speedometer or compass if required.

The forward deck section, with the steering head and front foil, hinge upwards for transport and easy launching, as do the motor and rear foil, which are mounted on a pivoted steel frame.

POWER PLANT: The craft can be fitted with any standard long-shaft outboard from 15-25 hp. A subcavitating propeller of about 9 in (229 mm) diameter is normally used.

DIMENSIONS:

Length overall, hull   8 ft 10 in (2·69 m)

Length waterline, hull   7 ft 10 in (2·3

Length overall, foils retracted

9 ft 10 in (2·99

Length overall, foils extended

8 ft 10 in (2·6

Hull beam   3 ft 5 in (1·0

Beam across foils   3 ft 5 in (1·0

Draft afloat, foils extended

2 ft 9 in (0·

Draft afloat, foils retracted   9 in (230

Draft foilborne   1 ft 4 in (0·

Freeboard   6 in (153

Height overall, foils extended

4 ft 2 in (1·2

WEIGHTS:

Craft and motor without fuel

300 lb (136

Max take-off weight with fuel driver

passenger   650 lb (294 kg)

RFORMANCE:

ax speed foilborne   30 mph (48·2 km/h)

ruising speed foilborne

         20 mph (32·2 km/h)

ax permissible wave height in foilborne
mode   12 in (306 mm)

Turning radius at cruising speed:

Number of seconds and distance to take-off
           5 secs, 60 ft (18·28 m)

Number of seconds and distance to stop
craft   3 secs, 60 ft (18·28 m)

Fuel consumption at max speed
          2½ gal. p/h (9·2 lit p/h)

Fuel consumption at cruising speed
          1½ gal/ p/h (6·7 lit. p/h)

COST:

Standard craft, f.o.b., less engine, £150

HYDROFOIL MANUFACTURERS
HYDROFIN: United Kingdom

Hydrofin
NEW HYDROFIN LTD

HEAD OFFICE:
Burfield Flat, Bosham Lane, Bosham,
Sussex

MANAGING DIRECTOR:
Christopher Hook

Christopher Hook's early Hydrofins demonstrated for the first time the stability and excellent seakeeping qualities of incidence-controlled, submerged foil craft, and marked a turning point in hydrofoil design.

Nearly seventy Hydrofins of various types have been built since 1949 in Norway, the USA, Poland and Israel. The company's latest design is the 22 ft Channel Skipper, a four-seat fibreglass-hulled runabout, the prototype of which is scheduled for completion in 1969.

CHANNEL SKIPPER

Developed from the earlier K2 Hydrofin, the K2D Channel Skipper is a four-seat sports hydrofoil fitted with mechanical wave sensors to control the incidence angle of the fully submerged main foils. Torsionetic universal joints are fitted to the propeller drive shaft to permit retraction.

FOILS: The fully submerged foil system is of "aeroplane" configuration with 65% of the weight carried on the two main foils and the remainder on the aft foil. All three foils

have swept back leading and trailing edges. A high-riding crash preventer plane is mounted ahead of and beneath the bow. The plane is also used as a platform for mounting a lightweight pitch sensor which is hinged to the rear. The sensor rides on the waves and continuously transmits their shape through a servo system and connecting linkage to vary the incidence angle of the main foils as necessary to maintain them at the required depth. A filter system ensures that the craft ignores small waves and that the hull is flown over the crests of waves exceeding the height of the keel over the water.

Two additional sensors, trailing from port and starboard beams immediately aft of the main struts, provide roll control. The pilot has overriding control through a control column, operated in the same manner as that of an aircraft

All three foils and the crash plane arm are retractable. The crash plane arm retracts into a hull slot; the two main foils swing forward above the displacement waterline and the rear foil strut assembly retracts upwards into the hull at the same time raising the propeller and drive shaft.

POWER PLANT: Motive power is provided by a single 80 hp Ford diesel engine, driving a 3-bladed propeller through a Vee-drive and a system of Torsionetic joints produced by the Eaton Spring Division of Eton, Yale and

Towne Inc. The joints are fitted betw the engine and the gearbox, and the gear and the drive shaft to permit retraction

DIMENSIONS:
Length overall	22 ft 0 in (6·71
Length waterline, hull	18 ft 0 in (5·48
Hull beam	6 ft 7 in (2·00
Length overall, foils extended	
	19 ft 7 in (5·96
Max beam, foils retracted	10 ft 9 in (3·27
Max beam, foils extended	13 ft 5 in (4·09
Draft afloat, foils retracted	1 ft 7 in (0·48
Draft afloat, foils extended	5 ft 3 in (1·60
Freeboard	2 ft 6 in (0·76

WEIGHTS:
Gross tonnage	1·8 t
Net tonnage	1·2 t
Light displacement	1·2 t
Useful load (fuel, water, passengers, b gage and crew)	1,300 lb (598

PERFORMANCE:
Cruising speed, foilborne 32 knots (51 km
Cruising speed, hullborne
        8-12 knots (14-21 km
Sea state capability   Unlimited in s
  corresponding to Barnaby's "aver
  rough sea" providing they conform
  regards proportions
Turning radius at cruising speed
    150 ft (45·7 m) fully banked on tu

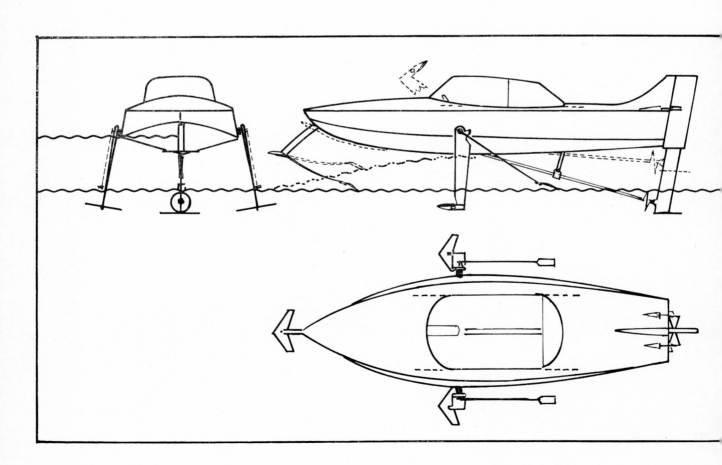

Hydrofin

uthern
THERN HYDROFOILS LIMITED

AD OFFICE:
Cumberland Place, Southampton
SO12BB

EPHONE:
outhampton 28831, STD 0703

LES:
ydrofoils Southampton

ECTORS:
. J. Sloss, Managing Director
mmander M. Thornton, DSO, DSC
. J. N. Bonner
F. Bridle
M. Thomson
M. Stacey CEng, AMRINA, Technical
Director

uthern Hydrofoils was founded in April
3 to design, manufacture and market
rofoils with fully-submerged systems.

small test craft was used during 1964-5
evelop a mechanical feeler arm system,
h was later improved by the addition of
electro-hydraulic response modification
. The systems is being employed in the
otype Sea Ranger 1, now under construc-
at Dartmouth, Devon.
sign studies for larger hydrofoils are in
.

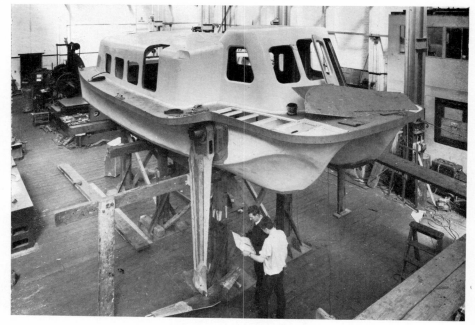

Prototype Sea Ranger

RANGER 1
a Ranger is an 8½ ton passenger hydrofoil
ered by two 283 hp General Motors
oit 8V53 diesels. Wave sensing arms
rol the incidence angle of the submerged
foils to maintain them at the required
h and provide the necessary hydro-
amic forces for stability.

e standard craft will seat up to 25
engers, but alternative versions, with
ified superstructure and internal arrange-
ts will be offered for a variety of applic-
ranging from fast naval, police and
oms patrol to ambulance duties.

LS: The foil system is fully submerged
of conventional "aeroplane" configura-
. The two bow foils are located slightly
ard of amidships and the single rear foil
tached to the propeller pod.

e angle of incidence of the two bow foils
ried by two wave-sensing arms extending
ahead of the main foil struts and
tting on the strut axes. Take-off,
ing and response modification is control-
ydraulically. A secondary function of
wave sensors is the provision of temporary
ort for the bow should there be a loss of
n either or both of the bow foils. Bow
rear foils and the two sensor arms are
d hydraulically above the waterline to
it manoeuvering in shallow water.

L: Designed for production in glass-
orced plastic, the wide "W" section,
-keel hull has high deadrise bows flatten-
o a planing surface aft. The main foils
sited within the hull beam to simplify
ing.

VER PLANT: Propulsion is supplied by
283 bhp General Motors Detroit Type
marine diesels. Power is transferred
ugh a hydrostatic transmission system to
ft 6 in (0·76 m) diameter fixed pitch

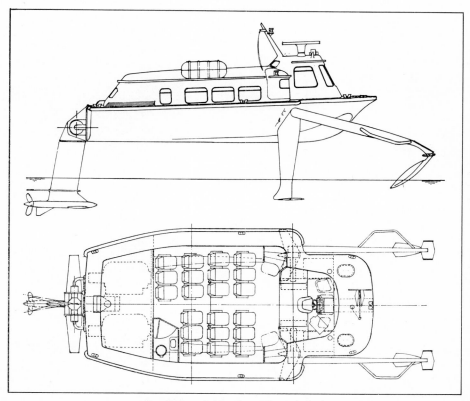

Sea Ranger inboard profile and deck

propeller. A retractable Volvo Penta outdrive unit housed in a well in the engine
compartment and driven hydrostatically
from either of the main engines, provides
auxiliary propulsion.

Total fuel (diesel) capacity is 140 gallons
(568 litres).

DIMENSIONS:

Length overall, hull	30 ft 0 in (9·140 m)
Beam overall, hull	15 ft 6 in (4·720 m)
Draft foils extended,	8 ft 5 in (2·56 m)
Draft, hullborne	1 ft 8½ in (0·52 m)

WEIGHTS:

Disposable load	5,600 lb (2,540 kg)
Displacement	8½ tons

PERFORMANCE (designed):

Speed, foils retracted	8 knots (14·7 km)
Max speed, fully loaded	40 knots (75 km/h)
Cruising speed	35/40 knots (65/75 km)

Fuel consumption at continuous rated speed
20 Imp galls per hour (91 litres per hour)
Fuel consumption at displacement cruise
speed 5 Imp galls per hour (22·7 litres per
hour)
Designed endurance and range at cruising
speed
7 hours/240 n. miles at 35 knots (64 km)

THE UNITED STATES OF AMERICA

Atlantic
ATLANTIC HYDROFOILS INC

HEAD OFFICE:
Box 1174, Stony Brook, New York 11790
TELEPHONE:
516 (Area Code) 751-0711
DIRECTORS:
John K. Roper, President

The Atlantic Hydrofoils' mechanically-controlled submerged foil system was the first to be approved for use on hydrofoil passenger ferries. The first order for craft employing this system, was placed by Sea World, Inc of San Diego. The success of the first 28-passenger, 30-knot craft ordered by the company resulted in orders for an additional three.

The Flying Cloud, described below, is a development of the Sea World craft and utilises a similar foil system. Two versions of the Flying Cloud were built, the first with two 600 hp Cummins Vimmer T diesels, production of which was abandoned, and the second with a Solar Saturn gas turbine.

FLYING CLOUD 2

The Flying Cloud 2 was the first gas-turbine powered hydrofoil built for commercial passenger services in the United States. Powered by a 1,100 hp Solar Saturn gas-turbine, it accommodates 70 passengers and a crew of 3.

FOILS: The foil system is of fully submerged aeroplane configuration with two split foils forward and an identical single foil aft. All three foils have trailing edge flaps, those of the forward foils being controlled by an automatic mechanical control device. Hinged vertical control flaps on the trailing edges of the forward struts automatically deflect the foil flaps to maintain the craft at a stable inflight attitude in all sea states. The aft foil can be adjusted in flight to compensate for changes in the longitudinal position of the centre of gravity. The aft foil-strut unit is steerable and acts as a rudder. All three foils retract clear of the water when not in use.

HULL: Laminated wood framing with plywood fibreglass-plating. Deck and superstructure are of plywood and fibreglass construction.

POWER PLANT: Power is provided by a Solar Saturn gas turbine with a normal service output of 1,100 hp, driving a 30 in (762 mm) diameter, 26 in (661 mm) pitch Columbian Style B propeller through a V drive. The turbine is mounted below deck amidships, with air intake apertures on the port side of the cabin superstructure. The exhaust stack discharges directly aft of the pilothouse.

ACCOMMODATION: Seats are provided in a comfortably appointed cabin for 70 passengers and a crew of three. Access to the cabin is through either of two doors located amidship, port and starboard. An emergency window exit is provided in the aft passenger compartment. A full range safety equipment is carried in accordance with US Coast Guard requirements.

DIMENSIONS:

Length overall, hull	61 ft 6 in (18·7
Hull beam	12 ft 0 in (3·6
Width across foils	28 ft 0 in (8·5
Draft afloat	7 ft 9 in (2·3
Forward foil area	30·6 sq ft (2·82
Aft foil area	15·3 sq ft (1·43

WEIGHTS:

Gross weight	46,000 lb (20,861
Max payload	11,500 lb (5,221
Fuel capacity	500 gallons (2,272 lit

PERFORMANCE:

Max speed	35 knots (64 km
Cruising speed	32 knots (57 km
Cruising speed hullborne	10 knots (14 km
Take-off speed	18 knots (32 km
Designed range at cruising speed	
	200 nautical miles (322

The Flying Cloud showing the mechanically operated submerged foil system. Hinged ver control flaps on the trailing edges of the forward struts automatically deflect the foil flaps to m tain the craft at a stable inflight attitude in all sea states

Flying Cloud, designed by Atlantic Hydrofoils Inc., and built by Teledyne Inc., of Gardena, California, is powered by a 1,100 hp Solar Satur gas turbine and has a service speed of 32 knots

eing

E BOEING COMPANY
vanced Marine Systems Organisation

AD OFFICE:
O Box, 3707 Seattle, Washington 98124

LEPHONE:
rea 206, 656-2121

ECUTIVE:
iro M. Gonnella, Manager, Advanced
arine Systems

he Boeing Advanced Marine Systems
ganisation was formed in 1959 to conduct
earch, development, design, manufacture
the testing of high performance marine
icle systems. Boeing also has a 60 per
t interest in Alinavi SpA, the Italian
drofoil company, with headquarters in
ne. Boeing's entry into the hydrofoil
l was announced in June 1960, when the
pany was awarded a $2 million contract
the construction of the US Navy's 120 ton
H-1 High Point, a canard design which
the outgrowth of experiments on a
ilar arrangement in the test craft Sea Legs.
eing has also built a jet-driven hydro-
le, the HTS, for testing foil models at
-scale velocity; the Fresh-1, a manned
t for testing superventilating or super-
itating foils at speeds between 60-100
ts and a water-jet test vehicle, Little
irt. The company has also completed a
er-jet propelled gunboat, the PGH-2
umcari, for the US Navy's Ship Systems
mand.

e Tucumcari is now based at San Diego
is serving with the US Navy Pacific
t Amphibious Command.

-1 HIGH POINT
eneral design of the PCH-1 High Point,
specified by the US Navy's Bureau of
is, with responsibility for detail design
construction assigned to Boeing. The
was accepted by the US Navy in August
3 and based at the Puget Sound Naval
yard at Bremerton, Washington. Since
it has been undergoing a wide range of
s to evaluate the performance of an
ore hydrofoil ASW system.

LS: The submerged canard foil system,
70 per cent of the foil area located aft,
trailing-edge flaps on all foils for lift
rol, is a scaled-up version of that employ-
on Sea Legs. The foil struts retract
ically into the hull. Foils and struts are
uilt-up construction in HY-80 weldable

L: The hull is of all-welded, corrosion
tant 5456 aluminium. Integral plate
ener extrusions are extensively used for
s and portions of the sides not having
ssive curvature.

VER PLANT: Foilborne propulsion is
rided by two Proteus Model 1273 gas
ines, each rated at 3,900 shp. The
ines are located aft and take air through
two towers housing the retracted foil
s. The exhaust is discharged directly
hrough the transom. Each gas-turbine
upled to a pair of contra-rotating, sub-
tating propellers, 29 in (737 mm) in
eter, through two right-angle gearboxes;
at the top of each aft strut and the others
ch of the underwater nacelles.
ullborne propulsion is supplied by a single
iss-Wright Model 1D-700 rated at 600 hp
continuous operation. The engine is

Boeing's FCH-1 is being employed by the US Navy to evaluate the performance of an inshore hydrofoil ASW system. In the above photograph the craft is seen equipped with high speed sonar
handling gear at the stern and lightweight homing torpedoes. In the background is the Tucumcari waterjet propelled hydrofoil gunboat

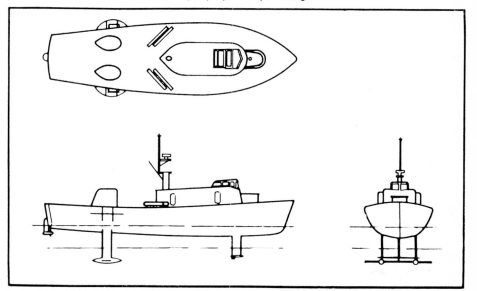

Boeing's PCH-1 High Point, a 120 ton experimental hydrofoil employed by the U.S. Navy since 1963
to evaluate the performance of an inshore hydrofoil ASW system

HYDROFOIL MANUFACTURERS
BOEING: United States of America

coupled to a 43 in (1,092 mm) diameter propeller through a retractable outdrive unit, which is steerable through 360 degrees and rotates about the axis of the horizontal shaft for retraction.

CONTROLS: The autopilot system, devised by Hamilton Standard, is designed to maintain the craft at a stable in-flight attitude in all sea states. It receives craft motion input from a sonic height sensor in the bow, and from roll and pitch gyros and vertical accelerometers. The information is processed by an electronic computer and fed continuously to hydraulic actuators of the foil control surfaces. The control surfaces develop the required hydrodynamic forces for stability manoeuvring and counteracting forces imposed by wave action.

The attitude control is entirely automatic except for steering. The take-off procedure on the PCH-1 is simply to set the desired flying height, then advance the throttles. At a gross weight of 117 tons take-off occurs at 27 knots with 3,880 total horsepower delivered to the transmission system, the speed stabilizing at 36·6 knots at that power setting. Minimum foilborne speed is 24 knots. At a cruising speed of 40 knots 4,400 hp is required, with propellers turning at 1,270 rpm.

DIMENSIONS, EXTERNAL:

Length overall, hull	115·7 ft (35·3 m)
Length, waterline, hull	110·0 ft (33·5 m)
Length overall:	
foils retracted	117·0 ft (35·7 m)
foils extended	117·0 ft
Max beam:	
foils retracted	31·5 ft (9·6 m)
foils extended	31·5 ft
Hull beam	32·0 ft (9·75 m)
Draught afloat, foils retracted	6·5 ft (2·0 m)
Freeboard	12·0 ft (3·7 m)

WEIGHTS:

Light displacement	93·0 tons
Max take-off displacement	120·0 tons
Useful load (fuel, water, equipment, armament, crew)	27·0 tons

PERFORMANCE:

Cruising speed:	
foilborne	in excess of 40 knots
hullborne	12 knots

ACCOMMODATION:

Crew	13

LITTLE SQUIRT

Little Squirt was designed and built by Boeing in 1962 as a company sponsored water-jet research vehicle.

FOILS: The three fully submerged, fixed foils have subcavitating sections with trailing edge flaps. Control of lift is obtained through variable incidence by rotating each foil. The flaps are for lift augmentation during take-off and are retracted for cruising. The foil arrangement, two forward and one aft, is tandem in the sense that the total forward foil area is equal to the aft foil area.

The foil incidence can be adjusted during operation, compounding the action of the moveable control surfaces. A Boeing automatic control system is installed that utilises craft motion and height inputs to maintain foilborne flight.

HULL: Built in plywood, the hull is of stepped "W" form. This configuration was chosen as it would provide greater roll safety for the craft.

Little Squirt is employed by Boeing for waterjet research. Propulsion water enters a scoop at base of the aft strut and is ducted upwards to a double-suction centrifugal pump powered Boeing 502 gas turbine

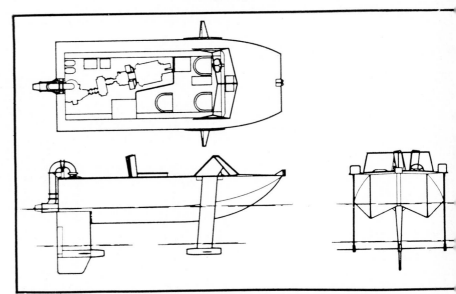

Little Squirt, Boeing's waterjet research craft

POWERPLANT: The waterjet is provided by a double-suction centrifugal pump powered through a reduction gearbox by a Boeing 502 gas-turbine rated at 450 hp. The propulsion water enters a ram scoop at the base of the aft strut and is ducted upward through the strut to the pump. At 2,360 rpm the pump absorbs 425 hp and produces a flow of 3,600 US gallons (13·63 m³) per minute at a pressure head of 400 ft (121·9 m). The craft had completed more than 140 hours of foilborne operation by mid-June 1968.

DIMENSIONS, EXTERNAL:

Length overall, hull	22 ft (6·71 m)
Length waterline, hull	17·1 ft (5·20 m)
Length over foils	22 ft (6·71 m)
Hull beam	8 ft (2·49 m)
Width across foils	11·25 ft (3·43 m)
Draft afloat	5·5 ft (1·68 m)
Draft foilborne	8 in to 2·5 ft (0·2 m to 0·7 m)
Freeboard	3·0 ft (0·91 m)

WEIGHTS:

Light displacement	2·28 tons
Max. take-off displacement	2·65 tons
Useful load	0·37 tons

PERFORMANCE:

Cruising speed, foilborne	48 k
Max permissible wave height in foilb	
mode	2·5 ft (0·762 m) w

ACCOMMODATION:

Crew

Passengers

FRESH-1

The FRESH-1 (Foil Research Su cavitating Hydrofoil) was built as par the US Navy's accelerated research and velopment programme aimed at gathe data for the design of large, high-sp ocean-going hydrofoils.

FOILS: The twin-hull catamaran arra ment provides a large, clear space betw the hulls, within which different foil syst can be mounted. The foils and struts attached to lateral beams between the h and may be positioned at several diffe longitudinal attachments point, providi great deal of freedom in the choice of the locations. The foils have been arranged conventional configuration, with two forward and one aft, and also in a ca

world's fastest hydrofoil is the 80-100 knot FRESH-I (Foil Research Supercavitating Hydrofoil) twin-hulled test craft.   Foils under test are attached to lateral beams which may be positioned at several different points between the hulls providing a choice of foil locations

figuration, with one foil forward and two s aft.

he first system tested comprised three ly submerged and fully flapped foils of mbered-parabolic blunt base section. The s, of machined 17·4 PH steel forgings, each l an area of 7·46 sq ft.   The foil loading s 1,600 lb sq ft.

WER PLANT: The choice of powerplant JT3D-3 fan-jet developing 18,000 lb 200 kg) st—means the propulsion system es not disturb the water flow around the t foils.

Iullborne propulsion is supplied by two hp outboard engines.

UXILIARY POWER: Electrical and hy-ulic power are furnished by a turbine-ven auxiliary power unit and by the main gine respectively. Auxiliary power systems ve been designed to accommodate a wide ge of future hydrofoil systems.

ILL: The catamaran hulls are in aluminium h steel truss members. The hull and cabin ve been constructed to withstand a variety oadings due to different attitudes of crash a result of system failures during tests.

ST EQUIPMENT: A most important l in the test programmes is the analogue nputer. An analogue simulation of the aracteristics of each foil configuration is eloped and maintained.

s the test data becomes available, the ulation is modified to ensure that it l duplicate the characteristics of the at as accurately as possible. Before h test is run, it is simulated. It is ssible in this way to analyse the system aviour and thus determine the safety of test. The accuracy of the simulation is st important if accidents or errors are to avoided, particularly when a test is ducted near the limits of the boat's ability.

n the design of FRESH-1, the problem of a acquisition was given as much attention the design of the craft itself. Because the rpose of the craft is testing untried foil tems, it was necessary to provide a data tem capable of recording instantaneous l continuous dynamic data.

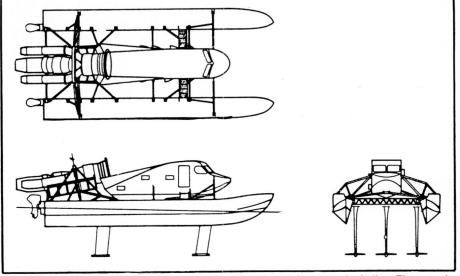

Foils under test on the FRESH-I are attached to lateral beams between the hulls.   They can be arranged in aeroplane configuration with two foils forward and one aft, and also in canard configuration.   Foilborne cruising speed is 80-100 knots

The data system utilizes a magnetic-tape recording system with instrumentation capable of providing 84 continuous channels, 82 commuted channels sampled 20 times per second, and 176 pressure channels sampled once per second.

SYSTEMS:

ELECTRICAL: Turbine-driven 120/208 volt, 3-phase 400 cycle generator with 30 KVA continuous rating.

HYDRAULICS: Dual system for foil flaps; pressure, 3,000 psi.

DIMENSIONS, EXTERNAL:

Length overall, hull	47·0 ft (14·33 m)
Length waterline, hull	45·0 ft (13·72 m)
Length over foils	57·3 ft (17·44 m)
Hull beam	22·5 ft (6·86 m)
Draft afloat	10·5 ft (3·20 m)
Freeboard	2·5 ft (0·76 m)

WEIGHTS:

Light displacement	12·4 tons
Max. take-off displacement	16·5 tons
Useful load	4·1 tons

PERFORMANCE:

Cruising speed, foilborne

80-100 knots (148-180 km/h)

Cruising speed, hullborne

4·5 knots (8·4 km/h)

ACCOMMODATION:

Crew   3

PGH-2 TUCUMCARI

A 58-ton waterjet-propelled hydrofoil gunboat, the PGH-2 was ordered from Boeing by the US Navy's Ship Systems Command in 1966, under a $4 million, fixed price PGH (Patrol Gunboat Hydrofoil) programme. Launched in July 1967, the craft first became foilborne in mid-October and was handed to the US Navy for testing and evaluation in February 1968.

The craft is now operating with the US Navy Pacific Fleet Amphibious Command and is based at San Diego.

FOILS: Like High Point, Tucumcari has a fully submerged canard arrangement with retractable foils. Unlike High Point however, the aft foils are divided for sideways retraction, instead of retracting vertically, and the single forward strut retracts forward into a slot in the bow. Doors preserve the hull lines when the strut is either fully extended or retracted.

Boeing PGH-2 Tucumcari hullborne with foils retracted clear of the water. The craft is now based at San Diego and is operating with the U.S. Navy's Pacific Fleet Amphibious Command

Main armament of the PGH-2 comprises a 40 mm gun forward of the bridge and an 81 mm mortar aft. Manually operated twin ·50 machine guns on ring mountings are sited aft of the wheelhouse on each side of the bridge superstructure. Foilborne cruising speed is in excess of 40 knots

Foils and their struts are fabricated in 17-4PH steel and have thin sections to avoid cavitation within the speed design range. Control flaps on the three foils are of marine aluminium alloy.

Both aft foils have anhedral to reduce their tendency to ventilate in bauked turns.

CONTROLS: A Boeing automatic control system stabilizes the craft in foilborne operation. This system consists of dual sonic height sensors; an inertial sensor package with vertical gyro, yaw rate gyro and vertical accelerometer; command signal equipment, control system computer and the hydraulically actuated control surfaces. The helmsman is responsible for controlling craft heading from the bridge through a wheel which controls the steerable bow foil. Height command is the only other manual input and this control is used primarily during take-off and landing.

HULL: The hull shape is designed to minimize the structural loadings due to wave impact. It has a 25 degree deadrise, rounded chines, a flaring bow and straight runs aft. Construction is entirely of welded aluminium and careful design has resulted in a relatively low hull weight of 10 tons. The deckhouse includes both welded and mechanically fastened aluminium structures. Four watertight bulkheads are incorporated.

POWER PLANT (foilborne): The waterjet propulsion system consists of a 3,200 hp Rolls Royce Proteus gas turbine driving a lightweight Byron Jackson two-element double suction centrifugal pump through a direct coupling.

Water is drawn into the system through two ports in the two aft foil/strut intersection pods then ducted up through the hollow struts to the pump's intakes, each strut supplying one pump element. From the pump it is discharged through two nozzles beneath the transom. The system ejects about 27,000 US gallons (102 m³) of water a minute, providing 24,000 lb (10,000 kg) thrust.

POWER PLANT (hullborne): A Buehler centrifugal pump, powered by a General Motors 160 hp diesel propels the vessel when

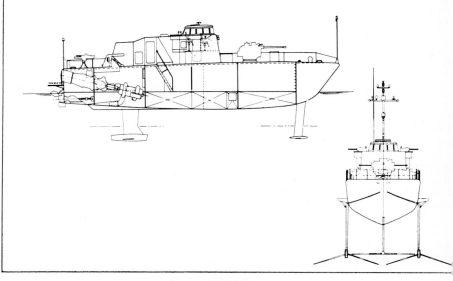

Boeing PGH-2 Tucumcari

hullborne. Steering and reversing are accomplished by vectoring the water jet exit flow, eliminating the need for reverse gearing.

The propulsion machinery space is divided into two watertight compartments. The hullborne diesel is located in one compartment and the Proteus in the other, permitting the craft to operate with either engine compartment flooded. Both foilborne and hullborne waterjet pumps are designed to operate under water in an emergency.

ARMAMENT: Main armament comprises a 40 mm gun forward of the bridge and an 81 mm mortar aft. Hand operated twin ·50 machine guns are sited each side of the bridge.

DIMENSIONS, EXTERNAL:
Length overall, hull   70 ft 1 in (21·64 m)
Length waterline, hull 66 ft 0 in (20·12 m)

Length overall:
foils retractad   80 ft 0 in (24·38 m)
foils extended   74 ft 6 in (22·71 m)
Hull beam   19 ft 6 in (5·94 m)
Max. beam:
foils retracted   25 ft 0 in (7·62 m)
foils extended   35 ft 4 in (10·77 m)
Draft afloat (foils retracted) 4 ft 6 in (1·37 m)
Freeboard   7 ft 0 in (2·13 m)

WEIGHTS:
Light displacement   40·8 tons
Max take-off displacement   57·4 tons
Useful load (fuel, water, equipment
armament and crew)   18·7 tons

PERFORMANCE:
Cruising speed, foilborne
in excess of 40 knots
ACCOMMODATION:
Crew

IC

C CORPORATION

dnance Engineering Division

AD OFFICE:

25 Coleman Avenue, Box 367, San Jose,
California

he Ordnance Engineering Division of
IC Corporation has engaged in concept,
earch, design, development and produc-
n of defence material for over 25 years,
rting early in World War II with the
sign and production of over 11,000 amphib-
us assault vehicles. Current activities
lude the development of amphibious
nicles, railroad cars, hydrofoil craft, landing
ft, airborne multipurpose vehicles, and
erations analyses studies.

During World War II, FMC designed,
veloped and produced seven versions of
Ts, under contract to the Bureau of Ships.
urrent amphibious vehicle programmes
ing conducted for the Bureau of Ships are:
nding Craft Assault (LCA), Landing
hicle Hydrofoil (LVHX2), Assault Am-
ibian Personnel Carrier (LVTPX12), and
nding Vehicle Tracked Family of Vehicles
VTP5A1).

The LVHX2 is the final product of a
ogramme which began in 1961 and included
sign, development, scale-model hull and
il testing, and fabrication of two full-scale
hicles. This vehicle is 38 ft long, capable
35 knot foilborne speed, and 40 mph land
eed while transporting a 5-ton cargo.

The division also designed and developed
e L312G hydrofoil test craft for the purpose
optimising hydrofoil system configurations
d draft control systems. This 30 ft craft
rries 12 passengers at speeds up to 45 knots.
he latest hydrofoil passenger craft built by
e company is the 48 passenger L548D.

VHX-2

Designed and built for the US Navy
ureau of Ships, the LVHX2 is an amphibi-
us, aluminium-hulled, 38 ft hydrofoil landing
raft with a cargo capacity of 10,000 lb. Its
ission is the high-speed transfer of cargo
nd equipment from ship to shore during am-
hibious assault operations. It operates
ilborne to the surf zone, negotiates off-shore
aters and the surf in the displacement
ode, then quickly moves inland on four
rge, sand-type tyres.

The maximum foilborne water speed is 35
nots. Maximum displacement speed is 12
nots, and maximum land speed on hard
urfaces is 40 mph.

FOILS: The foil system consists of split
orward surface-piercing foils and a rear foil
vhich remains fully submerged. The foil
truts retract vertically into the hull and the
inged sections of the forward foil fold up-
vard into recesses in the hull sides.

The foils may be retracted or extended while
n motion. A simple autopilot system is
used to provide a smoother ride in State 3
seas and to counteract adverse effects of a
following sea. The LVHX2 can be operated,
however, in the foilborne mode without the
autopilot.

POWER PLANT: The LVHX2 is powered
by an 1,100 hp Solar T1000-S27 two-shaft
gas turbine engine. The integrated drive
system permits use of marine and land power
simultaneously when needed. This system
also increases vehicle reliability and decreases

Land power for the LVHX2 is transmitted from the 1,100 hp Solar T 1,000-S27 gas turbine to the
wheels through an Allison TX 365-2 six speed transmission and non-slip differentials

The LVHX2, an amphibious hydrofoil landing craft built by FMC for the US marines. The craft
operates at 35 knots to the surf zone, negotiates shallow areas as a displacement craft, then moves
quickly inland on four sand-type tyres

HYDROFOIL MANUFACTURERS
FMC: United States of America

weight. Power for marine operation is transferred through a marine reverse gear to the vertically-retracting rear strut assembly of the aft foil. This arrangement provides full power transmission to the propeller when the strut is being extended or retracted. For land operation, the gas turbine engine is de-rated to the necessary power level. Land power is transmitted to the wheels through an Allison TX365-2 six-speed transmission and non-slip differentials. The craft is capable of negotiating 60% slopes in forward or reverse and can operate on 30% side slopes. CONTROLS: Three power-assisted steering modes are provided; conventional two-wheel steering, conventional four-wheel steering, and oblique four-wheel steering. The four wheels are individually suspended by a simple air-spring and hydraulic shock absorber system which provides a smooth ride over rough terrain. The wheels are retractable for water operation to facilitate loading and unloading in the land mode. Individual wheel retraction capability permits the vehicle to "kneel", "squat", or tilt, simplifying cargo loading and unloading on irregular terrain.

Air pressure in the 8·00 × 25 sand-type tyres can be varied by a central inflation system controlled by the driver.

Two LVHX2 prototypes have successfully completed Navy acceptance trials and are currently under test by the US Marine Corps.

DIMENSIONS:

Length overall	37 ft 0 in (11·28 m)
Vehicle width	10 ft 6 in (3·20 m)
Width over main foil	21 ft 6 in (6·55 m)
Freeboard, combat weight	
	3 ft 9 in (1·14 m)

WEIGHTS*:

Combat	17·4 tons
Net	12·9 tons
Payload	4·5 tons

PERFORMANCE:

Fuel capacity	430 US gal (1,625 litres)
Speed foilborne	35 knots (65 km/h)
Speed, afloat	12 knots (22 km/h)
Speed, beaching	8 knots (15 km/h)
Speed, land	40 mph (64 km/h)
Gradeability, forward slope	60%
Gradeability, side slope	30%
Turning radius, foilborne	300 ft (91·4 m)
Turning radius, afloat	75 ft (22·9 m)
Turning radius, land	35 ft (10·7 m)
Endurance on water at 35 knots	5 hrs
Endurance on land at 25 mph	10 hrs

*Weight

Combat: Weight of vehicle fully equipped and serviced for combat, including crew and payload for 10,000 lb.

Net: Weight of vehicle fully equipped and serviced for combat, including crew, but without payload.

L548D

Designed for fast, comfortable services across bays, lakes and sounds, the L548D hydrofoil passenger ferry has an operating cost of about 3½ cents per seat mile at 100% load factor. The prototype has logged over 3,500 miles during engineering tests in San Francisco Bay.

The maximum operating displacement is 14·29 long tons which includes 4·33 long tons of useful load. Design speeds are 45 mph maximum, 41 mph cruising and 10-11 mph during hullborne operation.

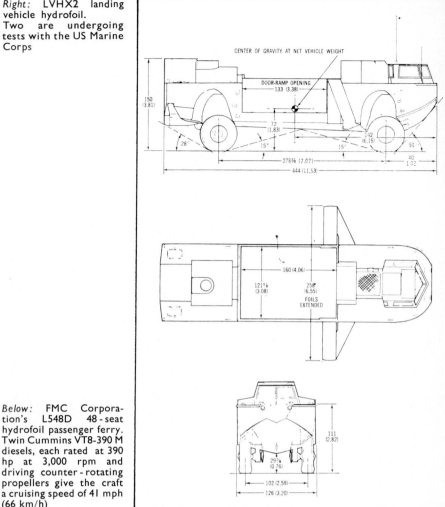

Right: LVHX2 landing vehicle hydrofoil. Two are undergoing tests with the US Marine Corps

Below: FMC Corporation's L548D 48-seat hydrofoil passenger ferry. Twin Cummins VT8-390 M diesels, each rated at 390 hp at 3,000 rpm and driving counter-rotating propellers give the craft a cruising speed of 41 mph (66 km/h)

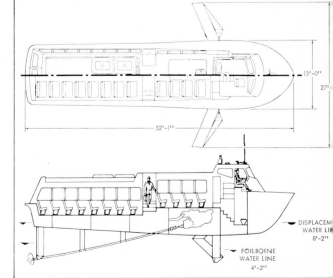

The L548D 48-seat passenger hydrofoil for bays, lakes and sounds

ating 12 passengers and capable of speeds in excess of 45 mph (72 km/h), the FMC L312G is a 30 ft (9·14 m) test and demonstration craft. It was used to obtain data for the design of the 48-passenger L548D

OILS: A combined surface piercing and bmerging foil configuration is employed, th two forward surface piercing foils pporting 70% of the load and two fully bmerged aft foils supporting the remainder. e foils, which are fixed, are built in minium. The foil configuration is design- to be inherently stable in any expected mbination of heave, pitch, roll and yaw. To prevent settling in a following sea and o to smooth out the ride generally, a amilton Standard stability augmentation stem automatically controls trailing edge ps on the forward foils to provide additional bility in heave and roll. Rudder flaps are ted to the trailing edges of the aft foil uts for steering control.

ULL: The craft is of welded aluminium con- ruction and carries 48 passengers in an at- active, soundproofed cabin with a temp- ature controlled ventilation system.

OWER PLANT: Power is provided by twin mmins VT8-390M watercooled diesels, ch with a normal service output of 390 hp 3,000 rpm. Each engine drives its own opeller shaft and the twin screws are ntra-rotating. Controls are all sited in an evated wheelhouse with a 360°-view at the re end of the passenger compartment. The engine transmission units are mounted a compartment below the forward passen- r deck. Removal seat deck sections and a movable roof hatch facilitate speedy placement of either unit.

CCOMMODATION: Passengers are accom- odated in a split-level cabin with 32 in the ain, aft compartment, and 16 in the forward

compartment. Access to both is through either of two gull-wing doors located amid-ships, port and starboard. Separate doors, port and starboard, are provided for the pilot and crew. An emergency window exit is provided in the aft passenger compartment.

A full range of safety equipment is carried, including four portable fire extinguishers, life jackets for each passenger and crew member, plus five additional children's life jackets. Inflatable rafts, catering for 50% of the passenger and crew capacity (minimum) are also carried.

SYSTEMS AND CONTROLS: Standard electrical equipment of the L548D includes a Raytheon Model DE-718A depth sounder, a Raytheon Model 1065C radio-telephone and Decca 202 radar.

DIMENSIONS:

Length overall, hull	52 ft 1 in (15·88 m)
Length waterline, hull	47 ft (14·32 m)
Hull beam	13 ft (3·96 m)
Width across foils	27 ft 8 in (8·43 m)
Draught afloat	8 ft 2 in (2·49 m)
Draught foilborne	4 ft 2 in (1·27 m)
Freeboard	5 ft 8 in forward (1·73 m)
	3 ft 6 in aft (1·07 m)

WEIGHTS:

Gross tonnage	36
Net tonnage	24
Light displacement	9·96 long tons
Max take-off displacement	14·29 long tons
Useful load	4·33 long tons

PERFORMANCE:

Cruising speed, foilborne	41 mph (66 km/hr)
	45 mph max (72 km/hr)
Cruising speed, hullborne	10-12 mph

Sea State capability	2
Design foilborne range	
	270 statute miles (334 km)
Turning radius at cruising speed	
	550 ft (167·6 m)
Fuel consumption at cruising speed	
	32 gal/hr (22·7 litres/hr)
Fuel consumption, hullborne	
	5 gal/hr (13·6 litres/hr)

L312G

After completing the basic design of the LVHX2, the FMC Ordnance Division con-ducted a company-sponsored research pro-gramme into hydrofoil systems. Following this investigation, it was decided to build a 30 ft test and demonstration hydrofoil to verify the results of the study and to provide a test vehicle for further research.

The L312G, an all-aluminium craft with surface-piercing main foils, was launched in September 1964.

Powered by a Daytona Marine rated at 380 hp at 3,800 rpm, it has a maximum speed of 50 mph. Seats for 12 passengers are provided in the enclosed cabin, or alternative-ly, 2,880 lb of equipment or cargo can be carried.

DIMENSIONS:

Length overall	30 ft (9·14 m)
Hull beam	9 ft (2·74 m)
Width across foils	17 ft 6 in (5·33 m)
Draught afloat	5 ft 3 in (1·6 m)
Draught foilborne	2 ft (0·6 m)
Displacement:	
Nett	5,900 lb (2,676 kg)
Gross	9,500 lb (4,309 kg)
Range at gross weight	120 mile (193 km)

HYDROFOIL MANUFACTURERS
GENERAL DYNAMICS: United States of America

General Dynamics
QUINCY DIVISION

HEAD OFFICE:

97 East Howard Street, Quincy, Massachusetts 02169

TELEPHONE:

617 471-4200

General Dynamics has entered into a licence agreement with Supramar Ltd of Lucerne, Switzerland, under which General Dynamics will manufacture and sell hydrofoil boats in the United States and other Western Hemisphere nations based on Supramar's patents and engineering drawings.

Responsibility for hydrofoil programmes has been assigned to the Convair Division in San Diego, California, which is exploring adaption of Supramar hydrofoil concepts for a number of military missions, including patrol boats, antisubmarine warfare air-sea rescue missions.

General Dynamics also will direct its effo to expand the use of hydrofoils as fast, sta passenger ferries on lakes, rivers and coas waters, for Coast Guard and customs wo and for use in connection with off-sh drilling operations.

~rumman
~UMMAN AIRCRAFT ENGINEERING ~ORPORATION

~AD OFFICE:
~ethpage, Long Island, USA

~BLES:
~rumair

~RECTOR:
~. C. Towl

~ORLDWIDE DISTRIBUTOR AND SALES AGENT
~OR THE DOLPHIN:
~he Garrett Corporation, 9851-9951, Sepulveda Boulevard, Los Angeles, California,
9009.

~IRECTORS:
~. H. Wetzel, President
~. J. Pattison, Vice-President, Sales and
Service
~. W. Calvert, Director of Hydrofoil Sales

Grumman entered the hydrofoil field in
~956 when it acquired Dynamic Develop-
~ents Inc. The initial product of this
~enture was the experimental XCH-4, built
~r the Office of Naval Research in 1955.
~owered by two aircraft engines with air
~ropellers, this eight-ton vessel established a
~orld's speed record for hydrofoil craft,
~xceeding 78 knots (145 km/h). In 1958,
~he 60-knot XCH-6 Sea Wings, the first boat
~o employ supercavitating foils and a super-
~avitating propeller, was also built for the

Office of Naval Research. In the same year
a hydrofoil kit designed by William Carl was
made available for do-it-yourself installation
on 14 to 16 ft (4·3 to 4·9 m) outboard runabouts.

In 1960, Grumman was awarded a contract
by the Maritime Administration for the
design and construction of the HS Denison,
an 80-ton open ocean research vessel which
was launched in June 1962. This craft
(described in the 1967/8 edition) has been
operated at speeds above 60 knots (111
km/h) demonstrating good foilborne man-
oeuverability and seakeeping ability in rough
water.

Grumman also designed the 320-ton, 212 ft
(64·6 m) AG(EH) for the US Navy. The
foils for this craft were the forerunners of
those used on the Dolphin and the more
recent PGH-1 Flagstaff.

The Flagstaff is currently being evaluated
by the US Navy. Dolphin class hydrofoils are
being built for Grumman by Blohm & Voss,
Hamburg, and the second craft was due to
be completed during the autumn of 1968.
Blohm & Voss will also build the 325 ton
Grumman Neptune, a description of which
appears in the entry for Blohm & Voss,
Germany.

DOLPHIN

A 64-ton hydrofoil ferry, the Dolphin is
designed to carry a maximum of 116 passengers over routes of up to 300 nautical miles.
Foilborne cruising speed of the vessel is 50
knots (93 km/h) and it can maintain schedules
in 8-10 ft (2·4-3 m) waves.

It incorporates several design features
resulting from operating experience with the
Denison, but unlike the Denison it has fully
submerged main foils. Foilborne power is
supplied by a single Rolls-Royce Type 621
gas-turbine driving a KaMeWa propeller.

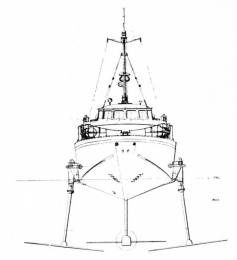

Blohm & Voss Hydrofoil 'Dolphin' end view

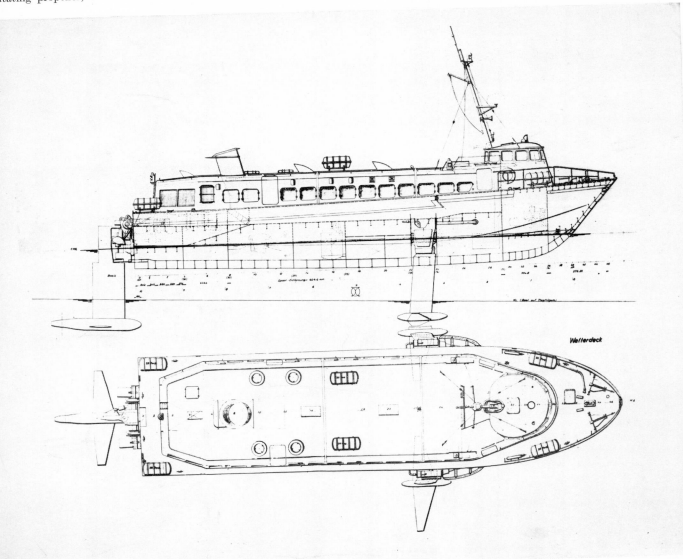

Dolphin—side and deck views

HYDROFOIL MANUFACTURERS
GRUMMAN: United States of America

The Dolphin is being built under contract by Blohm & Voss of Hamburg and marketed by the Garrett Corporation. The prototype was operated by Maritima Antares in the Canaries and has recently been purchased by an operator in the United States. The second Dolphin was due for trials in the autumn of 1968, and has also been sold to an American operator.

FOILS: The fully submerged foil system is of conventional aeroplane configuration with 70% of the weight supported by the two bow foils and 30% by the single tail foil, A Garrett electronic autopilot system controls the incidence angle of the three foils. The stern foil strut rotates for steering and all three foil struts are retracted hydraulically. The foils are of forged aluminium.

The Dolphin autopilot is fully automatic and can be programmed for specific water conditions. It consists of a bow-mounted height sensor, accelerometers, gyros, a solid state electronic computer and an electro-hydraulic foil control system. The sensor sends data on the height of water approaching the hull. The computer translates data from the height sensor, gyros and accelerometers into the optimum foil angle, and sends a continuous positioning signal to the control system.

HULL: The hull is of aluminium alloy construction. Transverse framing is utilised throughout and all frames and bulkheads are welded assemblies.

ACCOMMODATION: The elevated wheelhouse at the forward end of the passenger compartment provides side-by-side seating for the captain and an engineer. A single wheel is provided at the captain's station. All instrumentation is located so that it can easily be monitored. The crew normally comprises a captain, an engineer and one deck hand.

In addition to 116 and 60-80 passengers, first-class seating arrangements, low density luxury seating, workboat and cargo configurations are available. Crew and passengers' accommodation is air conditioned.

Tour operators can order sight-seeing versions of the Dolphin with full vision windows extending the length of the superstructure on both sides. Alternatively, the entire passenger superstructure can be omitted and, for excursion trips on sheltered water, a top provided to roll up or down as desired. With an open well deck, the Dolphin can also be used as a workboat for servicing offshore oil rigs, and carrying high priority cargo.

Access to the passenger compartment is through an aft door on the starboard side. There are three emergency exits. A full range of safety equipment is carried, including approved life rafts, sufficient for the crew and 116 passengers. Life jackets for adults and children are also provided. The safety arrangements have been approved by Seeberufsgenossenschaft, Germany.

POWER PLANT: Foilborne propulsion is provided by a single Rolls-Royce Tyne 621 marine gas turbine, rated at 3,600 bhp at 14,500 rpm. Power is transferred through a mechanical right-angle drive transmission to a KaMeWa supercavitating, controllable-pitch stainless steel propeller of 3 ft 9 in (1·140 mm) diameter at the end of a strut and pod assembly. Hullborne power is supplied by two 216 hp GM6 V-53 N diesels driving two waterjets, each fitted with a moveable nozzle and reversing bucket. An acoustic bulkhead and two rest rooms separate the power plant, which is mounted aft from the main passenger cabin.

COMMUNICATIONS AND NAVIGATION: Standard equipment includes an RCA Cruisephone 110 CRM P 12-A-100 radio telephone and Raytheon MP 1900 radar.

SYSTEMS:

AIR CONDITIONING: Anton Kaeser, type Granturbo HLHK IE 325.

ELECTRICAL: Diesel generator GM 3-53 N model 5034-8100/GE 40kW/225/450 V, 60 cps for auxiliary power, lighting, master warning, monitoring system and autopilot.

HYDRAULICS: 210 atu for strut retraction, foil incidence control and auxiliary power.

APU: Batteries for autopilot system.

DIMENSIONS, EXTERNAL:

Length overall, hull	74 ft 3 in (22·63 m)
Length waterline, hull	66 ft 8 in (20·32 m)
Length overall, foils retracted	86 ft 4 in (26·31 m)
Length overall, foils extended	89 ft 11 in (27·40 m)
Hull beam	18 ft 8 in (5·68 m)
Beam overall, foils retracted	32 ft 2 in (9·80 m)
Beam overall, foils extended	36 ft 10 in (11·24 m)
Draft afloat, foils retracted	4 ft 2 in (1·28 m)
Draft afloat, foils extended	12 ft 10 in (3·91 m)
Draft foilborne	3 ft 11½ in-8 ft 6 in (1·20 up to 2·60 m)
Freeboard	5 ft 9 in (1·75 m)
Height overall	45 ft 7 in (13·90 m)

DIMENSIONS, INTERNAL:

Superstructure includes the wheelhouse, passenger cabin, toilets and upper part of the plenum chamber. The wheelhouse, passenger cabin and toilets are separated by partitions; the plenum chamber by a bulkhead.

Length	42 ft 8 on (13·00 m)
Max width	15 ft 3 in (4·65 m)
Max height	6 ft 5 in (1·95 m)
Floor area	613 sq ft (57·00 m²)
Volume	(110·00 m³)

BAGGAGE: Racks for hand luggage passenger cabin, baggage hold in forepe

WEIGHTS:

Gross tonnage	83 to
Net tonnage	52 to
Light displacement	50 to
Normal take-off displacement	67 to
Max take-off displacement	69 to
Normal deadweight	17 to
Max deadweight	19 to
Normal payload	10 to
Max payload	12 to

PERFORMANCE (with normal payload):

Max speed, foilborne	50 knots (93 km/
Max speed, hullborne	10½ knots (19 km/
Max permissible wave height in foilbor mode	11 ft 6 in (3·5 m
Cruising speed, foilborne	48 knots (90 km/
Cruising speed, hullborne	10 knots (14 km/
Designed endurance and range at cruisin speed	approx 300 n.m
Turning radius at cruising speed	656 ft (200 m
Number of sec and distance to take-off	25 sec 590 ft (180 m
Number of sec. and distance to stop craf	6·2 sec 230 ft (70 m
Fuel consumption at max speed	257 gallons per hou
Fuel consumption at cruising speed	250 gallons per hou

SEA TEST: Tests have been undertaken i sea states 4, 5 and 6. In state 3 seas the maximum vertical acceleration has been 0.095 g. Beyond sea state 3 acceleration have been from 0.1 to 0.29 g. Accelerometers were located amidships.

PG(H)-1 FLAGSTAFF

The 65-ton PG(H)-1 Flagstaff hydrofoil gunboat was developed from the civil Dolphin. It was due to be delivered to the US Navy for trials in September 1968.

FOILS: The fully submerged foil system is of aeroplane configuration, with approximately 70% of the weight supported by two bow foils and 30% by the single tail foil. The three foils are incidence-controlled and operated by an electronic autopilot. The stern foil strut rotates for steering and all three foil struts retract hydraulically, completely clear of the water.

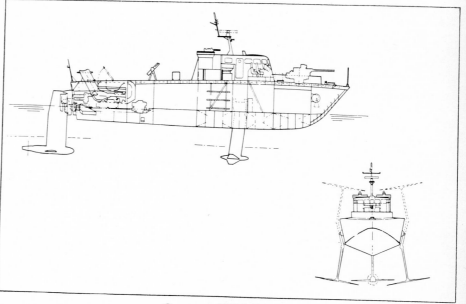

Grumman PGH-1 Flagstaff

e Grumman PGH-1 undergoing tests at the Naval Ship Research and Development Center's Hydrofoil Special Trials Unit, Bremerton, Washington

IULL: The hull is of aluminium alloy
nstruction. All frames and bulkheads are
lded assemblies and transverse framing is
ed throughout.
RMAMENT: The main armament comprises
40 mm gun mounted forward of the bridge
d an 81 mm mortar aft. Manually-
erated twin ·50 machine guns on ring
untings are sited each side of the bridge.
ROPULSION: The main engine is a
600 hp Rolls-Royce Marine Tyne 621
s-turbine driving supercavitating KaMeWa
ntrollable pitch propeller through a mech-
ical right-angle drive transmission. Hull-
rne power is supplied by two 320 hp
neral Motors diesels driving two waterjets.
MENSIONS:
Length overall   73 ft 0 in (22·2 m)
Length waterline, hull   66 ft 8 in (20·3 m)
Hull beam   21 ft 5 in (6·5 m)
Length overall, foils retracted
                                     86 ft 4 in (26·3 m)
Length overall, foils extended
                                     89 ft 0 in (27·1 m)
Max beam, foils retracted
                                     34 ft 0 in (10·3 m)
Max beam, foils extended
                                     37 ft 2 in (11·3 m)
Draft afloat, foils retracted   4 ft 3 in (1·3 m)
Freeboard, minimum   6 ft 6 in (1·9 m)
EIGHTS:
Max take-off displacement   65 tons app
ERFORMANCE:
Cruise speed, foilborne
           In excess of 40 knots (76 km/h)
Crew   13

G(EH)-1 PLAINVIEW
The 320 ton AG (EH)—the designation

means auxiliary general experimental hydrofoil—was built by the Lockheed Shipbuilding
& Construction Company, Seattle, Washington. It is being used by the US Navy's
Hydrofoil Special Trials Unit, Bremerton,
Washington to investigate the performance
of a large seagoing hydrofoil under operational conditions. The guidance design and
preparations of contract specifications were
undertaken by Grumman under the direction
of the Bureau of Ships.
Initially the craft will operate at subcavitating speeds below 60 knots, but the design
provides for subsequent doubling of power
and adaptation to high speed supercavitating
foils. The hull is therefore built to withstand
wave impacts at 90 knots.
FOILS: The foil system is fully submerged
and automatically controlled by a Hamilton
Standard autopilot system similar to that used
in High Point. The foil arrangement is of
the conventional "aeroplane" type with 90%
of the weight carried on the two main foils
and the remainder on the aft foil. The stern
foil strut rotates for steering and all three
foils struts retract completely clear of the
water. The three foils, which have considerable sweep and taper, are geometrically
similar with an aspect ratio of 3. The swept
back leading edges help to delay cavitation
and facilitate the shedding of seaweed and
other neutrally buoyant debris. They also
reduce impact loads associated with water
entry after foil broaching. The main foils
have some dihedral while the tail foil is flat.
All three foils are incidence controlled.
HULL: The hull is almost completely
fabricated of 5456 aluminium alloy. All

deck, side and bottom plating is made from
integrally stiffened, aluminium extruded
planks. The hull is predominantly welded
construction with the exception of the pilot
house and certain longitudinal hull seams
that act as crack stoppers.
The hull shape is designed to minimize the
structural loadings due to wave impact and
the bow shape has been developed for this
specific purpose. Bottom deadrise is carried
all the way to the transom with the objective.
POWER PLANT: Foilborne propulsion is
supplied by two General Electric LM 1500
gas turbines (marine version of the J-97) of
14,000 bhp continuous rating, connected by
shafting and gearing to two supercavitating
propellers at the end of the propulsion pods
on the main foils. The air inlet for the main
turbines is introduced at the top of the
deckhouse. Because of the need to prevent
ingestion of water or saltspray into the gas
turbines, there are lowered deflectors over
the inlet opening, followed by a bank of sheet
metal spray separators.
There is a dam for solid water separation
and four right angle turns before the air
reaches the engine bellmouths.
The hullborne powerplants are two Curtiss-
Wright Model 12v-142 diesels rated at 900 hp
maximum and 700 hp continuous. Each
diesel drives aft through a shaft to a right
angle gear drive resembling a large outboard
motor, mounted on the side of the hull. Each
of these right angle drives is retractable about
a horizontal axis and steerable about a
vertical axis through 360 deg. rotation. A
subcavitating propeller is mounted at the end
of each right angle drive.

HYDROFOIL MANUFACTURERS
GRUMMAN: United States of America

Auxiliary power is supplied by two Cummins VT8-430 diesels rated at 260 hp continuous and each is capable of providing all the ships' hydraulic and electric power. Normally one is operating while the other serves as a standby. In addition to the diesels a small gas turbine auxiliary power unit is carried, which drives a 200 hp hydraulic motor capable of starting both main engines simultaneously.

SYSTEMS:

AIR CONDITIONING: The pilothouse, CIC compartment, living, messing and berthing spaces are air-conditioned during the cooling season by a 13 ton capacity freon type compressor system. Sanitary and washroom areas, galley, displacement engine room, main engine room, windlass room and the engineers control booth are all mechanically ventilated.

DIMENSIONS:

Length overall	212 ft 0 in (64·6 m)
Max beam	40 ft 0 in (12·2 m)
Draught afloat, foils retracted	
	6 ft 0 in (1·8 m)
Draught afloat, foils extended	
	25 ft 0 in (7·6 m)

WEIGHTS:

Displacement	320 tons

PERFORMANCE:

Max speed foilborne	
	50 knots plus (8·29 km/h) plus

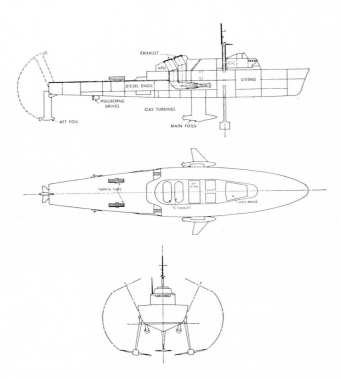

The US NAVY'S AG (EH) experimental hydrofoil designed by Grumman and built by the Lockheed Shipbuilding & Construction Company

The P-1 undergoing tests at the Naval Ship Research and Development Center's Hydrofoil Special Trials Unit, Bremerton, Washington

nold

WIG HONOLD MANUFACTURING
MPANY

D OFFICE:

ester Pike and Folcroft Avenue, Folcroft,
Pennsylvania

ne introduction of Albatross marked the
ry of the United States into the commercial
rofoil field. The first commercial hydro-
service in the New York area was
ugurated with the departure of an Alba-
ss with 16 passengers aboard from Port
shington, Long Island, bound for the foot
Vall Street in Manhattan, on July 15, 1963.
ne craft was designed by Helmut Koch
Ira Dowd's American Hydrofoils, Inc, and
prototype was built in Wilmington,
fornia. Production craft for the New
rk World's Fair service operated by
erican Hydrofoils Inc were built by
wig Honold.

merican Hydrofoils reported that during
World's Fair they carried just over
000 passengers for a total of 1,600,000
enger-miles (2,575,000 passenger-km),
out a single reported passenger injury.
batross operators currently include Unit-
States Hydrofoils, Miami, New York
lrofoils Inc and Crillion Tours Ltd, La
, Bolivia.

addition to the production-type Alba-
s, Ludwig Honold has developed a sports
ng model, equipped with fishing chairs in
rge cockpit and a flying bridge atop the
n.

ATROSS

ne Albatross was the first hydrofoil in the
ted States to be certificated by the
st Guard for passenger services in lakes,
s and sounds.

commodation is provided for 22 passen-
in twin, aircraft-type seats arranged two
ast along a centre aisle. On short routes
one crew member is normally carried to
igate the craft but two are carried at
t.

wer is supplied by a General Motors
53 diesel, developing 197 shp at 2,800
, and driving a single screw through a
: 1 reduction gear. The inclined drive
t is supported in the middle by a vee strut.
e hull, of the deep vee stepped type, is
ll-welded aluminium construction. All
panels throughout the cabin area and all
es beneath the passenger deck not utilis-

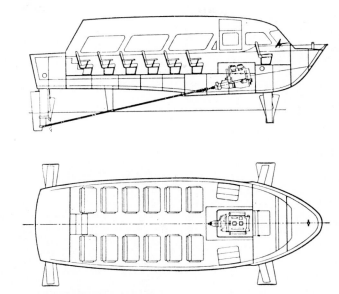

The 22-seat ALBATROSS—first hydrofoil to be approved by the
US Coast Guard for commercial passenger service

ed for machinery and control equipment are
filled with an approved foam for structural
reinforcement and buoyancy.

The fixed-surface piercing foils are of
welded aluminium construction and are
fastened, with their supporting struts, to the
hull attachment plates with stainless steel
bolts. These are designed to shear off to
prevent hull failure in case of grounding or
collision with a submerged object.

The rudder post is utilised for the rear foil
centre support, the propeller shaft bearing,
and to accommodate the engine cooling water
scoop and injection piping.

The navigation, fire protection and life-
saving equipment is as specified by the US
Coast Guard for small passenger craft. The
steering system is hydraulically operated and
a manual tiller is provided for emergencies.

DIMENSIONS:

Length	34 ft 1 in (10·39 m)
Beam	11 ft 4 in (3·45 m)
Width across foils	15 ft 2 in (4·62 m)
Draught afloat	6 ft 6 in (1·98 m)
Draught foilborne	2 ft 6 in (0·76 m)

WEIGHTS:

Displacement	6 tons

PERFORMANCE:

Cruising speed foilborne	28 knots
Max speed	35 knots

HONO-FOIL SPORTFISHERMAN

Sportfisherman is built to provide rapid
passage to and from fishing grounds. It is
basically similar in construction to the
Albatross, but equipped with a large cockpit
with fishing chairs aft of the cabin superstructure, and a flying bridge for improved
vision,

It is reported that interest in the Boston
area in a fast means of getting lobsters to
market may result in a cargo version based
on this design.

The cabin is 15 ft 6 in (4·72 m) long and has
6 ft 3 in (1·90 m) headroom. Sleeping
accommodation is provided for four. Standard equipment includes foam rubber cushions
on berths and dinette seats, enclosed head
with manually operated toilet, stainless steel
wash basin, vanity mirror and medicine
chest, and a complete galley with sink, two-
burner alcohol stove, ice-box glass and dish
rack, utensil drawer and food locker.

Basic equipment of the flybridge includes
two pilot folding seats with safety belts,
power steering, throttle and clutch, and a
complete dashboard with all switches and
gauges.

Weight of the craft is 11,000 lb (5,000 kg).
Dimensions and performance as for the
Albatross.

---

ernational Hydrolines
ERNATIONAL HYDROLINES INC

D OFFICE:

5 Park Avenue, New York 10017

EPHONE:

700

ECTORS AND OFFICERS:

rald O. Rennarts, President and Director

J. Roland Leduc, Vice President in charge
of Operations

Charles E. Laidlaw, Treasurer and Director

Howard F. Cerny, Secretary

Ira E. Dowd, Vice President and Chairman

Robert Arum, Director

Charles Plohn, Director

This company succeeds International Hydrofoils and Air Cushion Vehicles. Although
organised initially for the purpose of operating
hydrofoils, air cushion vehicles and surface
effect ships, it will also market these craft
and has been selected by Satra Corporation
as their representative for Sudoimport
hydrofoils in the Western Hemisphere.

HYDROFOIL MANUFACTURERS
LOCKHEED: United States of America

Lockheed
LOCKHEED SHIPBUILDING & CON-
STRUCTION COMPANY

HEAD OFFICE:

Seattle, Washington, USA

In June 1963 Lockheed Shipbuilding & Construction Company was awarded the contract for the detailed design and construction of the 320 ton AGEH-1 Plainview, the world's biggest hydrofoil to date.   The hull was launched in June 1965 and the US Navy took delivery of the craft in late 1967.   The craft successfully completed her maiden flight in Puget Sound on March 21st, 1968.

The AGEH-1 has been assigned to the US Navy's Hydrofoil Special Trials Unit and will undergo extensive evaluation for several years.   The potential of the craft as an ocean going vessel for the US Navy will be fully explored.   To facilitate analysis of data obtained from the extensive instrumentation installed aboard the craft, provision has been made for continuous and simultaneous recording of more than two hundred data channels on a single magnetic tape.

The power plant at present consists of two General Electric LM 1500 gas turbines, each driving one propeller through a right-angle bevel gear transmission.   The design will permit the addition of two more engines at a later date to enable the craft to achieve much higher speeds using a ventilated or supercavitating foil system.

Wheelhouse of the AGEH-1 Plainview

The Plainview is being tested by the Hydrofoil Special Trials Unit, Bremerton, Washington

yland

YLAND SHIPBUILDING AND
YDOCK COMPANY

O OFFICE AND YARD:

Box 537, Baltimore 3, Maryland

e HS Victoria, a 75-seat hydrofoil
enger ferry designed by Gibbs & Cox and
by Maryland Shipbuilding & Drydock
pany for Northwest Hydrofoil Lines
is now operating between Seattle and
oria BC. The craft operates a daily
ce, with two round trips per day on
ays, Saturdays and Sundays. Journey
is just under 2½ hours, reducing by two
s the time taken by conventional
es. The vessel has a fully submerged
system of canard configuration and is
ered by two LM100 gas-turbines driving
reversing water propellers. The foil
em is controlled automatically by a
eral Electric Foil-Borne auropilot system.
LS: A fully submerged canard configura-
is employed, with an incidence controlled
foil and two main foils with trailing edge
s. Approximately 20% of the weight is
orted by the bow foil and each of the
foils supports 40%. All foils have
ght taper in plan form. Fore and aft
ts are located approximately ¼ and ¾ of
length of the craft from the bow. The
struts are tapered from top to bottom.
t length was chosen to permit the craft
erform well in the design sea state without
ucing excessive strut deflection in turns.
ts and foils are constructed of HY80 steel
are non-retractable, but provision is made
retractable foils on subsequent vessels of
type.

TOPILOT. A Foil-Borne Control System,
gned and manufactured by the General
tric Defence Electronic Division is
ided to automatically maintain the
ility of the Victoria when foilborne and
ides height, heel, trim and heading
trol and power steering. It consists of
following components: (1) control com-
r; (2) three hydraulic actuators; (3) three
gyros; (4) vertical gyro; (5) height
or; (6) two accelerometers; (7) control
el; (8) directional compass system.
he system makes the maximum use of
d state electronics and of modular
struction. Individual modules have a
n Time Between Failure of 10,000 hours
mechanical components will provide
0 hours of operation between overhauls.
s designed to operate efficiently in a State
ea, which includes waves to a maximum
ght of 4·8 ft (1·21-2·43 m).

IGHT CONTROL: The height control
p maintains an altitude at the stern of
in (153 mm) of a set value in calm water,
uding effects of height and pitch control
ps in cascade. Vertical accelerations of
·15g are maintained in the designed sea
te.

CH: Pitch altitude is maintained within
one degree from the vertical in the designed
state. A signal from the pitch loop is
med at the port and starboard servo
plifiers with a signal from the roll loop.
e resultant signal, applied to a servo valve,
ses the actuator ram at the top of each
ut to activate the flap on each rear foil.
LL CONTROL: Roll attitude is maintain-

HS Victoria carries 75 passengers at 37-40 knots.   Powered by two 1,000 hp GE LM100 gas turbines
it is now operating between Seattle and Victoria BC

HS Victoria at speed in Puget Sound

ed within ± one degree from the vertical while
foilborne in the design sea state. Roll is
controlled by the differential motion of the
port and starboard flaps by means of the
servo-actuators. A roll trim control permits
the manual introduction of a small bank
angle during turns.

DIRECTION CONTROL: Control: The
directional control loop maintains the craft
to within ± one degree of a set course while
the craft is foilborne. For course correction
and normal power steering, steering wheel
torque acts on a torque transducer to control
the electrohydraulic servo system.

HULL: The hull, designed for two-compart-
ment subdivision (ie any two adjacent
compartments below the main deck may be
flooded and the vessel will remain afloat) has
a hard chine, high deadrise forward, planing
form selected for easy entrance, good
planing surface aft, and good re-entry
characteristics for take-offs and landings.
Approximately 65% of the main hull is
formed by extruded panels combining shell

plating and toe stiffeners. It is built in
5000 series aluminium.

ACCOMMODATION: The wheelhouse,
located forward, provides an unobstructed
360° view and is equipped with duplicate
steering controls for the captain and first
officer.

The passenger cabin is arranged in airliner
style with three and four seats abreast on
either side of a longitudinal aisle. The cabin
is accoustically and thermally insulated. It
is sheathed in aluminium, and the forward
and after cabin bulkheads are covered with
a Firn-a-Flex walnut wood veneer. The
passenger cabin deck is covered with acrylan
carpeting, and the reclining seats are vinyl
covered and equipped with foot rests and seat
belts. The cabin is complete with water
dispensers and overhead racks. Two
lavatories in the passenger cabin are located
one fore and one aft. All construction
materials, including curtains, are fireproof in
accordance with US Coastguard rules and
regulations.

HYDROFOIL MANUFACTURERS
MARYLAND: United States of America

Passenger and crew spaces are fully heated and ventilated by a hot air system. Air conditioning is optional.

The displacement drive compartment, auxiliary machinery space, fuel oil tanks, electronic compartment and baggage freight compartment are all located below the main deck.

A Carbon-Baron-Freon $(CBRF_3)$ fixed flooding fire fighting system is installed to protect compartments below the main deck and the gas-turbine sponsons. A sea water fire main runs the length of the Victoria with two fire stations located so as to reach any point in the vessel with a 25 ft (7·62 m) hose.

Four 25-man self-inflating life rafts of the latest type are provided, as required by the US Coast Guard.

POWER PLANT: Power is supplied by two General Electric LM100 marine gas turbines, each rated at 1,000 shp. The LM100 is equipped to burn Diesel 1D fuel. Other fuels can also be used.

The compression section of the engine is a 10-stage axial-flow unit which delivers more than 12 lb of air per second at a pressure ratio of 8 to 1. Inlet guide vanes and the first three stages of stator vanes are variable to allow rapid starting, acceleration and deceleration. Starting power is supplied by 28-volt batteries, and the turbine can attain full speed in less than one minute.

The gas-turbines are located in watertight sponsons outside the main hull and drive non-reversing propellers through a single train right angle reduction gear system consisting of a reduction gear, upper and lower spiral bevel gear pairs and vertical shafting.

A 100 hp Harnischfeger lightweight diesel with a Hydro-Drive retractable right angle drive unit is mounted in the stern for hullborne propulsion.

The starting and stopping operations of the main turbines and auxiliary diesel engine are remotely controlled from the wheelhouse. The remainder of the auxiliaries are remotely controlled from the control area of the main cabin.

COMMUNICATIONS AND NAVIGATION: Equipment includes a radio-telephone, a radio direction finder, radar, echo depth sounder, electric horn and three compasses.

SYSTEMS:

ELECTRICAL: The vessel is provided with an electric plant having a nominal 24 volts D.C. The power sources are: (a) two 500-amp, 30-volt, aircraft-type generators, one driven off each main turbine; (b) one 170-amp-hour (at the one-hour rate) 24-volt nickel cadmium battery; (c) one 35-amp-hour 24-volt nickel cadmium battery; (d) one 200-amp, 30 volt aircraft type standby generator, arranged for belt drive by the diesel engine.

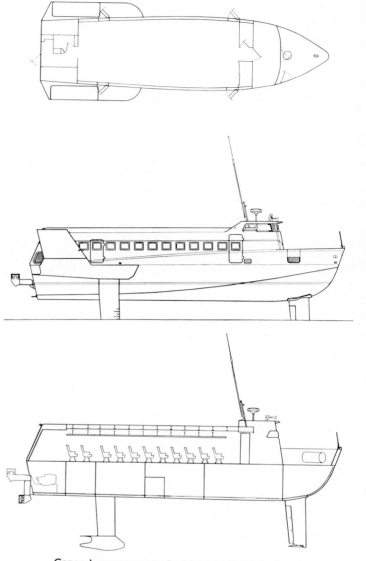

General arrangement drawing of HS VICTORIA

Quick-connecting, aircraft-type receptacles are provided on the weather deck of the craft for the connection of shore power while in dock. A separate shore power connection is provided for the lube oil heater.

HYDRAULICS: Hydraulic power for the foil control system is provided by three 5 hp constant pressure hydraulic oil pumps driven, one each, by the two GE gas turbines and the displacement diesel.

BILGE: A bilge main serves all compartments in the ship. The fire pump, driven by the displacement diesel engine, is self-priming and also serves the bilge main. Its capacity is 50 gallons per minute. This pump operates in the displacement condition. The salt-water cooling pump, which serves the lubricating oil cooler and hydraulic oil cooler, is self-priming and also serves the bilge system. It has a capacity of 60 gpm and operates when the craft is foilborne.

All bilge suction valves are mechanicall operated from the deck.

DIMENSIONS:

Length overall, hull	64 ft 9 in (19·7 m)
Hull beam	16 ft 0 in (4·87 m)
Beam overall, across foils	30 ft 6 in (9·29 m)
Draft afloat	14 ft 1 in (4·29 m)
Draft foilborne (full load, maximum)	7 ft 6 in (2·28 m)
Draft foilborne, minimum	4 ft 0 in (1·22 m)

WEIGHTS:

Maximum take-off displacement	40 tons
Gross tonnage	87 tons
Payload	10 tons

PERFORMANCE:

Cruising speed, foilborne	37 knots (69 km/h)
Max speed, foilborne	40 knots (74 km/h)
Range at 37 knots, full load	180 nautical miles (290 km)

g
ALD J. NIGG
RESS:
4 Fontana, Prairie Village, Kansas,
SA 66208
PHONE:
3-642-2002

e development of a practical sailing
rofoil has been the objective of a few
ginative designers for the past two
des. Fewer than a dozen full-scale
rimental craft have lifted from the
r surface under sail power alone, and
 has had its own unique problems.

true development class of sailing hydro-
has been slow to emerge, but Donald
's Flying Fish, which was successfully
d during the summer of 1968, may mark
peginning of such a class.

eoretical speeds of twice the wind
ity are the main attraction of these craft.
speed potential falls between that of the
ern catamaran and the ice-yacht.

velopment of the Flying Fish began in
 at Lake Quivira, an inland lake in
sas, Donald Nigg believed that if the
pole moment and vertical stability
lems could be solved, the front-steering
point suspension system typical of the
ern ice-yacht offered several advantages.
ious craft had often used three-point
ension, but all appear to have used rear
ing. To develop this new approach,
coetus, an experimental platform was
t. It was evolved through three distinct
ions during 1964-67 and established the
 feasibility.

terest in the experiments resulted in
erous requests for plans, but although
craft was ideal as a development platform,
as not a design suitable for home con-
ction. In response to these requests the
ng Fish was produced.

keep the costs to a minimum, the craft
signed to carry a sail area of 100-150
. It was anticipated that most of those
ested in building a sailing hydrofoil
d be small boat sailors, owning a boat
ving a mainsail of this size. The design
 allows the builder to share the sail and
ng with an existing dinghy.

 monohull and buoyant crossbeam of
'lying Fish represents a simpler and more
ed structure than that of the Exocoetus.
crossbeam provides stability when in
 and in a displacement condition at low
ds. At 2-3 knots the horizontal safety
 at the top of the Vee of the rear foils

Exocoetus on landing approach to dock

provide interim foil stabilization up to the
take-off speed of 5 knots and prevent dragging
an end of the crossbeam in the water. At
foilborne speeds the safety foils preclude the
possibility of an end of the crossbeam being
driven into the water by sudden heeling.

FLYING FISH

First of a development class of sailing
hydrofoils, the Flying Fish has been specially
developed for home builders. Built mainly
in wood and with a length overall of 16 ft
6 in (5·02 m), it has a maximum foilborne
speed of more than 30 knots.

The estimated cost of constructing a craft
of this type, less sail and rigging (the 125
sq ft mainsail and rigging from a Y-Flyer
were used for the prototype illustrated), is
$US 175·00.

FOILS: The foil configuration is surface
piercing and non-retractable with 16% of the
weight supported by the vee bow foil and the
remaining 84% by the outrigged main foils.
The latter are also of the vee type, with
cantilevered extensions at the apex.
Total foil area is 15·3 sq ft (1·42 m²) and the
foil loading is 300 lb sq ft max at 30 knots.
The front foil and its supporting strut are
built in aluminium and oak, and the main
foil is in oak only.

STEERING: A basic feature of the design is
the use of front rather than rear steering.
Directional control is provided by the movement of the hinged bow foil.

HULL: This is an all-wooden structure built
in fir plywood, ¼ in thick and sealed. Torque
load is carried by the skin, and bending loads
are carried by the skin and the internal beam
structure.

RIG: A catamaran rig of 100-150 sq ft
(92-13·9 m²) area is recommended.

DIMENSIONS:

Length overall, hull (plus boom overhang at
    rear, dependent on sail plan)
                          16 ft 6 in (5·02 m)
Length waterline, hull   16 ft 0 in (4·87 m)
Beam   20 ft 0 in (6·09 m)
Draft afloat (fixed foils) 3 ft 6 in (1·06 m)
Draft foilborne
    12-30 ins over operating speed range
Height, approx   24 ft 0 in (7·3 m)

PERFORMANCE:

Max speed foilborne
Over 30 knots, design cruise range
                optimized for 20-30 knots
Max speed hullborne   5 knots
Min wind for take-off   10 knots
Number of seconds and distance to take-off
    (theor. app)
3 secs with 50 ft (15·2 m) run in favourable
                                      wind
Number of seconds and distance to stop
    craft (theor. app)
Can land from 20 knots in 150 ft (45·6 m)
                        in about 6 seconds

The Flying Fish in a broad reach in a moderate
wind. Boat speed estimated at about 18
knots

SEA TEST: The craft has been tested in
10-25 knot winds on a relatively sheltered
inland lake, with a max chop of about 18
inches. Ten hours testing has been accrued
on the final design at the time of going to
press. Speeds up to approx 30 knots have
been attained. Enquiries regarding plans
should be made direct to Donald J. Nigg at
the address given above.

---

a
RA CORPORATION
O OFFICE:
Park Avenue, New York, NY 10016
ra is a New York trading corporation
ng the Sudoimport licence to import

Soviet hydrofoils. The corporation has
imported the Volga hydrofoil, which has been
restyled and marketed in the USA as the
Forte, and also the Raketa. A 100-passenger
Kometa is also being imported by Satra and

was expected to arrive in the USA in the
autumn of 1968. International Hydrolines
has been selected by Satra as the representative for Sudoimport hydrofoils in the
Western Hemisphere.

HYDROFOIL MANUFACTURERS
WYNNE-GILL: United States of America

Wynne-Gill

WYNNE-GILL ASSOCIATES, INC

HEAD OFFICE:
261 S.W.6th Street, Miami, Florida 33130

TELEPHONE:
(305) 373-3130

MARITIME FLIGHT 1

This 21 ft four-seat sports hydrofoil has been designed by international offshore powerboat champion Jim Wynne and his partner, John Gill, for the Maritime Corporation, Alliance, Ohio. The craft has a fully-submerged foil system, with mechanical wave sensors operating trailing edge flaps to maintain the foils at the required depth, and provide stability in all four axes—heave, pitch, roll and yaw. For the first time in hydrofoil design use has been made of Torsionetic Universal joints on the propeller drive shaft to permit retraction. The designed for construction in corro resistant aluminium alloy, the prototy of marine ply.

FOILS: The fully submerged foil syste of conventional "aeroplane" configura with about 80% of the load supported by two rectangular bow foils and the remai by the rear foil. All three foils ret

The Wynne-Gill Maritime Flight I 4-seat sports hydrofoil prototype. The craft has a fully submerged foil system with mechanical wave sensors o ating trailing edge flaps to maintain the foils at the required depth.

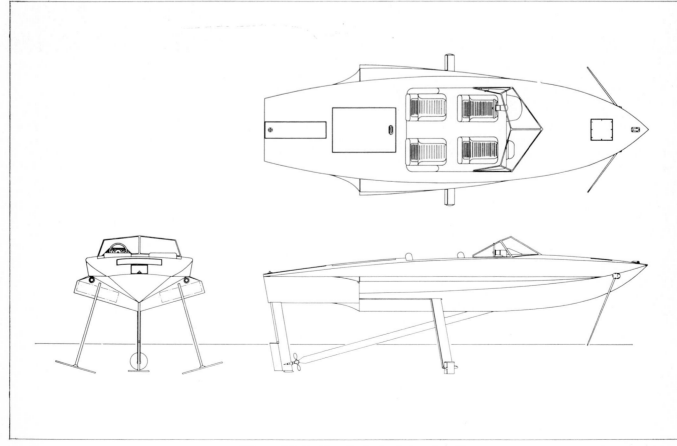

Wynne-Gill Maritime Flight I, out-board profile.

draulically. The two main units retract arwards into hull slots and the rear sembly retracts upwards through the hull, the same time raising the propeller and ive shaft.

Lightweight mechanical feeler arms trailing om the bow ride on the waves and continu- usly transmit their shape through a connect- ng linkage to adjust the angle of the trailing dge flaps on the main foils.

The driver has overriding control. By ushing the wheel forward, the craft rides ower; and by pulling it back it rides higher. When turned to the left or right, the hull will ank to the particular side. The rudder, at the trailing edge of the stern foil strut, is operated by foot pedals.

POWER PLANT: Motive power is provided by a single 200 hp Holman and Moody inboard engine driving a single 3-bladed propeller through a vee-drive and a system of Torsionetic joints, produced by the Eaton Spring Division of Eaton, Yale and Towne Inc. The Torsionetic joints are fitted between the engine and the gearbox and between the gearbox and the propeller shaft, enabling the shaft to be retracted.

HULL: Deep transverse frames on multiple longitudinal stringers with slotted sponsons and keel for foil retraction.

SYSTEMS:
ELECTRICAL: 12 volt
HYDRAULIC: 1,000 psi retraction cylinders
DIMENSIONS:

Length overall	21 ft 3 in (6·47 m)
Hull beam	7 ft 3 in (2·20 m)
Width across foils	9 ft 3 in (2·81 m)
Draft foils, lowered	4 ft 7 in (1·39 m)
Draft, foils retracted	2 ft 2 in (0·66 m)

WEIGHTS:

Light	2,250 lb (1,021 kg)
Max gross	3,200 lb (1,452 kg)

PERFORMANCE:

Max speed	45 mph (72 km/h)
Cruising speed	38 mph (61 km/h)
Take-off speed	20 mph (32 km/h)

THE UNION OF SOVIET SOCIALIST REPUBLICS

Sormovo
KRASNOYE SORMOVO SHIPYARD

HEAD OFFICE AND WORKS:
Gorki

OFFICERS:
M. Yuriev, Shipyard Director
Dr Rostilav Yergenievich Alexeyev, Head of the Central Design Bureau for Hydro-foil Vessels

OVERSEAS REPRESENTATIVES:
United Kingdom, Western Europe and British Commonwealth, Airavia Ltd, 20 North Road, Shanklin, Isle of Wight

TELEPHONE:
Shanklin 3643

USA and Western Hemisphere:
International Hydrolines, Inc, 245 Park Avenue, NY 10017, USA

TELEPHONE:
Murray Hill 2-0700

Krasnoye Sormovo is one of the oldest established shipyards in the Soviet Union. In addition to building displacement craft of many kinds for the Soviet River Fleet, including cargo-carrying catamarans, the yard constructs the world's widest range of passenger hydrofoils, the majority of which are equipped with the Alexeyev shallow draft submerged foil system. Dr Alexeyev started work at the end of 1945 on the design of his foil system which had to be suitable for operation on smooth, but open and shallow, rivers and canals. He succeeded in making use of the immersion depth effect for stabilising the foil immersion in calm waters by the use of small lift coefficients.

The system comprises two main horizontal lifting surfaces, one forward and one aft, with little or no dihedral, each carrying approximately half the weight of the vessel. A submerged foil loses lift gradually as it approaches the surface from a submergence of about one chord. This effect prevents the submerged foils from rising completely to the surface. Means therefore had to be provided to assist take-off and prevent the vessel from sinking back to the displacement condition. The answer lay in the provision of planing sub-foils, port and starboard, so located in the vicinity of the forward struts that when

they are touching the water surface the main foils are submerged approximately one chord.

The foils have good riding characteristics on inland waters and in small waters.

The system was first tested on a small launch powered by a 77 bhp converted car engine. Three more small craft were built to prove the idea, then work began on the Yard's first multi-seat passenger craft, the Raketa, the first of which was launched in June 1957.

The yard is also responsible for the development of seagoing craft with V-type surface piercing foils, similar in configuration to those of the Schertel-Sachsenburg system. Craft employing this system are generally described as being of the Strela-type, Strela being the first operational Soviet design to use V foils. Seating 90 passengers, the vessel is powered by two M-50 diesels and, visually speaking, is a cross between the PT 20 and the PT 50, though smaller than the latter. A military derivative is currently employed by the Soviet navy for coastal patrol in the Baltic and the Black Sea.

Several of the V-foil range have been designed in Leningrad, including the Nevka and Delphin. The latest Soviet hydrofoil to be announced is the gas-turbine powered, 90-seat passenger ferry Typhoon, the prototype which was due to be completed in 1968.

BUREVESTNIK

First Soviet gas-turbine hydrofoil to be designed for series production, the Burevestnik has two 2,000 hp marinized airarcft gas-turbines driving two three-stage water-jets. The prototype was launched in April 1964 and two models are now being built; one for medium range, non-stop inter-city services, seats 130 passengers, the other for suburban services, seats 150 passengers.

There is a four-man crew, comprising captain, engineer, motorman and a seaman.

After extensive trials the Burevestnik began operating on the Gorky-Kuibyshev route, about 700 km (435 miles), on April 26, 1968.

FOILS: There are two main foils and an auxiliary stabilizer foil sited behind the bow foil, all built in titanium alloy. Each is

square-tipped and slightly wedge-shape planform. The foils are secured to the h by columns and brackets. The columns welded to the upper surface of the foils, t bolted to the brackets, an arrangem allowing the angle of incidence to be chang when the craft is in dock.

HULL: The hull, which is divided into elev watertight compartments, is framed longitudinal and transversal formers w the aluminium alloy skins welded into pla

ACCOMMODATION: Saloons and cabins air-conditioned and are decorated w pastel-shade panels and soundproofed w glass-fibre insulation. The engine room is the stern and seperated from the saloon b sound-proof double partition.

POWER PLANT: The two 2,000 hp Ivch ko gas turbines, adapted from those of IL-18 airliner, operate on either kerosene light diesel fuel and have a consumption about 300 gallons per hour. Sufficient f can be carried to operate non-stop over range of 270 nautical miles (500 km). T shaft of each of the two three-stage wa jets is connected with the shaft of one of turbines by means of a flexible coupling, a reduction gear.

CONTROLS: Four rudders are fitted ad cent to the waterjet streams to provi directional control. Reversing is achiev by using a hydro-reversal system in whi two deflectors reverse the waterflow. T waterjets themselves are on fixed mountin and cannot be rotated.

Operation of the waterjets, turbines, rud ers and deflectors is all effected from t bridge by electro-hydraulic control.

DIMENSIONS:

Length	142 ft 0 in (43·3
Hull beam	22 ft 0 in (6·7
Draught afloat	5 ft 10 in (1·8
Draught foilborne	1 ft 4 in (0·4

WEIGHT:

Displacement, loaded	62 to

PERFORMANCE:

Maximum speed	60 knots (110 km
Cruising speed	52/53 knots (95-97 km
Crew	
Passengers, maximum	1

The gas-turbine powered Burevestnik, latest in the family of Soviet hydrofoils inspired by the Meteor. The craft cruises at 60 knots and opened service between Gorky and Kuibyshev in April 1968

~ELORUS

~his craft was developed from the Raketa ~ the Chaika for fast passenger services on ~ding rivers less than 3 ft (1 m) deep and ~ shallow for vessels of the standard type. ~ 1965 it was put into series production at ~ river shipyard at Gomel, in Byelorussia.

~ILS: The shallow draught submerged foil ~tem consists of one bow foil and one rear ~ and a midship subfoil. Main foils are ~welded stainless steel and the subfoil is of ~minium alloy plate.

~LL: Hull and superstructure are built in ~minium magnesium alloy. The hull is of ~ welded construction and the super- ~ucture is both riveted and welded.

COMMODATION: The craft seats 30 ~ssengers in aircraft-type seats.

~WER PLANT: Power is supplied by a ~ hp M-50 diesel. The wheelhouse is ~ed with an electro-hydraulic remote con- ~l system for the engine, reverse gear and ~l supply.

~RFORMANCE:

~laximum speed	42 knots (78 km/h)
~ruising speed	35 knots (60 km/h)

~IAIKA

~n experimental 30-passenger craft, Chaika ~ used as a test-bed for the development of ~sel-operated waterjet systems. It was ~signed initially as a 30 passenger waterbus ~ shallow rivers but was found to be un- ~itable for negotiating sharp river bends at ~gh speed.

~ULL: Hull and superstructure are built in ~miniuim magnesium alloy.

~WER PLANT: An M-50 diesel, developing ~200 hp drives a two-stage waterjet.

~NTROLS: Rudders adjacent to the water ~ream govern the flow of the ejected water ~r directional control.

~IMENSIONS:

~Length overall	86 ft 3 in (26·3 m)
~Hull beam	12 ft 6 in (3·8 m)
~Draught afloat	3 ft 10 in (1·2 m)
~Draught foilborne	1 ft 0 in (0·3 m)

~EIGHT:

~Displacement loaded	14·3 tons

~ERFORMANCE:

~ruising speed, foilborne	46·5 knots (86 km/h)

~ELPHIN

Only limited details of this craft have been ~ceived. Powered by a marinised aircraft ~s turbine, the Delphin is described as a ~ater member of the Strela family of ~ydrofoils''. A waterjet propulsion system

Byelorus, a 30-45 seat hydrofoil developed for fast ferry service on shallow waters, seen on the Irtysh river. Powered by a 735 hp M-50 diesel the craft cruises at 60 km/h

Chaika, an experimental 30 seat waterbus designed for shallow rivers. The craft is used as a test bed for the development of diesel-driven waterjet systems

is employed and the top speed is quoted as being in excess of 70 knots (130 km/h).

KOMETA

Seagoing version of the earlier Meteor, the Kometa prototype made its maiden voyage on the Black Sea in the summer of 1961. Seating 100 passengers in three heated and ventilated cabins it is designed for daytime operation on coastal services and has a cruising range of 311 miles (500 km).

Kometas are built at the Krasnoye Sormovo Shipyard, Gorki, but in addition a number have been assembled at Poti, one of the Black Sea Georgian Yards from prefabricated sections sent from Gorki. The craft has been exported to Yugoslavia, where five are in service, and another was due to be deliver- ed to International Hydrolines for services between Trinidad and Tobago and Grenada towards the end of 1968.

The vessel has proved to be exceptionally robust and has a good all-round performance. On one charter a Kometa covered 3,300 miles (5,310 km) by sea and river in 127 hours.

Kometa

HYDROFOIL MANUFACTURERS
SORMOVO: The Union of Soviet Socialist Republics

The Kometa operates as a hydrofoil in waves up to 4 ft 1 in (1·25 m) high and can travel hullborne in waves up to 8 ft 3 in-10 ft 0 in (2·5-3·0 m) high.

FOILS: Bow and rear foils are in welded stainless steel and the midship subfoil and stabiliser fin are in welded aluminium-magnesium alloy. The bow foil, struts and the outer struts of the rear foil can be unbolted from the hull for maintenance or replacement. Struts of the midship sub-foil and keel struts of the stabiliser fin and aft foil are non-detachable.

HULL: Similar in shape to that of the earlier Meteor, the hull has a wedge-shaped bow, raked stem and a spoon-shaped stern. Hull and superstructure are built in aluminium magnesium alloy; the hull is of all-welded construction and the superstructure is both riveted and welded. Below the freeboard deck the hull is divided by watertight bulkheads into thirteen compartments, which include the engine room, and the compartments for fuel, the fire-fighting system, tiller gear and the fuel transfer pump.

ACCOMMODATION: The standard version of the Kometa seats 100 passengers. It carries a four-man operating crew, comprising captain, engineer, motorman and a seaman, and also a barman. Embarkation platforms sited immediately below the wheelhouse provide access to the craft. Passengers are accommodated in three compartments, a forward saloon seating 24, and central and aft saloons seating 48 and 28 respectively. The central saloon has three exits, two forward, leading to the embarkation platforms, and one aft, leading to the promenade deck. This is located between the side spaces above the engine room and is partially covered with a removable metalic awning.

To the starboard side is a crew's off-duty cabin, hydraulic system pump room, bar

A Kometa on the Thames in August 1968 during a sales tour which took the craft from the Black Sea to the Baltic, Copenhagen, Antwerp, Rotterdam and London

store and bar, and to the port are two toilets, boiler room, battery room and a second crew cabin.

The aft saloon has two exits, one forward leading to the promenade deck, the other aft, leading to the weather deck, which is used for embarking and disembarking when the vessel is moored by the stern.

Floors of the passenger saloons, crew's cabins, bar and wheelhouse are covered in coloured linoleum and the deckhead in the passenger saloons, as well as bulkheads and the sides above the lower edge of the windows, are finished in light coloured pavinol. Panels of the saloons beneath the windows are covered with plastic.

Passenger saloons are fitted with upholstered chairs, racks for small hand luggage and pegs for clothing. The middle and aft saloons have niches for hand luggage and the former is fitted with cradles for babies. The bar is fully equipped with glass washers, an ice safe, an automatic Freon compressor, electric stove, etc. The wheelhouse is equipped with seats for pilot and engineer, a folding stool, chart table, sun shield and a locker for signal flags.

SAFETY EQUIPMENT: A full range of saving equipment is carried including inflatable life rafts, each for 25 persons, life jackets, and 6 circular lifebelts, two life lines and two with luminous buoys. rafts are located two on the forward spor and two on the aft sponsons. When th into the water the life rafts inflate autom ally. Life jackets are stowed under seats in all saloons, and the circular life are stowed on the embarkation and p enade platforms.

FIRE FIGHTING EQUIPMENT. An pendent fluid firefighting system is prov for the engine room and fuel bay. automatic light and sound system sign fire outbreak. The fire fighting syste put into operation manually from the co deck above the engine room door. spaces are equipped with hand-operated and CO_2 fire extinguishers, felt cloths fire axes.

POWER PLANT: Power is supplied by M-400 watercooled, supercharged 12-cyl V-type diesels, each with a normal se output of 900 hp at 1,650 rpm and a imum output of 1,100 hp at 1,800 rpm. engine drives via a reverse gear its inclined shaft and the twin propeller contra-rotating. The shafts are of stee are parallel to the craft.

The propellers are of five-bladed desig made of brass. Two sizes are avail 2 ft 2 in (0·65 m) diameter with 2 ft (0·80 m) pitch, and 2 ft 3 in (0·69 m) dia with 2 ft 6 in (0·76 m) pitch.

Main engine controls and gauges installed in both the wheelhouse and engine room. A diesel-generator-com or-pump unit is provided for charging st air bottles; supplying electric power wh rest; warming the main engines in weather and pumping warm air beneat deck to dry the bilges.

The Kometa entering Dover harbour during its visit to the United Kingdom in August 1968

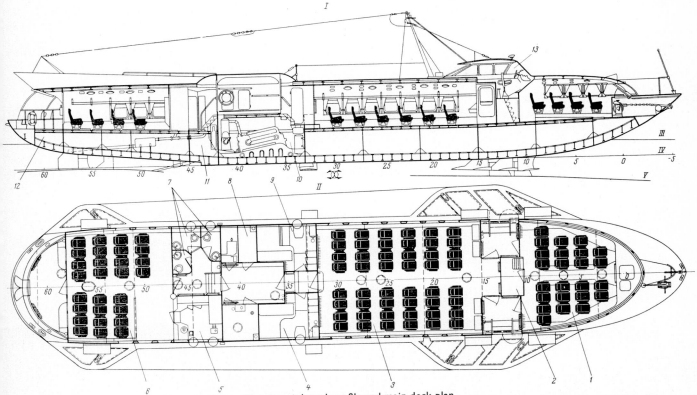

Kometa—inboard profile and main deck plan.

I inboard profile; II main deck; III waterline (afloat); IV keel; V foilborne waterline. I forward passenger cabin, seating 24; 2 accessories room; 3 main passenger cabin seating 48; 4 cloakroom; 5 bar; 6 aft passenger cabin seating 28; 7 WC/washbasin units; 8 storeroom; 9 duty cabin; 10 engine room; 11 firefighting equipment; 12 fuel tanks; 13 wheelhouse

Diesel oil tanks with a total capacity of 6,612 lb (3,000 kg) for the main engines and the auxiliary unit are located in the after-peak. Two lubricating oil service tanks and one storage tank located at the fore bulkhead of the engine room have a total capacity of 551 lb (250 kg). Diesel and lubricating oil capacity is sufficient to ensure a range of 230 miles (370 km).

CONTROLS: The wheelhouse is equipped with an electro-hydraulic remote control system for the engine reverse gear and fuel supply, fuel monitoring equipment, including electric speed counters, pressure gauges, lubricating and fuel oil gauges. The boat is equipped with a single, solid aluminium magnesium alloy balanced rudder, which is controlled through an electro-hydraulic steering system or a hand operated hydraulic drive. In an emergency, the rudder may be operated by a hand tiller.

SYSTEMS:

ELECTRICAL: Power supply is 24 volts dc. A 1kW dc generator is attached to each of the two engines and these supply power while the craft is operating. A 5·6 kW generator is included in the auxiliary unit and supplies power when the craft is at rest. It can also be used when under way for supplying the heating plant or when the 1·0 kW generators are inoperative. Four 12 volt acid storage batteries, each of 180 amp/hr capacity and connected in series to provide 24 volts, supply power during short stops.

HYDRAULICS: The hydraulic system for controlling the main engines and reverse gear consists of control cylinders located in the wheelhouse, power cylinders located on the engines, a filler tank, pipe lines and fittings.

COMMUNICATIONS: A radio transmitter/receiver with r/t and w/t facilities is installed in the wheelhouse for ship-shore and inter-ship communications on SW and MW bands.

A portable emergency radio and automatic distress signal transmitter are also installed in the wheelhouse. A broadcast system is fitted in the passenger saloons and a two-way crew communications system is installed in the wheelhouse, engine room, anchor gear compartment and mooring stations.

NAVIGATION: The following navigation aids are standard: a gyro compass, magnetic compass (reserve) and log.

DIMENSIONS:

Length	115 ft 6 in (35·2 m)
Beam	31 ft 6 in (9·6 m)
Overall height above water level when foilborne with mast raised	
	28 ft 7 in (8·7 m)
Draught, foilborne	4 ft 7 in (1·4 m)
Draught, hullborne	10 ft 6 in (3·2 m)

WEIGHTS:

Light displacement (max)	42 tons
Full-load displacement (max)	56 tons

PERFORMANCE:

Cruising speed (full load) Not less than 32 knots in calm water and in wind conditions up to Force 3

Sea State capability Craft is normally able to operate foilborne in waves up to 4 ft 1 in (1·25 m) high and can travel hullborne in waves up to 8 ft 4 in -10 ft0 in (2·5-3 m) high

Turning diameter 558-656 ft (170-200 m) when operating hullborne with the rudder shifted 35°; 1,640-1,804 ft (500-550 m) when foilborne with the rudder shifted 10-12°

METEOR

Dr Alexeyev's Meteor made its maiden voyage from Gorki to Moscow in the summer of 1960, bringing high performance and unprecedented comfort to the river boat scene, and setting the pattern for a family of later designs.

FOILS: The foil arrangement consists of one bow and one stern set, with the stanchions of the bow system carrying two additional planing subfoils. The foils are attached to the stanchions, which are of a split type, by flanges and bolts. The foil incidence can be altered when necessary by the insertion of wedges between the flanges and the foils when the craft is in dock.

HULL: With the exception of the small exposed areas fore and aft, the Meteor's hull and superstructure are built as an integral unit. The hull is framed on longitudinal and transverse formers and both hull and super-structures are of riveted construction with welded steel members.

POWER PLANT: The Meteor is powered by two 12-cylinder M-50 watercooled, super-charged V-type engines, each with a normal service output of 900 hp and a maximum output of 1,200 hp. Each engine drives its own propeller shaft and the twin-screws are contra-rotating. Controls are all sited in a small wheelhouse set above and at the rear of the fore saloon. Aircraft styling is used in the wheelhouse and the throttles are of dual-lever aircraft type.

ACCOMMODATION: Up to 150 passengers are seated in a short haul version built for suburban services, while alternative models for inter-city services, seat 116-130. Meteors are fitted with full air-conditioning, a bar and an aft promenade deck.

DIMENSIONS:

Length overall	112 ft 10 in (34·4 m)
Hull beam	19 ft 8 in (6·0 m)
Draught afloat	7 ft 6 in (2·3 m)
Draught foilborne	3 ft 11 in (1·2 m)

WEIGHTS:

Displacement loaded	52 tons

PERFORMANCE:

Max speed, foilborne	35 knots (65 km/h)
Maximum endurance	9 hours

HYDROFOIL MANUFACTURERS
SORMOVO: The Union of Soviet Socialist Republics

MIR

First Soviet passenger craft to use a surface piercing foil system was the MIR (Peace), built in the autumn of 1961. Described as the first Soviet seagoing hydrofoil it is in many respects similar to the Supramar PT 50. The hull is of welded aluminium construction and the foils are in high tensile stainless steel. It can undertake voyages in up to State 4 seas and has a maximum speed of 47 knots (87 km/h). Power is supplied by twin M-50 diesels driving twin screws. The engines are electro-hydraulically controlled from the wheelhouse, which has an auto-pilot system for emergencies.

MOLNIA

This popular six-seat hydrofoil sports runabout was derived from Alexeyev's original test craft. Many hundreds are available for hire on Russian lakes and rivers and in slightly modified form the type is now being exported to countries including the United Kingdom and the USA. The craft is navigable in protected off-shore water up to 2 miles from the land and has particular appeal for water-taxi and joy-ride operators.

FOILS: The hydrofoil assembly comprises two forward foils, one aft foil and planing sub-foils.

POWER PLANT: Powered by a 77 bhp CAZ652 Volga car engine, it has a top speed of about 32 knots (60 km/h) and a range of about 100 nautical miles (180 km).

HULL: Built in sheet and extruded light alloy, the hull is divided into three compartments by metal bulkheads. The forepeak is used for stores, the midship compartment is the open cockpit, and the compartment houses the engine, and gearbox. The cockpit is fitted with a steering wheel, throttle, reverse gear lever and an instrument panel adapted from that of the Volga car. Individual life jackets are carried for each passenger and are incorporated into the seat cushions.

DIMENSIONS:
Length overall	27 ft 11 in (8·50
Hull beam	6 ft 5 in (1·95
Draught afloat	2 ft 10 in (0·85
Draught foilborne	1 ft 10 in (0·55

WEIGHTS:
Displacement:
loaded	1·8 to
empty	1·25 to

PERFORMANCE:
Max speed at 1·8 tons displacement
	32 knots (60 km/
Fuel capacity	17 gall (80 litre
Range	97 nautical miles (180 k

NEVKA

This small fibreglass-hulled passenger fer is being built by a Leningrad yard and w be used initially at Black Sea and Bal holiday resorts.

FOILS: Bow and rear foils are both of fix V surface piercing type and made of ste The foils are detachable for maintenance replacement.

MOLNIA, a popular six-seat runabout, is said to be navigable in protected off-shore waters up to two miles from land, and ideal for water-taxi services and joy-ride operators. Top speed is 32 knots

The Nevka is available as a 12-14 seat open cockpit water-taxi, cabin cruiser or sightseeing craft with a transparent roof. A 250 hp diesel provides speed of 60 km/h

ULL/ACCOMMODATION: The hull is in
oulded glass fibre reinforced plastic, it can
 supplied with an open 12-14 seat cockpit
uipped with a wide windshield; as a cabin
iiser with a solid top or as a sightseeing
aft with a transparent cabin roof.
As a cabin cruiser, the craft is equipped
th bunks, a galley and toilet. The driving
nd can be located either at the fore end
 the cabin or in a raised position amidships.

OWER PLANT: Power is supplied by a
0 hp diesel driving a three-bladed propeller
ough, a vee drive.

MENSIONS:

.ength overall, hull	35 ft 11 in (10·9 m)
Beam	8 ft 11 in (2·7 m)
Width across foils	13 ft 2 in (4·0 m)
Draft foilborne	2 ft 9 in (0·8 m)
Draft afloat	5 ft 3 in (1·6 m)

EIGHTS:

Max take-off displacement	5·5 tons
Displacement, unloaded	4·1 tons

RFORMANCE:

Max speed, calm water	37 mph (60 km/h)
Cruising range	137 miles (220 km)

KETA

he prototype Raketa was launched in
57 and was the first multi-seat passenger
drofoil to employ the Alexeyev shallow
ught submerged foil system. Several
ndred are now in service on all the major
ers of the USSR.
ince 1960, an increasing number of export
lers have been placed for the craft. The
t, for two Raketa 340s, came from
ngary and these began operation during
 summer of 1962, one serving the route
dapest-Mohacs, 118 miles (190 km) to the
th, and the other between Budapest and
ergom. The following year the service
s extended to Vienna. Other countries
erating Raketas include Bulgaria and
land. Trinidad-Tobago Hydrolines, a
ision of the American owned International

Raketas are in service on all the major rivers of the U.S.S.R. and on the Danube. The first to be exported to North America is to operate a service in Trinidad between Port of Spain and San Fernando

Hydrolines Inc is planning to operate a Raketa between Port-of-Spain and San Fernando.

The Raketa is powered by a 1,200 hp M-50 diesel and cruises at 33·5 knots.

The craft is designed for services in daylight hours in protected waters under moderate climate conditions. It meets the requirements of Soviet River Register Class 'O'.

In October 1968 it was announced that the design of a new shallow draught variant had been completed. By changing the position of the propellers and regucind the hull weight, the draft will be reduced to 3 ft 11¼ in (120 cm) or almost halved. The modernised version is expected to have a speed of 43·5 mph (70 km/h). Seating arrangements vary from 50-64 passengers according to the route length and conditions. The crew consists of a captain, engineer, motorman, and barman.

FOILS: The foil system consists of one bow foil and one rear foil and two subfoils. The main foils are in welded stainless steel and the subfoils are of aluminium alloy plate.

HULL: The hull is framed on longitudinal and transverse formers and all the main elements—plating, deck, framing, partitions, bulkheads, platforms and wheelhouse—are of riveted aluminium alloy.

Beneath the freeboard deck the hull is divided by watertight bulkheads into six compartments.

ACCOMMODATION: The passenger saloon of the standard model seats 50 in aircraft-type seats. At the aft end of the saloon is a bar. The saloon has one exit on each side leading to the promenade decks and one forward, leading to the forecastle. Aft of the saloon is the engine room, toilet, a promenade deck with a sofa, and the embarkation companionway leading to the awning deck. Beneath the companionway is a store room.

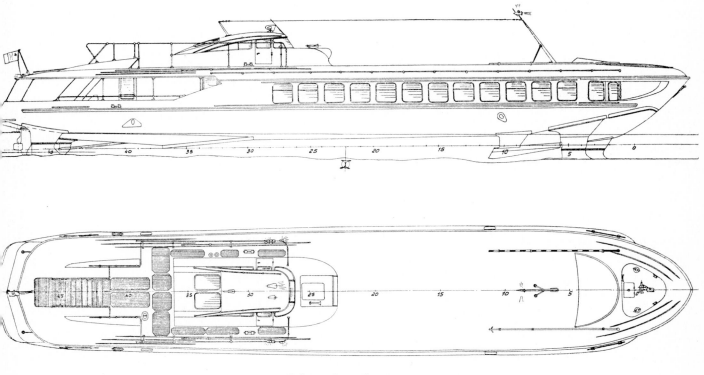

Raketa—General view

HYDROFOIL MANUFACTURERS
SORMOVO: The Union of Soviet Socialist Republics

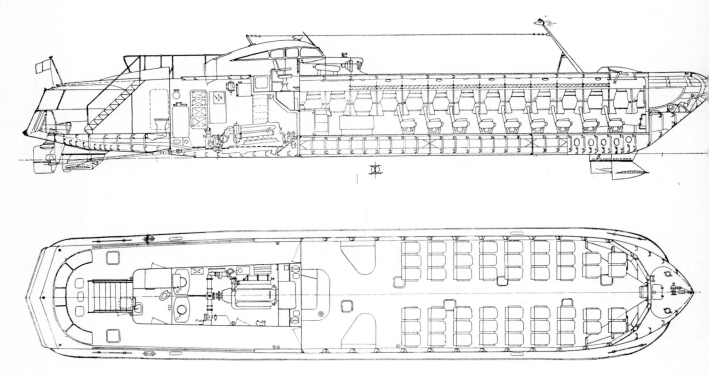

Inboard profiles and deck views of the Raketa

The craft carries a full range of life-saving and fire-fighting equipment. There are 54 life jackets stowed in the passenger saloon, and 4 circular lifebelts located on the embarkation and promenade decks. Firefighting equipment includes four foam and four CO_2 fire extinguishers, two fire axes, two fire buckets and two felt cloths.

POWER PLANT: Power is supplied by a single M-50 watercooled, supercharged 12-cylinder V-type diesel, with a normal service output of 850 hp at 1,600 rpm, and a maximum output of 1,100 hp at 1,800 rpm. Specific fuel consumption is approximately 193 g/hp/h and the engine service life is 1,000 hours. The engine drives via a reverse gear and stainless steel intermediate and propeller shafts, a six-bladed brass propeller. The fuel system comprises two fuel tanks with a total capacity of 2,204 lb (1,000 kg) a fuel priming unit, and a hand-fuel-booster pump and filter. Lubricating oil system consists of a 120 litre service tank, and an 80 litre oil storage tank. A compressed air system, comprising a propeller shaft-driven air compressor and two 40 litre compressed air bottles, is provided for main engine starting, operating the foghorn and scavenging the water intake.

CONTROLS: The wheelhouse is equipped with an electro-hydraulic remote control system for the engine, reverse gear and fuel supply. The boat is equipped with twin balanced rudders in solid aluminium alloy. The rudders are controlled by a hand-operated hydraulic drive and in emergency by a hand tiller.

SYSTEMS:
ELECTRICAL: Power supply is 24 volts dc. A 1 kW dc generator attached to the main engine supplies power while the craft is operating. Four 12 volt acid storage batteries, each of 180 amp/hr capacity and connected in series to give 24 volts, supply power during short stops.

HYDRAULICS: The hydraulic system for controlling the main engine, reverse gear and fuel supply, consists of control cylinders located in the wheelhouse, power cylinders located on the engine, a filler tank, pipelines and fittings.

HEATING AND VENTILATION: Passenger saloon and wheelhouse are provided with a natural ventilation system, using ram inflow when the boat is in motion. When at rest the saloon and wheelhouse are ventilated through open windows and by electric fans. In cold weather the cabin is heated by water from the main engine cooling system. A conventional motor radiator serves as the heat exchanging unit. Engine room, passenger saloon and wheelhouse are heated by electric heaters using a shore power supply when the craft is at rest.

COMMUNICATIONS: A radio-telephone with a range of about 19 miles (30 km) is installed for ship-to-shore and ship-to-ship communication. The craft also has a public address system and intercommunication speakers linking the engine room, wheelhouse and forecastle.

DIMENSIONS:

Length overall	88 ft 5 in (26·96 m)
Beam, amidship	14 ft 6 in (4·4 m)
Breadth, moulded	16 ft 5 in (5·0 m)
Draught, hullborne	5 ft 11 in (1·8 m)
Draught, foilborne	3 ft 8 in (1·1 m)
Freeboard	2 ft 8 in (0·8 m)
Height overall (without mast)	
	14 ft 7 in (4·46 m)

WEIGHTS:

Light displacement	17·93 tons
Loaded displacement	25·33 tons

PERFORMANCE:
Cruising speed 32-32½ knots (58-60 km/h)
Sea State capability Will normally operate foilborne in waves up to 1 ft 8 in (0·5 m) high and will operate in huilborne condition in waves up to 4 ft 1½ in (1·25 m) high

Diameter of turn hullborne
328 ft (100 m) with rudders shifted
Diameter of turn foilborne
820 ft (250 m) with rudders shifted
Time and distance required to beco
hullborne 1 min 25 sec (800-1,000
Time and distance required to stop craft
1 min 20 sec; (150-200

SPUTNIK

The 100-ton Sputnik was the first of Soviet Union's large hydrofoils. On maiden voyage in November 1961, prototype carried 300 passengers betw Gorki and Moscow in 14 hours. Althoug heavy autumn storm was encountered route the craft was able to continue un way at a cruising speed of 40 knots thro several large reservoirs with waves runn as high as 8 ft.

FOILS: The foil system comprises a bow rear foil with the outer struts of the b assembly carrying two additional plan subfoils.

HULL: The hull is welded in A1Mg aluminium-magnesium alloy. Adoption an all-welded unit construction facilita prefabrication of sections at the Sorm shipyard and elsewhere, the parts being s to other yards in the USSR for assemb One yard used for assembling Sputniks is Batumi, on the Caspian Sea.

POWER PLANT: Power is supplied by f 850 hp M-50 watercooled, supercharged type diesels, each driving its own propel shaft and controlled electro-hydraulica from the forward wheelhouse.

ACCOMMODATION: Passengers are acco modated in three saloons, a well-glazed f compartment seating 68, and central and compartments each seating 96. On sho high frequency services, the seating is incre ed to 108 in the latter compartments by t substitution of padded benches instead adjustable aircraft-type seats. Two separa

ydrofoils of the Soviet river fleet are playing an increasingly important part in the passenger transport scene on the Volga. In 1965 forty-one
ketas, Meteors and Sputniks carried over two million passengers on a route network on the river totalling 7,786 km. Above is a 110-ton
Sputnik, passing down the Volga at Gorki

luty cabins are provided for the 5-man
. The cabins are attractively finished in
el shades and fully insulated against heat
sound. Full fire fighting and other
rgency provisions are made and in
ition to lifebelts for all passengers and
bers of the crew, two inflatable rubber
s are carried.

IENSIONS:

ength overall	157 ft 2 in (47·9 m)
am overall	29 ft 6 in (9·0 m)
raught afloat	4 ft 3 in (1·3 m)
raught foilborne	2 ft 10 in (0·9 m)

IGHTS:

isplacement full load	110 tons

RFORMANCE:

uising speed	41 knots (75 km/h)

RELA

eveloped from the MIR and intended for
ices across the Black Sea, the prototype
la (Arrow) completed its acceptance trials
ards the end of 1961. The craft, which

Two fast patrol hydrofoils of the Soviet Navy photographed at sea in February 1968. This class
of vessel has been developed from the Strela commercial hydrofoil

is built by a Leningrad shipyard, was first put into regular passenger service between Odessa and Batumi, and later between Yalta and Sebastapol. More recently a Strela 3 has been operating a service between Leningrad and Tallinn. It covers the distance in four hours, ninety minutes faster than the express train service connecting the two ports.

Two 1,200 hp 12-cylinder V-type M-50s driving twin screws give the Strela a cruising speed of 40 knots (75 km/h). The craft can operate in State 4 seas.

'RELA (Arrow) a ninety-two passenger hydrofoil with a surface piercing foil system, operates between Yalta and Sevastopol on the Black Sea, and
tween Leningrad and Tallinn. Two 1,200 hp 12-cylinder supercharged V-type M-50 diesels driving twin screws give it a cruising speed of 40 knots

HYDROFOIL MANUFACTURERS
SORMOVO: The Union of Soviet Socialist Republics

TYPHOON

This new gas-turbine powered, seagoing hydrofoil is under construction at a Leningrad shipyard and was due to be completed during 1968. The foil system (it has not been stated whether this is fully or partly submerged) is controlled by an electronic autopilot. Craft motion input is fed into and processed by a small computer.

The craft seats 90 passengers and is designed to maintain a speed of 38 knots in severe storms.

Power is supplied by two 1,700 hp gas turbines. No further information was available at the time of going to press.

VIKHR

Seagoing version of the Spuntik, Vikhr is the biggest passenger hydrofoil operating today. Described as a 'coastal liner' which can operate as far as 50 miles from the shore, the craft has been designed for regular, year-round coastal services on the Black Sea.
FOILS: Compared with the Sputnik, innovations include more sharply swept-back foils, a form of auto-stabilisation, and sets of subfoils amidships in addition to those fore and aft, to increase seaworthiness and stability.
POWER PLANT: Power is provided by four 1,200 hp M-50s each driving its own propeller.
CONTROLS: Engines and rudders are controlled from the wheelhouse electro-hydraulically.
ACCOMMODATION: As with the Sputnik, there are three passenger saloons. The fore saloon seats 70, the central saloon seats 96 and the aft 94. At the rear of the central cabin is a large buffet and bar, beneath which is the engine room. From the bar, double doors lead to the off-duty quarters for the seven-man crew,

In high seas passengers board from the stern, across the promenade deck. In normal conditions embarkation takes place amidships through a wide passageway across the vessel between the fore and middle saloons. Seats are arranged in three rows of four abreast across each cabin with two aisles each one metre wide between, to ease access to the seats.

DIMENSIONS:

Length	156 ft 0 in (47·5 m)
Beam	37 ft 9 in (11·5 m)

WEIGHTS:

Displacement, full load	110 tons

PERFORMANCE:

Max speed	43 knots (78 km/h)
Cruising speed	40 knots (73 km/h)

VOLGA

Export version of the Molnia sports hydrofoil, the Volga incorporates various design refinements including a completely redesigned bow foil. The craft has been exported to countries including the United Kingdom and the United States. The USA model, which has been re-engined and re-styled, is known as the Forte.
FOILS: The foil system consists of a bow foil with stabilizing subfoil and a rear foil assembly. The foils are of stainless steel.
HULL: Built in sheet and extruded light alloy, the hull is divided into three compartments by metal bulkheads. The forepeak is used for stores, the midship compartment is the open cockpit and the aft compartment houses the engine and gearbox.

Seagoing variant of the 300 passenger Sputnik, the Vikhr has been designed for regular, year-round services on the Black Sea. Innovations include an amidships subfoil for improved stability and electronic autopilot system

Underside of the Volga showing the bow and rear foil assemblies.

ACCOMMODATION: Seats are provided for six—a driver and five passengers. The controls, instruments, magnetic compass and radio receiver are grouped on a panel ahead of the driver's seat. A full range of safety equipment is provided, including life jackets for six, life line, fire extinguisher and distress flares. A folding awning can be supplied.
POWER PLANT: Power is supplied by a 77 hp M652-Y 6-cylinder automotive engine, which drives a 3 bladed, stainless steel propeller through a V drive. The shafting comprises an intermediate shaft, propeller shaft, stern gland with rubber bearings, propeller shaft coupling boxes with reduction gear and propeller shaft bracket.

SYSTEMS:
ELECTRICAL: 12 volt dc. Starti instrument and navigation lights and sir are provided by an engine-mounted genera and an acid storage battery.

DIMENSIONS:

Length overall	27 ft 11 in (8·5
Beam	6 ft 11 in (2·1
Draught afloat	2 ft 9½ in (0·85
Draught foilborne approx	1 ft 8 in (0·5

WEIGHTS:

Total displacement	3,090 lb (1,886
Fuel	141 lb (64

PERFORMANCE:

Cruising speed	32 knots (60 km
Range	112 miles (180 k

HYDROFOIL OPERATORS

HYDROFOIL OPERATORS

AMERICA, NORTH

USA

Operator: New York Hydrofoils Inc
Type(s): Albatross, 2 (Honold)
Route: East 90th Street-Wall Street. Commuter service

Operator: US Hydrofoils
Address: DuPont Plaza Marina, Florida
Type(s): Albatross, 3 (Honold)
Route: Biscayne Bay, Miami

Operator: Northwest Hydrofoil Lines Inc
Address: 1412 Vance Building, 3rd and Union, Seattle, Washington 98101
Type(s): Victoria (Maryland)
Route: Daily service between Seattle and Victoria (BC); two round trips on Fridays, Saturdays, Sundays.

Operator: International Hydrolines, Inc
Address: 245 Park Avenue, New York, NY 10017
Telephone: MUrray Hill 2-0700
Type(s): Raketa, Kometa (Krasnoye Sormovo)
Routes: The company's initial area of operation is the Caribbean. Its first craft, a Raketa, will operate in Trinidad between Port-of-Spain and San Fernando. In late 1968 the company was due to take delivery of a Kometa to operate from Trinidad to Tobago and Granada.

Operator: US Navy Pacific Fleet Amphibious Command
Type(s): Boeing PGH-2 Tucumcari
Base: San Diego

Operator: US Naval Ship Research and Development Center
Type(s): High Point, PCH-1; Plainview AGEH-1; Flagstaff, PGH-1
Purpose: US Navy hydrofoil development programme

AMERICA SOUTH

ARGENTINE

Operator: Alimar SA
Type(s): PT 50, 3 (Rodriquez)
Route: Buenos Aires-Colonia-Montevideo

BOLIVIA

Operator: Crillon Tours Ltd
Address: PO Box 4785 Av Camacho 1223 Ed, Krsul, La Paz
Type(s): Albatross, 2 (Honold), modified by Helmut Kock
Route: Lake Titicaca

VENEZUELA

Operator: Compania Shell
Type(s): PT 20, 4 (Werf Gusto)
Route: Offshore oil drilling operations on Lake Maracaibo

Operator: Naveca SA
Type(s) PT 20, 4 (Rodriquez)
Route: Maracaibo-Cabimas

EUROPE

CHANNEL ISLANDS

Operator: Condor Hydrofoil Services, Guernsey
Type(s): PT 50, 1 (Rodriquez)
Route: Guernsey-Jersey-St Malo

DENMARK

Operator: Danish Railroad
Type(s): PT 50, 1 (Westermoen)
Route: Copenhagen-Malmo

FINLAND

Operator: Paijanteen Kantosiipi Oy
Type(s): Raketa, 1 (Krasnoye Sormovo)
Route: Lahti-Jyvaskyla, across Lake Päijäne

FRANCE

Operator: Navite SA
Type(s): PT 20, 2 (Rodriquez)
Route: Cannes-Nizza-Monte Carlo-San Remo

GERMANY

Operator: Water Police
Type(s): PT 4, 3 (German Shipyard)
Route: Patrol service on the Rhine

Operator: Hamburg Transport Dept
Type(s): Seaflight P46, 2
Routes: In Hamburg harbour

GREECE

Operator: John Latsis
Type: PT 50
Route: Athens-Passalimini-Hydra

HUNGARY

Operator: Hungarian Navigation Company
Type(s): Raketa, 2 (Krasnoye Sormovo)
Route: Budapest-Vienna

ITALY

Operator: ENIT
Type(s): P 46, 2
Route: Cruise routes

Operator: SNAV, Messina
Type(s): PT 50, 3; PT 20, 1 (Rodriquez)
Route: Naples-Capri-Ischia

Operator: Aliscafi SpA
Type(s): PT 20, 5; PT 50, 1 (Rodriquez)
Route: Messino-Reggio-Isole Liparre

Operator: SAS Trapani
Type(s): PT 50, 1; PT 20, 3 (Rodriquez)
Route: Trapani-Egadi Islands

Operator: Tourist Ferryboat Co.
Type(s): P 46, 2; H 57, 1
Routes: Messina-Reggio Calabria

Operator: Adriatica SpA di Navigazione Venezia
Type(s): PT 50, 1 (Rodriquez)
Route: Tremoli-Isoledi Tremiti

Operator: Ministry of Transport, Milan
Type(s): PT 20, 3 (Rodriquez)
Route: Lake Garda

Operator: Compagnia di Navigazione
Type(s): PT 20, 1 (Rodriquez)
Route: Lake Maggiore

Operator: Compagnia di Navigazione
Type(s): PT 20, 1 (Rodriquez)
Route: Lake Como

Operator: Lauro Navigation Co
Type(s): H 57, 2
Routes: Naples-Capri; Naples-Ischia

Operator: Fiera Internationale Genova
Type(s): PT 20, 1 (Rodriquez)
Route: Liguria Riviera-Genoa

Operator: SAS and SNAV
Type(s): PT 50, 1 (Rodriquez)
Route: Palermo-Eolian Islands

Operator: Societa Sirena, Palermo

Type(s): PT 50, 1; PT 20, 1
Route: Palermo-Ustica

Operator: Societa Tosco Sarda di Nav P. Ferraio
Type(s): PT 20, 2
Route: Piombino-R. Marina-P. Azzutto

MALTA

Operator: Malta Aliscafi Ltd
Type(s): PT 20, 1 (Rodriquez)
Route: Malta-Cozo

NORWAY

Operator: Stavangerske Dampskibsselsk.
Type(s): PT 50, 2; PT 20, 1 (Rodriquez)
Route: Stavanger-Haugesund-Bergen

Operator: Hardanger Sunnhordelandsk. Dampskibsselskab
Type(s): PT 20, 1 (Rodriquez)
Route: Bergen-Tittelsness

Operator: Hydrofoilrutene Oslo
Type(s): PT 20, 2 (Westermoen)
Route: Oslofjord

POLAND

Operator: Central Board of Inland Navtion
Type(s): ZRYW-1
Route: Szczecin-Swinoujscie

SOVIET UNION

The Soviet Ministry of the River F operates approximately 700 hydro passenger ferries employing the Alexe foil system on routes which cover practic all the major rivers, lakes, canals reservoirs from Central Russia to Sib and the Far East. In addition Strela-t hydrofoils operate services in the Gul Finland between Leningrad and Tallinn supported by Kometas and Vikhrs, pro year-round services between ports the Black Sea. Strelas are likely to joined in 1969 by the new gas tur powered Typhoon, built in Leningrad. Typhoon seats 90 passengers, has an a stabilised foil system, and is designed operation in Sea State 5.

There are now 54 hydrofoil services on Volga alone, operated by vessels of Meteor, Raketa and Spuntik series. T older, diesel powered designs were joinec the Volga on April 26 1968 by the protot Burevestnik, which is now operating betw Gorky and Kuibyshev, a distance of miles (700 km).

The Burevestnik is powered by gas-tur driven waterjet units and has a service sp of 95-97 km/h. It seats up to 150 passen on shorter range routes and 130 on non-intercity services.

SWEDEN

Operator: AB Sundfart Malmo
Type(s): PT 50, 1; PT 20, 2 (Western
Route: Copenhagen-Malmo

Operator: Svenska Rederiaktiebolaget Oeresund
Type(s): PT 50, 2 (Rodriquez)
Route: Copenhagen-Malmo

Operator: Gothenburg-Fredrikshavn Lin
Type(s): PT 150 (Westermoen)
Route: Gothenburg-Aalborg-Fredriksha

EDEN/DENMARK

Operator: Oerosund AB

Type(s): PT 50, 2 (1 Rodriquez, 1 Wester-
en)

Route: Copenhagen-Malmo

TZERLAND

Operator: Societé de Nav. sur le Lac Léman

Type(s): PT 20, 1 (Rodriquez)

Route: Lake Léman

TED KINGDOM

Operator: Red Funnel Steamers Ltd

Type(s): Seaflight H57

Route: Southampton-Cowes

OSLAVIA

Operator: Split Airport/Globtour

Type(s): Kometa, 6 (Sormovo)

Route: Pula-Dubrovnik

PT

Operator: Ministry of Commerce, Cairo

Type(s): PT 20, 3 (Rodriquez)

Route: Abu Simbel-Asswan

Operator: Suez Canal Administration

Type(s): PT 4, 1 (Werf Gusto)

Route: Suez Canal

A, AUSTRALIA & NEW ZEALAND

TRALIA

Operator: Port Jackson & Manly Steamship,
Sidney

Type(s) PT 20, 2; (Hitachi and Rodriquez)

Route: Sydney bay and coastal services

HONG KONG

Operator: Shun Tak Co

Type(s): PT 20, 1 (Rodriquez)

Route: Hong Kong-Macao

Operator: Hong Kong Macao Hydrofoil Co

Type(s): PT 20, 4; PT 50, 4 (Rodriquez)

Route: Hong Kong-Macao

Operator: Far East Hydrofoil Co

Type(s): PT 50, 3 (Hitachi)

Route: Hong Kong-Macao

INDONESIA

Operator: Indonesian Government

Type(s): PT 20, 1 (Rodriquez)

Route: Patrol

JAPAN

Operator: Biwako Kisen Co Ltd

Type(s): PT 3A, 1 (Hitachi)

Route: Biwa Lake

Operator: Kyushu Shosen Co Ltd

Type(s): PT 3A, 1 (Hitachi)

Route: Misumi-Shimabara

Operator: Nishisskutajimamura Kotsubu

Type(s): PT 3A, 1 (Hitachi)

Route: Kagoshima-Hakamakoshi

Operator: Innoshima Suichu Yokusen Co Ltd

Type(s): PT 3A, 1; PT 3B, 1; PT 5, 2
  (Hitachi)

Route: Onomichi-Innoshima

Operator: Neitetsu Kaijo Kanko Co Ltd

Type(s): PT 20, 2 (Hitachi)

Route: Nagoya-Gamagori; Toyohsahi-Toba

Operator: Kansai Kisen Co Ltd

Type(s): PT 20, 2; PT 50, 1 (Hitachi)

Route: Osaka-Takamatsu

Operator: Setonaikai Kisen Co Ltd

Type(s): PT 20, 3 (Hitachi); MH 30, (Mitsubishi)

Route: Matsuyama-Hiroshima; Onomichi-
  Imabari

Operator: Hankyu Maikai Kisen Co Ltd

Type(s): PT 20, 2 (Hitachi)

Route: Kobe-Naruto

Operator: Iwasaki Kisen Co Ltd

Type(s): PT 20, 1 (Hitachi)

Route: Matsuyama-Hiroshima

Operator: Neitetsu Kaijo Kanko Co Ltd

Type(s): PT 50, 1 (Hitachi)

Route: Nagoya-Gamagori

Operator: Nihon Kosokusen Co Ltd

Type(s): PT 50, 1 (Hitachi)

Route: Enoshima-Atami

Operator: Shimakatsuurakankokisen

Type(s): MH 30, 3

Route: Gamagori-Toba-Nagoya

NEW ZEALAND

Operator: Kerridge Odeon Corporation

Type(s) PT 20, 1 (Rodriquez)

Route: Auckland-Waiheke Island

PHILIPPINES

Operator: Tourist Hotel and Travel Corporation

Type(s): PT 20, 2 (Rodriquez)

Route: Manila-Corregidor

Operator: Philippine Navy

Type(s): PAT 20, 2 (Rodriquez); PT 32 2
  (Hitachi)

Coastal Patrol

Operator: Sundaharya Corp, Djakarta

Type(s): PT 20

Route: Indonesian Coast

REPORT ON
HYDROFOIL DEVELOPMENT

REPORT ON HYDROFOIL DEVELOPMENT

Four vessels—the Tucumcari, Plainview, Victoria and PT 150—demonstrated in 1968 how far and how fast hydrofoil technology has advanced since the PT 20 prototype opened the first-ever scheduled hydrofoil sea service twelve years ago.

The superb performance of the Tucumcari waterjet-propelled hydrofoil gunboat prompted four European navies to send observers to study the craft at Seattle. A key point in their interest is that the Tucumcari is suitable for patrolling long coastlines at well over 40 knots and can operate without difficulty in heavy seas.

It is being argued increasingly that naval patrol vessels of the future must be small and fast. Twenty-five to thirty rocket-equipped hydrofoil warships, for example, would provide twenty-five points of naval fire, and because of their size and speed would be far less vulnerable to air or guided missile attack than a conventional cruiser.

The Italian Navy has shown particular interest in the Tucumcari, and is reported to be considering an order for thirty, which would be built in Italy. Airo M. Gonnella, head of Boeing's Advanced Marine Systems Organisation, which designed and built the craft, estimates there is a market for 200-300 military hydrofoils in Europe initially.

The Tucumcari is now in its home port of San Diego, operating with the US Navy Pacific Fleet Amphibious Command, where it is due to be joined by the Grumman Flagstaff. Both craft will be evaluated by the US Navy which, according to a press report, is considering an initial purchase of about 30 of one of the two gunboat designs.

Boeing dismisses the debris "problem" as a highly localised one, confined to only a few areas such as Puget Sound, where the Tucumcari was tested extensively. The craft struck debris several hundred times and splintered every log it hit, including one 25 ft long, 18 in diameter timber weighing $1\frac{1}{2}$ tons. The hull structure is designed to crumple under severe impact, absorbing the force before the strut is damaged or sheared off.

Debris in other areas, the Mediterranean for example, might be up to the size of a railway tie, but no larger, and craft like the Tucumcari can withstand strikes of objects that size without damage. Debris will not present any serious problems in naval operations, and as vessels get larger, the problem of sustaining foil damage in this way, will disappear altogether.

Just how large hydrofoils will become eventually seems to be anyone's guess. At one time it was considered that because of the size of the foils required, and the performance of the powerplants available, hydrofoils would be limited in size to about 1,000 tons displacement. Today this figure appears to be on the conservative side. Relatively small high-lift foils, new marine gas-turbines with twice the output, and new, less complex propulsion systems are being developed which could lead to the construction of hydrofoils several times the size of craft envisaged ten to twelve years ago.

Not long ago the design of a hydrofoil capable of operating in the Atlantic was thought to be out of the question. Now most hydrofoil designers concede that this is feasible.

Certainly projects for much larger craft are beginning to take shape. Boeing states that the company could build boats of up to 1,000 tons, employing the same basic technology as that of the Tucumcari, and having similar performance.

Meanwhile, the world's biggest hydrofoil to date is the 320 ton USS Plainview, which successfully completed her maiden flight at Puget Sound on March 21, 1968. The craft will provide the first opportunity to evaluate the potential of submerged foil craft for full ocean-going naval service. The guidance design was completed by Grumman and the contract for detailed design and construction was awarded to Lockheed Shipbuilding & Construction Company. In addition to its large size, its design is substantially different to that of the PCH-1, the US Navy's experimental hydrofoil patrol boat. Foil lift variation is effected on the Plainview by changing the incidence angle of both the main foils and the tail foil. Ultra-sonic height sensors are mounted both at the bow and the stern.

Initally the powerplant comprises two General Electric LM1500 gas turbines, each driving one propeller through a right-angle bevel gear transmission. Provision has been made however for adding two more engines to permit much higher speeds to be attained. A ventilated or supercavitating system would be fitted to the craft in this form. The AGEH-1 has been assigned to the US Navy's Hydrofoil Special Trials Unit at Bremerton, Washington, and will undergo extensive evaluation for a period of several years. Grumman has now completed the design of a commercial derivative—the 325 ton Neptune. The standard version, designed for mixed traffic, will accommodate 302 passengers on the upper deck and 37 cars on the vehicle deck beneath. The craft will be capable of operating in sea state 6 and will have a cruising speed of 50 knots. Blohm & Voss AG of Hamburg, which built the first two Grumman Dolphins, will also build the Neptune and handle its sale in Europe.

After various delays, the HS Victoria, built by Maryland Shipbuilding & Drydock Co. for William I. Niedermair, President, Northwest Hydrofoil Lines, got away to a flying start on its scheduled service between the heart of Seattle and Victoria B.C. in the summer of 1968. By the end of August the craft was operating with clockwork regularity and carrying capacity payloads. To cope with the traffic, the service has been increased to two round trips per day on Fridays, Saturdays and Sundays. Journey time is just under $2\frac{1}{2}$ hours, reducing by two hours the time taken by conventional ferries.

Victoria, one of the world's most sophisticated passenger hydrofoils, was designed by Gibbs & Cox. The vessel carries a crew of four and 75 passengers and will operate in

8-10 ft waves at 37-40 knots. It has a f submerged foil system of canard configu tion and is powered by two LM1500 turbines driving non-reversing water pro lers. The incidence controlled bow foil the trailing edge flaps of the main foils controlled automatically by a Foil-Bo Control System designed and manufactu by General Electric Defense Electro Division.

In complete contrast to the electro employed to stabilise Tucumcari, Plainv and Victoria is the Schertel-Supra stabilisation system employed on the wor biggest commercial hydrofoil to date— 150 ton Supramar PT 150 built by Wes moen for the Gothenburg-Fredrikshavn L Latest in the long line of Supramar desi the craft is the first to be built for fast fe services in unprotected waters away fi the coast. Originally the PT 150 was inte ed as a 250 seat passenger ferry, but at request of the operating company, the b design was modified to allow an alterna payload of 150 passengers and 8 cars to carried.

The craft has a surface-piercing bow and a fully submerged rear foil. Stabilit maintained jointly by the inherent stabi of the bow foil and the air stabilisat system fitted to the rear foil. Separate p and starboard systems are installed to sta ise rolling and pitching. The system fe air from the free atmosphere through exits to the foil upper surface (the low pres region) decreasing the lift. The amount lift is varied by the quantity of air admitt this being controlled by a valve actuated a damped pendulum and a rate gyro. craft is stabilised by decreasing the availa air volume for the more submerged side a increasing that of the less submerged o The bow foil centre section is also to provided with submergence depth stabil tion, the quantity of air admitted be varied with the degree of submergence.

During the first two months of service, craft carried more than 25,000 passengers the Gothenburg-Fredrikshavn route. journey time, compared with that taken conventional ferry boats, was reduced fr four hours to one hour and forty minut The costs per seat/mile ranged betwe $2\frac{3}{4}$d and 3d. A second PT 150 is under c struction by Rodriquez.

Supramar refers to the craft as being 'par stabilised'. In 1968 the first of a n generation of "fully stabilised" Supran craft was being evaluated in the Mediterra ean. The craft, an ST 3 (formerly PT test bed, with a fully submerged foil syste is powered by a GE LM100 gas turbine, a has been operated at speeds up to 56 kno

Two Soviet-built hydrofoils that ma news in 1968 were the Kometa, the seago version of the earlier Meteor, and the new f patrol derivative of the 90-passenger Str hydrofoil ferry. The Kometa visited Lond and the Isle of Wight at the end of a sa tour which took the craft from Poti, on t Black Sea, to the Baltic. Copenhag

twerp and Rotterdam en route. The
ft proved to be exceptionally robust and
have a good all-round performance. It
s a cruising speed of 32 knots and is
rmally able to operate foilborne in waves
to 4 ft (1·25 m) high. It can travel
llborne in 8-10 ft (2·5-3 m) waves. Export
lers for the Kometa continue to grow.
k have been supplied to Yugoslavia, which
s recently increased this order, and one is
ing shipped to International Hydrolines of
w York for a service between Trinidad
d Tobago.

nterest has been shown in the craft by
tential operators in the United Kingdom,
d one is on order through Airavia Ltd, the
doimport representatives, for delivery in
rly 1969 for a service in the UK, subject
a passenger licence being granted by the
ard of Trade.

Photos of the new Soviet coastal patrol
drofoil reveal few details of the craft or
armament, apart from the use of a Scher-
-Sachsenburg type surface-piercing bow
l, and what appears to be a remotely-
erated bow turret mounting twin machine
ns. It is possible that the design has been
veloped from the Strela via the new 90-
ssenger Typhoon, and like the latter has a
s turbine powerplant and a form of
tostabilisation. Craft of this class are
ely to be operated in the Baltic, Black Sea
d the Caspian Sea.

A number of new craft with mechanically-
erated incidence control systems are
rrently being developed. The latest are
e Wynne-Gill Maritime Flight 1, a 21 ft
ur-seat sports hydrofoil designed by
ternational offshore powerboat champion
m Wynne, and his partner, John Gill, for
e Maritime Corporation, Alliance, Ohio,
d the New Hydrofin Ltd's Channel Skipper,
Maritime Flight 1 has a fully-submerged
il system with mechanical wave sensors
erating trailing edge flaps to maintain the
ils at the required depth. For the first
ne in hydrofoil design, use is made of

Torsionetic universal joints on the propeller
drive shaft to permit retraction. Top speed
is about 40 knots. Christopher Hook's
Channel Skipper is developed from his
earlier K2 Hydrofin, and is also a four-seater.
A high-riding crash preventer plane is mounted ahead as a platform for mounting a lightweight pitch sensor which is hinged to the rear.
The sensor rides on the waves and continuously transmits their shape through a servo
system and connecting linkage to vary the
incidence angle of the main foils. A filter
system ensures that the craft ignores small
waves and that the hull is flown over the
crests of waves exceeding the height of the
keel over water. The prototype is expected
to be completed in 1969.

A growing range of sports hydrofoils is
becoming available. The best known are
the Molnia and Volga, of which several
thousand have been built (the Forte, on sale
in the USA, is a derivative); the Hungarian-
built Nikex (production of which has now
ceased) and the very successful Water Spyder
series, constructed by Water Spyder Marine
Ltd, Downsview, Ontario. In 1969, two
new Polish designs will be added to the
range—the six-seat WS-6 Eros and the
four-seat WS-4 Amor. The craft, which are
designed by Gdansk Ship Research Institute,
have glass fibre hulls and will go into series
production.

If hydrofoil enthusiasts prefer sail to power,
they can build a new class of sailing hydrofoil
—the Flying Fish—designed by Donald J.
Nigg. The estimated cost of constructing
this craft, which is capable of more than 30
knots, is $US 175·00, less sail and rigging.
The design allows the builder to share the
sail and rigging with an existing dinghy.

Another new craft due to be completed in
1969, will be the prototype Seaflight L.90, a
100-120 seat passenger ferry which has been
designed by this Italian company for export.
The craft has been developed from the
successful 60-seat Seaflight H.57, one of
which has been ordered by Red Funnel

Steamers Ltd for services between Southampton and Cowes, Isle of Wight.

Like its forebears, the L.90 incorporates
a foil system in which the foil automatically
assumes the best angle of incidence in relation
to the wave condition. The split bow foil
combines a horizontal submerged centre
section with inclined surface piercing areas,
and the geometry of the bow and rear foils
is such that it is possible to beach the vessel
on a falling tide on a nearly flat sandy bottom,
the hull remaining stable.

Seaflight vessels are now in service in Hamburg and are operating an increasing number
of scheduled passenger services around the
Italian coastline. Several have been employed for holiday cruises and have operated to
the coast of North Africa. Variants of the
C.46, H.57 and L.90 include fast luxury yachts
and fast coastal patrol craft.

In 1968 hydrofoils were operating in
increasing numbers and spreading to more
and more countries. Progress in the past
has been painfully slow, but the tremendous
growth in the use of commercial hydrofoils
during the past few years, combined with the
increasing interest of the world's navies,
suggests that the opposite will be true in the
future.

Even in the United Kingdom, which unlike
most other European countries, still has no
scheduled hydrofoil ferry services, there is
an awakening to its possibilities. Desmond
Plummer, leader of the Greater London
Council, foresees a future for them on the
Thames. He says: "We are finding out it if
is going to be practicable for hydrofoils to be
employed on inter-city services. These craft
have also, I am sure, a great future on
passenger ferry services within London. I
look forward to the day when the worker in
Central London can be carried speedily from
his home at Thamesmead, our new town
near Erith, free from the weary journey on
overcrowded trains. The visitor to London
may, before long, be able to enjoy high speed
travel to the Continent by water, as well as
by air".

AIR CUSHION VEHICLE and HYDROFOIL POWERPLANTS

FRANCE

Turboméca
SOCIÉTÉ TURBOMÉCA

HEAD OFFICE AND WORKS:
Bordes (Basser-Pyrénées)
PARIS OFFICE:
1 Rue Beaujon, Paris 8e
PRESIDENT AND DIRECTOR GENERAL:
J. R. Szydlowski

The Société Turboméca was formed in 1938 by MM. Szydlowski and Planiol to develop blowers, compressors and turbines for aeronautical use.

In 1947 the company began development of gas turbines of low power for driving aircraft auxiliaries and for aircraft propulsion. Since then it has evolved about 50 different types of powerplants, of which 15 have gone into production and 10 have been manufactured under licence in five foreign countries.

These engines have proved so successful that about 7,000 had been delivered to customers in France and in 54 foreign countries by early 1966. Many thousands have been built under licence successively by Blackburn Engines Ltd and Bristol Siddeley Engines Ltd (merged with Rolls-Royce Ltd in April 1967), in the United Kingdom, the Continental Aviation and Engineering Corporation in the United States, ENMA in Spain and a state factory in Yugoslavia. Present production by Turboméca totals approximately eighty engines per month.

The Bertin Terraplane BC 8 has a single 500 shp Turboméca Artouste shaft turbine driving two airscrews for propulsion, and the lift system is powered by a Turboméca Marboré.

The Naviplane N 300, under development by SEDAM, is powered by two Turmo III D3s. The new Bertin Aerotrain high-speed research vehicle is powered by three Turboméca Astazou gas turbines, two driving centrifugal fans for the lift and guidance pads, and one for the propeller.

The description that follows apply to standard aviation versions of the engines. Details of specific installations in the French ACVs listed have not been received.

TURBOMÉCA ARTOUSTE IIC

The Artouste II is a shaft turbine. The two-stage turbine uses part of the available power to drive the compressor, the remaining power being free to drive a power take-off shaft.

By January 1966, Turboméca had completed the delivery of 1,395 Artouste II engines. Many more have been built by Blackburn and Bristol Siddeley in England.

A single Artouste drives the two propulsion airscrews on the Naviplane BC 8 and the lift/propulsion system on the Naviplane N 102
TYPE: Gas-turbine with centrifugal compressor, an annular combustion chamber and a two-stage turbine.
COMPRESSOR: Single-stage centrifugal compressor. Two diffusers, one radial and the other axial, aft of compressor. Pressure ratio at 34,000 rpm at S/L 3·88 : 1. Air mass flow 7·05 lb/sec (3·2 kg/sec) at 34,000 rpm at S/L.
COMBUSTION CHAMBER: Annular type, with rotary atomiser fuel injection. Torch igniters.

FUEL: AIR 3405 turbofuel. Normal aviation gasoline for starting.
OIL: AIR 3512 (mineral) oil.
TURBINE: Two-stage axial type. Blades integral with discs. Row of nozzle guide vanes before each stage.
JET PIPE: Fixed type. Diameter of diffuser exit 12·5 in (318 mm). Exhaust gas speed 328 ft/sec (100 m/sec) maximum. Exhaust gas temperature 500°C maximum.
STARTING: Labavia 2,500-watt starter. Two Turboméca igniter plugs.
DIMENSIONS:

Length	56·7 in (1,440 mm)
Height	21·5 in (545 mm)
Width	15·35 in (390 mm)

WEIGHT (Dry):

Equipped	315 lb (143 kg)

PERFORMANCE RATINGS:

T-O	523 shp at 34,000 rpm
Max cont	473 shp at 34,000 rpm

FUEL CONSUMPTIONS:

At T-O rating	436 lb (198 kg) hour
At max cont rating	414 lb (188 kg) hour

TURBOMÉCA ARTOUSTE IIIB

This is a developed version of the Artouste II to power the Sud-Aviation Alouette III helicopter. It is a member of the second generation of Turboméca engines with two-stage axial-centrifugal compressor and three-stage turbine. It has a pressure ratio of 5·2 : 1. Air mass flow is 9·5 lb/sec (4·3 kg/sec) at 34,000 rpm.

Type approval at the rating given below was received on May 25, 1961, following completion of a 150-hour official type test. By January 1966, a total of 595 Artouste IIIB's had been built, with orders in hand for a further 80. In addition Artouste IIIB's are being built under licence in India by Hindustan Aeronautics Ltd.
DIMENSIONS:

Length	71·46 in (1,815 mm)
Height	24·68 in (627 mm)
Width	19·96 in (507 mm)

WEIGHT:

Dry	287 lb (130 kg)

PERFORMANCE RATINGS:
T-O and max cont rating 586 ehp (550 shp, at 33,500 rpm (6,000 output shaft rpm)
Fuel consumption 0·716 lb (0·325 kg) ehp/hr

TURBOMÉCA TURMO III

The Turmo is a free-turbine engine with a two-stage compressor, consisting of a single axial stage followed by a single centrifugal stage, an annular combustion chamber, two-stage compressor turbine and single-stage (two-stage on later versions) power turbine. Several versions are in current production or under development, as follows.

Two Turmo IIID3s power the SEDAM Naviplane 300.

Turmo IIIC. This shaft-turbine version powers the Sud-Aviation Frelon prototypes. Its gas-generator is fitted with a governor which compensates for altitude and limits acceleration. The free-turbine is fitted with limiters for both torque and acceleration. Pressure ratio 5·8 : 1. Air mass flow 13·4 lb/sec (6·1 kg/sec) at 33,500 rpm. Gas temperature 545°C at 23,150 rpm. Max rating 1,814 shp at 5,700 output shaft rpm.

Turmo IIIC.2 Development of IIIC. imum rating 1,282 shp.
Turmo IIIC3. Development of IIIC. stage power turbine. Maximum ratir 1,480 shp at 33,700 rpm.
Turmo IIID. Turboprop version, simi basic construction to Turmo IIIC, but generator output rpm limited to (Gas-producer is mounted beneath the o shaft, which is driven by the free-tur The overhung forward drive leads thro freewheel and dog-clutch to the pro reduction gearbox, which gives a final at 1,200 rpm. A drive pad at the rear primary box enables the engines of a m engined aircraft to be coupled togethe spanwise shafting, as is done on the Tu powered Breguet Br 941 and 942. Max rating 1,208 ehp (1,149 shp).
Turmo IIID.3 Development of Rated at 1,430 ehp at 33,500 rpm. Pr ratio 5·5 : 1. Air mass flow 13 lb (5·9 kg
DIMENSIONS:
Length:

IIIC3	77·8 in (1,976
IIID	75·6 in (1,920

Width:

IIIC3	27·3 in (693
IIID	37·0 in (940

Height:

IIIC3	28·2 in (7,171

WEIGHT (Dry):

IIIC3 with standard equipment	485 lb (22
IIIC3 as complete power plant	639 lb (29
IIID with standard equipment	694 lb (31

PERFORMANCE RATINGS:
Max T-O:

IIIC	1,184 shp at 23,150 free-turbin
IIIC2	1,282 shp at 24,700 free-turbin
IIIC3	1,480 shp at 33,700 (5,700 output shaft
IIID	1,20
IIID3	1,430 ehp at 33,500

Max cont:

IIIC	1,06
IIIC2	1,18
IIIC3	1,208 shp at 32,300

FUEL CONSUMPTION:
AT T-O rating:

IIIC3	0·595 lb (270 gr) s
IIID	0·657 lb (298 gr) s

At max cont rating:

IIIC3	0·633 lb (287 gr) s
III	0·683 lb (310 gr) s

TURBOMÉCA MARBORÉ VI

The Marboré is the most widely us Turboméca's range of gas-turbine en By January 1966, Turboméca had 3,850 of the original Marboré II and orders for another 90. Continental built about 3,700 in the United States the designation J69. Others have produced in Spain.

The Marboré powers the lift system Bertin Terraplane BC8.
TYPE: Centrifugal-flow turbojet.
AIR INTAKE: Annular sheet metal intake bolted to front of light alloy con sor casing.

MBUSTION CHAMBER: Composed of
er and outer sheet metal casings, forming
ular flame tube. Air from compressor
ses through both radial and axial diffuser
es and divides into three main flows, two
nary for combustion and one secondary.
o primary flows enter combustion zone
n opposite ends of chamber: the rear
am through turbine nozzle guide vanes
ich it cools. Secondary flow enters
ough the outer casing for dilution and
ling of combustion gases. Two torch
iters.

EL SYSTEM: Fuel, pumped through
low impeller shaft, is fed to combustion
e by rotating injector disc, around
iphery of which are a number of vents
ich act as nozzles. Fuel is vented by
trifugal force, being atomised in the
cess. Fuel delivery at low thrust settings
ulated by by-pass valve.

EL GRADE: Air 3405 (JP-1).

ZZLE GUIDE VANES: Twenty-five
ow sheet steel guide vanes cooled by part
primary combustion air.

RBINE: Single-stage turbine with thirty-
en blades integral with steel disc. Bolted
main shaft and tail shaft, latter supported
rear roller bearing for rotating assembly.
temperature 613°C at 21,500 rpm.

MPRESSOR: Single-sided impeller mach-
l from two alloy forgings, shrunk on steel
ft and locked and dowelled to maintain
nment. Externally finned light alloy
pressor casing supports front ball-bearing
rotating assembly in a central housing
ported by three streamlined struts. This
sing also contains gears for accessory
ves. Pressure ratio 3·84 : 1. Air mass
21·6 lb (9·8 kg) sec.

T PIPE: Inner and outer sheet metal
ings, latter supported by three hollow
ts. Inner tapered casing extends beyond
of outer casing to induce air-flow through
ts to cool rear main bearing and inner
ng.

CESSORY DRIVES: Gear casing in
tral compressor housing with drives for
and oil pumps. Connecting shaft to
lerside of accessories gear case above
pressor casing. Accessorues include
hometer generator and electric starter.
ke-off (4 hp continuous) for remotely-
ven accessory box.

BRICATION SYSTEM: Pressure type.
gle gear type pump serves front gear
ing, two main bearings and rpm governor.

Three scavenge pumps return bearing oil to
tank *via* cooler. Normal oil pressure 40
lb/sq in (2·8 kg/cm²).

OIL SPECIFICATION: Air 3152.

MOUNTING: Four points, with Silentbloc
rubber mountings, two at front and two at
rear.

STARTING: Air Equipement 24-volt electric
starter or compressed air starter. Two
Turboméca igniter plugs.

DIMENSIONS:

Length with exhaust cone but without tail-
pipe 55·74 in (1,416 mm)
Width 23·35 in (593 mm)
Height 24·82 in (631 mm)

WEIGHT (Dry):
Equipped 309 lb (140 kg)

PERFORMANCE RATINGS:
T-O 1,058 lb (480 kg) st at 21,500 rpm
Cruising 925 lb (420 kg) st at 20,500 rpm

SPECIFIC FUEL CONSUMPTION:
At T-O rating 1·09
At cruising rating 1·07

TURBOMÉCA ASTAZOU II

The Astazou is another of the second-
generation Turboméca engines, incorporating
the experience gained with earlier series and
making use of new design techniques. It has
an extremely small gas-producer section and
has been developed both as a shaft-turbine
and as a turboprop, driving a variable-pitch
propeller.

The two-stage compressor consists of an
axial stage followed by a centrifugal stage,
with an annular combustion chamber and
three-stage turbine. Accessories are mounted on the rear of the main intake casting.
Pressure ratio is 6 : 1 and air mass flow 5·5
lb/sec (2·5 kg/sec) at 43,500 rpm.

Three different reduction gears are available
on the turboprop version, to give nominal
propeller rpm of 2,200, 2,080 and 1,800
respectively. In the shaft-turbine, the speed
of the output shaft is 6,000 rpm.

Three Astazous power the new Bertin
Aerotrain high speed research vehicle. Two
will drive centrifugal fans feeding the lift
and guidance pad and one the propeller.

The Astazou II turboprop powers the Sud
Aviation Marquis, Mitsubishi MU-2 and
Pilatus Turbo-Porter. Type approval at the
ratings quoted below was received on May
29, 1961, after completion of a 150-hour
official type-test.

The shaft-turbine version of the Astazou II
powers the Sud-Aviation Alouette-Astazou
helicopter.

By January 1966, Turboméca had built a
total of 270 Astazou engines of all marks and
had orders for 125 more.

The Astazou has a unique control system
under which the pilot selects the desired rpm,
after which engine power is varied entirely
by use of the propeller-pitch control. When
this control is not moved, the shp is balanced
automatically against airspeed. Overspeed-
ing is prevented by automatic pitch limit
stops.

DIMENSIONS:

Length overall:
Turboprop 75·3 in (1,913 mm)
Shaft turbine 50·1 in (127,3 mm)
Diameter 18·1 in (460 mm)

WEIGHT (Dry):
Turboprop 271 lb (123 kg)
Shaft turbine 269 lb (122 kg)

PERFORMANCE RATINGS (turboprop
with 9·0 in = 228 mm diameter jet-pipe):
T-O 555 ehp (523 shp) at 43,500 rpm
Max cont 503 ehp (475 shp) at 43,500 rpm

PERFORMANCE RATINGS (shaft-turbine
with 10·25 in = 260 mm diameter jet pipe):
T-O 546 ehp (523 shp)
Max cont 494 ehp (475 shp)

SPECIFIC FUEL CONSUMPTION:
At T-O rating:
Turboprop 0·586 lb (266 gr) ehp/hr
Shaft turbine 0·599 lb (271 gr) ehp/hr
At max cont rating:
Turboprop 0·602 lb (273 gr) ehp/hr
Shaft turbine 0·604 lb (274 gr) ehp/hr

TURBOMÉCA ASTAZOU XII

The Astazou XII turboprop is a development of the Astazou II from which it differs
by the addition of a second stage of axial-
flow compression, giving a pressure of 7·8 : 1.
It powers the Short Skyvan and Potez 842
transport aircraft, and is an alternative to
the Astazou II in the Pilatus Turbo-Porter.

DIMENSIONS:
Length with propeller 75·27 in (1,912 mm)

WEIGHTS (Dry):
Engine with standard equipment
281 lb (128 kg)
Complete power plant 395 lb (163 kg)

PERFORMANCE RATINGS:
T-O rating 671 shp (731 eshp) at 43,000 rpm
Max fuel at S/L 631 shp (690 eshp)

FUEL CONSUMPTION:
At T-O rating 0·536 lb (240 gr) eshp/hr
At max cont rating
0·538 lb (241 gr) eshp/hr

GERMANY

Maybach Mercedes-Benz
MAYBACH MERCEDES-BENZ MOTORENBAU GmbH

HEAD OFFICE:
  799 Freidrichshafen, Postfach 298
DIRECTORS:
  Dipl Ing Carl Böttner
  Rolf Breuning
  Dipl Ing Markus von Kienlin

Both the MB 820 and the MD 1081 series of diesel engines have been specially designed for hydrofoils. The 30-ton Supramar PT20 is powered by a single MB 830, the 63·5 ton PT 50 is fitted with twin MB 820s, and the new 150-ton PT 150 has twin MD 1081s.

The new PT 70 will be available with two MB 835s or two MB 655/18 diesels.

MB 820 Bb/Db, PT 20/61

Single-engine set, MB 820 Db/h rated at 1,350 hp, 1,500 rpm. This consists of the diesel engine Vulkan coupling: intermediate shaft; cardan shaft 367/6 1/2; ZF marine reverse-reduction gearbox BW 800 ES (input and output ends on the same side) and propeller shaft.

The engine is electrically started with mechanical control of the engine and electrical gearbox control from the bridge. Cooling is by means of heat exchanger.

PT 50

Twin-engine set comprising 2 × MB 820 Db/h providing 2 × 1,350 hp at 1,500 rpm. This consists of the diesel engines—Vulkan couplings—ZF marine reverse-reduction gearbox BW 800 E (input and output ends on opposite sides)—propeller shafts. Otherwise as type PT 20/61.

MB 820

TYPE: 6 cylinder in-line; 12 and 16 cylinder Vee type, 4-cycle, water cooled.
CYLINDERS: Bore 6·89 in (175 mm). Stroke 8·07 in (205 mm). Swept volume 4·93 litres per cylinder. Compression ratio 16 : 1. Cast iron cylinder liners and individual cylinder heads.
PISTONS: Light metal alloy pistons with three compression rings and two oil control rings. Nitro steel floating gudgeon pins.
CONNECTING RODS: Special steel case hardened connecting rods. Lead-bronze bearings with steel cups; bronze bushes.
CRANKSHAFT: Special steel case hardened. Lead-bronze bearings with steel cups.
CRANKCASE: Upper and lower parts of cast-iron or light-alloy.
VALVE GEAR: Two inlet and two exhaust overhead valves per cylinder, operated through push rods and rocker arms. Two piece camshaft of high grade special steel, located in upper part of crankcase.
FUEL INJECTION: Bosch injectors with one Bosch pump in 6 cylinder engine, and two in 12 cylinder.
TURBOCHARGER: Büchi system, exhaust gas driven, made by Brown Boveri.
FUEL: Diesel fuel having a specific gravity of 0·81 to 0·87 (17°C) with a calorific value of at least 9.800 calories.
LUBRICATION: Pressure feed with two toothed wheel pumps. Oil cooled in heat exchanger.

The MB Db/h 12-cyl four-cycle V-engine, rated at 1,350 hp

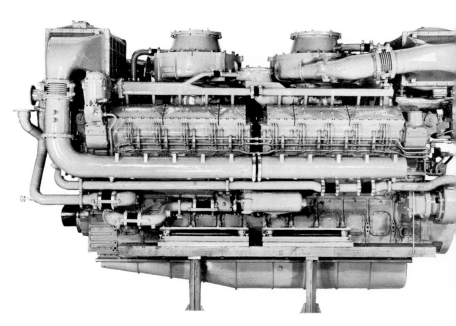

The MD 1081, water-cooled 20 cylinder four-cycle V-engine, rated at 3,440 hp

OLING SYSTEM: Sectional radiator with
mler-Benz centrifugal pump.
ARTING: Bosch electric starter or
pressed air.
UNTING: Two engine bearers, fixed
nting.

SEL ENGINE MD 1081, PT 150DC
vin-engine set 2 × MD 1081
gine output   3,540 hp at 1,790 rpm
tput when lifting 4,080 hp at 1,840 rpm
termittent output) (minutes)
th flange-mounted converter KSUW 40
ardan shaft; ZF marine reverse-reduction
box BW 1200 HS, reinforced type (input
  output ends on the same side) and
eller shaft.
gine and gearbox are pneumatically
trolled from the bridge, with mechanical
rgency control from the engine room.
ge-mounted converted automatically
nging over from multiple-disc clutch
ine speed 600-800 rpm) to converter,
ation, then again operation through
tiple-disc clutch when moving on foils.

Series
atures of the Maybach MD series of high
d diesel engines are the special design of
kshaft and crankcase, and the standard
of cylinder for all models throughout the
re power range. On the crankshaft the
odox two crank webs serving adjoining
nders, with the main bearings between
n, are all completely replaced by a single
e diameter disc around which is fitted a
r type main bearing. These bearings are
nted into individual cross walls in the
piece crankcase, the completely assembl-
crankshaft being inserted through the
t end of the engine, into what appears
e a tunnel, hence the name "tunnel type".
PE: 4 and 6 cylinders in-line; 8, 12 and
ylinders Vee type, 4-cycle, water cooled.
LINDERS: Bore 7·28 in (185 mm). Stroke
 in (200 mm). Swept volume 5·375 litres
cylinder. Wet cylinder liners of cast
. Individual cast iron cylinder heads
central combustion chamber.
TONS: Maybach divided pistons with
e compression rings and two oil control
s, one above and one below fully floating
geon pin.
NECTING RODS: Heat treated steel
lead-bronze precision type bearing and
ze bushes.
NKSHAFT: Induction tempered disc
bed crankshaft with roller bearings.
NKCASE: Cast iron or welded steel,
nel" type.
LVE GEAR: Three inlet and three
aust silichromiun disc valves per cylinder
e seats cast into cylinder head. Gear
el driven cramshaft.

Mayback Mercedes-Benz MD 655/18 water cooled diesel rated at 1,700 hp

The MB 839Bb rated at 2,600 hp at 1,460 rpm

FUEL INJECTION: Maybach L'Orange unit
injector.
TURBOCHARGED: Maybach exhaust tur
bo-charger.
FUEL: Gas oil.

LUBRICATION: Pressure feed with three
gear pumps. Water cooled oil cooling.
COOLING SYSTEM: Pipe radiator with
Maybach centrifugal pump.
STARTING: Electric or compressed air.

AIR CUSHION VEHICLE AND HYDROFOIL POWERPLANTS
C.R.M. / DAVEY PAXMAN: Italy / United Kingdom

ITALY

C.R.M.
C.R.M. FABRICA MOTORI MARINI

HEAD OFFICE:
20121 Via Manzoni, Milan 12
TELEPHONE:
708. 326/327
CABLES:
Cremme

CRM has specialised in building lightweight diesel engines for more than twenty years. The company's engines are used in large numbers of motor torpedo boats, coastal patrol craft and privately-owned motor yachts. Two 1,350 hp CRM 18 D/S diesels are specified for the new Seaflight L. 90 100-120 seat hydrofoil ferry. A single CRM 18 D/2 rated at 800 hp continuous at 1,650 hp is installed in the Raketa 340 hydrofoil operated by Päijäntteen Kantosiipi OY across Lake Päijänteen, Finland.

CRM 18 D/S

TYPE: 18 "W" cylinders, 1,350 hp supercharged diesel with hydraulically-controlled reverse gear.
COMBUSTION SYSTEM: precombustion chamber.

BORE: 5·91 in.
STROKE: 7·09 in.
INDIVIDUAL PISTON DISPLACEMENT: 194,166 cu in.
OVERALL PISTON DISPLACEMENT: 3,459 cu in.
COMPRESSION RATIO: 16·25 : 1.
CYLINDER OVERLOADING: by two turbo charges driven by exhaust gas, and intermediate air cooling.
INJECTION EQUIPMENT: Pumps fitted with variable speed revolution control and pilot injection nozzles.
COOLING: Fresh water.
LUBRICATION: Pressure type by a gear pump.
OIL COOLING: By salt water circulating through a heat exchanger.
STARTING: Electric motor 15 hp 24 volts and 1,000 Watt generator for battery charge or compressed air.
REVERSE GEAR: Bevel crown wheels with hydraulically controlled band brake.

REDUCTION GEAR OR OVERDRI (optional): Spur gear. Reduction ra 0·561-0·640-0·730-0·846. Overdrive ra 1·181.
PROPELLER THRUST BEARINGS: corporated in the reduction gear or overdr Axial thrust 6,620 lb at 1,176 rpm.
WEIGHTS:
Dry engine 3,96
Reverse gear, generator starter 94
Reduction gear 330 lb operation w
longitudinal and transversal angle inclination of up to
OPERATING PERFORMANCE:
Continuous service 1,040 shp at 1,900 r
Intermittent service 1,250 shp at 2,020 r
Maximum hp 1,350 bhp at 2,075 r
SPECIFIC FUEL CONSUMPTION:
At continuous service 0·37 ± 5% lbs/bh
LUBRICANT OIL CONSUMPTION:
At continuous service 0·011 lbs/bh
Recommended fuel fuel oil 8·830 × 0·
Recommended lubricant oil mineral oil type SAE 40

UNITED KINGDOM

Davey, Paxman
DAVEY, PAXMAN & CO LTD (A member of English Electric Diesels Ltd)

HEAD OFFICE AND WORKS:
Colchester, Essex
DIRECTOR:
B. R. Bensly, Managing Director

Specialising in Vee-form engines for over 36 years, Davey, Paxman & Co build a wide range of lightweight four-stroke diesel engines.

The company's Ventura engine is being incorporated in several current designs for hydrofoils and rigid sidewall ACVs. It is available in 6, 8, 12 and 16-cylinder sizes, turbocharged and with or without intercooling.

The Ventura range with powers up to 2,400 bhp, will be extended with the introduction of a Mark 111 version which is now in an advanced stage of development. With ratings up to 3,000 bhp the new engine is designed to provide the power required by large surface skimmer types.

VENTURA (YJ) DIESEL

TYPE: Direct injection 60°, vee-form 6, 8, 12 and 16-cylinder, turbo-charged or turbo-charged and aftercooled four stroke diesel engine.
OUTPUT: 450-2,400 bhp, 1,000-1,600 rev/min.
BORE AND STROKE: 7·75 × 8·5 in (197 × 216 mm).
SWEPT VOLUME (per cylinder): 401 cu in (6·67 litres).
HOUSING: Fabricated high quality steel plate.
CRANKSHAFT AND MAIN BEARINGS: Fully nitrated shaft carried in aluminium tin pre-finished steel-backed main bearings. Engine fully balanced against primary and secondary forces.

Paxman 'Ventura' 16 YJCM 16-cylinder pressure-charged and intercooled diesel engine for the Ro Canadian Navy's FHE hydrofoil built by De Havilland Aircraft of Canada Ltd. This engine provic the hullborne power developing 2,400 bhp for lift-off and 2,000 bhp cruising

CONNECTING RODS: Fork and blade type with steel-backed, lead bronze lined, lead tin flashed bearings.
PISTONS: Conventional aluminium alloy, oil cooled with Alfin bonded insert for top ring. Three compression and two oil control rings (above and below floating gudgeon pin).

CYLINDER HEAD: Cast aluminium of hi grade cast iron carrying four valve dir injection system.

LINERS: Wet type seamless steel tub chrome plated bore and water side surfac honeycombed for surface oil retention.

L INJECTION: External Monobloc ps located below air manifolds. Pump gers and camshaft lubricated from main ne pressure system. Feed and injection p driven from engine drive and gear a; a fuel reservoir and air bleed system d. Injectors of the multi-hole type y fuel into the toroidal cavity in the top iston. Injectors retained by clamp and external to head cover.

ERNOR: Standard hydraulic 'Regulat-Europa' unit with self-contained lubric-g oil system; mechanical, electrical or matic controls. Alternative makes lable.

PRESSURE CHARGING AND INTER-COOLING: Napier water-cooled exhaust-gas-driven turboblowers mounted above engine. Air to water intercooler of Serck manufacture for after-cooled version.

LUBRICATION: Pressure lubrication to all bearing surfaces; separate pressure and cooling pumps. Oil coolers mounted externally and integral with engine. Full flow single or duplex oil filters can be supplied. Centrifugal filters fitted as standard.

FRESH WATER COOLING: Single pump at free end, shaft-driven from drive end gear train. Thermostatic control valve mounted above pump, giving quick warm-up and even temperature control of water and oil circuits.

EXHAUST: Single outlet from turbo-blower(s).

STARTING: Air, electric or hydraulic starting.

FUEL: Gas oil to BS.2869/1967 Class A1 and A2 or equivalent, and certain gas turbine fuels. Other classes of fuel subject to specification being made available.

LUBRICATING OIL: Oils certified to MIL-L-2104B.

OPTIONAL EXTRA EQUIPMENT: Gear-boxes, starting control systems, and all associated engine ancillary equipment necessary for marine applications.

---

ls-Royce Ltd
LS-ROYCE INDUSTRIAL & MARINE AS TURBINE DIVISION

D OFFICE:
sty, Near Coventry, Warwickshire

ECTORS:
F. Saxton (Managing Director)
H. Lindsey
T. Blakey
H. Fletcher
Jubb
V. Cleaver
W. F. Farthing

April 1967 Rolls-Royce Limited formed w division merging the former industrial marine gas turbine activities of Rolls-ce and Bristol Siddeley. The new sion is known as the Industrial and ine Gas Turbine Division of Rolls-Royce. offers a wider range of industrial and ine gas turbines based on aero-engine generators than any other manufacturer e world. It has available for adaptation whole of the gas turbine range being ufactured and under development by Rolls-Royce Aero Engine Division, the tol Engine, and Small Engine Divisions. inised gas turbines at present being luced and developed by the Company ade the Gnome, Proteus, Tyne, Dart and mpus.

ore than 500 of these marine and indus-l engines are in service or have been red for operation around the world and total value of the export orders received to mid-1968 was approximately £19 ion. Thirteen navies have selected the pany's marine gas turbines to power al craft. following the initial orders from Royal Navy in the late 1950s.

DROFOILS: The Boeing PCH High nt is powered by two Proteus gas turbines a single Proteus also powers the Boeing H-2 Tucumcari. A Tyne powers the mman designed Dolphin and PG(H)-1 gstaff.

VERCRAFT: The Gnome powers the C SR.N3, SR.N5 and SR.N6. The teus powers the SR.N4 and the BH.7 and esignated for the BH.8.

RINE DART
PE: Gas turbine, turbo-shaft.
R INTAKE: 15°C axial.
MBUSTION CHAMBERS: Seven.
EL GRADE: Light distillate.
RBINE—ENGINE: Two stage axial flow.

TURBINE—POWER: Single stage.
BEARINGS: Four ball bearings, 2 roller bearings.
JET PIPE: Exhaust duct to suit installation.
ACCESSORY DRIVES: All accessories are self contained.
LUBRICATION SYSTEM: Pressure system of dry sump type. There are separate systems for gas generator and power turbine.
OIL SPECIFICATION: D.E.R.D. 2487.
MOUNTING: Gas generator is carried on cantilever supports above the frame which supports the power turbine.
STARTING: Electric.
DIMENSIONS (Complete Unit):

Length	11 ft (3·3 m)
Width	3 ft 6 in (1·06 m)
Height	3 ft 3 in (0·99 m)
Weight	1,933 lb (876 kg)

PERFORMANCE RATING:

Max	1,750 bhp

SPECIFIC FUEL CONSUMPTION:
0·75 lb/bhp/hr

OIL CONSUMPTION: 1 pt/hr

MARINE GNOME
TYPE: Gas turbine, turboshaft.
AIR INTAKE: Annular. 15°C.
COMBUSTION CHAMBER: Annular.
FUEL GRADE:
D.E.R.D. 2494 Avtur/50 Kerosene.
D.E.R.D. 2482 Avtur/40 Kerosene.
TURBINE: Two-stage axial-flow generator turbine and a single-stage axial-flow free power turbine.
BEARINGS: Compressor rotor has a roller bearing at the front and a ball bearing at the rear. Gas generator turbine is supported at the front by the compressor rear bearings, and at the rear by a roller bearing.

Single stage power turbine is supported by a roller bearing behind the turbine disc and by a ball bearing towards the rear of the turbine shaft.
JET PIPE: Exhaust duct to suit installation.
ACCESSORY DRIVES: Accessory gearbox provides a drive for:—The fuel pump, the hydro-mechanical governor in the flow control unit, the centrifugal fuel filter, the dual tachometer and the engine oil pump.
LUBRICATION SYSTEM: Dry sump.
OIL SPECIFICATION: D.E.R.D. 2487.
MOUNTING: Front: Three pads on the front frame casing, one on top, one on each side. Rear without reduction gearbox, mounting point is the rear flange of the exhaust duct centre-body. With reduction gearbox mounting points are provided by two machined faces on the reduction gearbox.
STARTING: Electric.
DIMENSIONS:

Length	70·8 in (1,800 mm)
Width	12·36 in (314 mm)
Height	20·4 in (518 mm)
Weight (with reduction gearbox)	444 lb (201·4 kg)

PERFORMANCE RATINGS:

Max	1,050 bhp
Cont	900 bhp

SPECIFIC FUEL CONSUMPTION:

Max	0·625 lb (283 gr) bhp/hr
Cont	0·650 lb (295 gr) bhp/hr

OIL CONSUMPTION:

	1·2 pints (0·67 litre)/hr
Power Turbine	1·5 pints (0·84 litres)/hr

MARINE OLYMPUS
Gas generator and single stage power turbine
TYPE: Gas turbine, turbo-jet.
AIR INTAKE: 15°C.
COMBUSTION CHAMBER: Eight.
FUEL GRADE: Diesel fuel B.S.S. 2869 Class A. DEF 2402 or NATO F. 75.
TURBINE (ENGINE): Two stage, each stage driving its own respective compressor—5 stage low pressure or 7 stage high pressure.
TURBINE (POWER): Single stage axial-flow.
BEARINGS: Compressor rotor forward end supported by a roller bearing and rear end by a duplex ball bearing.

The power turbine rotor assembly and mainshaft are supported as a cantilever in two white metal bearings housed in a pedestal.
JET PIPE: Exhaust duct to suit installation.
ACCESSORY DRIVES: Power turbine. Accessories are mounted on the main gearbox which is a separate unit transmitting the turbine's power output to the propeller shaft. These include pressure and scavenge oil pumps, speed signal generator, iso-speedic switch and rev/min indicator.
LUBRICATION SYSTEM: The gas generator has its own integral lubrication system which is supplied with oil from a 27 gal tank. Components in the system are:—A pressure pump, main scavenge pump, four auxiliary scavenge pumps and an oil cooler.

Power Turbine. Bearings are lubricated and cooled by a pressure oil system.
OIL SPECIFICATION: Gas generator. D. Eng R. D. 2487. Power turbine. O.E.P. 69.

AIR CUSHION VEHICLE AND HYDROFOIL POWERPLANTS
ROLLS-ROYCE: United Kingdom

Rolls-Royce Marine Gnome gas turbine installed in a BHC SR.N6 hovercraft

MOUNTING: The mounting structure depends on the customer's requirements for a particular application.
STARTING: Air and electric.
DIMENSIONS:
Gas Generator:

Length	11 ft 9 in (3·6 m)
Width	4 ft 3 in (1·29 m)
Weight	6,500 lb (2·94 kg)

Power Turbine:

Length	12 ft 9 in (3·9 m)
Width	8 ft 0 in (2·4 m)
Height	9 ft 9 in (3 m)

Complete Unit:

Length	22 ft 3 in (6·8 m)
Width	8 ft 0 in (2·4 m)
Height	9 ft 9 in (3 m)
Weight	21 tons

PERFORMANCE RATING:
27,200 bhp
SPECIFIC FUEL CONSUMPTION:
Max   0·49 lb (226 gr) bhp
OIL CONSUMPTION:
Gas Generator:
Max   1·5 pints (0·84 litre)
Power turbine   1·5 pints (0·84 litre)

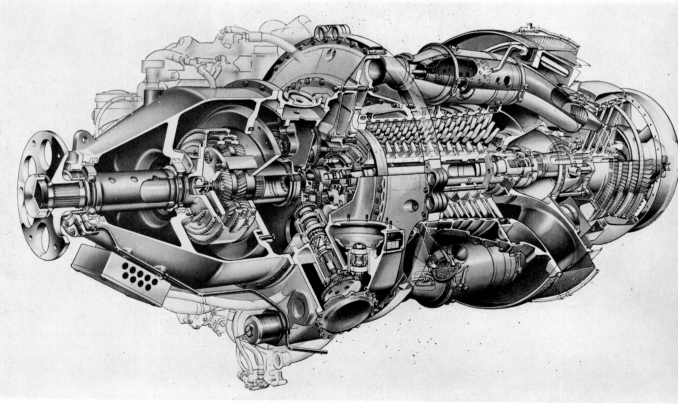

Cutaway of the Marine Proteus

MARINE PROTEUS

TYPE: Gas-turbine, turboshaft.

AIR INTAKE: Annular between the compressor and turbine sections of the engine.

COMBUSTION CHAMBERS: Eight, positioned around the compressor casing.

FUEL GRADE: DEF 2402—Distillate diesel

TURBINE: Four stages coupled in mechanically independent pairs. The first coupled pair drive the compressor, the second pair drive the free power turbine, which drives the output shaft.

BEARINGS: HP end of compressor rotor is carried by roller bearing. The rear end by thrust bearing. Compressor turbine rotor shaft is located by a ball thrust bearing, as the power turbine rotor.

JET PIPE: Exhaust duct to suit installation.

ACCESSORY DRIVES: All accessories are driven by the compressor or power turbine systems. Compressor driven accessories are: compressor tachometer generator, fuel pump and centrifugal oil separator for the breather. The power turbine tachometer generator and governor are driven by the power turbine. The main oil pressure pump and also the main and auxiliary scavenge pumps, are

driven by both the compressor and power turbines through a differential gear.

LUBRICATION SYSTEM: The engine is lubricated by a single gear type pump connected by a differential drive to both the compressor and power turbine systems.

OIL SPECIFICATION: OEP 71. D.E.R.D. 2479/1 or D.E.R.D. 2487 (OX 38).

MOUNTING: Three attachment points comprise two main trunnions, one on each side of the engine close to the diffuser casing and a steady bearing located beneath the engine immediately aft of the air intake.

STARTING: Electric, air or hydraulic.

DIMENSIONS:

Length	113 in	(2,870 mm)
Diameter	42 in	(1,067 mm)
Weight (dry)	3,118 lb	(1,414 kg)

PERFORMANCE RATINGS:

Max	4,250 bhp
Cont	3,600 bhp

SPECIFIC FUEL CONSUMPTION:

0·565 lb (256 gr) bhp/hr

OIL CONSUMPTION:

Average 0·5 pints (0·28 litres)/hr

MARINE TYNE

TYPE: Gas-turbine, turbo-shaft.

AIR INTAKE: 15°C.

COMBUSTION CHAMBERS: Turbo annular containing ten flame tubes.

FUEL GRADE: D.E.R.D. 2482 Avtur 40. D.E.R.D. 2494 Avtur 50.

TURBINE: Three stage low pressure turbine and a single stage high pressure turbine.

BEARINGS: The rotor and reduction gearbox units are mounted on ball and roller bearings.

JET PIPE: Exhaust duct to suit installation.

ACCESSORY DRIVES: Drives for oil and fuel pumps. starter and speed measurement are all contained within the engine.

LUBRICATION SYSTEM: The engine has its own integral oil system.

OIL SPECIFICATION: Aviation turbo oil 35. Aeroshell 750.

MOUNTING: To suit installation requirements.

STARTING: Electric or air.

DIMENSIONS:

Length	86 in	(2,184 mm)
Diameter	48 in	(1,219 mm)
Weight	1,900 lb	(861·8 kg)

PERFORMANCE RATING:

Max	4,500 bhp
Cont	3,600 bhp

SPECIFIC FUEL CONSUMPTION:

Max	0·495 lb (222 gr) bhp/hr
Cont	0·530 lb (240 gr) bhp/hr

OIL CONSUMPTION:

Max	1 pint (0·57 litre/hr)

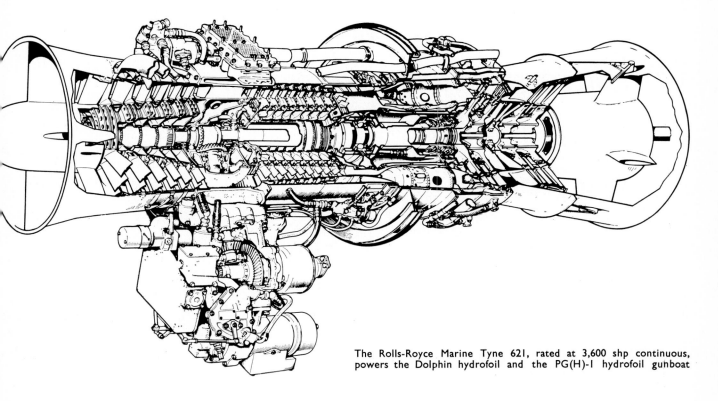

The Rolls-Royce Marine Tyne 621, rated at 3,600 shp continuous, powers the Dolphin hydrofoil and the PG(H)-1 hydrofoil gunboat

THE UNITED STATES OF AMERICA

AiResearch

Airesearch TMP831-401 turbomarine power unit, rated at 400 shp

AiRESEARCH MANUFACTURING COMPANY OF ARIZONA, a division of the Garrett Corporation

EXECUTIVES:

Ivan E. Speer, Vice President and Manager

AiResearch Manufacturing Company, Phoenix, Arizona is the world's largest manufacturer of small gas turbines. Since 1951, AiResearch has produced turbine engines for use in aerospace, commercial, industrial and marine applications. The firm occupies approximately 850,000 sq ft of facilities on 100 acres of land adjoining Phoenix Sky Harbour Airport. Its employees number over 4,000.

Two turbomarine power systems with continuous power ratings of 400 shp and 500 shp have been designed. The 400 shp system, designated the Model TMP831-401, is fully developed and currently available. A 500 shp Model TMP831-501 system is under development.

TMP831-401

COMPRESSOR: Two-stage centrifugal.

TURBINE: Three-stage axial.

RATING: 400 shp continuous.

RATED ROTOR SPEED: 41,730 rpm.

SYSTEM OUTPUT SPEED: Varies linearly with output power from 5,433 rpm at zero hp to 5,240 rpm at 400 hp.

DIRECTION OF ROTATION: CW (facing shaft).

Max. EGT: 980°F.

OUTPUT PAD(S): Shaft.

INLET AREA: 216 sq in (0·135 m²) (9 (229 m) × 24 in (610 mm) rect)

EXHAUST AREA: 11·5 in (292 mm) dia Fuels: ASTM D975 (1D/2D), VV-F- (DF 1/2), MIL-F-1684; ASTM D 1655 (J A-1 and B) and MIL-T-5624 (JP-4, JP- OILS: MIL-L-7808, MIL-L-23699, MIL 16672.

WEIGHT: 1,317 lb (complete packa (597·5 kg).

LENGTH: 76 in (1,932 mm).

WIDTH: 41 in (1,044 mm).

HEIGHT: 38·8 in (986 mm).

OPERATING ENVIRONMENTS: Temp ature —30°F to 130°F. Altitude 1,000 max at 80°F max.

Cummins

CUMMINS ENGINE COMPANY INC

OFFICES:

Cummins Engine Company Inc, International Division, 100 Fifth Street, Columbus, Indiana

Cummins Engine Company Ltd, Coombe House, St Georges Square, Malden Road, New Malden, Surrey

DIRECTORS:

J. I. Miller
E. R. Black
C. R. Boll

J. B. Fisk
H. H. Helm
H. L. Hilman
P. L. Miller
G. W. Newlin
R. B. Stoner
E. D. Tull

The Cummins Engine Company was formed in 1919 in Columbus, Indiana. It produces a wide range of marine diesel engines which are now manufactured and distributed internationally. In addition to five manufacturing plants in the United States the company

also produces diesel engines in nine plant Australia, Germany, India, Japan, Mex and the United Kingdom. All these pla build engines to the same specifications t ensuring interchangeability of parts and same quality standards.

Cummins marine diesels power the Seafli 46 (two VT8N-370-M), the FMC L548D (t VT8-370-M) and the Hovermarine H sidewall hovercraft.

On the latter two VT8-370-Ms, each dera to 320 bhp, supply propulsive power, an single V6-215-M, derated to 185 bhp, dri the lift fans.

AIR CUSHION VEHICLE AND HYDROFOIL POWERPLANTS
CUMMINS / GENERAL ELECTRIC: The United States of America

DEL:	V6-215-M	VT8-370-M
ing (60°F—29·95 In.HG)		
termittent	215 bhp at 3,000 rpm	370 bhp at 3,000 rpm
ontinuous	160 bhp at 2,600 rpm	270 bhp at 2,600 rpm
oe	90°V *Form Diesel*	90°V *Form Diesel*
Cylinders	6	8
e and Stroke	$5\frac{1}{2}$ in × $4\frac{1}{8}$ in	$5\frac{1}{2}$ in × $4\frac{1}{8}$ in
con Displacement	588 cu in (9,635 cm³)	785 cu in (12,863 cm³)
erating Cycle	4	4
oiration	Natural	Turbocharged
cific Fuel Consumption:		
ttermittent	0·409 lb/bhp/hr	0·402 lb/bhp/hr
ontinuous	0·381 lb/bhp/hr	0·394 lb/bhp/hr
Consumption	$\frac{1}{2}$ pint/hr	$\frac{1}{2}$ pint/hr
t Weight (with std accessories)	2,325 lb (1,055 kg)	2,775 lb (1,259 kg)
nensions (with reverse gear):		
ength	5 ft 4 in (1·62 m)	5 ft 9 in (1·75 m)
idth	3 ft 3 in (0·99 m)	3 ft 3 in (0·99 m)
eight	2 ft 9 in (0·83 m)	2 ft $10\frac{1}{2}$ in (0·87 m)

Cummins VT8-370-M marine diesel, rated at 370 bhp at 3,000 rpm

neral:	
arting	Electric
earings	Precision type, steel backed inserts
ccessory drives	By 'V' belts from free end crankshaft or from PTO pulley above flywheel housing.
ibrication	Force feed to all bearings—gear type pump
ounting	Rubber in shear type vibration isolators
1el Specification	Class A gas oil
ıb. Oil Specification	US Military specification MIL-L-2104A
	British Defence specification DEF-2101B

neral Electric
NERAL ELECTRIC COMPANY AIRCRAFT ENGINE GROUP

ADQUARTERS:
)00 Western Avenue, West Lynn, Massachusetts 01905

E PRESIDENT AND GENERAL MANAGER:
erhard Neumann

JNSEL:
W. Sack

he General Electric Company entered the -turbine field in about 1895. Years of neering offort by the late Dr Sanford A. ss produced the aircraft turbosuperrger, successfully tested at height in 1918 I mass-produced on World War II for US iters and bombers.

The company built its first aircraft gas-turbine in 1941, when it began development of Whittle-type turbojets, under an arrangement between the British and American Governments.

Since that time, General Electric has produced a series of successful designs, from the J47, which powered the Boeing B47 and the North American F 86 series of aircraft, to the J79, the first US production engine capable of powering aircraft at Mach 2 speeds.

Three General Electric marinized gas-turbines are now available, the LM100, the LM1500 and the new LM2500. The LM100 powers the Bell SK-5 -6 and -9, and the HS *Victoria* hydrofoil, and the LM1500 powers

the AG(EH)-1 *Plainview* and the HS *Denison* hydrofoils.

LM100

Earliest marine application of the LM100 was in the 24-foot experimental hydrofoil vessel *Sea Wings*, developed for the Bureau of Ships. The craft was propelled at high speeds by a single LM100 gas turbine to explore the validity of supercavitation principles. Later, it was selected as the docking and harbour manoeuvering engine for the Maritime Administration's hydrofoil ship Denison.

The LM100 is an outgrowth of the GET58 helicopter engine, which underwent some six years of development and has amassed more

General Electric LM100 2 shaft, axial flow engine (1,150 shp)

AIR CUSHION VEHICLE AND HYDROFOIL POWERPLANTS
GENERAL ELECTRIC: The United States of America

General Electric LM500 2 shaft axial flow engine, rated at 15,500 shp

than 700,000 hours of operation. Rolls-Royce (previously Bristol Siddeley Engines Ltd) are manufacturing the T58 under licence in the United Kingdom as the Gnome, and this type is also being built under licence in Germany and Japan.

TYPE: 2-shaft, axial flow, simple cycle.

AIR INTAKE: Axial, inlet bellmouth on duct can be customized to installation.

COMBUSTION CHAMBER: Annular.

FUEL: Kerosene, JP-4, JP-5, diesel, natural gas.

TURBINE: 2-stage gasifier, 1-stage power turbine.

JET PIPE: Customized to fit installation.

OIL SPECIFICATION: MIL-L-23699, MIL-L7808F and commercial equivalents.

MOUNTING: At power turbine and compressor front frame.

STARTING: Normally electric.

DIMENSIONS:

Length overall	6 ft 4 in (1·924 m)
Width overall	1 ft 8 in (0·508 m)
Height overall	2 ft 10 in (0·864 m)
Performance rating 1,100 shp at 80° F SLS	
Specific fuel consumption	·61 lb shp/hr
Oil consumption	0·5 pint (0·29 litre)/hr

LM1500

The GE LM1500 turboshaft engine is the result of a company investment in a programme to adapt the J79 jet engine to a free power turbine for commercial and marine use.

On the US Navy's newest aluminium-hulled PG84 class gunboats, an LM1500 gas turbine is used to supplement two regular diesels whenever high speed operation is desired. By combining reduction gears, the LM1500 is used to drive two propellers.

Twin LM1500s supply foilborne propulsive power for the USS *Plainview* (AGEH), and a growth version of the craft will use four engines of this type. A single LM1500 is the main propulsion unit of the HS *Denison* hydrofoil.

TYPE: 2-shaft, axial flow, simple cycle.

AIR INTAKE: Axial, inlet bellmouth on duct can be customized to installation.

COMBUSTION CHAMBER: Canannular.

FUEL GRADE: JP, aviation kerosene, diesel.

TURBINE: 3-stage gas generator, 1-stage power turbine.

JET PIPE: Customized to fit installation.

OIL SPECIFICATION: MIL-L-23699, MIL-

General Electric LM2500 2-shaft simple cycle marine gas turbine derived from the TF 39 h bypass turbofan. Performance rating at 80°F is 25,000 shp

L-7808F and commercial equivalent.

MOUNTING: At power turbine and compressor front frame.

STARTING: Pneumatic, hydraulic, electric.

DIMENSIONS:

Length overall	25 ft 0 in (7·62 m)
Width overall	6 ft 6½ in (2·0 m)
Height overall	6 ft 11 in (2·11 m)
Performance rating	
	15,000 shp at 80°F (27°C)
Specific fuel consumption	
	·51 lb (0·25 kg) shp/hr

LM2500 GAS TURBINE

The LM2500 marine gas turbine is a 2-shaft, simple cycle, high efficiency engine. Derived from the GE TF39 High Bypass Turbofan engine for the US Air Force C-5 transport, the engine incorporates the latest features of compressor, combustor, and turbine design to provide maximum progression in reliability parts life, and time between overhaul. The engine has a fuel rate 25% better than that of current production marine gas turbines. This

is made possible by high compressor press ratio, high turbine inlet temperature improved cycle efficiency.

TYPE: 2-shaft, axial flow, simple cycle

AIR INTAKE: Axial, inlet bellmouth duct can be customized to installation.

COMBUSTION CHAMBER: Annular.

FUEL GRADE: Kerosene, JP4, JP5, Die Navy Multipurpose.

TURBINE: 2-stage gas generator, 6-st power.

JET PIPE: Customized to fit installation.

OIL SPECIFICATION: Synthetic Turb Oil (MIL-L-23699) or equal.

MOUNTING: At power turbine and co pressor front frame.

STARTING: Pneumatic, hydraulic.

DIMENSIONS:

Length	12 ft 6 in (3·8
Width	7 ft 7¼ in (2·3
Height	7 ft 6¼ in (2·6
Performance ratings	25,000 shp at 8
Specific fuel consumption	0·38 lb/hp

tt & Whitney
PRATT & WHITNEY AIRCRAFT VISION OF UNITED AIRCRAFT CORPRATION
AD OFFICE AND WORKS:
ast Hartford, Connecticut 06108
ECTORS:
ernard A. Schmickrath, Division President
ruce M. Torell, Division Executive Vice-President
oss H. Begg, Asst to Division President
ichard T. Baseler, Division Vice-President, Engineering
ames S. Lee, Division Vice-President, Marketing
, J. McNamara, Division Vice-President, Product Support
, Parmakian General Manager, Airport and Overhaul Department)
onald J. Jordan, Engineering Manager
. G. Phinney, Chief, Engineering Operations
illiam Sens, Chief Engineer, Advanced Gas Turbines
. D. Pascal, Chief Engineer, Production
illiam Podolny Chief Engineer, Advanced Power Systems
ugustine De Camillis, Manufacturing Manager

Since 1948, Pratt & Whitney has manufactured a total of more than 30,000 military and commercial gas-turbine engines. These engines had accumulated about 80,000,000 engine flying hours in military and commercial service by the end of 1955.

In the spring of 1961 the Bureau of Ships initiated competitive procurement to develop a 30,000 hp marine gas-turbine, suitable for hydrofoil applications. Subsequently Pratt & Whitney was selected to develop the FT4A engine, utilising the J75 jet engine as the basic generator with the addition of a power turbine. The company's current marinized turbines are the FT4, FT12 and ST6.

The FT4A-2 is the main powerplant of the FHE 400 ASW hydrofoil of the Royal Canadian Navy and the ST-6 provides the craft with foilborne auxiliary power. An ST-6 also powers the Cushioncraft CC-7.

FT4A-2
TYPE: A simple cycle two spool free turbine engine. ALP compressor driven by a two stage turbine and HP compressor driven by a single stage turbine. The burner section has 8 burner cans with duplex fuel burners. The free power turbine has two stages and its shaft extends through the exhaust duct.
AIR INTAKE: Fabricated steel casing with

17 radial struts support the front compressor bearing hot bleed air anti-icing system.
COMBUSTION CHAMBER: 8 burner cans located in an annular arrangement and enclosed in a one piece steel casing. Each burner has six duplex fuel nozzles.
FUEL GRADE: PWA 522, 527, 532, MIL-J5624, MIL-F-16884.
TURBINE (GAS GENERATOR): Steel casing with hollow guide canes. Turbine wheels bolted to the compressor shafts and are supported on ball and roller bearings. A single stage turbine drives the high compressor and a two stage turbine drives the low compressor.
TURBINE (POWER): The engine is available with either (clockwise or counter clockwise) rotation of the power turbine. Desired direction of rotation specified by customer. Free turbine housing is bolted to gas generator turbine housing. The two stage free turbine is straddle mounted and supported on ball and roller bearings. The output shaft is bolted to the hub of the power turbine rotor and extends through the exhaust duct.
LP COMPRESSOR: Eight stage axial flow on inner of two concentric shafts driven by two stage turbine and supported on ball and roller bearings.

Pratt & Whitney ST6A simple cycle free turbine engine, rated at 390 shp continuous

A marinized FT4 is prepared for test at Pratt & Whitney's Willgoos Turbine Testing Laboratory, East Hartford, Connecticut

AIR CUSHION VEHICLE AND HYDROFOIL POWERPLANTS
PRATT & WHITNEY / SOLAR: United States of America

HP COMPRESSOR: Seven stage axial flow on outer hollow shaft driven by single stage turbine and runs on ball and roller bearings.

BEARINGS: Anti-friction ball and roller bearings.

JET PIPE: Exhaust duct—31·5 sq ft (2·9 m²).

ACCESSORY DRIVE: Starter, fluid power pump, tachometer drives for low compressor, high compressor and free turbine. Inching motor drive for low pressure rotor and free turbine.

LUBRICATION SYSTEM: Return system inertial pressure and scavenge pumps.

OIL SPECIFICATION: PWA 521, MIL-L-23699.

MOUNTING: Horizontal-5 degrees nose up or nose down. 15 degrees either side of vertical. Momentary inclination for periods of 10 seconds; pitch 10 degrees nose up or down and up to a 45 degree either side of vertical.

STARTING: Pneumatic or hydraulic.

DIMENSIONS: Length 312 in (7,925 mm), width 76 in (1,930 mm), height 85 in (2,159 mm).

PERFORMANCE RATING: 30,000 shp max intermittent; 25,500 shp max continuous; 21,500 shp normal, all ratings at 3,600 rpm shaft speed and 80°F sea level.

SPECIFIC FUEL CONSUMPTION: 0·49 lb (222 gr) shp/hr max int; 0·50 lb (226 gr) shp/hr max cont; 0·52 lb (235 gr) shp hr normal. Fuel LHV 18,500 Btu/lb.

OIL CONSUMPTION: 0·4 gal (1·82 litres) hr max. Service operation average 0·1 gal (0·45 litres) hr.

FT12A-3
TYPE: A simple cycle free turbine engine. Single spool gas generator. Multi stage compressor driven by a two stage turbine. Burner section has 8 burner cans with downstream injection. The two stage free turbine is directly connected with the output shaft.

AIR INTAKE: Fabricated steel casing with 15 radial struts supporting the front compressor bearing.

COMBUSTION CHAMBER: One piece steel

Pratt & Whitney FT12A-3 simple cycle free turbine, rated at 3,200 shp, max continuous output

case containing eight burner cans with duplex fuel nozzles providing downstream fuel injection.

FUEL GRADE: PWA 522, 527, or 532 MIL-J-5624.

TURBINE (GAS GENERATOR): A two stage turbine drives the compressor. The turbine wheels are bolted to the rotor shaft supported on ball and roller bearings.

TURBINE (POWER): Engine is available with either direction of rotation of the power turbine, clockwise or counter clockwise. Desired direction of rotation specified by customer. Free turbine housing is bolted to gas generator turbine casing. The two stage turbine wheels are overhung mounted on the output shaft and supported on ball and roller bearings.

COMPRESSOR: The axial flow compressor has 9 stages and is contained in a two piece steel casing. The front compressor case is equipped with an automatic bleed valve for starting.

BEARINGS: Anti-friction—ball and roller bearings.

JET PIPE: Exhaust duct 570 sq in (27·9 m²).

Exhaust duct may be positioned in increments of 10 degrees through 260 degrees

ACCESSORY DRIVES: Starter-generator, gas generator and free turbine rotor tachometer, fluid power pump.

LUBRICATION SYSTEM: Rotor system internal pressure and scavenge pumps 45

OIL SPECIFICATION: PWA 521, MIL 23699.

MOUNTING: Horizontal—10 degree nose or nose down. 20 degrees either side vertical. Momentary inclination for period of 11 seconds; pitch 20 degrees nose up down and up to 45 degrees either side vertical.

STARTING: Electric starter generator pneumatic or hydraulic.

DIMENSIONS:

Length	99 in (2,515 mm)
Width	33 in (838 mm)
Height	36 in (914 mm)

PERFORMANCE RATINGS:

Max intermittent	3,770
Max continuous	3,200
Normal all ratings at 9,000 rpm shaft speed	
80°F and sea level	2,500

Solar
Solar Division of International Harvester Company
HEAD OFFICE:

2200 Pacific Highway, San Diego, California, USA

The Saturn gas-turbine has been designed specifically for marine and industrial applications.

CONSTRUCTION: A rugged, simple cycle axial-flow design, it powers the Bell Aerosystems SKMR-1 Hydroskimmer, the US Marine Corp's FMC LVHX2 amphibious hydrofoil, and the Flying Cloud passenger hydrofoil.

SATURN 10MV
TYPE: Simple axial-flow.

DIMENSIONS:

Maximum hp	1,100
RPM at max hp	6,050
Continuous hp	1,020
RPM at cont hp	6,000
SFC at cont hp; LB/HP-HR	0·63

Solar Saturn simple cycle axial flow marine gas-turbine rated at 1,020 hp continuous

Turb Inlet temp at cont hp, °F:	1,450	Width	3·75 ft (1·0
Weight, dry, lb	950 lb (431 kg)	Height	3·66 ft (1·0
Spec weight lb/hp (cont)	0·93	Volume	77 cu ft (2·1 cu
Length	5·6 ft (1·6 m)	Spec volume cu ft/hp (cont)	0·0

THE UNION OF SOVIET SOCIALIST REPUBLICS

IVCHENKO

The design team headed by general designer Ivchenko is based in a factory at Zaporojie in the Ukraine, where all prototypes and pre-production engines bearing the "AI" prefix are developed and built. Ivchenko is assisted by chief designer Lotarev and chief engineer Tichienko. The production director is M. Omeltchenko.

First engine with which Ivchenko was associated officially was the 55 hp AI-4G piston-engine used in the Kamov Ka-10 ultra-light helicopter. He has since progressed via the widely used AI-14 and AI-26 piston-engines, to become one of the Soviet Union's leading designers of gas-turbines engines.

Two AI-20s in de-rated, marinised form and driving two 3-stage waterjets power the Burevestink, the first Soviet gas-turbine hydrofoil to go into series production, and a single AI-24 drives the integrated lift/propulsion system of the Sormovich 50 passenger ACV.

AI-20

Ivchenko's design bureau is responsible for the AI-20 turboprop engine which powers the Antonov An-10, An-12 and Iluyshin Il-18 airliners and the Beriev M-12 Tchaika amphibian.

Six production series of this engine had been built by the Spring of 1966. The first four series, of which manufacture started in 1957 were variants of the basic AI-20 version. They were followed by two major production versions, as follows.

AI-20K. Rated at 3,945 ehp. Used in Il-18V, An-10A and An-12.

AI-20M. Uprated version with T-O rating of 4,190 ehp (4,250 ch e). Used in Il-18D/E, An-10A and An-12.

The AI-20 is a single-spool turboprop, with a 10-stage axial-flow compressor, annular combustion chamber with ten flame tubes, and a three-stage turbine, of which the first two stages are cooled. Planetary reduction gearing, with a ratio of 0·08732 : 1, is mounted forward of the annular air intake. The fixed nozzle contains a central bullet fairing. All engine-driven accessories are mounted on the forward part of the compressor casing, which is of magnesium alloy.

The AI-20 was designed to operate reliably in all temperatures from —60°C to +55°C at heights up to 33,000 ft (10,000 m). It is a constant speed engine, the rotor speed being maintained at 21,300 rpm by automatic variation of propeller pitch. Gas temperature after turbine is 560°C in both current versions. TBO of the AI-20K was 4,000 hours in the Spring of 1966.

WEIGHT (Dry):

AI-20K	2,380 lb (1,080 kg)
AI-20M	2,270 lb (1,030 kg)

PERFORMANCE RATINGS:
Max T-O:

AI-20K	3,945 ehp (4,000 ch e)
AI-20M	4,190 ehp (4,250 ch e)

Cruise rating at 390 mph (630 kmh) at 26,000 ft (8,000 m):

AI-20K	2,220 ehp (2,250 ch e)
AI-20M	2,663 ehp (2,700 ch e)

SPECIFIC FUEL CONSUMPTION:
At cruise rating:

AI-20K	0·472 lb (215 gr) hp/hr
AI-20M	0·434 lb (197 gr) hp/hr

OIL CONSUMPTION:

Normal	1·75 Imp pints (1 litre) hr

AI-24

In general configuration, this single-spool turboprop engine, which powers the An-24 transport aircraft, is very similar to the earlier and larger AI-20. Production in 1960 and the following data refer to engines of the second series, which were in production in the Spring of 1966.

A single marinised version, developing 1,800 shp, drives the integrated lift/propulsion system of the Sormovich 50-passenger ACV.

An annular ram air intake surrounds the cast light alloy casing for the planetary reduction gear, which has a ratio of 0·08255 : 1. The cast magnesium alloy compressor casing carries a row of inlet guide vanes and the compressor stator vanes and provides mountings for the engine-driven accessories. These include fuel, hydraulic and oil pumps, tacho-generator and propeller governor.

The 10-stage axial-flow compressor is driven by a three-stage axial-flow turbine, of which the first two stages are cooled. An annular combustion chamber is used, with eight injectors and two igniters.

The engine is flat-rated to maintain its nominal output to 11,500 ft (3,500 m). TBO was 3,000 hours in the Sprimg of 1966.

DIMENSIONS:

Length overall	95·87 in (2,435 mm)

AMERICAN SURFACE EFFECT SHIP ACTIVITIES

by E. K. LIBERATORE

AMERICAN SURFACE EFFECT SHIP ACTIVITIES

E. K. Liberatore

1. BACKGROUND

Government interest in the large, high speed, ocean going SES dates back to the early 1960's. Both the US Navy and the Maritime Administration (MARAD) recognised the potential of the SES and supported programmes that would lead to the realisation of large ocean going types. Around the time the 22-ton SKMR-1 was procured the Navy considered a 400-500 ton SES as the smallest operational size.

In 1963 Booz-Allen Applied Research, Inc completed a study for MARAD of the large surface effect ship in the Merchant Marine. This study produced three final reports (Reference 1). Design interest was then focused on the sidewall configuration and Booz-Allen produced two follow-on studies (Reference 2). On the basis of these studies MARAD was ready to proceed on the development of a 100-knot, 4-5,000 ton SES. Before this programme made much headway a committee was established to evaluate the feasibility of the large SES. This committee, called SESOC (Surface Effect Ships for Ocean Commerce), produced its final report in 1966 (Reference 3). Essentially its conclusions were to proceed in smaller steps to the large size.

As a result of this activity, the MARAD-Navy Joint SES Project Office (JSESPO) was formed in June, 1966. JSESPO's long range plans include immediate development of a 80-100 knot, less than 100-ton sidewall test craft. This is to be followed by a 500-ton SES in the 1970's. The 4,000-5,000 SES would then be procured in the early 1980's. The 15-ton XR-1A prototype captured air bubble is considered the first of the series leading to the 4-5,000 ton SES.

To mid-1968 JSESPO programmes were directed toward component research and development. Several of their programmes are discussed subsequently. The general significant trends of JSESPO programmes reflect the aerospace origins of project personnel.

(a) A purposeful, goal-orientated series of research and development programmes directed toward scalability of the 4,000-5000 ton, water propelled sidewall SES. The immediate goal is a less than 100-ton test craft prototype.

(b) The application of formal systems engineering concepts to the 100-ton test craft programme, at a level consistent with the programme scope. This included development of a series of general regulatory specifications applicable to the sidewall type SES.

(c) The R/D programmes attacked the major problem areas of propulsion, vehicle dynamics, bubble system, and lift-drag clean up, as well as the general design approach to a prototype test craft.

Another significant trend in the "second generation" of design tools is the imposing of habitability requirements on the design of the cushion lift-fan system. These requirements specify the "g" comfort levels to which the lift system is to be designed.

Always in the foreground of the design approach is the economic justification of the SES. This demonstrates the viability necessary for MARAD support of the SES programme. The commercial SES will move the type of cargo going by air. Therefore the C-5A aircraft becomes a strong competitor. In a recent study, freight rate dollars per ton mile were compared against range. The chemically fueled SES showed freight rates half those of the C-5A in the 2,000 mile range. In the 6,000 mile range the relationship was substantially reversed. However, the nuclear powered SES showed lower rates over the 2-10,000 mile range, obviously increasing with distance. At 6,000 miles the nuclear SES freight rates are about half those of the C-5A. Literally and figuratively, the long range prospects of the SES look very good. The principle activities of JSESPO have been carried along on the basis of this rationale. The discussions that follow primarily concern the Navy-MARAD programmes. However Navy/Marine Corps and Army programmes also are described.

2. JOINT NAVY-MARAD SPONSORED PROGRAMMES

Conceptual and Parametric Design Studies for an SES test craft were undertaken in 1967 by Electric Boat Div. of General Dynamics Corp, Bell Aerosystems, and Aerojet-General. These three programmes for a less than 100-ton test craft served to demonstr feasibility of the sidewall concept. From the project viewpo supporting three companies strengthened the competitive base procurement planned for late 1968. The test craft requireme published in *Jane's Surface Skimmer Systems* 1967-68 Adder include the following:

Max speed	80-100 kr
Range	1,500 nautical m
Turn radius (at all speeds above hump)	8,000 ft (2,432
Speed in 6-ft waves	10 knots above hump sp
Accommodations for crew operations	up to 24 hc

The design requirements explicitly emphasised safety and re bility. The Conceptual and Parametric design follow-on tasks each of the three firms included the development of a set of gramme specifications for the SES test craft as a system. system included a test vehicle and port support facility. C currently JSESPO developed a set of regulatory specifications the SES in the areas of design, handling qualities (through Aerosystems), and structural design criteria. The design specif tions for SES are anologous in content to the "General specificat for Ships of the United States Navy". The applicable p of these design specifications became part of Type or Detail Specif tion of the particular SES under design. This fully develo specification becomes the basis of a hardware contract.

Other follow-on programmes included flexible seal tests sidewall model hydrodynamic tests. These were undertaken Electric Boat Division. The Conceptual and Parametric stu of the three firms were completed in 1968.

In parallel with the Conceptual and Parametric study program JSESPO supported several programmes in the area of propulsi These went to a different group of firms specialising in this fi The programmes in the propulsion area pertain to supercavitat propellers and jet pumps. Some development work has b accomplished under other hydrofoil programmes. However higher speeds (80-100 kt) of the SES create problems requir special treatment. Two types of supercavitating propellers being evaluated. One is the fully submerged type. The othe semi-submerged in which the major portion of the propeller including the hub is out of the water. The intent of this arran ment is to minimize pod drag at high speed. Naval Ship Rese and Development Command (NSRDC) have tested propeller mod of this configuration. The propulsive efficiencies are compare for the semi and fully submerged propeller. In the supercavitat propeller development, Hydronautics has conducted a design st of a variable pitch type. A hardware study of the variable pi propeller was undertaken by Hamilton-Standard.

The water jet programmes consist of the following:

(1) XR-1A jet pump installation with ST-6 turbine. (UAC/Pratt Whitney programme)

(2) Gas turbine—water jet development. (UAC/Pratt Whitney Programme)

(3) Jet pump inlet studies. (Lockheed Programme)

In addition to the above there is 550-ton SES water jet stu conducted by Rocketdyne. This company is utilizing its roc pump technology as background for the task. In the 4,000- size, hydrojet propulsion was studied in 1967 by NSRDC. The w is documented in Reference 4. The hydrojet pump is a stro contender as the propulsion means for large surface effect sh Problem areas include pump cavitation at take off, the design the inlet, and water intake fluctuation in waves. Generally inlet is located in the sidewall and it experiences the same broach as the sidewall does. As with air systems, water boundary la intake improves the overall propulsive efficiency of the water j

Another major problem area covers the dynamics of the S An extensive programme in craft dynamics has been undertal by Aerojet-General. The major areas of investigation consisted

(1) Theoretical analysis of stability and control.

2) Seal design analysis.

3) XR-3 test and evaluation.

An objective of the stability and control analysis is to ascertain the feasibility of designing passive or inherent stability into the SES. This analysis is based on a computer simulation programme. It is expected that a generic mathematical model will be an output of this study. This mathematical model would be developed iteratively through model (tank) testing and full tests of the XR-3. Considering the variety of sidewall possibilities, including seal variations, this can develop into a massive programme.

An objective of the seal programme is to establish the criteria which characterise desirable forward and aft seals. The programme includes testing a series of candidate seals on a "dry rig" simulating sea conditions. A computer response study is part of this task. One of the significant requirements of this computer simulation is the imposing of a ·10g limit on vertical accelerations in continuous operation of the SES. With this philosophy habitability is designed into the system.

A similar seal programme (outside the Aerojet contract) and noted previously was undertaken by Electric Boat Division in conjunction with Goodyear Aircraft. This seal work was narrower in scope and directed toward the specific flexible structure used in the E.B. Sidewall SES.

The intent of the third part of the Aerojet Programme, XR-3 test and evaluation, is to provide quantitative data on craft motions, loads, resistance, and manoeuvrability. Also the XR-3 tests permit a qualitative appraisal of sidewall handling and control characteristics.

Developing the equations of motions for an SES is relatively more complicated than those for an aeroplane. The degrees of freedom are greater and the sea as a forcing function is irregular. Regular "sine wave" seas simplify the problem. Reducing the degrees of freedom to pitch and heave yields a further simplification. In these simplified modes lies the current state of dynamic analysis. Hull-borne ship studies with recent attention being given to stable platforms apparently are in the early stages of modelling. As a result there is no extensive library of ship dynamics in waves to draw from.

As noted in the Background the imposing habitability requirements on the cushion system design is a significant advance in creating an operationally suitable SES. This programme was undertaken in 1968 by Electric Boat Division in conjunction with the Electrodynamics Division, also part of General Dynamics Corp. The study programme addressed itself to three sizes of CAB sidewall SES: 100, 500, and 4,000-ton. The programme included development of a mathematical model and a computer simulation of the SES in waves. Study results included the detailed design and power requirements for the cushion or bubble system. The problem of habitability and its effect on power have been discussed by Cockerell (Reference 5) and Beardsley (Reference 6).

In waves, the SES can behave as a "constant volume" or "constant pressure" vehicle. These are the extremes. High accelerations but relatively low cushion power are associated with a constant volume SES. The reverse is true for a constant pressure system. As the term suggests there is no cushion pressure change and in theory no accelerations transmitted to the hull. In flight and for certain wave forms, wave pumped air within the SES length will increase and decrease its volume cyclically. How the SES responds to this depends on the design. The periodic variation in cushion pressure will be minimized if the excess air is allowed to escape through the hull by one-way venting and instantaneously replaced by the fan. This design approach characterizes a constant pressure low "g" system. If the excess air is not relieved within the cushion it results in periodic over and under pressure on the hull. This produces relatively high periodic accelerations, and a rough ride. The fact the cushion air is somewhat compressible helps reduce the acceleration, but it is not completely compensating.

ACVs built to-date behave more like constant volume than constant pressure systems. This is very likely due to the fact no particular attention was given to this problem and intuitively an air cushion should provide a "soft" ride. It does in calm water but not in waves. In general there is an apparant trade off between a given "g" level and cushion power requirements. For any given flight speed the designer has many choices between low cushion power and relative high "g" to low "g" and high power. It appears that with present, relatively crude analytical and design techniques the "g" levels of present designs can be reduced 50% with small power increases.

Taking a broad look at the SES habitability problem one sees an analogy with the hydrofoil. The constant volume SES responds in a manner similar to the rough riding, surface piercing hydrofoil. The SES design tools directed toward constant pressure parallel those used with the fully submerged foil system. The SES deal with fan characteristics, air flow hull vents, and power, while the hydrofoil deals with automatic stabilization, submerged foils, and controllable flaps.

A JSESPO programme directed towards improving range performance was undertaken by Hydronautics Corporation. This advanced lift drag ratio study has as its goal a substantial improvement in sidewall SES L/D. The programme includes consideration of such advanced techniques as hull lubrication. The work here is a reflection of MARAD interest in an SES that exhibits economic feasibility. Another design parameter with an economic impact is SES ratio of empty to gross weight. JSESPO has not emphasized research in weight reduction. Apparently the ratios given by Bell Aerosystems, Aerojet, and Electric Boat Division in their Conceptual and Parametric Studies were acceptable from the economic viewpoint. Two other parameters related to operating economics are the engine SFC and SES propulsive efficiency. At present and discounting nuclear propulsion, improvements in these parameters is relatively costly in relation to the potential gains by improving L/D.

As noted in the Background, JSESPO planned for procurement of a prototype test craft of under 100 tons. The design competition open to Bell Aerosystems, Aerojet, and Electric Boat Division was under way in mid-1968 with the contract award to be made late that year. In conjunction with this plan, a test site study was given to Booz-Allen. This task is a survey of various areas of the US where a suitable SES test base can be established.

There are two programmes in what may be considered the operational area:

(1) Military Requirements for 100-500 ton SES.

(2) Economic Opportunity Study.

The first programme is a mission-orientated study undertaken by Booz-Allen. The Economic Opportunity Study undertaken by Stanford Research Institute apparently is a refinement and fresh look at the Booz-Allen studies of the early 1960's. The immediate objectives of the economic study are to identify the MARAD cargo trade areas or routes suitable for SES operations and to evaluate their operational and economic feasibility on these routes. The study is to detail where in the commercial transportation spectrum between ships and aircraft is the domain of the SES. The emphasis is on operational characteristics, support requirements, investment requirements, operating costs, revenues, and profitability. A broad range of configurations are covered including ACV's, ram wings, wings in ground effect, and other high speed types. The MARAD trade routes for study are separated into short range, medium range, and trans-ocean. Short and medium ranges cover routes within the Great Lakes and along the US coasts between the US and Alaska and among the Hawaiian Islands. They also include routes from the US to nearby islands and selected ports in Canada and Mexico.

Identifying trade areas and SES configurations serve as starting points for the economic study. These are followed by an analysis of the cargo potential of the routes. Once a transportation system is postulated, including patterns of operation and schedules, the system support can be determined. Various SES systems are evaluated within this framework. Operational and economic feasibility then become study outputs. A part of this programme compares the SES with the C-5A.

In mid-1968 a design criteria study for ocean going SES was undertaken by Bell Aerosystems. This programme represents a broad look at the 80-100 knot SES, exploring the upper range of sizes for chemical and nuclear fueled SES in the 1957 time frame. The programme studies the interaction of performance and design and their effect on the parameters that measure economic efficiency. These parameters include lift drag ratio, ratio of empty to gross weight, chemically fueled engine SFC, propulsion efficiency and nuclear powerplant weights per horsepower. The payload-range matrix for the study is 1,100 tons for 1,000 to 9,000 statute miles and 500 tons for 3,000 statute miles. Operating cost studies are conducted using optimum designs in ship fleet sizes of 10, 50, 300, and 500.

The preceding discussions summarise the joint Navy-MARAD sponsored studies. As noted previously, the biggest programme scheduled for contracting in late 1968 is the procurement of a less than 100 ton test craft system including one test craft and a port

AMERICAN SES ACTIVITIES

support facility. This programme includes a comprehensive test and evaluation phase. Essentially full scale data will be collected in the areas of propulsion, performance, structural loads, and craft dynamics. The programmes undertaken in 1967 and 1968 provide a solid engineering background for the evaluation of the design and operational test data to be collected.

3. OTHER PROGRAMMES

There are other programmes in the US which include Navy, Marine Corps, and Army activities.

Navy procurement and employment of three Bell SK-5s in Vietnam in 1966 has been well-publicised. Of interest is the fact the Army then evaluated the SK-5s toward the end of their tour of duty. The favourable evaluation led to the 1968 Army purchase of armoured SK-5s. These also were deployed in Vietnam.

An independent Navy study programme to a Philadelphia concern is to investigate the operational design features of a nuclear powered aircraft carrier. This study was under way in 1968.

Two programmes directed toward Marine Corps requirements are:
(1) USN Assault Craft Design Study.
(2) Riverine Warfare ACV Design Study.

The assault craft study, completed in 1967, was undertaken through Gibbs and Cox. The ACV study was part of a larger programme to provide assault craft characteristics to a computer study conducted by Stanford Research Institute. This SRI study is to investigate for the assault mission: ACVs, the hydrokeel, and the hydrofoil as replacements for current hullborne amphibious types. The ACVs studied had payloads from about 4 to 190 tons. This runs the payload gamut from the current LARC-5 amphibian to the LCU landing craft. Companies that participated in this programme include Electric Boat and Quincy Divisions of General Dynamics, Bell Aerosystems, Atlantic Hydrofoils, and Aerojet-General. The lower range (4-5 tons) represents one of the most difficult design problems for any vehicle. It is to be amphibious and operate on a highway, which limits its dimensions. LARC type amphibians are slow in the water and vulnerable in the transition to the beach. The shift here is from propellers to wheels. There can be a dead zone where the beach is too soft for wheels and propellers are ineffective. Amphibious hydrofoil types are mechanically complicated and must stop at the shore to retract their foils and extend their wheels. The best current transition vehicle is the tracked LTV series. Tracks provide positive traction at the beach but they are slow in the water and slow and noisy on land. However the LTV is a basic military amphibian. The ACV provides high speed over water and across the beach. The complexity develops when the wheeled, highway operation requirement is imposed.

The riverine warfare design studies were undertaken in 1968 by Bell Aerosystems, Electric Boat Division, and Aerojet-General. The mission requirements are for a utility river warfare boat.

Although there is no active programme in the area, there is a group within the Navy who advocate development of the high density SES. This design approach is the conventional displacement ship utilising the air cushion principle for modest speed increases up to around 50 knots. In 1966 Electric Boat Division also investigated the concept and conducted tank tests with a catamaran hull. This programme was in conjunction with their FDL ship studies. A particular requirement was to unload a ship containing about 1,000 vehicles plus supplies in 20 hours. The air bubble catamaran would permit beaching the ship, thereby eliminating waterborne lighterage in heavy seas. The concept was too advanced for the FDL Contract Definition programme and work was transferred to the SES project office at Electric Boat. Due to the 80-100 kt speed interest the catamaran hulls became thinner and the sidewall SES overshadowed the other programme. A study of the buoyant sidewall (or catamaran) hull with water jet propulsion is discussed in Reference 4. The MARAD view of the 50-knot concept is apparently not favourable. From the economic viewpoint 80-100 kt is preferable.

4. CONCLUDING REMARKS

A significant distinction to be made in following joint Navy-MARAD programmes is the basic difference in objectives. The Navy, as a military arm, is primarily mission-oriented. Once a mission requirement is defined the system providing the least life cycle cost would be the most cost effective. Thus any new concept, as the SES, enhancing mission capabilities is a candidate for development.

MARAD as a commercial arm is primarily concerned with operating economics and developments leading to its improvement. Any new system that is competitive or superior in such terms as freight rate in cents per ton mile becomes a candidate for development.

Joint funding of an SES programme therefore imposes conditio on developments, military mission effectiveness, and commerc operating economies. This combination is unusual in the devel ment of transportation vehicles. Usually they are sequential following the military then the commercial route. The helicop programmes in the US are an example of the latter. This vehi is still in the military circuit.

Fortunately the SES is equal to the task. More than one stu has shown the potential of the SES in Naval applications. Similar in commerce the concepts of roll on-roll off cargo, high ocean tran time, and high turn around time are natural elements of the nucle powered ocean going SES. Compared with existing shipping t overall time from the shipper to receiver is reduced substantial The shipper at present must contend with delays at the terminal transfer of cargo. The ship operator lives with the fact more ti is spent in port than at sea. The latter is one reason it is diffic to sell speed to a displacement hull ship operator. But the S does not compete commercially with the surface vessel. The natu SES cargo consists of non-bulk items such as consumer goo packaged or mobile machinery and mechanical parts, perisha foods, and miscellaneous high density items.

Comparative studies such as these are essential but they do tell the whole story. To day the SES is often judged not on own terms but on those of the aeroplane. On its own terms, t commercial SES can and will open up an entirely new market t is non-existent to-day. It will create the era of global mass tra portation. The nuclear powered SES is a natural link in the roll roll-off system of cargo and auto ferry movement across the ocea As a private passenger auto-ferry it serves as the ocean highw moving travellers faster across the ocean than their cars could ta them the same distance under their own power. The convenier of taking a car and family on a trans-ocean trip requiring less th 24 hours will open up this new market in global travel. There nothing inherent in the system that precludes a low fare. C hundred C-5A's will never equal the task of one 15,000-ton SES. T social impact of such a mass intermingling of societies will acco plish more in solving the world's big problems than any ot single activity. On its own terms the SES will not only hold own but lead the way in global mass travel and in the mass mo ment of cargo.

5. REFERENCES

1. *The Surface Effect Ship in the American Merchant Mari* Booz-Allen Applied Research, Inc.
   Final Reports—January, 1964—Contract MA-3232.
   PART I —An Economic Feasibility Study of the 100-t MARAD SES (Columbia).
   PART II —The Technical and Economic Feasibility Study a Nuclear Powered Surface Effect Ship.
   PART III—Comparative Performance and Cost Characterist of Four Types of Surface Effect Ships.
2. Booz-Allen Applied Research, Inc.
   Follow-on—MARAD Contract MA-3742.
   PART IV —A Comparative Study of the Economic Feasibil of Two Sidewall Concepts with Other Surf Effect Ships. (March, 1965).
   PART V —An Analysis of the Economic Potential of t Captured Air Bubble SES in the Future Tra oceanic Competitive Environment, Compared w Cargo Aircraft and Displacement Ships. (July, 1965).
3. *Surface Effect Ships for Ocean Commerce (SESOC).*
   Final Report on a study of Technology Problems by the SESO Advisory Committee.
   Washington, DC—US Government Printing Office—Februar 1966.
4. Garrett, J.
   Preliminary Design of Water-Jet Propulsion Systems for 4,00 ton Captured Air Bubble (CAB) Ship.
   Report 41/67—March, 1967—Marine Engineering Laborator Naval Ship Research and Development Command.
5. Cockerell on Seaworthiness and Economics.
   Flight International Supplement—19 October, 1967.
6. Beardsley, M. W.
   Wave Pumping and Its Effects on the Design and Operation Air Cushion Ships.
   Report 48/67—March, 1967—Marine Engineering Laborator Naval Ship Research and Development Command.

SAFETY, RELIABILITY AND MAINTAINABILITY OF SUPRAMAR COMMERCIAL HYDROFOIL BOATS

by BARON HANNS VON SCHERTEL

SAFETY, RELIABILITY AND MAINTAINABILITY OF SUPRAMAR COMMERCIAL HYDROFOIL BOATS

by

BARON HANNS VON SCHERTEL
SUPRAMAR LTD., LUCERNE

INTRODUCTION

Hydrofoil boats are a comparatively new means of transportation. With their arrival a new era in short distance water communications began. For the first time in the history of transportation a waterborne vehicle was capable of competing successfully with fast land vehicles wherever such competition was geographically possible. Hydrofoil boats can also compete in profit and even in journey time with short distance airliners because they operate from place-to-place, rather than from airport-to-airport.

However, a rapid passenger service is only justified if the timetable can be strictly adhered to. Frequent long delays would destroy the advantage over slower communications and many passengers would, no doubt, turn to the shipping lines which guarantee punctual arrival. This illustrates the importance of safety and reliability of operation for rapid means of transportation.

It is obvious that in the case of a long distance service in unprotected waters profitable operation can only be expected if the vessel has sufficient riding comfort. But the system employed for obtaining smooth performance in rough seas should be of simple design and reliable. Experience has shown that sensitive high cost foil systems, requiring specialist engineers for maintenance, are of little appeal to a commercial operator, however impressive the sea performance may be, because he will fail to get an adequate return on his investment.

Figure 2. The 63 ton PT 50, seating 130 passengers

COMMERCIAL HYDROFOILS IN THE PAST DECADE

Before we investigate how the requirements for safety, reliability and maintainability are met by the hydrofoils operating in passenger service at present, let us briefly review the developments of commercial hydrofoils in the past decade.

The first regular public hydrofoil serv in the world was inaugurated in 1953 Supramar Ltd., on Lake Maggiore in north Italy. With experience gained from t service and with the hydrodynamic a technical knowledge in hydrofoil constr tion gathered since prewar times, the co pany was in the position to plan larger a more economical passenger vessels. 7 recognition that complicated devices red reliability and require increased maintenar which affects profits, led to the decis to use only simple components with prov reliability and durability. This policy l contributed towards having hydrofoil cr accepted as a commercial means of passen transportation.

If we disregard the Russian governme operated craft, no other type of hydrof could be used profitably up to the prese on public passenger lines.

The first foilborne passenger-carrying cr to be approved by classification societ for coastal service, was a Supramar desig 30 ton craft, the PT 20, built in the Ro riquez Shipyard (Fig. 1).

After successful and profitable operatic with this boat, a 63 ton vessel, the PT (Fig. 2) was constructed in 1958, to be us on off-shore routes. The machinery this 91 ft boat consists of two of the sar diesel units as used in the smaller typ and seating is provided for 130 passenge

Figure 1. The PT 20, first passenger carrying hydrofoil to be approved by classification societies for coastal services

June 1968, a third type was added to ⎟fleet, the PT 150, the world's largest ⎟⸱oing passenger hydrofoil and first to ⎟⸱y cars over long distances. The prototype, ⎟"Expressan" is now plying between ⎟⸱den and Denmark and can accommodate ⎟⸱ passengers or 8 cars and 150 passengers ⎟⸱. 3). This ship is provided with the ⎟⸱st comprehensive safety equipment ever ⎟⸱d for a hydrofoil, as we shall see later. ⎟⸱uring operation these vessels are being ⎟⸱stantly improved in line with the results ⎟⸱ day-to-day endurance tests, thus over- ⎟⸱ming development troubles successfully. ⎟⸱Iore than one hundred craft of Supramar ⎟⸱⸱ign have been built. They have a total ⎟⸱ting capacity of over 8,000 passengers ⎟⸱l are operating throughout the world. ⎟⸱ey cover an accumulated daily distance ⎟⸱ about 22,000 nautical miles, which is the ⎟⸱iivalent to a daily circle around the ⎟⸱rld. The total number of passengers ⎟⸱rried to date is estimated to be 35 ⎟⸱llion persons, and the total distance ⎟⸱velled by all passenger craft more than ⎟⸱ million nautical miles.

Figure 3. The prototype PT 150 Expressan passenger/car ferry, now operating between Sweden and Denmark

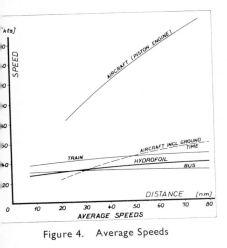

Figure 4. Average Speeds

To illustrate why hydrofoils can compete ⸱uccessfully with transportation by train, ⸱ar, bus and aeroplane, a comparison of speed ⸱nd fares has been made. Figure 4 shows ⸱hat the mean speeds of land vehicles come ⸱ery close to that of the hydrofoil which ⸱enerally has in straight course a shorter ⸱oute; and that also the total air trip speed ⸱f a short-haul domestic liner is not greatly ⸱uperior if ground travelling time to and ⸱rom the airport is added which, today, ⸱uns up to about 70% of the total elapsed ⸱ime. Figure 5 shows that only the bus ⸱ares are lower than those of the hydrofoil.

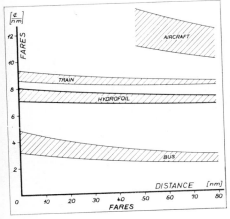

Figure 5. Fares Chart

The very extensive experience obtained through the operation of Supramar craft has enabled the company to analyse and discuss in detail the safety reliability and maintainability of these craft.

SAFETY OF THE PASSENGER-CARRYING HYDROFOIL

Our first consideration is the operational safety of the passenger-carrying hydrofoil. Fourteen years of regular passenger service have shown that the performance is safer than most means of transportation. Indeed in about one billion passenger miles no life has been lost, and only in very few cases have passengers sustained slight injuries when foils hit rocks or in one instance a large buoy. According to statistics as represented in Figure 6, 1 fatal accident happens in trains, 2 in buses, 6 in airlines and 27 in motor cars in the same passenger-mile range.

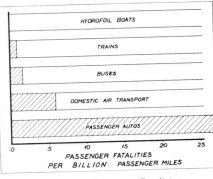

Figure 6. Passenger Fatalities

The exceptionally good, fatality free performance of the hydrofoil boat must be attributed to the following performance characteristics:

The Supramar boats are provided with surface-piercing front foils which are distinguished by their simplicity of construction and inherent stability. These foils have a higher static and dynamic transverse stability in flying condition than conventional ships. In addition, they provide a strong damping effect in waves. In hullborne

condition at low speeds the stability is again greater, due to the foil weight below the hull, as compared with ordinary ships. The low centre of gravity in floating condition combined with the motion damping action of the foils provides an important safety factor. Indeed, not one hydrofoil craft of this type has ever capsized.

By the 1950s the prototype of the smaller PT 20 had already proved the sea-keeping qualities of the 68 foot vessel. Forced down by a severe storm off the coast of Greece, it was possible for her to continue in sea waves in the order of 13 ft and a speed of 15 knots. At a later date, a PT 20 came into the tail of a hurricane in the Caribbean with very long waves of up to 16 ft in height and was able to remain foilborne. These examples show that a commercial hydrofoil is not endangered if she meets by accident a sea state which has not been foreseen.

The distance required for a complete stop from full speed is in the order of 500 ft. The inherently good stopping ability in addition to the rapid response to rudder deflections ensures adequate manoeuvrability at high speed. The turning radius of the boat is approx. 300 ft when speed is reduced to below 30 knots.

It is often believed that floating debris offers a considerable danger. Experience has, however, shown that even quite large pieces of driftwood are either broken or tossed aside by the foils. It appears that the kinetic energy of the heavy steel foils is sufficient for an uneventful outcome for such collisions. Scale model tests in the Berlin towing tank confirmed that the decelerations of 1 g for 1/10 sec are too short to be dangerous and that after the collision the hull always comes down onto the water in an essentially horizontal position.

We shall now see to what extent safety precautions are applied on hydrofoil craft.

Commercial hydrofoils meet all passenger protection safety regulations set up by the shipping authorities. If a boat is serving on international routes also, the requirements of SOLAS convention are observed. The hull is divided into several compart-

Figure 7.   Bow foil of PT 20 swings backward if the craft is grounded or hits a heavy obstacle

ments so that buoyancy is ensured even when two neighbouring compartments are flooded. The life saving equipment on board is made up by life jackets, belts and rafts. In the new PT 150 car ferry (Fig. 10) for instance, fire protection includes an A 60 insulation in both engine room and car deck, fire-fighting plant with two fire pumps, 2 powder extinguishers in every room and an automatic sprinkler installation with its separate pump. An automatic starting emergency power station with a power output of 75% of the normal electric supply is provided on deck to ensure operation in all eventualities. Navigational aids are duplicated with all wiring arrangements. A total additional weight of 13·5 tons is added in the interests of passenger's safety. This weight increase corresponds to a carrying capacity loss of more than 140 passengers.

RELIABILITY AND SAFETY OF FOILS, HULL STRUCTURE AND PROPULSION SYSTEM

We shall now consider reliability and safety of the foil system, hull structure and propulsion plant.

The first stage of development revealed that the foil system is not so vulnerable as was initially suspected. This has been demonstrated several times involuntarily. Due to a wrong gear shifting of an unskilled pilot a PT 20 prototype crashed into an iron jetty with the outer section of the front foil. The jetty was quite badly bent whereas the boat suffered only buckling of the hull plating in the vicinity of the foil attachment, and service was continued for a month before she underwent routine repairs. Another hydrofoil cut up the sidewall of a cement carrying wooden barque of about 150 tons displacement in a collision. The sinking barque was beached, but the hydrofoil continued service after inspection.

In cases of grounding or hitting heavy obstacles, the bow foil adjusting lever of the PT20, which is attached to the foil supporting

tube, first bends and absorbs part of the shock energy before breaking. The foil system then swings backwards on the bearings of the supporting tubes (Fig. 7). On the PT 50, the bolts which fasten the front foil system to the hull shear off and the foil separates. In both cases the hull suffered no damage. In only one incident, in bad weather conditions, when a captain went off course in dangerous waters, were both foils so heavily damaged that repairs were exceedingly difficult. The picture shows the bow foil after the accident (Fig. 8). The rear foil detached entirely from the transom but the hull remained watertight. No passenger came to grief. The latter is an example of the good protection the foils give to the hull. It shows that the passengers' safety has not been in any way impaired through their use. A conventional boat would have suffered extensive hull damage and would probably have sunk.

The specific load factors of foils w determined over long operating peri and by aid of load measurements. In f foil failures have never been experien when the periodical inspection inclu welding of the small cracks which may oc occasionally. In this respect it must noted that the surface piercing foil sys provides an additional safety factor wh is not considered in stress analysis. For front foil represents a multiple indetermin system in which stress displacements t place from temporarily overloaded portions to less stressed parts.

With regard to the hull, it is very of believed that it requires thicker plating th conventional ships, because of the bend moments to which the hull is exposed w being sustained by two foils separated considerable distance. This is not tr The thickness of the plating is determined the local stress imposed by wave imp on the bottom which exceeds the bend stress. However, the plating at the bott must not be as thick as that required surface craft due to the described dampen effect of the foils.

A safety factor of 1·5 against calcula wave impact stress is introduced in the design. With this safety assumption o once was damage experienced in a stro gale. The boat involved was the PT Condor I, which is plying between the Chan Islands under definitely too heavy sea c ditions. The skin and several frames of bow part section were pushed in. Than to the deformability of the aluminium al used, the hull remained watertight as other cases when the hull parts were invol in collisions. In all cases when commerc hydrofoils have suffered hull damage, th have safely reached harbour.

When considering reliable operation propulsion plant is of prime concern. S ramar hydrofoil ferries are powered Maybach Mercedes-Benz diesel engin which underwent severe endurance test in Trans European Express trains. W the experience obtained in rail traction a marine service, safety of operation cou be so much improved that motors and ge are now capable of achieving at least 10,0

Figure 8.   Bow foil of the PT 50 after grounding in dangerous waters

Figure 9. Inclined shaft transmission on a Supramar hydrofoil

riding comfort in comparison with the conventional PT 50 in a seaway.

Regarding the reliability of the air feed lift control system, experience shows that the air outlets at the foil for the air supply are never blocked by soiling due to the prevailing suction and can therefore be regarded as fail-safe. The structural simplicity of the part-air-stabilized craft and the stabilization unit, which does not need a power supply, ensures a high degree of operational safety. One such unit is provided for each foil half, and each is capable of maintaining stability on its own. In this way the reliability of the system is further increased. In fact, the new stabilization of the "Expressan" (Figure 10) worked faultlessly from the first trial run until the vessel was put out of service at the end of the 1968 season. In the improbable event of a simultaneous failure of both stabilization units, the boat can still continue the trip at decreased flying height, with however, somewhat reduced seakeeping capability. This is an important advantage over craft with fully submerged foils which

rs between overhauls. Marine gas ines, on the other hand, have offered ⁓ a fraction of this life until now so that a seasonal service of 3-4,000 hours, money had to be spent for a spare turbine in ition to the high initial costs of the inal installation. This explains why PT 150 is also provided with diesel engines. ut with the steady progress in gas turbine elopment we can envisage that the time ear when turbine driven hydrofoils can pete profitably with diesel propulsion. here are three main systems to transmit ver to the thrust generating device.

he inclined shaft as transmission between tor and propeller (Figure 9) is not an ideal ation, particularly because it sets limits the hull clearance with regard to sea aviour. But again, after evaluating the ses of fractures on a dozen shafts, this smission has proved to offer greatest ty at lowest costs. The double bevel r transmission is technically difficult and not been sufficiently tested for endurance. satisfactory water jet propulsion has y been achieved recently by the Boeing npany, though its efficiency is about % lower than that of propellers. Both se solutions reduce, however, the economy a hydrofoil service due to the initial costs ich are higher than that of inclined shaft pulsion. The high speed propellers had the first years a rather short life—they re either destroyed by cavitation erosion damaged by floating debris. By placing propellers behind the rear foil and apply-careful design methods the life of the pellers could be increased up to 4,000 irs.

GULARITY OF PASSENGER ERVICE

he regularity of passenger hydrofoil vices, as a measure of their reliability, can ly be assessed from the information made ailable by operators. The percentage of e of scheduled service in well organized es, which operate under normal seaway ditions, is 96-98%. Only 1-2% of the lures are caused by mechanical mishaps d the rest by bad weather.

Figure 10. Stability of the PT 150 is maintained jointly by the surface piercing bow foil and the air stabilised rear foil

RELIABILITY OF AIR-STABILIZED CRAFT

Supramar has designed two air-stabilized craft which have both been built at the Westermoen Shipyard in Norway. These craft are provided with a dihedral surface piercing bow foil and a fully submerged rear foil. Stability is maintained jointly by the inherent stability of the front foil and air stabilization which causes a change of lift on the rear foil, in a restoring sense, when the boat is leaving her normal position in a seaway, thus reducing roll and pitch angles. Lift variation is produced by the Schertel-Supramar-System by the admittance of air drawn from the free atmosphere into the suction areas of the foil, the quantity of air being automatically controlled. A craft with this system, which is rather simple in its conception, can be designated as "partly stabilized".

In 1966 an air-stabilized PT 50 underwent successful trials and proved to have superior

in the event of a failure can only proceed in a displacement condition.

MAINTENANCE AND MAINTAINABILITY

The Supramar foil system requires only modest maintenance and this is more or less limited to cleaning, smooth-finishing, and corrosion protection measures. This is a routine job and has to be done at intervals of a fortnight to 3 months, depending on sea conditions and the marine growth development in the operating area. Because of the sturdiness and simplicity of the structure, maintenance can be further reduced by devoting special attention to the selection of materials with reciprocal low potential differences to avoid electrolytic corrosion. The use of non-corrosive steel for the foils is another means of reducing maintenance.

During maintenance the ship is either drawn onto a slip, raised by a crane, or she is tended by divers. Maintainability is simplified considerably when the foils are retractable. Foil retraction is acceptable as an additional technical mechanism in the case of fully submerged foils, whereas for surface piercing foils the additional costs resulting from retractability are in most cases not compensated by the advantage of easier cleaning. Therefore, Supramar applies retractable foil systems only where necessary, such as operation in shallow waters.

The danger of corrosion of light metal hulls cannot be excluded. However, if care is taken to avoid strong electrolytic potentials between plates, rivets, interior components and steel foils, then the useful life of the bottom aluminium plates alloyed with less than 5% magnesium has reached up to 8 years before replacing. This presupposes that bottom painting is done every 3 to 4 months.

Between major overhauls, engine and gear are subject to routine maintenance on board. At the request of the surveying authorities the engine is opened up every year for random inspection of one piston rod bearing.

To maintain these vessels, including repairs, cleaning and painting, some 1,800 man-hours are required on an average each year. If we assume that each craft has an annual utilisation of 2,500 hours, then maintenance hours are in the ratio of 70 to 100 operating hours which is reasonably low as compared, for instance, with the competing helicopter, where we have to allow 400-600 maintenance hours for every 100 operating hours. The maintenance costs of a hydrofoil amount to 12-15% of the total operating costs against 18-19% for an airplane.

RELIABILITY AND SAFETY OF FUTURE HYDROFOIL BOATS

Finally, let us try to visualise the reliability and safety which can be expected of future hydrofoils. The seagoing hydrofoil of the second generation must inevitably be of more sophisticated design to meet modern requirements for better riding comfort in a seaway, and increased complexity poses new problems for operational safety. However, when speaking of the future, only craft for open sea service are generally considered and it is not realized that the demand for foilborne transportation in inland waters and protected sea areas will continue to expand. Here the hydrofoil of tomorrow will be basically the same as today and only its speed, safety and reliability will increase in the course improved technology.

It is believed that in future there will be seagoing types, the partly and the fstabilized craft. The first type which have already described will be for off-sl service and is an intermediate low solution, since it is a cross between ves with rigid surface piercing and fully subm ed controlled foil systems. Sea performa of the first comes close to that of the la but its structural sturdiness, simplicity ease of handling provide a higher ability and economy. However, the fu hydrofoil for severe sea conditions will, doubt, have fully submerged controlled f although many technical difficulties involved which are liable to impair profit ity and safety of operation. Problems a from the required large hull clearance lea to intricate propulsion systems and from foil lift control which must be comple fail-safe and easy to maintain. The air-system for controlling fully submerged f could bring second generation hydr designs closer to the requirements of econ and reliability.

GLOSSARY OF AIR CUSHION VEHICLE AND HYDROFOIL TERMS

GLOSSARY OF ACV AND HYDROFOIL TERMS

abeam. Another craft or object seen at the side or beam.

ACV. Air cushion vehicle.

aeration. See **air entry.**

aeroglisseur, (French, air-glider). Name given to range of passenger-carrying amphibious ACVs designed in France by Société Bertin & Cie in conjunction with Société D'Études et de Développement des Aéroglisseurs Marins (SEDAM). The name **Aerobac** is given to mixed passenger/car ferries and freighters designed by Bertin and SEDAM.

aeroplane foil system. Foil arrangement in which the main foil is located forward of the centre of gravity, to support 75% to 85% of the load, and the auxiliary foil, supporting the remainder, is located aft as a tail assembly.

Aerotrain. Generic name for a range of tracked air cushion vehicles under development in France by Société de l'Aerotrain.

aft. Towards the stern of the craft.

air bleed (hyd). See **air stabilisation.** Occasionally used instead of aeration or air entry.

air bleed (ACV). One method of preventing "plough in" on a skirted ACV is to bleed air from the cushion through vent holes on the outer front of the skirt to reduce its water drag by air lubrication.

aircraft-in-ground-effect. An aircraft designed to fly at all times in close proximity to the earth's surface to take advantage of the so called "image flow" that reduces induced drag by about 50%.

air cushion vehicle. A vehicle capable of being operated so that its weight, including its payload, is wholly or significantly supported on a continuously generated cushion or 'bubble' of air at higher than ambient pressure. The air bubble or cushion is put under pressure by a fan or fans and generally contained beneath the vehicle's structure by flexible skirts or sidewalls. In the United States large or ship size air cushion vehicles are called **surface effect ships**

air entrainment. See **air entry.**

air entry. Entry of air from the atmosphere that raises the low pressures created by the flow due to a foil's cambered surface.

air gap; also **daylight gap, daylight clearance** and **hover gap.** Distance between the lowest component of the vehicle's understructure, e.g. skirt hem, and the surface when riding on its cushion. **air gap area**; area through which air is able to leak from a cushion.

air pallet, also **hoverpallet.** Air cushion supported, load-carrying structure, which bleeds a continuous low pressure volume of air between the structure and the reaction surface, creating an air film.

air pad. Part of an air pallet assembly into which compressed air is introduced and allowed to escape in a continuous flow through communicating holes in the diaphragm.

air-port system, also **thrust port.** See **puff-port.**

air-rider. Alternative generic name for air cushion vehicles or weight carrying structures lifted off the surface by a cushion or film of air.

air stabilised foils. See **foil systems.**

amidships. (1) Midway between the stem and stern of a hull. (2) abbreviated to **midships** and meaning the rudder or helm is in a mid-position.

angle of attack. The angle made by the mean chord line of an aero- or hydrofoil with the flow.

angle of incidence. The angle made by the mean chord line of a hydrofoil in relation to the fixed struts or hull.

annex foil. A high speed foil system designed for the US Navy and employing a super-cavitating section. A strengthening extension or annex is added to the foil base and this remains unwetted within the cavity at high speed. A large take-off flap is fitted to the undersurface for increased lift up to about 30 knots, and retracts into the cavity at higher speeds. A small split flap on the undersurface provides lift control at cruising speed, and a third flap, on the upper surface, acts as a spoiler to reduce lift at high speed. Designed for fully ventilated operation, the system includes blunt based struts with side flaps to induce ventilation and channel air to the low pressure areas of the foil.

Aquavion type foil. Adapted from the Grunberg system. About 85% of the load is carried by a mainfoil located slightly aft of the centre of gravity, 10% by a submerged aft stabilizer foil, and the remainder on a pair of planing sub-foils at the bow. The planing sub-foils give variable lift in response to wave shapes, whether skimming over them or through them, and so trim the angle of the hull, in order to correct the angle of attack of the main foil.

aspect ratio. (1) the measure of the ratio of a foil's span to its chord. It is defined as

$$\frac{span^2}{total\ foil\ area}$$

(2) for ACVs it is defined as $\frac{cushion\ beam}{cushion\ length}$

athwart, athwartship. Across the hull, from one side of the craft to the other.

axial-flow lift fan. A fan generating an airflow for lift that is parallel to the axis of rotation.

backstrap. A fabric strap used to secure a lift jet exit nozzle in a flexible skirt at the correct angle.

baffle plates. See **fences.**

ballast. Fuel, water or solids used to adjust the centre of gravity or trim of a craft.

ballast tank or box. Box or tank containing the liquids or solids used to trim a craft.

ballast system. A method of transferring water or fuel between tanks to adjust fore and aft trim. In Mountbatten class ACVs, four groups of tanks, one at each corner of the craft, are located in the buoyancy tanks. A ring main facilitates the rapid transfer of fuel between the tanks as ballast and also serves as a refuelling line.

beam. Measurement across a hull at a giv point.

bilge. Point of the hull where the side a the bottom meet. Also water or fuel accu ulated in the bilges.

bilge system. A pumping system devised dispose of water and other fluids which ha accumulated in the bilges. In air cushi vehicles bilge systems are installed to cle the buoyancy tanks. Small craft general have a hand operated pump which connec directly to pipes in the tanks. In larg craft, like the 165-ton BHC Mountbatte because of the large number of buoyan compartments, four electrically driven pum are provided, each of which can drain o compartment at a time.

boating. Expression used to describe an a cushion vehicle when operating in displace ment condition. The boating or **semi-hov** mode is used in congested terminal are when lift power and spray generation is ke to a minimum. Some craft have water su face contact even at full hover for stabili requirements.

bow. Forward part of a craft.

bow-up. Trim position or attitude when craft is high at the bow. Can be measur by eye or attitude gyro.

breast, to. To take waves at 90° to the crests.

bridge. Elevated part of the superstructu providing a clear all round view, from whi a craft is navigated and steered.

broach, to. Sudden breaking of the wat surface by a foil, or part of a foil, resulti in a loss of lift due to air flowing over t foil's upper surface.

to broach to. Nautical expression meani to swing sideways in following seas und wave action.

bulkheads. Vertical partitions, either tran verse or longitudinal, which divide or su divide a hull. May be used to separa accommodation areas, strengthen the stru ture, form tanks or localise fires or floodin

buoyancy. The reduction in weight of floating object. If the object floats i weight is equal to (or less than) the weig of fluid displaced.

buoyancy chamber. A structure designed such a way that the total of its own weig and all loads which it supports is equal (or less than) the weight of the water displaces.

buoyancy, reserve. Buoyancy in excess that required to keep an undamaged cra afloat. See **buoyancy.**

buoyancy tubes. Inflatable tubular membe providing reserve buoyancy. May be use as fenders if fitted to the outer periphery a craft.

CAB. Captured Air Bubble.

camber. (1) A convexity on the upp surface of a deck to give it increased strengt and/or facilitate draining. (2) The conve form on the upper surface of a foil. The hig speed flow over the top surface causes decrease in pressure and about two-thirds the lift is provided by this surface.

nard foil system. A foil arrangement in which the main foil of wide span is located near the stern, aft of the centre of gravity, and bears about 65% of the weight, while a small central foil is placed at the bow.

ptured air bubble craft (see also sidewall aft and surface effect ship). Vessel in which the cushion (or air bubble) is contained by rigid sidewalls and flexible bow and stern skirts. Occasionally used for any air cushion craft in which the air cushion (or air bubble) is contained within the cushion periphery with minimal air leakage.

vitation. The formation and collapse of vapour bubbles due to pressure decrease on the upper surface of a foil or the back of a propeller's blades at high speeds. Cavities or cavitation bubbles of aqueous vapour form near the foil's leading edge and extend downstream expanding and collapsing. At the points of collapse positive pressure peaks may rise to as high as 20,000 psi. These cause corrosion and pitting of the metal. Cavitation causes an unstable water flow over the foils which results in abrupt changes in lift and therefore discomfort for those aboard the craft.

Foil sections are now being developed which either delay the onset of cavitation by reduced camber, thinner sections, or sweepback, or, if the craft is required to operate at supercavitating speeds, provide a smooth transition between sub-cavitating and super-cavitating speeds.

ntrifugal flow lift fan. A cushion lift fan which generates an airflow at right angles to the axis of rotation.

ain ties. Chains used to maintain the correct shape of an air jet exit nozzle on a flexible skirt.

ord. The distance between the leading and trailing edges of a foil section measured along the chord line.

nord-line. A straight line joining the leading and trailing edges of a foil or propeller blade section.

assification, also certification. Seagoing and amphibious craft for commercial application are classified by mode and place of construction, in the manner of the registration system started in the City of London by Edward Lloyd, and continued since 1760 by Lloyd's Register of Shipping. Outside the British Isles classification societies now include Registro Italiano Navale, Germanischer Lloyd, Det Norske Veritas, American Bureau of Shipping and the Japanese Ministry of Transport.

A classification society's surveyors make a detailed examination of craft certificated by them at regular intervals to ensure their condition complies with the particular society's requirements.

ontinuous nozzle skirt. See skirts.

ontour, to. The motion of an air cushion vehicle or hydrofoil when more or less following a wave profile.

P shifter. A control system which moves the centre of pressure of an air cushion to augment a craft's natural stability in pitch and roll.

raft. Boats, ships, air cushion vehicles and hydrofoils of all types, regardless of size.

ew. Those responsible for manning a craft of either boat or ship size, including the officers. The company of an ACV or hydrofoil.

ross-flow. The flow of air, transversally or longidutinally within an air cushion.

cushion-borne. A craft borne above the sea or land surface by its air cushion.

cushion. A volume of higher than ambient pressure air trapped beneath the structure of a vehicle and its supporting surface causing the vehicle to be supported at some distance from the ground.

cushion area. Area of a cushion contained within a skirt or sidewall.

cushion beam. Measurement across an air cushion at a given point.

cushion length. Longitudinal cushion measurement.

cushion length, mean. Defined as:
$$\frac{\text{cushion area}}{\text{cushion beam}}$$

cushion seal. Air curtains, sidewalls, skirts, water-jets or other means employed to contain or seal an air cushion to reduce to a minimum the leakage of trapped air.

cushion thrust. Thrust obtained by the deflection of cushion air.

CWL. Calm water line.

daylight clearance. See air gap.

daylight gap. See air gap.

deadrise. The angle with the horizontal made at the keel by the outboard rise of a vessel's hull form at each frame.

diffuser-recirculation. See recirculation system.

displacement. The weight in tons of water displaced by a floating vessel. Light displacement is the craft weight exclusive of ballast.

ditch, to. An emergency landing on water while under way due to a local navigation hazard, loss of cushion air or failure of a powerplant.

down-by-the-head. Trim or sit of a craft with its bow more deeply immersed than the stern. The opposite expression is 'down by the stern'.

drag. (1) ACVs—aerodynamic and hydrodynamic resistances encountered by an air cushion vehicle resulting from aerodynamic profile, gain of momentum of air needed for cushion generation, wave making, wetting or skirt contact.
(2) hydrofoils—hydrodynamic resistances encountered by hydrofoils result from wave making, which is dependent on the craft shape and displacement, frictional drag due to the viscosity of the water, the total wetted surface and induced drag from the foils and transmission shafts and their supporting struts and structure, due to their motion through the water.

draught. Depth between the water surface and the bottom of a craft. Under the Ministry of Transport Merchant Shipping (Construction) rules, 1952, draught is defined as the vertical distance from the moulded base line amidships to the sub-division load waterline.

draught marks. (1) marks on the side of a craft showing the depth to which it can be loaded. (2) figures cut at the stern and stem to indicate draught and trim.

drift angle. Difference between the actual course made and the course steered.

elevator. Moveable aerodynamic control surface used on small hovercraft to provide a degree of fore and aft trim control. Elevator surfaces are normally located in the slipstream of the propulsive units in order to provide some control at low speed.

fathom. A depth of 6 ft.

ferry. A craft designed to carry passengers across a channel, estuary, lake, river or strait.

fetch. The number of miles a given wind has been blowing over open water or the distance upwind to the nearest land.

finger skirt. See skirts.

fire zone. A compartment containing a full supply and ignition source which is walled with fire resisting material and fitted with an independent fire warning and extinguishing system.

flexible skirt. See skirts.

flying bridge. A navigating position atop the wheel or chart house.

foilborne. A hydrofoil is said to be foilborne when the hull is raised completely out of the water and wholly supported by lift from its foil system.

foil fence. Small partitions placed at short intervals down the upper side of a hydrofoil tending to prevent air from passing down to destroy the lift. They are attached in the direction of the flow.

foil flaps. Foils are frequently fitted with (a) trailing edge flaps for lift augmentation during take-off and to provide control forces, (b) upper and lower flaps to raise the cavitation boundary.

foil systems. Foil systems in current use are generally either surface piercing, submerged or semi-submerged. There are a number of craft with hybrid systems with a combination of submerged and surface piercing foils, recent examples being the Supramar PT 150 and the De Havilland FHE-400.

Surface piercing foils are more often than not vee-shaped, the upper parts of the foil forming the tips of the Vee and piercing the surface on either side of the craft. The vee foil, with its marked dihedral is area stabilised and craft employing this configuration can be designed to be inherently stable, and, for stability, geometry dependent.

The forces restoring normal trim are provided by the area of the foil that is submerged. A roll to one side means the immersion of increased foil area, which results in the generation of extra lift to counter the roll and restore the craft to an even keel.

Equally, a downward pitching movement at the bow means an increase in the submerged area of the forward foil, and the generation of extra lift on this foil, which raises the bow once more. Should the bow foil rise above its normal water level the lift decreases in a similar way to restore normal trim. This type of foil is also known as an emerging foil system.

As the vee-foil craft increases its speed, so it generates greater lift and is raised further out of the water—at the same time reducing the wetted area and the lift. The lift must be equal to the weight of the craft, and as the lift depends on the speed and wetted foil area, the hull rides at a pre-determined height above the water level.

ladder foils. Also come under the heading surface piercing, but are rarely used at the present time. This is one of the earliest foil arrangements and was used by Forlanini in his 1905 hydro-aeroplane, which was probably the first really successful hydrofoil. In 1911 Alexander Graham Bell purchased

Forlanini's patent specifications and used his ladder system on his Hydrodrome, one of which, the HD-4, set up a world speed record of 61·5 knots in 1919. Early ladder foils, with single sets of foils beneath the hull, fore and aft, lacked lateral stability, but this disadvantage was rectified later by the use of two sets of forward foils, one on each side of the hull. The foils were generally straight and set at right angles to their supporting struts, but were occasionally of vee configuration, the provision of dihedral preventing a sudden change of lift as the foils broke the surface. Both the vee foil and the ladder systems are self stabilising to a degree. The vee foil has the advantage of being a more rigid, lighter structure and is less expensive.

Primary disadvantages of the conventional surface-piercing systems in comparison with the submerged foil system are: (a) the inability of vee-foil craft without control surfaces to cope with downward orbital velocities at wave crests when overtaking waves in a following sea, a condition which can decrease the foil's angle of attack, reducing lift and cause either wave contact or a stall; (b) on large craft the weight and size of the surface piercing system is considerably greater than that of a corresponding submerged foil system; (c) restoring forces to correct a roll have to pass above the centre of gravity of the craft, which necessitates the placing of the foils only a short distance beneath the hull. This means a relatively low wave clearance and therefore the vee foil is not suited to routes where really rough weather is encountered.

shallow-draught submerged foil system. This system is employed almost exclusively on hydrofoils designed and built in the Soviet Union and is intended primarily for passenger carrying craft on long, calm water rivers, canals and inland seas. The system, also known as the immersion depth effect system, was evolved by Dr. Rostislav Alexeyev. It generally comprises two main horizontal foils, one forward, one aft, each carrying approximately half the weight of the vessel. A submerged foil loses lift gradually as it approaches the surface from a depth of about one chord, which prevents it from rising completely to the surface. Means therefore have to be provided to assist take-off and prevent the vessel from sinking back into the displacement mode. Planing subfoils, port and starboard, are therefore provided in the vicinity of the forward struts, and are so located that when they are touching the water surface, the main foils are submerged at a depth of approximately one chord.

submerged foils have a greater potential for seakeeping than any other, but are not inherently stable to any degree. The foils are totally immersed and a sonic-cum-electronic, mechanical or air stabilisation system has to be installed to maintain the foils at the required depth. The system has to stabilise the craft from take-off to touchdown in all four axes—pitch, roll, yaw and heave. It must also see that the craft makes co-ordinated banked turns in heavy seas to reduce the side loads on the foil struts; ensure that vertical and lateral accelerations are kept within limits in order to prevent excessive loads on the structure and finally, ensure a smooth ride for the passengers and crew.

The control forces are generated either by deflecting flaps at the trailing edge of the foil or varying the incidence angle of the entire foil surface. Incidence control provides better performance in a high sea state.

A typical sonic electronic autopilot control system is that devised for the Boeing PGH-1 High Point. The key element is an acoustic height sensor located at the bow. The time lag of the return signal is a measure of the distance of the sensor from the water. Craft motion input is received from dual sonic ranging devices which sense the height above the water of the bow in relation to a fixed reference; from three rate gyros which measure yaw, pitch and roll; from forward and aft accelerometers which sense vertical acceleration fore and aft and from a vertical gyro which senses the angular position of the craft in both pitch and roll. This information is processed by an electronic computer and fed continuously to hydraulic actuators of the foil control surfaces, which develop the necessary hydrodynamic forces for stability producing forces imposed by wave action manoeuvring and correct flight.

mechanical incidence control. The most successful purely mechanically operated incidence control system is the Hydrofin autopilot principle, designed by Christopher Hook, who pioneered the development of the submerged foil. A fixed, high-riding crash preventer plane is mounted ahead of and beneath the bow.

The fixed plane, which is only immersed when the craft is in a displacement mode, is also used as a platform for mounting a lightweight pitch control sensor which is hinged to the rear.

The sensor rides on the waves and continuously transmits their shape through a connecting linkage to vary the angle of incidence of the main foils as necessary to maintain them at the required depth. A filter system ensures that the craft ignores small waves and that the hull is flown over the crests of waves exceeding the height of the keel over the water.

Two additional sensors, trailing from port and starboard immediately aft of the main struts, provide roll control. The pilot has overriding control through a control column, operated in the same manner as that in an aircraft.

air stabilisation system. A system designed and developed by Baron Hanns von Schertel of Supramar AG, Lucerne. Air from the free atmosphere is fed through air exits to the foil upper surface (i.e. into the low pressure regions). The airflow decreases the lift and the flow is deflected away from the foil section with an effect similar to that of a deflected flap, the air cavities extending out behind producing a virtual lengthening of the foil profile. Lift is reduced and varied by the quantity of air admitted, this being controlled by a valve actuated by signals from a damped pendulum and a rate gyro. The pendulum causes righting moments at static feeling angles. If exposed to a centrifugal force in turning, it causes a moment, which is directed towards the centre of the turning circle, thereby avoiding outside banking. The rate gyro responds to angular accelerations and acts dynamically to dampen rolling motions.

following sea. A sea following the same or similar course to that of the craft.

forward. Position towards the fore end of a craft.

freeboard. Depth of the exposed or free side of a hull between the water level and the freeboard deck. The degree of freeboard permitted is marked by load lines.

freeboard deck. Deck used to measure or determine loadlines.

free power turbine. A gas turbine on which the power turbine is on a separate shaft from the compressor and its turbine.

full hover. Expression used to describe the condition of an ACV when it is at its design hoverheight.

GEM. Ground effect machine.

gross tonnage. Total tonnage of a vessel, including all enclosed spaces, estimated on the basis of 100 ft^3 = 1 ton.

ground effect machine. Early generic term for air cushion vehicles of all types.

ground crew and **ground staff.** Those responsible for craft servicing and maintenance. Also those responsible for operational administration.

Grunberg foil. A foil system based on main amidship foil which carries about 90 of the load and small planing foils, s forward, carrying the remainder of the loa

heave. Vertical motion of a craft in respon to waves.

hover commander. Senior crew memb aboard a hovercraft. Equivalent in rank airliner or ship's captain. Alternative term pilot, driver, captain, helmsman and coxwai

hovercraft. Generic name for craft usin the patented peripheral jet principle invente by Christopher Cockerell CBE, in which th air cushion is generated and contained by jet of air exhausted downward and inwa from a nozzle at the periphery at the base the vehicle.

hover gap. See **air gap.**

hover height. Vertical height between th hard structure of an ACV and the supportin surface when a vehicle is cushion-borne.

hover-listen. Expression covering ACVs er ployed for anti-submarine warfare whi operating at low speeds to detect a targe

hover-pallet. See **air pallet.**

hover-time. Time logged by an air cushic vehicle when cushion borne. Often calle **power hours.**

hump. The "hump" formed on the grap of resistance against the speed of a displac ment vessel or ACV. The maximum of th "hump" corresponds to the speed of th wave generated by the hull or air depression

hump speed. Critical speed at which th curve on a graph of wave making drag of a ACV tends to hump or peak. As speed increased, the craft over-rides its bow wav the wave making drag diminishes and th rate of acceleration rapidly increases.

hydrofoils. Small wings, almost identical section to those of an aircraft, and designe to generate lift. Since water has a densit some 815 times that of air, the same lift a an aeroplane wing is obtained for only $\frac{1}{81}$ of the area (at equal speeds).

hydroskimmer. Name given originally t experimental air cushion vehicles built unde contract to the US Navy Bureau of Ship Preference was given to this name since gave the craft a sea-service identity.

inclined shaft. A marine drive shaft used i small vee foil and shallow-draught submerge foil craft, with keels only a limited heigh above the mean water level. The shaft generally short and inclined at about 12°-14 to the horizontal. On larger craft, designe for operation in higher waves, the need t fly higher necessitates alternative driv arrangements such as the vee drive an Z-drive, the water jet system or even ai propulsion.

induced wave drag. Drag caused by th hollow depressed in the water by an ACV air cushion. As the craft moves forward th depression follows along beneath it, buildin up a bow wave and causing wave drag as i a displacement craft until the hump spee has been passed.

integrated lift-propulsion system. An ACV lift and propulsion system operated by common power source, the transmission an power-sharing system allowing variation i the division of power.

keel. (a) The "backbone" of a hull (b) An extension of an ACV's fore-and-af stability air jet, similar in construction and shape to a skirt, and taking the form of an inflated bag.

tmesh pads. Thick, loosely woven pads, either metal or plastic wire fitted in the ~~ine air intake to filter out water and solid ~~ticles from the engine air.

ot. A nautical mile per hour.

d, to. At the end of its run hydrofoils ~~l ACVs are said to "settle down" or ~~nd".

ding pads, also **hard points.** strengthened ~~as of the hull on which an ACV is sup~~ted when at rest on land. These may also ~~vide attachment points for towing equip~~nt, lifts and jacks.

fan. See also **axial flow lift fan** and ~~trifugal flow lift fan.** A fan used to ~~ply air under pressure to an air cushion, ~~/or to form curtains.

off. An ACV is said to lift off when it ~~es from the ground on its air cushion.

gitudinal framing. Method of hull con~~uction employing frames set in a fore and ~~ direction or parallel to the keel.

utical mile. A distance of 6,080 ft, or one ~~nute of latitude at the equator.

viplane. Name for the overwater or ~~phibious air cushion vehicles developed ~~ France by SEDAM.

t tonnage. Total tonnage of a craft based ~~ cubic capacity of all space available for ~~rying revenue-producing cargo less allow~~ce for the engine room, crew quarters, ~~ter ballast, stores and other areas needed ~~ operate the craft.

ital motion. Orbital or circular motion of ~~ water particles forming waves. The ~~cular motion decreases in radius with ~~reasing depth. It is the peculiar sequence ~~ the motion that causes the illusion of wave ~~nslation. In reality the water moves ~~ry little in translation. The circular ~~ections are: up at the wave front, forward ~~ the crest, down at the wave back and ~~ck at the trough.

ripheral jet. See **air curtain** and **hover~~ft.**

ripheral jet cushion system. A ground ~~shion generated by a continuous jet of air ~~ued through ducts or nozzles around the ~~ter periphery of the base of a craft. The ~~shion is maintained at above ambient ~~essure by the horizontal change of mo~~ntum of the curtain.

ripheral trunk. See **skirt.**

ch. Rotation or oscillation of the hull ~~out a transverse axis in a seaway. Also ~~gle of air or water propeller blades.

ch angle. Pitch angle a craft adopts ~~ative to a horizontal datum.

atform, to. Approximately level flight of ~~ hydrofoil over waves of a height less than ~~e calm water hull clearance.

num. Space or air chamber beneath or ~~rrounding a lift fan or fans through which ~~ under pressure is distributed to a skirt ~~stem.

num chamber cushion system. The most ~~ple of air cushion concepts. Cushion ~~essure is maintained by pumping air ~~ntinuously into a recessed base without ~~e use of a peripheral jet curtain.

"plough in" A bow down attitude resulting from the bow part of the skirt contacting the surface and progressively building up drag. Unless controlled this can lead to a serious loss of stability and possibly an overturning moment.

With the skirt's front outer edge dragging on the water towards the centre of the craft (known as 'tuck under') there is a marked reduction in righting moment of the cushion pressure. As the downward pitch angle increases, the stern of the craft tends to rise from the surface and excessive yaw angles develop. Considerable decceleration takes place down to hump speed and the danger of a roll over in a small craft is accentuated by following waves which further increase the pitch angle.

Solutions include the provision of vent holes on a skirt's outer front to reduce its drag through air lubrication, and the development of a bag skirt which automatically bulges outwards on contact with the water, thereby delaying tuck under and providing a righting moment.

power take off unit. Unit for transmitting power from the main engine or engines, generally for auxiliary services required while a craft is under way, such as hydraulics, alternators and bilge pumps.

PTO. See **power take-off unit.**

puff ports. Controlled apertures in a skirt system or cushion supply ducting through which air can be expelled to assist control at low speeds.

ram wing. Term used originally for an air cushion vehicle with an understructure taking the form of a box with the bottom and frontside removed. As it gathers speed close to the ground, ram air pressure builds up beneath the base giving a lifting force. Recently the term has been extended to ACV types which, in order to reduce the power requirements of the air curtain system, use an aerodynamic lifting body for support at high speeds. As speed increases the cushion lift fans are cut out and only the propulsion engines are left in operation.

recirculation system. An air curtain employing a recirculating air flow, which is maintained within and under the craft.

roll. Oscillation or rotation of a hull about a longitudinal axis.

roll attitude. Angle of roll craft adopts relative to a longitudinal datum.

SES. See **surface effect ship.**

sidewall vessel. An ACV with its cushion air contained between immersed sidewalls or skegs and transverse air curtains or skirts fore and aft. Stability is provided by the buoyancy of the sidewalls and their planing forces.

significant wave height. Average height of the largest 1/3 well formed and defined waves.

single shaft gas turbine. A gas turbine with a compressor and power turbine on a common shaft.

strake. (a) a permanent band of rubber or other hard wearing material along the sides of a craft to protect the structure from chafing against quays, piers and craft alongside. (b) lengths of material fitted externally to a flexible skirt and used to channel air downwards to reduce water drag.

multiple skirt. System devised by M. Jean Bertin, employing a number of separate flexible skirts for his system of individually fed, multiple air cushions.

skirt. Flexible fabric extension hung between an ACV's metal structure and the surface to give increased obstacle and overwave clearance capability for a small air gap clearance and therefore reduced power requirement. The skirt deflects when encountering waves or solid obstacles, then returns to its normal position, the air gap being increased only momentarily. On peripheral jet ACVs the skirt is a flexible extension of the peripheral jet nozzle with inner and outer skins hung from the inner and outer edges of the air duct and linked together by chain ties or diaphragms so that they form the correct nozzle profile at the hemline.

skirt, bag. Simple skirt design consisting of an inflated bag. Sometimes used as transverse and longitudinal stability skirts.

skirt, finger. Skirt system designed by Hovercraft Development Ltd, consisting of a fringe of conically shaped nozzles attached to the base of a bag or loop skirt. Each nozzle or finger fits around an air exit hole and channels cushion air inwards towards the bottom centre of the craft. The most successful skirt design developed so far, it produces substantially less drag through surface contact in calm water and wave conditions and also reduces the amount of spray normally generated by cushion air by about 75%.

skirt shifting. A control system in which movement of the centre of area of the cushion is achieved by shifting the skirt along one side, which has the effect of tilting the craft. Pitch and roll trim can be adjusted by this method.

semi-submerged propeller. A concept for the installation of a partially submerged, supercavitating propeller on ship-size air cushion vehicles, driven through the sidewall transom. The advantages of this type of installation include considerable drag reduction due to the absence of inclined shafts and their supporting structures, and possibly the elimination of propeller erosion as a result of appendage cavity impingement.

set down. To lower an air cushion vehicle onto its landing pads.

split foil. A main foil system with the foil area divided into two, either to facilitate retraction, or to permit the location of the control surfaces well outboard, where foil control and large roll correcting moments can be applied for small changes in lift.

stability curtain. Transverse or longitudinal air curtains dividing an air cushion in order to restrict the cross flow of air within the cushion and increase pitch and roll stability.

stability skirt. A transverse or longitudinal skirt dividing an air cushion so as to restrict cross flow within the cushion and increase pitch or roll stability.

strake. See **rubbing strake.**

submerged foil system. A foil system employing totally submerged lifting surfaces. The depth of submergence is controlled by mechanical, electronic or pneumatic systems which alter the angle of incidence of the foils or flaps attached to them to provide stability and control. See **foil systems.**

supercavitating foil. A general classification given to foils designed to operate efficiently at high speeds while fully cavitated. Since at very high speeds foils cannot avoid cavitation, sections are being designed which induce the onset of cavitation from the leading edge and cause the cavities to proceed downstream and beyond the trailing edge before collapsing. Lift and drag of these foils is determined by the shape of the leading edge and undersurface.

superventilated foil. A system of forced ventilation designed to overcome the reduction in lift/drag ratio of a foil at supercavitating speeds. Air is fed continuously to the upper surface of the foil un-wetting the surface and preventing the formation of critical areas of decreased pressure. Alternatively the air may be fed into the cavity formed behind a square trailing edge.

surface effect ship. Term implying a large ship-size ACV, regardless of specific type.

take-off speed. Speed at which the hull of a hydrofoil craft is raised clear of the water, dynamic foil lift taking over from static displacement or planing of the hull proper.

tandem foils. Foil system in which the area of the forward foils is approximately equal to that of the aft foils, balancing the loading between them.

thickness-chord ratio. Maximum thickness of a foil section in relation to its chord.

Tietjens-type foil. Named after Professor Tietjens, this system was based on a forward swept (surface piercing) main foil located almost amidships and slightly ahead of the centre of gravity. It was intended that the pronounced sweep of the vee foils would result in an increasing area of the foil further forward coming into use to increase the bow up trim of the craft when lift was lost. The considerable length of unsupported hull ahead of the centre of gravity meant the craft was constantly in danger of "digging in" in bad seas and it was highly sensitive to loading arrangements.

transcavitating foil. Thin section foil designed for smooth transition from fully wetted to supercavitating flow. By loading the tip more highly than the root, cavitation is first induced at the foil's tip, then extends spanwise over the foil to the roots as speed increases.

transit foil. See **transcavitating foil.**

transisting foil. See **transcavitating foil.**

transom. The last transverse frame of a ship's structure forming the stern board.

trapped air cushion vehicle. A concept for a skirt-type surface effect ship with 20 ft skirts separated from the water surface by a thin film of air lubrication.

trim. Difference between drafts forward and aft in a displacement vessel and, by extension of the general idea, ACV and hydrofoil hull attitude relative to the line of flight.

ventilation. See **air entry.**

water wall ACV. A craft employing a curtain of water to retain its air cushion instead of an air curtain.

waterjet propulsion. A term now applied to a propulsion system devised as an alternative to supercavitating propellers for propelling high speed ship systems. Turbines drive pumps located in the hull, and water is pumped through high velocity jets above the water line and directed astern. The system weighs less than a comparable supercavitating propeller system and for craft with normal operating speeds above 45 knots it is thought to be competitive on an annual cost basis. First high speed applications include the Soviet Burevestnik and Chaika hydrofoils and two products of the Boeing Company—the Little Squirt and the PGH-2 hydrofoil gunboat.

The system employed on the 55 ton PGH hydrofoil is similar to that of the experimental Little Squirt gas turbine waterjet power testbed, which, with a commercially available double-suction centrifugal pump, attained propulsive coefficient of 0·48 at a speed 50 knots.

Waterjets are also being employed propulsion at relatively low speeds. In Soviet Union the Zarya shallow-draught waterbus (24 knots) and the Gorkovchan sidewall ACV are propelled by waterjets In the USA the Dolphin, Denison PGH-1 and PGH-2 hydrofoils use waterjets for hullborne propulsion. The jet can be turned easily give side propulsion to facilitate docking which is not so easy for a normal propeller

wave height. The vertical distance from wave trough to crest or twice the wave amplitude.

wave length. The horizontal distance between adjacent wave crests.

wave velocity. Speed at which a wave form travels along the sea surface. (The water itself remaining without forward movement.)

yaw angle. Rotation or oscillation of a craft about a vertical axis.

yaw-port. See **puff port.**

Z-drive. A drive system normally employed on hydrofoils to transmit power from the engine in the hull to the screw. Power transmitted through a horizontal shaft leading to a bevel gear over the stern, then via vertical shaft and a second bevel gear to horizontal propeller shaft, thus forming "Z" shape.

ADDENDA
United Kingdom: BRITISH HOVERCRAFT CORPORATION

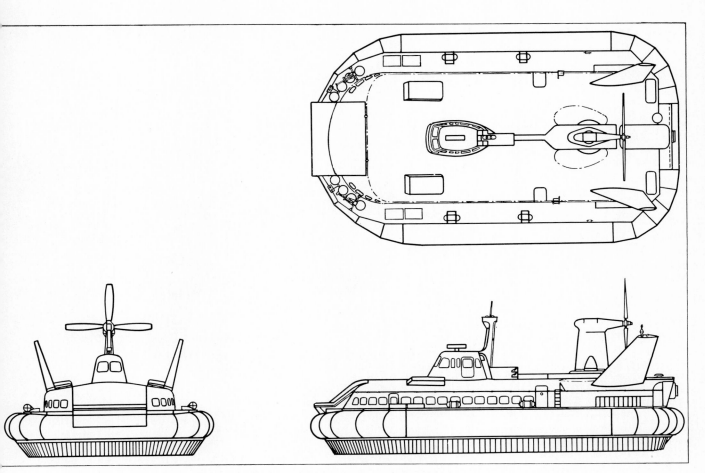

General arrangement of the B.H.C. B.H.7 Wellington (Commercial) showing the revised skirt system

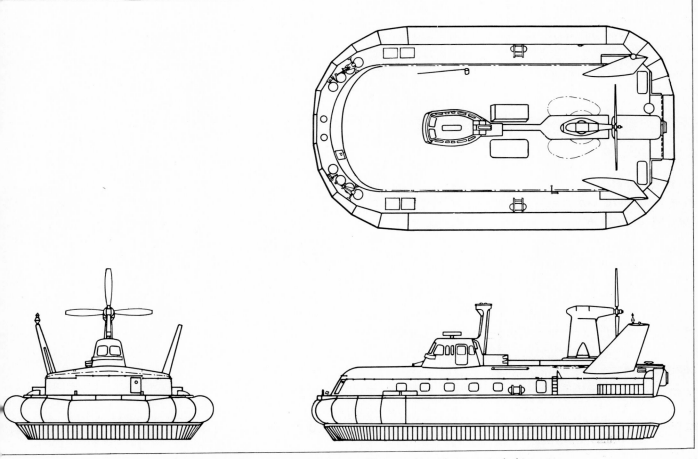

General arrangement of the B.H.7 Wellington (fast attack) with its revised skirt system

ADDENDA
ACV SECTION: United Kingdom

Airavia

AIRAVIA LTD.

HEAD OFFICE:
20 North Road, Shanklin, Isle of Wight

TELEPHONE:
Shanklin 3643

DIRECTORS:
See Hydrofoil Section

Airavia is the sales representative for

Sudoimport air cushion vehicles and hyd‍‍
foils in the United Kingdom, British comm‍‍
wealth countries, Scandinavia and West‍‍
Europe. The company is also planning‍‍
lease air cushion vehicles on wet or c‍‍
charters in these areas.

Hatton & Bass
HATTON & BASS LTD

HEAD OFFICE:
Botolph Bridge Works, Oundle Road, Peterborough

TELEPHONE:
Peterborough 67843

DIRECTORS:
Geoffrey Hatton
Richard Bass

Hatton & Bass Ltd was formed in September 1966 to design and build a range of lightweight ACVs which could be operated at fun fairs and amusement parks. The company's first craft were the Midget and Trident each designed to carry a child. These were followed by the Major and Minor, which are capable of carrying up to two passengers of average size. All four craft have an integrated lift/propulsion system, and are intended for operation over smooth, flat surfaces only. The company is now developing a new range of skirted amphibious sports and utility craft. Capable of operating over open, rough ground and farmland. The first of these is the Mistral.

Two miniature ACVs built by Hatton & Bass for fun fairs and amusement parks: the Midget (for‍‍ ground) powered by a 3½ h.p. Aspra 4-stroke, and the Minor, with a 13½ hp VLO. Over smoo‍‍ flat surfaces the Midget will travel at 5-10 mph (8-16 km/h) and the Minor at 10-15 mph (16-24 km/‍‍

MISTRAL

This is basically a fibreglass-hulled two-seater, but it can be quickly adapted into a form suitable for a range of light utility roles including crop-spraying by removing the rear section of the cabin and replacing it with a load-carrying platform. In this configuration it will carry a driver and a payload of up to 400 lb (181 kg).

LIFT AND PROPULSION: Motive power is supplied by two 30 bhp, 600 cc twin-cylinder JLO engines, one driving a 27 in (0·68 m) diameter 10-bladed lift fan, the other a 4 ft 6 in (1·37 m) diameter Rollason propeller for thrust.

Twin rudders operating in the propeller slipstream provide directional control.

HULL: The craft has a glass fibre hull wit‍‍ built-in buoyancy. A bag type skirt‍‍ fitted.

DIMENSIONS:
Length overall	15 ft 0 in (4·57 n
Width overall	8 ft 0 in (2·43 n
Height overall	4 ft 6 in (1·37 n

HYDROFOIL SECTION: United Kingdom

New Hydrofin
NEW HYDROFIN LTD
SAILING HYDROFIN

The Sailing Hydrofin adopts the Hook system to the requirements of sail. A 7 ft long prototype model of the craft is now under construction.

The foils are of the fully submerged incidence-controlled type, with full retraction. The foil system is of 'aeroplane' configuration, with the main foils carried on outrigged sponsons. The foil struts are inclined outwards so that the lift on the foils can offset the sail thrust.

Stability is maintained by feeler arms adjusting the angles of the foils as necessary. A control column is used to give more angle

to the lee foil and less to the windward t‍‍ maintain the craft in the upright sailin‍‍ position.

The first production craft will be a two-sea‍‍ model for sailing enthusiasts, but a muc‍‍ larger craft is envisaged which would b‍‍ employed in the South Seas, where commer‍‍ cial operation of the craft would be practica‍‍ because of the strong, regular trade wind‍‍

CORRIGENDA

1. Page 64   Caption at bottom of page should be transposed with the one at the bottom of page 66.
2. Page 74   The Dobson photograph is the Model B, not Model D.
3. Page 80   US Army Aviation Laboratories. The Commanding Officer is Col. Eduardo M. Soler; the ACV Project Engineer ‍‍ William E. Sickles.
4. Page 40   Express two-seat Air Riders at the first Inter-Schools hovercraft building contest.